Johnny Rogan became a full-time author following postgraduate work on Spenser's *The Faerie Queene*. He has written extensively on the contemporary music scene. STARMAKERS AND SVENGALIS is his seventh book.

By the same author

Timeless Flight: The Definitive Biography Of The Byrds
Neil Young: Here We Are In The Years
Roxy Music: Style With Substance — Roxy's First Ten Years
Van Morrison: Portrait Of The Artist
The Kinks: The Sound And The Fury
Wham! Death Of A Supergroup (Confidential)

STARMAKERS
AND
SVENGALIS

Johnny Rogan

Futura

A Futura BOOK

Copyright © Johnny Rogan 1988

First published in Great Britain in 1988 by
Queen Anne Press, a division of
Macdonald & Co (Publishers) Ltd
London & Sydney

This edition published in 1989 by
Futura Publications, a division of
Macdonald & Co (Publishers) Ltd
London & Sydney

Picture credits: BBC Hulton Picture Library (plates II, V, XIII);
Jayne Houghton Photography (plate XVII); London Features
International (plate VIII); Barrie Wentzell/Melody Maker (plates IV, XII);
Rex Features (plates VI, X, XIV, XV); Andrew Catlin/Some Bizzare Records
(plate XVI); Virginia Turbett (plate I); Universal Pictorial Press
(plates VII, IX, XI); Mike West (plate III).

ISBN 0 7088 4004 3

Reproduced, printed and bound in Great Britain by
Hazell Watson & Viney Limited
Member of BPCC plc
Aylesbury, Bucks, England
Typeset by Cylinder Typesetting

Futura Publications a division of
Macdonald & Co (Publishers) Ltd
Greater London House
Hampstead Road
London NW1 7QX

A member of Maxwell Pergamon Publishing Corporation plc

If you want to fight me, you fight me, but remember one thing: when you fight the champion you go 15 rounds . . . You say what you like. I don't have to answer to you or to anybody. You've been warned. I'll take you with one hand strapped up my arse.

Don Arden

It seems these pop stars present one side of their profile to the public and enjoy it — but do not like it when the warts are shown on the other side. If you don't like the glare, stay out of the limelight.

Lord Justice Lawton

I think that almost anything a manager might do, however harmless or trivial, could induce hatred and distrust in a group of highly temperamental, jealous and spoilt adolescents.

Lord Justice Salmon

CONTENTS

ACKNOWLEDGEMENTS

I would like to extend my thanks to the many individuals who contributed their time and conversation during the research period for this book. I am especially grateful to the following managers: Danny Betesh, Vic Billings, Harry Dawson, Rob Gretton, Ken Howard, Eddie Kennedy, Terry King, Robert Last, Alan McGee, Malcolm McLaren, Harvey Lisberg, Gordon Mills, Simon Napier-Bell, Dave Nicolson, Larry Page, Larry Parnes, Tam Paton, Don Paul, Kenneth Pitt, Phil Solomon, Stevo, Tony Stratton-Smith, Jazz Summers, Robert Wace and Peter Walsh.

The following musicians/performers also provided interesting insights into the many entrepreneurs featured in this book: Peter Astor, Chris Britton, Joe Brown, Stuart Colman, Tony Dangerfield, Robbie Hood (Mike West), Matt Johnson (The The), Billy J. Kramer, Little Lenny Davis (Dick Hayes), Stephen Mallinder, Steve Marriot, Millie (Small), Ian Mitchell, Mitch Mitchell, Tony Murray, Ray Phillips, Brian Poole, Reg Presley, Danny Storm (Dave Hurren), Screaming Lord Sutch, Ronnie Wells, Mike Willett and Marty Wilde.

Other interviewees whose comments proved particularly useful included Rob Collins, Roger Cook, Raymond Cotter, Phil Coulter, Sam Curtis, Mark Dean, Clive Epstein, Nick Kent, Dick Leahy, former Detective Chief Superintendent John MacNamara, Brian Matthew, Rory Robertson, Dick Rowe, Shel Talmy, Chip Taylor and Ron Watts.

Thanks also to Keith Altham, Peter Doggett, Detective Sergeant Ian Foster, Spencer Leigh, Philip Norman, Tony Peake, David St George and Sara Wheeler.

The obsession to complete this book without a prior commission resulted in some hardship and tested friendships. I am extremely grateful to Paddy and Nora Nolan for again providing me with free use of the inspirational cottage in Tramore. During my three years of homelessness, J.L. Pooley allowed me to sleep on his floor for many months, provided a table on which to type and only ever required a contribution to gas and electricity. Others, including Cathy Shea, Dorothy Fisher, George Kenyon and Wally Hammond looked after some precious books and records which might otherwise have ended up on a skip. John Graves saved me money in xerox fees and Cathy Shea and Dorothy Fisher provided fictitious addresses and telephone numbers when I was homeless and intimidated. I thank them all.

Useful agencies consulted during my period of research included the Old Bailey, New Scotland Yard, the Society of Authors, *Melody Maker*, Lady Margaret Hall, Oxford law faculty and Colindale Newspaper Library. Quotations cited in the text are taken from my interviews with the above participants during the period 1982–7. Additional quotations are from the following sources: *Melody Maker* (140, 187-8, 239, 338); *News of the World* (133b, 135, 139, 151); BBC *Checkpoint* (145, 147); *Daily Mail* (234); *Disc* (243a).

Finally, and certainly not least, I would like to thank Peter Frame for feedback, support and inspiration, not to mention a number of unsolicited meals and drinks throughout the five-year period in which I wrote this book.

Johnny Rogan

INTRODUCTION

The idea of writing a history of British pop management from the fifties to the present had been germinating in my mind since early 1982. It was an area that had never been adequately explored in the many books and major articles written about rock music over the years, and I found this both perplexing and frustrating. Virtually every major artiste that I had previously written about was the beneficiary of strong managerial direction and, in many respects, their success was the product of someone else's vision. Remarkably, however, these architects of fame had either been completely forgotten or ludicrously undervalued. Intentionally or otherwise, the media has consistently served to perpetuate pop star propaganda, rarely venturing behind the scenes to investigate the non-musical factors that determine an artiste's rise and fall.

Compiling the case studies that are used in this book was no easy task. Before even beginning the marathon interviewing sessions, I had to read through every British weekly music paper from 1954 to the present. Armed with copious notes and a detailed cross reference of British artistes/managers, I produced a formidable list of candidates. Deleting short-listed case histories was not as difficult as it first seemed. I quickly discovered that many famous figures in the history of British pop have been erroneously referred to as managers when, in fact, they were primarily producers, agents, impresarios or record company executives. Occasionally, somebody would ask me 'Is *x* in your study?' and the reply would be 'Well, actually, he's not really a manager'.

After several years' full-time work on this project, I finally completed 25 case-study chapters which were presented to my agent as a manuscript of 1048 pages. That was just the beginning. Since no publisher could cost out the unexpurgated tome, I restructured the book, dropped some chapters and judiciously edited the remainder.

My final selection of case studies was carefully compiled to reflect the diversity and change that British pop management has undergone since the fifties. The pop landscape presented herein reveals the legendary and the obscure jostling for power in the hope of establishing themselves and their artistes as the new élite. In pop management the line between millionaire success and near bankruptcy, greatness and infamy, and survival and death has often proved remarkably thin. Ego, ambition, greed, power, corruption, faith, dedication, love and uncanny luck have all played their part in motivating the myriad figures of British pop management. What emerges most clearly, however, is the tendency of managers to reflect and even determine the political pop climate in which they function. The fifties was an age of managerial autonomy mirroring the power that the four major companies had over the fate of so many artistes; the sixties was an age of entrepreneurial expansionism in which managers and groups rivalled each other for creativity and charisma; the early seventies represented the rejection of the old-style tycoon, ushering in a period when accountants and solicitors replaced romantic visionaries thereby ensuring that the only sparkle left in British pop was that of artificial glitter; the late seventies and early eighties heralded the return of the young, inexperienced manager and saw an equally frequent turnover of musical styles and sub-cultural fashions. The lessons of history are informative. All managers are, to some extent, creators and victims of their own times.

PARADIGMS OF POP MANAGEMENT

Although all managers perform a range of similar functions, their individual strategies are often miles apart. All managers and artistes indulge in some form of role play and their performances frequently follow a specific pattern. The most familiar caricature of a pop manager would appear to be the cigar-smoking hustler, who takes advantage of starstruck adolescents. Once, this stereotype probably had some validity, though no manager I interviewed blew cigar smoke in my face or acted out the time-honoured proprietorial role. However, I was introduced to a rich variety of managerial types, many of which fell into easily recognizable categories. The following is a selection of the most common types, a number of which will come to life in the succeeding case studies.

The Autocratic Manager

The autocratic manager always thinks he knows what must be done to achieve success and pursues those aims efficiently and ruthlessly. Often, he treats his artistes as pure commodity and is quick to arrest artistic progress if it conflicts with commercial demands. His strength lies in an ability to fight tooth and nail for his artiste, particularly in the financial sphere. All too often, however, he falls victim to greed. Many groups have found themselves virtually bankrupt by allowing a money-orientated manager complete control over their artistic and financial destiny. Today, autocratic managers are regarded by most artistes as somewhat anachronistic and the long history of litigation over allegedly unfair contracts has encouraged both parties to seek independent advice in legal and accounting matters.

The Concerned Parent

Many managers find it easy to slip into the role of the stern, but benevolent, parent. Often, their groups are taught rules and drills that must be obeyed. The Parnes 'code of conduct' and Epstein's famous typed memos to the Beatles were indicative of this mentality. However, these two legendary managers always balanced the cold formality of rules and regulations with a genuine caring approach to their artistes' needs and problems. Parnes and Epstein were capable of great sentimentality and frequently regarded their charges almost as members of the family.

The Indulgent Manager

Altruistic, artiste-orientated managers are rare in pop and rock, but they do exist. At best, they can act as patrons for a major talent by investing huge amounts of money, time and energy in the firm belief that their love and industry will be rewarded. Many sensitive or neurotic performers would never have lasted the course without the dogged persistence of such backers. Unfortunately, it is equally easy to spoil an artiste by over indulgence. Some managers unwittingly create a comfortable environment where the need for hard work and artistic progress becomes irrelevant. A manager with too much heart, too much money and too much faith can sometimes do more harm than a shady hustler in search of a quick financial killing.

The Neophyte
In the early days of British pop, managers tended to be considerably older than their protégés, but the sixties youth explosion changed all that. A new breed of young entrepreneurs led by Andrew Oldham looked and even acted like stars themselves. The image of the youthful tycoon was revived in the wake of punk when many young groups appointed close friends as 'managers'. Some succeeded, diversified, formed independent record labels and established themselves in their own right, but the majority were chewed up and spat out either by the industry they had wooed or the fickle artistes in their charge. History has shown that the greatest problem for a neophyte is not failure but instant, unexpected success. If the hits come instantly and effortlessly, the performer often takes full credit and comes to regard the manager as a hanger-on who struck lucky. In such circumstances, the group becomes easy prey for a 'poacher' or 'inheritor'.

Poachers and Inheritors
It is important to distinguish between 'poachers' and 'inheritors': the former is a predator, the latter an unassuming collector of talent. Both types are experienced and often ruthless businessmen whose promises of fame and wealth frequently prove irresistible to an ambitious or avaricious artiste. An inheritor is usually approached by a group in search of a better deal or more professional representation. Sometimes, a neophyte manager who realizes that he is out of his depth will make the first move in order to prove that he is acting in the best interests of his artiste. This will normally save him from being unceremoniously sacked and encourage the group or inheritor to offer a fair settlement. In such circumstances, the inheritor generally buys the management contract or pays the neophyte a compensatory long-term percentage. There is little hope of such mercy from a seasoned poacher. At his worst, he is Lucifer incarnate, tempting the group with sweet words and fanciful

percentages. He will not hesitate to poison the relationship between an act and their manager for his priority is to win the group for nothing. Far too often, he succeeds.

The Neutered Lackey
Numerous neophytes have survived the onslaught of poachers and inheritors and established themselves with hit groups. Many are managers in name only and spend less time negotiating deals than running around performing demeaning tasks. Occasionally, such lackeys are not even on a percentage, but accept a meagre weekly wage in return for the reflected glory of their spurious status. Paradoxically, there is a growing trend among certain artistes to sign such doting devotees to some form of exclusive contract, thereby denying their managerial services to other rivals. All too often, this is akin to neutering a pet cat. The 'manager' looks the same but his power and virility have been greatly reduced. Such enforced subservience can transform a potentially good manager into a yes-man whose clout in the industry is inevitably non-existent.

The Dilettante Manager
The dilettante is a dangerous species. His motives for entering pop management can range from short-term ego gratification to the equivalent of a financial flurry on the racecourse. The dilettante believes that he has tremendous wisdom to impart to his charges, though he is seldom greatly interested in them as individuals. A hit record will rouse his interest and allow him to bathe in the limelight. Unless success comes quickly and regularly, however, his butterfly mind will move on to other projects, leaving the artiste feeling totally dejected and disillusioned.

The Fatalistic Manager
In attempting to resolve the many ambiguities implicit in the decision-making process, it is not surprising that many managers find themselves overwhelmed with pressure from record companies, agents, accountants and self-conscious artistes. The manager knows that if he ignores the demands of a record company executive, the act may be dropped from the label; if new product is late, finances or lucrative live work may be jeopardized. Conversely, however, the long-term interests of the artiste must be protected from the paranoia of myopic money-grabbers. The effective manager will always be aware of the conflicts between his performers, himself, the record company and other agencies, but the lazy manager, overwhelmed by confusion, is likely to adopt a fatalistic philosophy. He will scorn long-term plans and feebly tackle each problem as it

arises. At such a stage in his career, the manager is merely relying on luck. He no longer manages the events determining the fate of his artistes — they manage him. Inevitably, the result will be illogical advice and desperate gambles as the manager plunges headfirst into self-inflicted chaos.

The Overreachers

In the mid-sixties, pop management was filled with charismatic young figures who saw themselves as moguls capable of establishing hit groups, forming independent record labels, music publishing outlets and production companies. The ultimate dream was to build the biggest financial empire in the music business, and management was often seen as the first crucial step. The relentless ambition of these moguls often produced great innovation and millionaire success, but their impatience and constant need for ego gratification also resulted in premature expansionism and the courting of financial disaster. The spectacular bankruptcies of the Australian entrepreneur Robert Stigwood and the liquidation of Andrew Oldham's Immediate empire pinpoint the pitfalls of relying too heavily on personal flair. Great overreachers love to rise from the dead, but it is never easy.

The Scapegoat Manager

Perhaps the saddest figure in pop is the failed manager who loyally struggles on with a no-hoper group until they split up amid acrimony or disillusionment. Unless he has had success elsewhere, the manager will likely be used as a scapegoat for the performers' own lack of drive or talent. Most scapegoat managers without a hit act or track record quickly disappear from the business and never return.

The Dual Role

Many producers, agents and promoters have dabbled in management over the years with varying degrees of success. Usually, they lose interest quickly and prefer to service an established act rather than spend time developing the career of a rough diamond. Of course, many large, established agencies provide management facilities via employees as a matter of course, often recruiting former independent managers of some standing. In this sense, however, the manager is an adjunct to the agency and his relationship with an artiste tends to be less close.

Co-Management and Team Management

Co-management deals have always been popular with certain managers and artistes. From the management side, it splits the work load and halves the financial risk, while also allowing time to cover options by taking on other acts. For worldly-wise groups who demand a greater say in management decisions, a dual set-up may well produce a more democratic forum for voicing their views. Since the concentration of power often tends to corrupt, co-management structures may appear an ideal and more sophisticated alternative to the rather dated notion of the autocratic svengali. Unfortunately, few of these partnerships have proved long-lasting or successful. Creative managers are independent by nature and their visionary zeal seldom allows compromise. Team management, for all its apparent democracy, can easily create administrative nightmares. The tripartite set-up involving Larry Page, Grenville Collins and Robert Wace ended in a wearying three-year court case. History has shown that such partnerships are more likely to succeed if the individuals are complementary rather than similar (i.e. a creative and business manager combining their respective expertise). All too often, two 'creative' managers controlling one artiste is a recipe for disaster.

The Record Company Manager

By the late sixties there were relatively few established entrepreneurs specializing in the management of albums bands. It was not surprising, therefore, that the new, progressive labels, such as Island and Chrysalis, frequently managed their own acts rather than farming them out to traditional Tin Pan Alley merchants. As a result of this trend, figures such as Chris Blackwell and Chris Wright gained some fame as 'managers' though, in truth, their primary role was record company mogul. Other new labels increasingly placed their artistes' affairs in the hands of trusted employees. The 'in-house' label manager ensured smooth relations between the artiste and record company but, occasionally, he would be placed in an invidious political position as a result of his lack of independence. When such role conflict became unbearable, it was not unusual for a record company manager to leave an organization, taking the artiste with him.

Larry Parnes, the most famous British pop manager of the fifties and, some claim, the greatest of all time, has avoided the regal limelight in recent years and maintained an uncharacteristically low profile. Bouts of poor health are probably part of the reason and Larry himself says that one illness nearly cost him his sight. While researching this book, I was astonished to hear wild rumours circulating from certain quarters that Larry Parnes was dead. It was a surprise, therefore, to meet a sprightly, exuberant man, far removed from the walking corpse of some people's imagination. Indeed, Parnes looked more healthy and youthful than the majority of his once-great contemporaries. During a twelve-hour discussion, including a seven-hour taped interview, Parnes never once showed signs of flagging and our conversation was interrupted only by the arrival of several birds on his penthouse roof at 6.45 a.m. Like his former protégé, the late Billy Fury, Parnes is a great animal lover with a long history of involvement in various animal charities. As the evening progressed, he frequently alluded to Prince and Duke, his long-serving dogs whose cremated remains are displayed in a vase, surrounded by photographs and a personalized epitaph. He clearly grieves for them and betrays a sense of overwhelming loss that is most disconcerting and difficult to rationalize. In more revealing moments, he confesses that he is presently going through a rather negative period in his life but hopes this outlook will alter in the near future. For all his show business achievements and reputed wealth, Parnes seems an unusually solitary figure and gives the impression of a man marking time.

For almost a decade, Larry was celebrated as the great connoisseur of the pop world with his stylish clothes and exotic tastes in food and wine. Nowadays, he prefers to live more simply though he retains some of the trappings of a flashier youth including a Jaguar, a Knightsbridge flat and a propensity for lavishly prepared Chinese food.

Parnes comes across very much as an old sentimentalist and displays a fierce loyalty towards his former artistes. Although most of his acts left him over two decades ago, his rose-coloured perception of their talents remains undarkened. His comments sound like public-relations hyperbole until you realize that he passionately believes every word. The stream of compliments ranges from plausible ('Billy Fury was the most important rock 'n' roll singer Britain ever produced') to fanciful ('Marty Wilde could go into

films and out-act 500 people currently on the screen') contentious
('Marty has a better voice and stage presence than Cliff') and nigh
heretical ('Tommy Steele was a much better stage performer than
Elvis'). Indeed, Larry elaborates on that last comment to imply
that the main reason Elvis never toured Britain was because he
knew that our Tommy would show him up as a one-dimensional
performer. Even his second division acts receive warm praise and
Larry fights a stirring verbal battle on their behalf, often expressing
puzzlement at their lack of chart success. His unswaying commitment to his artistes is unquestionably his most distinctive characteristic as a manager. What makes him more important is his
historical role as Britain's first pop mogul. Parnes was *the* trailblazer
— there is no comparable figure in fifties rock to match his entrepreneurial power or skill.

Often, people speak of born singers, born musicians or born
actors, but Larry Parnes was a most unlikely specimen — a born
impresario. At the precocious age of eight, he organized his first
show in Cliftonville, Kent, featuring a cast of child artistes. The
performance produced a grand profit of £2. 15s. The road from
Cliftonville to the London Palladium was a considerable distance
and, for a long time, Parnes seemed unsure of the route. Partly
financed by his family, he bought three ladies' fashion shops, but
only one proved a successful business venture. Soon, Parnes was in
debt, a disillusioned shopkeeper with an uncertain future.

By the mid-fifties, Larry was leading a quiet, unexciting life, far
removed from the glamorous world of show business. That situation
gradually changed following a series of happy accidents. A friend who
worked for BOAC took a look at Larry one night and told him he led a
much too insular life and should spend more time enjoying himself.
The reluctant socialite was taken to *La Caverne,* a subterranean bar
in Romilly Street in London's West End where the governors allowed
after-hours drinking for a select clientele. Soon, everybody proceeded
to get half drunk except the sober-blooded young Parnes. He had
never taken a drink in his life. As the night wore on, the two
proprietors became embroiled in a discussion which swiftly developed
into a slanging match. Ever the peacemaker, Larry intervened and
after calming them down attempted to sort out their problems. It
soon transpired that the two partners found it impossible to work
together so, in a moment of madness, Parnes offered to buy one of
them out. Of course, there was one major problem — Parnes had
almost no money. Fortunately, one of the partners was so anxious
to leave that he agreed to accept £500 on an instalment basis. The
following morning, Parnes rushed to his solicitor who drafted a

contract which was immediately signed. Larry was back in business!

In order not to offend altruistic customers, the new teetotal proprietor reluctantly began drinking Scotch in minimal amounts. Often, Parnes would sit alone for four or five hours surveying the bar like a king watching over his realm. *La Caverne* had style, but no stairs. Probably half the fun was watching people climbing up and down the ladder that was the only entrance to the bar. Its setting seemed to attract an intriguing clientele and Larry soon began to recognize important playwrights, famous actors and show business personalities.

One evening, a mischievous prankster decided to have some fun at Larry's expense by challenging him to a whisky-drinking contest. Parnes blithely accepted and within an hour found himself staggering along the streets of the West End lost in a euphoric drunken haze. When he failed to return to *La Caverne* his concerned friend set off in hot pursuit only to discover Larry outside the London Pavilion singing a selection of Johnnie Ray songs to a bemused and enraptured crowd. Within seconds, he was huddled into the back of a car, driven home, and left to sleep off his midnight revelries.

The following morning the whisky-drinking champion awoke with a pounding headache. His hangover was interrupted by a knock on the door where he was greeted by a distinguished gentleman with horn-rimmed glasses and an expensive briefcase. The man explained that he was here to discuss 'the play'. It soon transpired that during the previous evening Larry had agreed to produce a new play called *The House of Shame*. The gent standing in front of him was producer Geoff Wright and the truth was he needed an 'angel' to finance the project. Seduced by the glamour of the theatre, Larry agreed to another investment by instalment. The play toured throughout 1955 but seemed destined to run at a substantial loss until Wright recruited a young publicist named John Kennedy. He immediately persuaded his employer to change the title of the play to the more provocative *Women Of The Streets* and in a brilliant publicity stunt persuaded a couple of the actresses to stand outside the stage door during the interval. Dressed as prostitutes, the girls caused an absolute sensation and soon found themselves under police arrest. The national press picked up on the story and, as a result, the play took off. At the end of the year, Parnes received a balance sheet and was amused to discover that he had made a total profit of £2. 15s. — precisely the amount taken at that Cliftonville show many years before.

In spite of his flirtation with West End theatres and clubs, Parnes still felt unfulfilled. Even a three-week Scandinavian holiday with an American friend seemed only a prelude to an anti-climactic return to London. On the evening that his friend departed for the States, the travel-weary Parnes returned home and at 7 p.m. crept into bed. Two hours later, he was still awake and extremely bored. Eventually, he roused his spirits sufficiently to get dressed and drive towards Soho, still feeling very negative and unsure what was drawing him towards London's most lively but notorious square mile. Parking his car in Wardour Street, he suddenly found himself outside a coffee bar, The Sabrina. The joint was obviously named after the busty starlet who was then Britain's parodic equivalent of Jayne Mansfield. Larry had met Sabrina several times, and the association of her name with the coffee bar encouraged him to enter the place. As he walked in, a hand tapped him on the shoulder and Larry looked around to see a vaguely familiar face. It was John Kennedy. The young publicist explained that he had been mysteriously fired during the closing run of *Women Of The Streets* and wanted to know why. Larry couldn't provide the answer, but agreed to join John in a commiserative cup of coffee. They adjourned to a table in the gallery and while studying their respective menus, an unusual conversation ensued. Kennedy asked the great Parnes his opinion of rock 'n' roll. Larry completely misheard the question and, scouring the menu, explained that he didn't like rock cakes and would much prefer a sandwich to a roll. The publicist dropped his menu and exclaimed excitedly 'No, rock 'n' roll! The big thing that's sweeping America.' A rather embarrassed Parnes was forced to admit that he had never even heard the term. The admission was nothing less than extraordinary. By mid-1956, Teddy Boys were terrorizing the streets; Bill Haley had already charted with 'Shake, Rattle And Roll' and 'Rock Around The Clock'; *The Blackboard Jungle* had reached our screens and Elvis was in the charts with 'Heartbreak Hotel'. Yet, Parnes was strangely unaware of the rock 'n' roll revolution and seemed still lost in the sobs of Johnnie Ray. What Kennedy started that evening was to transform the face of British popular music for the next five years.

While Larry drank his coffee, the garrulous publicist explained that he had found a boy who could be Britain's first rock 'n' roll sensation. The kid was barely 20, a merchant seaman, and had played several shows in American servicemen's camps. All he needed was the right management and some financial backing to achieve national success. Parnes considered this latest deal but became slightly sceptical when he learned that the potential star was named Tommy Hicks. Kennedy brushed that objection aside and begged Larry to come and see the boy perform at the Condor Club. 'Where's that?', enquired Parnes. 'Above this coffee bar!'

replied Kennedy. Unfortunately, Parnes was in such an apathetic mood that he couldn't even muster the enthusiasm to travel that far. After finishing his coffee, he wearily arose and returned to his car. Clutching at straws, Kennedy invited his reluctant companion to attend Hicks' next performance at Regent Street's Stork Room. Grudgingly, Larry accepted and following a series of pestering phone calls turned up at the club the following week.

When the singer bounded on to the grand stage of the Stork Room Parnes received a pleasant surprise. Three months earlier he had seen the same performer singing for his supper at the Gyre and Gimble, a small coffee shop behind the Strand. Parnes had been mildly impressed then, but at the Stork Room Hicks was even better: 'I watched him . . . It was a very hard club. They weren't teenagers and this was a night club with a tough audience, but they loved him. He brought the place to life. He had charisma and a great personality.'

After the show, Parnes was introduced to the young singer who studied his features very closely. The lad then turned to John Kennedy and said: 'I like him. He's got honest eyes.' Brimming with confidence, Hicks proceeded to inform the startled Parnes 'You and he are going to be my managers'. Larry was about to interject when he received a sharp kick from John Kennedy. A long conversation followed, and it became increasingly obvious that Hicks, Kennedy and Parnes were a lethal combination. Although Larry was ignorant of rock 'n' roll, he had seen hundreds of kids screaming at Johnnie Ray and frequently wondered why Britain could not produce a similarly sensational home-grown star. All it required, in Parnes' mind, was the right combination of talent and image. Tommy had already demonstrated his talents and John Kennedy, as a master publicist, could be relied upon to develop the perfect image. By the end of the evening Larry felt committed to the partnership and a management contract was signed a few weeks later in September 1956. Initially, Parnes and Kennedy met some resistance from their old friend Geoff Wright, who, in conjunction with businessman Roy Tuvey, claimed prior rights on Hicks' contract. It was soon pointed out, however, that Tommy had never signed an agreement with them and was perfectly entitled to appoint new advisers. Kennedy had put the matter beyond doubt by securing the signatures of Hicks' parents. According to legend, Kennedy's confidence was so great that he promised to tear up the contract if the management failed to make the boy a national star within three months. It was like a crazy Hollywood movie script with Kennedy playing the fast-talking, streetwise starmaker. Yet his brash assurances were to prove remarkably prophetic.

During the early stages of Hicks' career, Kennedy was undoubtedly the major creative force and provided Parnes with a number of ideas and strategies that were successfully developed with other artistes in later years. First, there was the all-important rechristening of Thomas Hicks who was transformed into Tommy Steele — a neat amalgam of the homely and the sexual. However, Kennedy was careful to keep Steele's sexuality submerged and maintain his clean-cut wholesome image. The press had already denounced razor-slashing Teddy Boys and in many people's eyes rock 'n' roll was synonymous with hooliganism and venereal disease. As Britain's first rock 'n' roll star, Steele had the power to reverse this blanket condemnation of teenage music and introduce the record industry to a new generation of young artistes. His success, however, depended on good publicity and the willingness of record companies, agents and theatre managers to accept that there was life after Variety. Remarkably, this was all achieved in the short space of six weeks. Within days, Kennedy was knocking on record company doors and although he received a terse rejection from EMI's George Martin, the powers at Decca were not so myopic. Their A & R (artistes and repertoire) manager, Hugh Mendl, agreed to cut a record immediately, while Kennedy embarked on a vigorous promotional campaign. Using the old 'working-class boy makes good' angle, John placed the chirpy cockney in the unlikely setting of a debutante's ball. Class-conscious Fleet Street lapped up the idea of Tommy as the 'Deb's delight' and immediately took him to their hearts. Meanwhile, Decca rush released the debut single 'Rock With The Caveman' which was showcased on BBC's *Off The Record*. The television exposure and attendant publicity were sufficient to provide a Top 20 hit, followed by a nationwide tour. Tommy Steele had truly arrived.

Strangely enough, Steele's second single, 'Doomsday Rock/Elevator Rock', was a complete flop, but the management were unfazed by this setback, as Parnes recalls:

> We never had time to worry. We always had such enormous faith in Tommy's talent that one record didn't make any difference. In those days records weren't as important as the artiste and the talent, and when you've got a super talent like Tommy Steele, why worry about one record. We never looked at Tommy as a recording artiste.

The management's confidence was vindicated when a cover of Guy Mitchell's 'Singing The Blues' reached number 1 in January 1957. Since there was effectively no competition from any other young

British singer, Steele could do no wrong. His tours proved spectacularly successful and for the music press of the period he personified British rock 'n' roll. Without resorting to sexual suggestiveness or onstage violence, he managed to provoke mass teenage hysteria unseen since the days of Johnnie Ray.

After six months on the road with Steele, the restless Kennedy became bored and decided to return to London. Relations between the publicist and his star were often strained and more than once Parnes had been forced to intervene as peacemaker. Larry was pleased to assume Kennedy's role on tour and it was at this stage that he emerged as a creative force in his own right. While Kennedy had been content to allow Steele to perform a raucous, non-stop rock 'n' roll set, Parnes suggested a more professional approach. He encouraged Tommy to project his personality by talking to audiences and injecting humour into the show. During perform-ances, the manager would be out front taking notes on the success or failure of particular ad libs and later advising which routines should be incorporated in the set. In effect, Parnes was negating the precious little crudity that still existed in Steele's already polished anglicized rock 'n' roll.

Although rock purists may accuse Parnes of heresy, his desire to transform his protégé into an all-round entertainer was eminently logical. In 1956, British rock 'n' roll could not develop in a vacuum outside the sphere of traditional show business. From the outset, conformity was implicit in Steele's rise to fame and any real rebellion would have been snuffed out immediately. Even his major rock 'n' roll hit had achieved success partly through the comic notion of rocking with a caveman. The fact that rock 'n' roll was regarded as a 'craze' rather than a powerful movement precluded any thoughts about achieving a long-term career in that area. It would be tanta-mount to expecting a sixties artiste to survive indefinitely on twist records. The state of the art and the industry in 1956 had a powerful influence on Parnes from which he never fully recovered. He became the champion of rock 'n' roll, but never saw it as an end in itself; it was an important apprenticeship probably lasting two or three years after which the artiste would move into other areas of show business, preferably theatre or films. Steele was a great disciple of Parnes in this respect and eventually achieved more success in traditional show business areas than he ever did in rock 'n' roll. His career development appeared to vindicate Parnes' general philosophy. Larry came to regard pure rock 'n' rollers like Gene Vincent as excellent, yet limited. Similarly, although he rightly derides the fifties music press for describing Tommy Steele as 'Britain's Answer To Elvis Presley', it is not because the epithet is flattering nor, indeed, because his artiste was innocuous by comparison. What irks Parnes is that Tommy should be bracketed alongside a seemingly one-dimensional artiste:

> Tommy was nothing like Presley. He never looked like Presley, he never acted like Presley. Tommy was a much better stage performer than Elvis . . . The press saw Marty Wilde as Britain's Elvis Presley. They saw Billy Fury as Britain's Elvis Presley. The British press was always calling my artistes Elvis Presley. It was a load of rubbish. To be frank, Elvis Presley, with all due respect, may have been a great star and a legend but he could never have gone on to the heights that Tommy achieved. Not in the areas that Tommy achieved them. Never.

At heart, Parnes was a show business tycoon rather than a lover of pure rock 'n' roll, but at least he recognized its potency. For the next few years, Parnes would nurture British rock 'n' roll more lovingly than any entrepreneur of his era. Like a protective parent, however, he trusted that his offspring would one day grow up and marry into the powerful, secure and richer family of show business.

By mid-1957, Steele was fulfilling the career plan that he and Parnes had unconsciously mapped out. During one summer week he had four songs in the Top 30 but none could be classified as rock 'n' roll. In spite of these hits, recording became very much a secondary issue as the Bermondsey boy sought far greater heights. A bit part in a film starring Pat O'Brien, *Kill Me Tomorrow*, led to a contract for an autobiographical movie based on his remarkable rise to fame. The resulting musical, *The Tommy Steele Story*, even spawned a book of the same title written by John Kennedy. That the life of a British rock 'n' roller should be deemed worthy of a film and a book was in itself remarkable for the period, indicating how successfully Steele had captured the public's imagination.

The importance of Tommy Steele as a prototype for English rock 'n' roll singers prior to the Beatles is undeniable. What seems most extraordinary, however, is the way Parnes and Kennedy maintained his standing as a rock 'n' roller even while he was moving into other fields of entertainment. Whether it was playing before debs, performing at the Café Royal, or appearing in panto-mime, Tommy's achievements were paradoxically publicized as those of a rocker. In this way, Parnes and Kennedy were able to capture young and old alike without seeming to compromise. Even as late as May 1958, Steele caused a riot when he appeared at Dundee's Caird Hall. Fans crowded on to the stage, pulled his hair, tore his shirt and actually knocked him unconscious. He might even have died if the gallant Parnes hadn't pushed his way through the hordes of fans to rescue his fallen star. Yet, within a month of this pandemonium, Tommy effectively abdicated his rock 'n' roll throne by announcing his engagement. The publicity caused great concern to his managers who felt that the betrothal should have remained a secret for a further year. In effect, it made little difference to Steele's popularity since his younger fans were already discovering new heroes. Although Steele continued to live a dual life as a rock 'n' roller cum family entertainer, his original persona gradually faded as the fifties wound to a close. Further movie success in *The Duke Wore Jeans* (1958) and *Tommy The Toreador* (1959) helped redefine his image, while also restricting the time available for touring. In recording terms, 1959 saw the final throes of Tommy the rocker with covers of Ritchie Valens' 'Come On Let's Go' and Freddy Cannon's 'Talahassee Lassie'. The year and decade ended, however, with the novelty children's number 'Little White Bull' and after that it had to be goodbye to rock 'n' roll.

The management continued to advise Steele during the second stage of his career, but prior to that they had consolidated their position as the decade's most successful discoverers of teenage talent. Kennedy attempted to recreate the Steele magic by launching Tommy's younger brother, Colin Hicks, in the autum of 1957. Ever ambitious, Kennedy began negotiating film contracts and arranged several foreign tours in the hope of breaking the boy abroad. His strategies remained undeveloped, however, for in the same month that Steele became engaged, Hicks' contract was terminated. Strangely enough, his mother took over the management reins, aided by the Fosters Agency. For Kennedy, that was effectively the end of his career as a full-time pop manager. He eventually split with Parnes and pursued other interests outside show business.

Meanwhile, Larry became more intrigued by rock 'n' roll and his entrepreneurial ambitions increased accordingly. Having helped launch the career of Tommy Steele, he lusted for further success and spent much time scouring coffee bars and dance halls in search of another star. It was Lionel Bart, co-writer of several Tommy Steele hits, who first informed Parnes about Reg Smith (né Patterson), the latest singing sensation of the Condor Club. Larry was so impressed by Bart's testimonial that he immediately went to the establishment only to find that the singer had left. The following day Smith received a big surprise. Having discovered his address, Parnes turned up at his house and presented the kid with a management contract. As the star elect later observed: 'It was typical

Larry. The contract even had my name on it, and I'd never met the guy before!' Suddenly, Parnes was demonstrating fast talking and creative skills the equal of John Kennedy. The boy was taken away and neatly groomed into a potential teenage star. This meant purchasing new clothes from the best tailors, meeting important journalists and learning to appear relaxed and confident in any social situation. Although Smith accepted Larry's training programme, he had a strong will of his own and challenged many decisions. Their first major disagreement occurred when Parnes announced that Reg Smith was dead. Henceforth he would be known as Marty Wilde. It was an inspired rechristening, combining the wild side of the kid's nature with the sentimentality of Marty, the anti-hero portrayed by Ernest Borgnine in the film of the same name. Unfortunately, Smith hated his new name and gamely resisted Parnes' persuasion. Eventually, both parties agreed to decide the issue by tossing a coin. Reg lost both spins and was forced to surrender his Christian name and surname, much to his later relief:

> Once I'd been going a year I realized how lucky I was to have that name. I'm very grateful really. It's a fantastic stage name; it always looked good in print or on a poster. In the old days my name used to stand out. Always.

A flash name was not enough to break a teenage singer in Britain during 1957, and in spite of a lucrative contract with Philips, Wilde's early releases failed to chart. This was of little consequence, however, as Parnes' control of the means of hit production was growing with each successive month. After plugging Wilde consistently throughout 1957, Larry eventually won the ear of television producers. By the New Year, Marty was Britain's most famous non-chart singing idol and frequently hogged BBC's 6.5. *Special* for stretches of four weeks. In February, he appeared on both channels during the same evening, a remarkable achievement by fifties standards. With such extensive media exposure it was inevitable that Marty would chart eventually and in June he finally broke through with a cover of Jody Reynolds' 'Endless Sleep'. Meanwhile, negotiations were completed for a television deal that would put Wilde's supremacy beyond doubt. The man who held the key to his future was the most powerful and influential purveyor of teenage talent that British television has ever known.

Jack Good, a bombastic, outrageous and passionate believer in the power of pop had singlehandedly attempted to transform BBC's 6.5. *Special* into a platform for energetic, rebellious teenage music.

He used every trick in the book to try and fulfil that dream, including bluff, braggadocio and downright deception. In order to satisfy prying executives, he displayed safe, standard scenery that would later be discarded minutes before a show. Suddenly, a throng of teenagers would surround bemused cameramen and stars alike causing an electric atmosphere in the studio. It was a great idea that remained undeveloped. The spectacle proved far too anarchic for the conservative controllers of British broadcasting and Good was immediately forced to modify his innovative schemes. For the most part, he remained a rock 'n' roll evangelist outnumbered by pagan worshippers of showbiz shlock. Fortunately, there was one person who shared his vocation and religiously devoted himself to the deification of the teenage pop star. Larry Parnes was both soulmate and ally in the fight for televised rock 'n' roll for he knew that the support of this flamboyant producer meant exposure to millions of potential record buyers. Conversely, Good was very much aware that the continued support of Parnes would ensure a steady flow of teenage talent.

When the BBC brought in a new co-producer to oversee Good, he moved to independent television and announced plans for a new pop programme, *Oh Boy*. As soon as he heard this news, Larry was on the phone, nominating Marty Wilde as the resident star of the series. For a month, the arrangement worked perfectly, then disaster struck. Jack took an intense dislike to Wilde's latest single, 'Misery's Child', and refused to allow him to perform the song. The record flopped and Parnes was less than pleased. His anger increased upon learning that Good had discovered a new kid whose talents were so impressive that he was immediately booked for the show. The mystery star was Cliff Richard and to add salt to the wounds Larry remembered turning him down at a recent audition. At that stage, the boy had his own group, but now Good was pushing him as a soloist in direct competition to Marty Wilde. The consequences were unthinkable and Parnes regarded the producer's decision as little short of treasonable. In a huff, he stormed into the studio and physically dragged Marty from the set. The music press were informed that Wilde was boycotting *Oh Boy* because the producer was unfairly developing the career of 'a virtually unknown artiste'. Cliff didn't stay unknown for long. Within days of his television debut, the sublime 'Move It' rocketed to number 2. Cliff was unstoppable.

The loss of Jack Good was a terrible blow to Marty and he placed the blame firmly on Parnes' shoulders. Suddenly, Larry found himself in a nightmarish situation. He had alienated the most important producer in pop and now his artiste was threatening mutiny. Standing firm, Parnes informed the press that he would not be releasing Wilde from his management contract. The stalemate continued until December when, in true festive spirit, Good, Parnes and Wilde reconciled their differences. Larry remembers the happy conclusion:

> I knew Jack's temperament. I did blow my top and I regretted it because I had no desire to upset Jack or Marty. But I did have an arrangement whereby Marty would be the star of *Oh Boy* and I objected strongly that somebody else was going to be brought in . . . That was loyalty to my artiste. I think Jack recognized that . . . I had a great respect for Jack Good and if I hadn't Marty would not have been back in *Oh Boy*.

Like Tommy Steele, Marty chose 1959 as the symbolic final year of his career as a rock 'n' roller. He achieved spectacular success with such songs as 'Donna', 'Teenager In Love', 'Sea Of Love' and 'Bad Boy', almost keeping pace with Cliff's own chart achievements. However, any hopes of prolonging his career as a rock idol were abandoned following his announcement to Parnes that he intended to marry Joyce Baker of the Vernon Girls. According to Marty, such a statement was the fifties equivalent of a modern pop star telling the world he hated all Jews and blacks. Fortunately, Parnes took the news philosophically, as Marty reveals:

> I didn't give Larry a choice on the matter. I said, 'I'm going to get married. It's my decision.' We then had a business meeting. He laid out my future on the table and he told me my career would suffer badly. Very badly. He wanted to move me into films and other areas . . . He was quite good about it really. A lot of managers would have pulled some dirty tricks and he did have a lot of power.

In effect, Marty's engagement allowed Parnes to plot the second stage of his career. Several months before the wedding, Wilde announced that he would be abandoning rock 'n' roll in favour of classy Sinatra-style ballads. His new image was unveiled in the latest Jack Good pop show *Boy Meets Girls* in which Marty was the boy compere. The show included several visiting American rock 'n' roll stars, including Gene Vincent and Eddie Cochran, whom Parnes had booked for a UK tour. Apart from such highlights, however, the programme was a poor successor to *Oh Boy*, lacking the drive, energy and innovation that had made its predecessor such a landmark in British television pop history.

The seven-month run of *Boy Meets Girls* was merely a prelude to the elaborate long term career plans that Parnes had been hatching for his semi-retired rock 'n' roller. Like Tommy Steele, Marty was guided into film and theatre work. A starring role in the West End production of *Bye Bye Birdie* convinced Parnes that he was potentially a great actor, but the manager's dream of Hollywood stardom remained unrealized:

> We had differences. I didn't want him to go on making rock 'n' roll records like a lot of people were doing. Marty had such talent that he could have progressed in several different directions of show business. But that's where we differed. Marty didn't see himself as an actor, which has always amazed me.

Wilde's reluctance to adhere to Parnes' career plan left him in a barren wilderness for much of the sixties. According to his manager, Marty foresaw the era of the beat group years before any of his predecessors. Unfortunately, he was at odds with Philips' producer, Johnny Franz, who preferred lush orchestration to the loud sound of guitars and drums.

Rather than fulfilling Parnes' dreams, Wilde struggled on as a rock 'n' roller until the advent of the Beatles, after which he was regarded as an anachronism. There are no easy answers to the questions that Wilde's career provokes. Arguably, Parnes was not radical enough in his championing of rock 'n' roll, though by the early sixties even the American greats were veering towards MOR (middle of the road). The fact that Marty had not developed as a songwriter was also unfortunate, though this could hardly be blamed on Parnes. Indeed, it was Larry who insisted that Wilde release his own composition, 'Bad Boy', rather than the Mort Shuman/Doc Pomus flip, 'It's So Nice', which the artiste preferred. Such differences of opinion continued until 1963 when Marty finally left his long-term manager:

> Things were moving fast at the time and Larry didn't seem to be into the music. But, on reflection, I wasn't successful in the Beatles era. I like to think of us as being pretty good for the time. People have a go at artistes for being short term and, of course, it is marvellous to be a long-term artiste. But if you can hit the big time and hold it for two years, whether you're well-off or not financially, you've cracked it. You can't do much more than that.

Wilde claims that it was difficult to convince Larry to release the management reins and the leaving was a long drawn-out process. Parnes does not refute this but maintains that his motive was to persuade Marty to reconsider the possibility of pursuing an acting career. Much to his manager's amazement and frustration, Wilde refused to be drawn and went his own way.

The career of Marty Wilde was paralleled in microcosm by Parnes' third discovery, Vince Eager, who was launched during the spring of 1958. As his name suggests, Eager was a vivacious, hard-working performer, perfectly suited to the pop television shows of the period. Indeed, thanks to Jack Good, he became a minor star of *Oh Boy*. Vince was ambitious and this led to rivalry between himself and Marty, who felt that he was deliberately aping his act and often performing the same material. Parnes naturally harnessed this friction between the performers in order to keep them on their toes. Eager continued to live up to his name and accepted any booking that his manager negotiated. During the Parnes/Good feud, he could be found in Southport playing Simple Simon in a Mother Goose pantomime. Without doubt, he had showbiz potential, and the television exposure seemed to guarantee a hit single. Yet, despite a series of 1959 singles written by such big names as Floyd Robinson, Marty Robbins, Conway Twitty and Gene Pitney, the unfortunate Eager failed to chart. Parnes remained actively involved in his career throughout this period and achieved a major coup when he secured him a regular starring spot on BBC's *Drumbeat*. The show was a poor man's *Oh Boy*, designed to cash in on Jack Good's success on independent television, but it was popular enough to make Eager a household name.

Parnes' business relationship with Eager did not survive the *Drumbeat* series. Although he religiously appeared every week to attend the star during rehearsals, Eager became resentful of his presence. Shortly after this rebuttal, Larry received a visit from Vince's brother-in-law who requested that their contract be terminated. Parnes recalls the outcome:

> I said, 'All right, take over his contract!' This was while he was still on *Drumbeat*. He had the exposure and every opportunity to become a great big star. People liked Vince; he was a wonderful stage artiste and a good recording artiste. I can only tell you that a few months later his brother-in-law walked into my office and said, 'Larry, I can't manage Vince. I wish I'd never taken it on in the first place!' I could never understand it.

Without Parnes, Eager had little hope of extending recording or television contracts and his career quickly floundered. He remains a curious footnote in rock history, top of Parnes' second division, yet doomed to be dismissed as a Presley clone. The ever-patriotic

Parnes deplores such classifications and insists that all his artistes were true originals. Time has a delightful way of compounding such ironies, however, and it may be worth noting that Vince Eager was last heard of playing the leading role in the stage production of *Elvis*.

The power that Larry Parnes wielded during the pre-Beatles era of rock 'n' roll met little challenge from his contemporaries. Paul Lincoln, the proprietor of the Two Is, managed a couple of minor figures, most notably Terry Dene; the agent Tito Burns nabbed Cliff Richard for a spell, and the ageing queen of show business, Eve Taylor, mothered Adam Faith. Parnes was light years ahead of them all as a manager and, whatever errors he may have made, his reputation as the Great Provider of British rock 'n' roll was consummated in September 1958 at the Essoldo Cinema, Birkenhead. It was there that a gutsy teenager, guitar in hand, briskly walked into Marty Wilde's dressing room and asked to play a few songs. Parnes was so enthralled that he actually included the kid in that evening's performance. Suddenly, Ronald Wycherley was no longer a tugboatman. The furore he had created that evening had transformed him into the next Parnes creation — Billy Fury. Larry immediately approached Marty Wilde's label, Philips, but, incredibly, they turned the boy down. An audition was next held in the Midlands and several companies were notified, including Decca. Although Hugh Mendl, 'the gent of A & R', had already worked with Tommy Steele, it was Dick Rowe, the company 'spiv', who travelled to the audition that fateful afternoon. Rowe recalls what happened:

> When I got there and saw him I was mesmerized. I couldn't wait to take the boy back to London and get him in the studio. Jack Baverstock from Fontana was behind me, so I knew I had to act quickly. I told my boss, 'He's sensational. We've got to have him!' He phoned Larry who said, 'Delighted . . . but I don't want Dick Rowe to produce'. I was very upset.

Rowe believes that at that stage Parnes was reluctant to take a chance so elected to work with a senior producer. Dick was so disappointed with Decca that he left the company for a spell and joined the Rank Organization, producing for their label, Top Rank. He would not return for another year, but by that time both Larry and Billy would be waiting with open arms.

Meanwhile, Parnes had already begun building Billy's career. Within weeks, the boy successfully auditioned for a part in a television play, *Strictly For The Sparrows*, a prestigious start for an unknown. Next there was the inevitable audition for *Oh Boy*. Jack Good needed little convincing that Parnes' latest discovery was his greatest yet. The kid was a television producer's dream, a veritable rock 'n' roll icon. Visually, he exuded all the characteristics of a teen idol: high cheekbones, a perfectly-chiselled nose, brooding eyes and slicked-back hair that drooped over his forehead whenever he bent forward. His stage movements revealed a sexual intensity reminiscent of early Elvis, complete with swaying hips and an over-fondness for the microphone. It was hardly surprising when his risqué act later led to a ban in Eire. This was the stuff of rock 'n' roll heroes. Marty Wilde watched his early performances on *Oh Boy* and felt convinced that Billy would take over completely from himself and Cliff.

Unlike his contemporaries, Fury launched his career with a string of original compositions. More importantly, he created one of the rare examples of classic British rock 'n' roll with a 10-inch album, *The Sound Of Fury*. His influence on later UK rock stars was profound and Parnes frequently received flattering comments from the most unlikely sources:

> As far as pre-sixties British rock 'n' roll is concerned, Billy should be credited as the most important figure this country ever produced. Even David Bowie once told me he modelled himself on Billy. He said his brother used to take him to the shows and he thought Billy was wonderful. I think that's a great compliment.

In spite of the accolades, Billy's early recordings were not the monster hits that Parnes expected. While both Marty and Cliff effortlessly ripped into the Top 10, the Fury phenomenon had yet to be translated into record sales. Whatever plans Parnes plotted for his great discovery were also seriously hampered by a startling disclosure. Less than one year after his rise to fame, Larry learned that the teenager had a serious heart condition. His childhood had been plagued by constant illness following a bout of rheumatic fever which left him a walking time bomb. While his competitors were expected to tour throughout the year, Fury could not possibly survive the strain of endless road work that the early sixties demanded from rock performers. Consequently, he was forced to alter the nature of his appeal, though it is doubtful whether he would have remained a rock 'n' roller even if his health had been perfect. The balladeering success of Elvis and Cliff proved irresist-ible to record company producers and managers alike, and Fury found it easy to slip into this niche. The appointment of Dick Rowe as Billy's producer confirmed his move into the world of high ballads, almost all of them cover versions. Rowe had an unfortunate habit of serving up old chestnuts from bygone years, but with Fury he also kept a close eye on the American charts and snapped up fine songs by writers such as Goffin and King and Don Covay. The result was a string of hits that continued even through the ravages of Beatlemania. There could be no argument that Parnes handled Fury's career transition with great astuteness.

The cumulative success of Steele, Wilde, Eager and Fury were impressive achievements for a fifties entrepreneur and towards the end of the decade Larry branched out still further. With *Oh Boy* offering him television exposure to over nine million viewers, there was every incentive to increase his roster of artistes and blitz the country with a battalion of talented teenagers. It almost worked too, but, eventually, Larry was to fall victim to the law of diminishing returns. Significantly, the earliest signings from this second wave were the strongest. The first to emerge was Richard Knellar, a modest young man whom Parnes felt totally underestimated his own talent. In order to instil some self-belief in the lad, Larry christened him Dickie Pride. Following a number of appearances on *Oh Boy*, Pride was signed to Columbia and achieved a minor hit single, 'Primrose Lane'. Parnes held great hopes for his future, but Pride sabotaged his own career by breaking his manager's strict code of conduct. When Larry learned that the boy was taking drugs, he simply tore up his contract. Having witnessed the fall and degradation of Terry Dene, Parnes was well aware of the disastrous effects of bad publicity. Any scandal attached to even one of his artistes would reflect badly on the others, several of whom were heading for Royal Variety Performances and acting roles. Pride's drug abuse not only cost him his career but his life. Parnes mourns the tragic waste of potential:

> Dickie, poor Dickie, he died very young, but there was an artiste. He made a wonderful album called *Pride Without Prejudice*, which I named. He had a superb recording voice and stage act. I remember Tommy Steele standing in the wings and saying, 'Boy, that fellow has got talent!'

Within a couple of months of Pride's launching, Larry had already found another great young hope in the form of Ray Howard, lately renamed Duffy Power. He had been 'discovered' one morning at a dance contest, specially put on for the children of Shepherd's Bush. According to Larry, the main reason for the signing was because 'he was such a good mover'. Power specialized in rock 'n' roll covers such as 'Ain't She Sweet' and gamely resisted Parnes'

advice to record a catchy ballad written by his good friend Lionel
Bart. The song, 'Living Doll', was eventually passed over to deadly
rival Cliff Richard and rapidly soared to number 1. Poor Duffy
looked on enviously but in spite of several near misses and years of
hard touring he failed to achieve the major breakthrough that had
seemed so tantalizingly close in 1959.

Parnes was driven by a strange, intense urge during 1959. No
longer satisfied with developing an artiste over a two-year period,
he seemed to be signing new singers every month, almost as if the
end of the fifties signalled the extinction of the British teenager.
With their exotic titles, these boys sounded less like pop stars than
allegorical figures from a medieval moral pageant. The struggles
between the Proud and the Eager, the Power and the Fury and the
Wilde and the Gentle were no longer restricted to Miracle plays,
French Romances or Spenserian epics: they had escaped the confines of these fictional and theatrical landscapes and now inhabited
the pop universe of *Oh Boy, Drumbeat* and *Boy Meets Girls*. Parnes
had virtually transformed pop into his own technicolour epic where
moral conceits and aspects of personality took on human form,
sang songs, became stars and lived out their lives in the *real* world.
This was more than rock management, this was almost a new form
of art. Jean-Paul Sartre once argued that in order to be truly
realistic, fiction must somehow completely escape the hand of the
artist and function in an independent, self-sufficient universe.
Books must somehow become like trees or dogs, living, organic
objects outside the control of the author. This was a crazy cosmo-
logical concept way beyond the experimental work of Woolf, Joyce
or Kafka, who were writers, not gods. But Parnes had become a
god, and in the microcosm of pop had unwittingly fulfilled Sartre's
dream — the transmogrification of art into life.

The proliferation of teenage pop artistes under Parnes' aegis
inevitably attracted media attention. The documentary programme
Panorama included a special feature on the 'beat svengali' and the
national press soon followed their lead. However, rather than
hailing Parnes as a twentieth-century conceptualist, they branded
him a stud farmer. His protégés became known as the 'stable of
stars' and much time was spent explaining precisely how they had
been 'groomed'. During interviews of the period, Larry would
settle into his starmaker role and provide revealing tips on how to
breed these teenage idols:

> They go through a very extensive grooming. It is sometimes five
> months before they appear on a stage or three months before I let them
> do any recording. To start with, they have physical grooming. I have

their hair cut — that is very important. Sometimes, they may have bad skin which has to be attended to. Then I get them suitable clothes and provide them with comfort. I like them to have a touch of luxury from the start so that if they make the big time they don't lose their heads. I like them to live in a good home, get three good meals a day, get to bed early and have plenty of fresh air.

Today, Larry plays down the almost matronly image fostered in those early interviews and suggests that the artistes were very much in control of their own destinies:

I looked at it as advice, not grooming. Nobody had to groom Tommy, Marty or the others. It was a question of receptiveness on their part. Listening, taking it all in. If they didn't listen and they didn't have the talent, they didn't get anywhere . . . I always used to sit down and talk for a long time with my artistes about their careers, their stage performance and what they were going to try and do. But I didn't believe in *controlling* people's careers.

Other people from the period remember it differently. Marty felt Larry could be very authoritarian and stubborn, while Dick Rowe noted humorously: 'He ruled them with a rod of iron!' The image that emerges most often is that of a stern but benevolent headmaster, overseeing a class of mixed-ability young hopefuls. For the press, however, Larry remained inextricably linked with horsing imagery and few journalists could resist commenting on his grooming techniques.

Not surprisingly, there was a mild flurry when it was learned that a filly had joined the stable. The girl in question, Sally Kelly, had been signed by Larry after appearing on a television talent show. Parnes wisely resisted the temptation of hyping the singer as the glamour girl of the stable, but built her confidence gradually during a series of nationwide package tours. In spite of several recordings, however, it proved impossible to capture her vivacious stage presence in the studio and Sally soon fell into obscurity.

From the number of artistes he was recruiting in 1959, it was clear that Parnes was working on instinct. A known gambler, he was now taking chances on more teenagers than ever. Incredibly, he even became involved with the unfortunate Terry Dene whose image had been badly tarnished following appearances in court for drunkenness and vandalism, and a melodramatic discharge from the army. Shunned and discredited, Dene was now a manager's nightmare. It was a magnanimous gesture by Parnes to give the erring lad a second chance and on several occasions he defended the disparaged idol with great eloquence. Interviewed in August 1959 about Dene's disastrous history, he explained:

> One couldn't blame the boy entirely. Given a fair amount of under-standing he has a lot of good in him. It is my intention that he should have the right kind of publicity in future. If Terry is to get back to being a very big star it is going to mean six months hard work on all sides.

In spite of Parnes' optimism, the reformation of Dene could not undo the errors of the past and his comeback was short lived. He eventually retired in disillusionment, only to re-emerge in the sixties as a street-preaching evangelist and more recently as a cabaret artiste on the nostalgia circuit.

Larry's late fifties run of short-term artistes ended with a winner — Joe Brown. The blond tousled-haired guitarist was first spotted by Jack Good during an audition for *Boy Meets Girls*. After witnessing his exuberant performance, the ever alert producer had only one question to ask the bemused youngster, 'Who's your manager?' Sensing a new signing, Parnes abruptly stepped in and announced, 'I am!' From that moment, Joe became part of the famous stable and looked set to undergo the inevitable grooming process. However, unlike his more pliable contemporaries, the strong-willed guitarist was an inveterate rebel. When Parnes rechristened his animated discovery Elmer Twitch, the lad's dis-believing grin confirmed that the pseudonym would never be used. In spite of boasting one of the most common names in pop-star history, the guitarist insisted on remaining plain Joe Brown. More surprisingly, he was granted a luxury afforded few artistes in Parnes' employ — his own backing group, the Bruvvers. By this stage, Larry had hired a number of musicians to work for his firm and they backed virtually all the acts rather than being allocated to one star. That Brown could convince his manager to alter this arrangement says much about his powers of persuasion. Similarly, although he accepted the Parnes code of behaviour and always dressed smartly in public, he seemed immune to any grooming strategies:

> With me, he didn't have much luck there! I was a different sort of act. I went out there and appealed to the geezers playing Chuck Berry stuff. I don't know whether Larry realized that I had a mind of my own, but he seemed to let me get on with it. I was treated differently from the others. Perhaps he realized that I wasn't relying on a load of screaming kids, so he let me have my head.

What seems more likely is that Larry recognized Brown's wilfulness and playful humour as natural traits that could be used to enliven and personalize his act. For Brown was both a genuine rock 'n' roller and a throwback to the cheeky cockney chappie of the music-hall era.

Like many of his fellow artistes, Joe quickly became aware of Parnes' stubbornness, a trait that manifested itself in a number of humorous ways. One of the drawbacks of Larry's Sunday concerts was the observance law which decreed that musicians were not allowed to wear stage clothes or make-up on the Sabbath. In an attempt to dazzle his audience, Joe had ordered a specially-made suit, the right half of which was red and the left half yellow, with accompanying shoes of similar hues. When he turned up for rehearsals he was immediately ordered off the set and requested to change into sober day clothes. Characteristically, an indignant Larry intervened and explained that the two-tone suit did constitute normal day wear for his colourful star. The accuser remained unconvinced and argued that nobody in his right mind would wear such an outfit in public. Unfazed, Parnes arose from his seat and ordered the perplexed Brown to walk along the Blackpool sea front in order to prove the point. A bizarre scene ensued with Joe attracting stares from every person on the prom, while Larry and the officials stalked his every move. Following the display, it was agreed that Joe could wear the outfit, much to Parnes' satisfaction.

The amusing tales that Brown recalls from this period are frequently punctuated by complimentary comments on Parnes' parents. The overall impression conveyed is that relations between himself and his manager were cordial. Surprisingly, however, Joe suggests that there was also friction and incompatibility:

> The sad thing about Larry Parnes is that we never got on well together. I did have a lot of respect for Larry and I think he had a lot of respect for me . . . But I don't think he liked me very much. I was a cheeky bastard and used to take the mickey out of him. When the option for our contract came up after three years I'd given him such a hard time that he let me go.

Perhaps the passage of time may have distorted old memories, but Parnes remains blissfully unaware of any personality clash:

> I didn't find Joe difficult to work with. He was always on time, gave a very consistent performance, never over ran his time and always dressed well . . . I can't think where he was a problem. I could name others that were a lot more troublesome than Joe. We had differences

of opinion, but I had that with a lot of my people. It was sometimes difficult to get through to Joe on certain points, but I wouldn't say we didn't get on. We had a lot of fun and laughs.

The split between Parnes and Brown after three years proved reasonably amicable. As part of the terms of his release, Joe agreed to play two six-week seasons for Larry who, in turn, raised the guitarist's salary in order to secure that option. Before they parted, Joe was told by his manager that if his work progressed he would one day star in a West End musical. Several years later, Parnes fulfilled his prediction by casting Brown as Stubbs in the hit musical *Charlie Girl*. From playing nightly rock 'n' roll gigs for almost three years, Joe finally emerged as an all-round entertainer in classic Parnes tradition.

By 1960, Larry had acquired a nickname from the press that stuck — Mr Parnes, Shillings and Pence. It was a clever and amusing title that accurately conveyed his sharpness as a business manager. Unfortunately, the words also suggested that Parnes' primary motivation in life was a desire for money. Although his consistent nurturing of young talent seemingly demonstrated that such a theory was cruelly inaccurate, the media remained suspicious and occasionally hinted that his discoveries were merely saleable commodities. When *Panorama* produced their feature on the stable of stars, great stress was placed upon the market value of the boys and several of them were asked whether they felt manipulated or exploited. The fact that several of his artistes happened to be living at his flat during this period added weight to the notion that Larry was totally in control of their lives. When Parnes himself slipped into his paternal persona he virtually gave the interviewer a new round of ammunition. Suddenly, Larry began explaining that he preferred his boys not to be out after midnight and liked them tucked up in bed by a certain hour. His self-image seemed that of a protective parent guiding his young charges through a tricky show business adolescence. However, cynical television viewers must have pondered the same nagging question as the *Panorama* interviewer who immediately turned to one of the artistes and asked him if he felt like a puppet. His reply was hardly relevant; Larry Parnes was now a svengali, surrounded by naïve and impressionable teenagers.

The svengali persona has proved a potent and enduring image. Parnes has been parodied on Peter Sellers' comedy records and outrageously caricatured as the camp starmaker 'Harry Charms' in the film *Absolute Beginners*. Even in the unlikely setting of a Who biography Parnes found himself demeaningly portrayed as the fifties equivalent of a nineteenth-century factory owner, churning out teen idols whose ambition was supposedly circumscribed by a weekly wages system. Such one dimensional portraits seldom question the amount of money Parnes poured into his acts or look closely at the terms offered. As early as 1959, Larry explained that his policy was to offer artistes two types of contract, a straight percentage or a guaranteed salary over five years plus 60 per cent of record royalties. Parnes maintains that this resulted in substantial overheads:

> There was their food, their clothes, their living accommodation, the people that looked after them, their instruments, their stage clothes, their travel. You add all that up; I bet on what some of these people earned I wasn't getting 1½% commission! . . . I did what I felt was right for their careers at the time. I didn't make any money from them, my accountants can tell you that. It's a good job I diversified, otherwise I'd be sleeping on the embankment!

That last sentence overstates Parnes' case, but it is undoubtedly true that most of his money came from promotion rather than management. Moreover, the artistes in his employ who have since achieved great success readily acknowledge his shrewdness, but do not question his integrity or generosity.

The key to Parnes' nickname did not lie in parsimony but solicitude. He was always acutely aware of the need to keep his artistes' feet firmly on the ground and prevent the unhealthy egotism and insidious insularity that has destroyed so many entertainers. Joe Brown recalls with some amusement nonchalantly tipping a cabbie to the tune of one shilling. When he dutifully informed his manager of this undue extravagance, Larry hammered his fist on his desk and uttered the immortal words: 'Thruppence is quite sufficient'. So it was that Joe Brown learned the need to curb his spendthrift instincts.

By sixties standards, Parnes' management commission was very high, but the service he offered could not be matched by any other entrepreneur of the era. Marty Wilde, who was receiving a 60 per cent cut, still argues that it was a fair deal: 'Even if it had been 40 per cent or even 20 per cent, it would still have been good. Until he signed too many artistes, most of the people that went with him had success'. It is also interesting to note the circumstances surrounding Joe Brown's decision to leave Parnes. Far from feeling neglected or exploited, Joe's main worry was a lack of independence stemming from his manager's over-protective nature:

> I think Larry came out of it all right, but he paid all my expenses.

What worried me was that Larry was paying for my house. My mother and brother were living there, and Billy Fury as well. I thought to myself 'I've got nothing if I'm not with Larry Parnes. I haven't got a hope. I haven't got anything. What the hell's going to happen to me?' I didn't like that hanging over my head. I thought, I've got to take a chance now, otherwise I'll be relying on Larry entirely and I'll never grow up.

Clearly, Parnes was far removed from those small-time fifties managers who carved up most of their artistes' earnings and left them in near penury. Looking back at those early days, Parnes argues that his image as a ruthless businessman was a media distortion that ironically disguised his softness in dealing with music business accountants and solicitors. The Mr Parnes, Shillings and Pence image was accurate in one sense, but it was also a misnomer. Certainly, Parnes made money and his artistes worked hard, but he was not avaricious and even touring acts such as the Viscounts told me that they received a very fair rate of pay. Perhaps the last word on the integrity of Mr Parnes, Shillings and Pence should go to Harry Dawson, who later worked with Joe Brown:

> Larry was the cleverest person in the pop field. He wasn't a con man; he was a businessman. If I phoned Larry Parnes or Danny Betesh over a deal I wouldn't need a contract or even a letter. They are men of their word.

By the dawn of the sixties, Parnes' recent flurry of signings was considerably curtailed. However, he still managed to squeeze two more singers into his already overcrowded stable. Nelson Keene was a good-looking kid who had a brief run supporting Parnes' first division acts. Welshman Peter Wynne (his real name!), also disappeared quickly, though Larry claims that he was a better singer than Tom Jones and could have broken through later in the Engelbert Humperdinck era. The middling success of these second division acts was hardly surprising for Parnes was now more interested in promoting than star grooming. Ever since the 'Extravaganza' tour of 1958, he had been organizing bigger and better package tours and by the early sixties he was probably the most famous impresario in Britain. It was more a matter of circumstance than intention. The closure of many traditional music halls and variety theatres had forced Parnes to create his own package tours in order to provide his artistes with both publicity and live experience. The system ensured that they received lucrative work and enabled Parnes to supervise their activities simultaneously rather than choosing between them. As a result, the less popular acts on his books did not feel neglected and were encouraged to work harder.

The Parnes package tour became a major event in the early sixties British rock 'n' roll calendar and the billing always reflected the grandiloquent nature of its creator. Who could forget 'The Big New Rock 'n' Roll Trad Show', 'The Rock 'n' Roll Trad Spectacular', 'The Big Star Show of 1962', 'The Mammoth Star Show of 1962' or the glittering 'Star Spangled Nights'? Certainly not the artistes who rehearsed *ad infinitum* until Parnes the perfectionist was satisfied with the results. The impresario was equally industrious during the long months of preparation for these shows. His office resembled a military headquarters with maps on the wall and flags denoting dates and destinations. Demographic surveys of towns, cinema security and even atmospheric conditions were each taken into consideration as Larry plotted his final course. Often, the last detail would be the careful selection of a guest performer. The fee usually dictated Larry's choice, though his speciality was booking an act that was likely to be riding high in the charts at the time of the tour. This usually required a combination of intuition and luck, and as Parnes' career has proven, he had both in abundance.

Luck, fate and tragedy are words that recur throughout the Larry Parnes story. It may be possible to chart the history and development of rock 'n' roll through chance meetings, lost opportunities, lucky breaks and dramatic deaths. All these factors not only affected the Parnes stable but were also evident in Larry's association with other great artistes. The strangest series of historical events involving Parnes as a bit player occurred in the early months of 1960 when, in his role as the Great Provider, he had imported two of the era's most famous rock 'n' roll stars for a UK tour. The first to arrive was Gene Vincent, a partially-crippled, heavy-drinking misanthrope who seemed to epitomize the worst excesses of the rock 'n' roll lifestyle. Unfortunately, when he disembarked at Heathrow airport the original bad boy of rock appeared both well-dressed and unassuming. It took the perverse flair of Jack Good to transform the quiet American into a cross between Hamlet and Richard III, complete with black leather and an accentuated limp. From the moment he appeared on *Boy Meets Girls*, the sinister-looking Vincent guaranteed Parnes sell-out shows throughout the country. The second part of this heroic rock 'n' roll double act arrived several weeks later in the person of Eddie Cochran. The 21-year-old Oklahoman had already entranced a generation of English youngsters with vignettes of American teenage life, conjuring up visions of high school romance, cars and the coolness of rebellion against teachers, parents and any other authoritarian figure. Songs such as 'Twenty Flight Rock', 'C'mon Everybody' and, most crucially, 'Summertime Blues' were regarded as teen anthems by British kids still coming to terms with their new-found autonomy. Vincent and Cochran were brilliantly complementary figures and Parnes could not have chosen a more interesting package for the discerning British rock 'n' roll fan.

Larry dutifully attended the shows throughout the 13-week tour, including the one at Liverpool where history of a different chapter was already in the making. For scattered among the milling crowds at the Empire Theatre were three-quarters of the million-pound quartet that would later produce the greatest phenomenon in popular-music history. A no less important figure at that stage was a lowly coffee bar proprietor named Allan Williams. He pulled off a remarkable deal in which Parnes agreed to promote an additional show featuring the Vincent/ Cochran package backed by several Liverpool groups.

The triumphant Williams was still calculating his profit margins when a car carrying Vincent, Cochran and his songwriter girlfriend Sharon Sheeley careered from a Wiltshire road on Easter Sunday and crashed into a tree. Vincent and Sheeley suffered minor injuries but the ill-starred Eddie Cochran died the following afternoon.

The death of Cochran did not deter Williams from staging the show. Parnes was duly impressed by his tenacity. Several weeks later, Larry contacted the stocky Liverpudlian promoter with the intention of securing some durable backing musicians for his own artistes' regional tours. An audition was hastily arranged.

The arrival of Parnes, accompanied by his Liverpudlian chart star Billy Fury, caused pandemonium among the team of musicians that worked for Williams. The fact that Larry was merely searching for a temporary backing group was conveniently forgotten. Most of the musicians interpreted his visitation as a golden opportunity to win a one-way ticket from Merseyside obscurity to national stardom. Among the most vociferous self-campaigners was John Lennon, who persuaded Williams to allow his group their chance of glory.

The venue chosen for the famous audition was the Wyvern working men's club, a stone's throw from Williams' Jacaranda club. There, Parnes and Fury spent several hours listening to a primitive backbeat that would later become world renowned as the phenomenal Merseysound. All the groups had their strong points, but the Silver Beetles were encountering unforeseen problems. Whatever hope they had of impressing the London impresario seemed doomed when their newly-recruited drummer, Tommy Moore, inexplicably failed to appear until two-thirds of the way through the audition. In desperation, the boys had turned to Johnny Hutchinson, one of the most accomplished drummers in the area, whose group Cass and the Cassanovas were also competing for Parnes' favours. Conflicting loyalties ensured that his performance was at best lacklustre. Nevertheless, Parnes saw some spark of originality in the Silver Beetles and on his notepad he wrote next to their name 'Very good — keep note for future work'. In the meantime, it was Hutchinson's own group that were awarded the dubious distinction of backing Duffy Power on a strenuous Scottish tour.

The events of that historic day have produced conflicting accounts in a number of Beatles biographies. According to one source, Parnes was overwhelmed by the Silver Beetles and offered to sign them on the spot if they fired their inept bassist Stu Sutcliffe. Another story suggests that the smart-suited impresario was mildly interested but took exception to the group's scruffiness and lack of decorum. Both these accounts still perplex Parnes who has no memory of offering Williams or the Silver Beetles any firm deal:

> I was just looking for a backing group that day; I wasn't interested in signing groups. Groups, as far as I was concerned, didn't exist then. It would have been a question of signing four or five people, which I didn't want.

Certainly, Parnes' aversion to groups was a constant throughout his managerial career and it seems improbable that he would have had the foresight to recognize the Beatles' hidden potential as early as 1960, particularly when the remainder of his stable consisted of traditional teen idols.

The strangely confusing and contradictory accounts of Parnes' visit to Liverpool will probably never be resolved to everyone's satisfaction, but his own memories of that day add a completely new perspective to a well-worn tale:

> The most distinctive thing I remember is that four of them had these special haircuts and wore black trousers. They stood out amongst the others in the room. Their dress impressed me tremendously. But one of them dressed differently . . . I liked their style and music, but I told them they needed a more powerful drummer, somebody to drive their music along.

Interestingly, Parnes notes that he had no objections to bassist Stu Sutcliffe whose looks and image seemed consistent with the others. It was the 36-year-old drummer with the different uniform that clearly upset Larry. Poor Tommy Moore made the worst possible impression that afternoon. Parnes seldom looked kindly on unpunctual musicians and there was little time to explain that Moore was a hard-working fork-lift-truck driver with considerably more commitments than his fellow members. His arrival, late in the audition, unsettled the performers and with little chance to warm up, Tommy played below his best. Amidst this comedy of errors, the irrepressible John Lennon attempted to ingratiate himself with Larry, and midway through the afternoon asked for some extra time to play a couple of self-penned numbers. Parnes told him to come back after the audition when he promised to allow the group an additional 10 minutes. It was a lucky break, no doubt resulting from Lennon's earthy charm. After listening for a few minutes Larry politely praised the boys' songwriting abilities and left the club shortly afterwards. As far as the Silver Beetles were concerned that was the end of the matter.

Several weeks after returning to London, Larry found that he needed an additional backing group to accompany Johnny Gentle on a two-week tour of Scotland. Johnny Askew was a gentlemanly merchant seaman originally signed in 1959, but in spite of a record contract with Philips, his career was now in the descendent. Since the tour was especially arduous, Larry decided to enlist another of those rugged Liverpudlian units. Perusing his old notepad he came across the words 'Silver Beetles: Very Good; keep note for future work' and remembered the dark-clothed youths who had cheekily requested a second audition. Without hesitation, he wrote to Allan Williams offering the Silver Beetles the job. Their reaction was predictably exuberant and they wasted no time extracting themselves from various academic and occupational entanglements. Even the veteran Tommy Moore was reunited with his erstwhile colleagues for their first professional tour.

The lingering dreams of stardom were soon replaced by a rude awakening as the boys struggled through a series of one-night-stands in obscure towns throughout the North. Morbid discussion of the recent Eddie Cochran tragedy depressed them further and in a remarkable act of self-fulfilling prophecy there was a car crash in which Tommy Moore was concussed and taken to hospital. The injured drummer played on through several hazy gigs with the aid of painkilling drugs, but even these could not blot out the tedium and bickering that followed each performance. By the end of the tour, the unfortunate drummer was estranged from the others, especially Lennon whose cruel sarcasm proved intolerable.

This second saga in Parnes/Beatles history has produced some strangely conflicting viewpoints. Beatles biographer Peter Brown claims that Johnny Gentle intensely disliked his backing group, a view allegedly shared by promoters who supposedly complained to

Parnes about their poor standard. Brown has not disclosed the source of this contentious information which is contradicted by other commentators, denied by Gentle and totally confuted by Larry's own recollection of the events:

> Johnny used to phone me virtually every night and say 'Come up to Scotland and see these boys. I've given them a spot in my act and they're doing better than I am'. He was very honest. I always said that if I'd found the time to go up to Scotland he might have been the fifth Beatle. Who knows?

Parnes' blind spot for groups would probably have encouraged him to install Johnny as the 'leader' of the Beatles. The notion of a third party vying for power alongside Lennon and McCartney is an intriguing but ultimately inconceivable historical fantasy.

Parnes' cameo role in the Beatles' story did not end in 1960. Remarkably, he was offered another chance to sign the future megastars but once again allowed them to slip through his fingers. Marty Wilde remembers entering Larry's office one day and seeing some headed notepaper with the name Beatles next to his own. Several weeks later, he noticed that the name had been crossed out and uttered the memorable words, 'What ever happened to those Beatles?' It was a strange story that has never previously been documented. The period was late 1962, several months before the Beatles' meteoric rise to fame. Brian Epstein was still a novice in the music business and had no conception of the market value of his young protégés. While attempting to organize regular concert bookings, Epstein approached Parnes, whose Sunday shows at the Brittania Pier Pavilion were a welcome stepping stone for any up-and-coming act. Larry wanted the boys for 11 concerts but disagreed with Epstein over an appropriate fee. The bartering continued, but Parnes was in poor spirits due to the imminent retirement of his long-serving secretary. Ironically, her last duties consisted of relaying calls from the frantic and impatient Liverpudlian. On her final day, she waltzed into her employer's office and chided: 'Don't be silly, Larry. Come on, do the deal'. Like a disgruntled schoolboy Parnes retorted, 'No! If you weren't leaving me it might be different'. By the time his secretary left, the deadline had passed. Larry Parnes had lost the Beatles. The amount of money sacrificed that fateful afternoon remains incalculable. In his desperation and insecurity, Brian had been searching for a reputable co-promoter, and the proposed Brittania concerts were merely the first clause of a complex contract that offered a percentage of world touring rights spanning several years. The implications of the contract even included future NEMS acts in an almost never-ending spiral of multiplying revenue. For the sake of a measly few pounds a night, the obdurate emperor of fifties British rock 'n' roll had turned his back on a veritable goldmine.

It is fascinating to speculate what might have happened if Parnes had secured managerial control of the Beatles at this early stage of their career. Larry modestly shrugs his shoulders and notes that they might not have happened at all. This seems unlikely, especially when one considers the power and influence that Parnes wielded in the music industry at that time. Certainly, the Beatles early struggles to achieve recognition would have been greatly alleviated. The historically maligned Dick Rowe would have been credited as the most perceptive A & R person of his era for simply accepting another Parnes act. Without a doubt, Rowe would have signed the Beatles on Larry's recommendation alone, for he valued astute management above almost any other criterion. While realizing that Parnes would have secured a higher royalty rate and more secure deal, Rowe feels that the Beatles were probably better served by the man he rejected:

> I think Larry would have been too strong for them. Parnes had the experience. He was quite sure about everything he was doing. The Beatles were able to persuade Epstein to do things their way and he was weak enough to listen. And they were right . . . With Larry, they would never have been able to get themselves heard.

Rowe's argument sounds convincing, but his stress on Parnes' authoritarianism is rejected by Marty Wilde as an irrelevant side issue:

> Larry might not have been the right manager in the creative sense, though from what I can gather, the group handled themselves in that area. The Beatles were a tough bunch, nobody could harm them, all they could do was make money. Parnes always said, and I know it's a fact, that if he'd been handling the Beatles they'd be earning four times as much as they did. He said that at the time. What they needed was a brain to make money and Larry had all that experience.

Wilde went on to discuss the controversial merchandising deal that lost the Beatles millions of dollars and noted wryly: 'Larry would never have allowed anyone the choice of a figure'. Marty's thesis is probably sound, yet it is also likely that Epstein's initial naïveté and passion for the Beatles contributed to the accident of history which produced the Fab Four phenomenon. For all his commitment to his artistes, it is difficult to imagine Parnes matching the intense conviction that Epstein felt for the Beatles at that crucial point in their development. Yet, there is a certain magic in the thought of the two greatest managers in British pop music history merging their entrepreneurial talents to mastermind the career of the ultimate show business phenomenon of our time.

The burgeoning beat boom in Liverpool and other provincial cities heralded a new era in British pop music history but, sadly, Parnes chose not to celebrate the revolution. The Great Provider of the previous decade remained steadfast in his desire not to sign groups and even the Rolling Stones failed an audition at one stage. Only once was Parnes persuaded to co-manage a group and the experience proved unrewarding. The idea came from Billy Fury, who was in the process of changing backing groups to suit his new image as a balladeer. Previously, he had been accompanied by the Blue Flames, whose pianist, Clive Powell, had been rechristened Georgie Fame by the ever vigilant Parnes. Their replacements were the Tornadoes, a session group originally formed by producer Joe Meek. Unfortunately, the eccentric producer was so absorbed in his studio work that he had little time to administer their affairs, so Parnes was reluctantly roped in as co-manager. In truth, Larry only accepted the job to please Billy Fury who wanted the security of a backing group entwined with his management. Parnes' appointment coincided with the Tornadoes' sudden rise to the top of the charts with the million-selling 'Telstar'. When the instrumental also zoomed to number 1 in America, Larry began negotiations for a nationwide US tour. It was at this stage that he encountered resistance from Meek who insisted that the Tornadoes remain in Britain. Larry could not fathom his peculiar logic and always argued that a great opportunity was missed. The co-management deal barely lasted a year and was continually frustrated by conflicting loyalties within the group. Sensing their lack of support, Parnes bowed out, never to return to group management for the remainder of his career.

The worldwide success of the Beatles must have pleased Parnes in spite of his failure to clinch a satisfactory deal. During 1962, he had consistently voiced a nationalistic disdain for American acts and made vast claims in defence of seemingly minor British talents. Within two years of his outburst, however, Britain was the pop capital of the world for the first time in its history. Parnes, meanwhile, had wound down his famous pop school in order to pursue a career in theatre. He retained only two acts, one of whom was his first discovery, Tommy Steele. By this stage, the former merchant seaman was a successful actor moving confidently from *She Stoops*

To Conquer at the Old Vic to the West End hit musical *Half A Sixpence*. When that show transferred to Broadway for a highly successful run, Parnes felt that a long-term ambition had been achieved. In 1965, he ended his nine-year association with Britain's first rock 'n' roll star.

In common with several of his artistes, Larry's transition from rock 'n' roll to show business proved remarkably successful and his involvement in musicals such as *Charlie Girl* and *Chicago* confirmed that his old astuteness had not been lost. Although the pop world was rapidly becoming ancient history to Parnes, he continued to guide the career of Billy Fury throughout the sixties. The singer was cast in a couple of films, *Play It Cool* and *I Gotta Horse* (which Parnes co-produced) but neither proved memorable. Although Fury's recording career was threatened by marauding beat groups, he continued to chart until as late as 1966. Further achievements might have been forthcoming but for frequent bouts of illness which curbed Parnes' starmaking strategies:

> One had to be awfully careful about placing Billy's work, so many nights on, so many nights off. His health was against him from the start. He didn't know how ill he was because I didn't tell him. Billy would have been an international star if one could have gone all over the world on strenuous tours.

In 1967, Fury began vomiting blood and following a period in hospital it was revealed that one of the valves in his heart had closed up. For a time, he retired to a Sussex farm leaving Larry to administer his business affairs. When Parnes himself fell seriously ill at the end of the decade, it seemed an appropriate time to terminate their long-standing relationship:

> Billy and I had the most tearful parting. I was in hospital at the time. We'd been together for nearly 11 years and I had to tell him that I felt I could not do his career justice anymore. It was a lot to do with my health and knowing about his health. Frankly, I felt if I couldn't do the job properly I wouldn't do it at all.

On 28 January 1983, Billy Fury suffered a fatal heart attack.

Parnes' absence from the sixties pop pantheon has partly obscured his crucial importance in the history and development of British rock music. So much has been written about the sixties that even middling managers of that period are almost as famous as the Great Provider. Yet no figure over the past 30 years has ever matched the power that Parnes enjoyed during the fifties. In many respects, Larry Parnes reigned alone and like many great rulers fell victim to a historical inevitability — the destruction of one set of values by another. In Parnes' case it was the evolution of the fifties singing star into the sixties pop group that precipitated his retirement. With keener foresight he might have netted the Shadows, Beatles or Stones and extended his influence over pop music into a second decade, but his lust for power was far from all-embracing:

> I never set out to have control of the whole era. You're saying I could have had an entire monopoly of British pop up until the Beatles. And I could have had the Beatles as well if that had been my intention . . . but I had no designs. I didn't want to be Brian Epstein; I wasn't in the business to create monopolies. You say I was the pioneer of this era. Inevitably, a pioneer gets talked about but they never get the medals. That's not a bad thing because you introduce something to the business that other people follow. Hardly a week goes by where I don't turn on the television and see somebody that I either helped or discovered and that gives me the most satisfaction.

Surprisingly, Parnes' subsidiary interests in publishing and the short-lived record label Elempi both proved unsuccessful. The mogul in Parnes was always subservient to the imaginative impresario. His career, like that of his most consistently successful artistes, gradually moved from rock 'n' roll to traditional show business, and it was a logical development. The truth was Parnes became exhausted and probably rather bored with pop management by the early sixties and sought new avenues for creative diversion and entertainment. His veritable abdication of big-time management was premature, but probably wise. Without doubt, he would have been hard pushed by the flashier, group-orientated sensationalists such as Oldham, Page, Secunda, Lambert and Napier-Bell who all jostled for power amid the mid-sixties beat explosion. It is difficult to imagine Parnes ever feeling happy with the public behaviour of acts such as the Rolling Stones, the Kinks, the Who or the Move.

It is all too easy for critics to deride Parnes' old-fashioned professionalism and dismiss his artistes as manufactured, light-weight copies of genuine American rock 'n' rollers, but a historical context is necessary before passing judgement. In an era when Cliff Richard was seen as a devil, there was little opportunity to unleash rock 'n' roll sexuality of Presley proportions, nor were there under-ground performers of such power and originality being handled by lesser managers. What Larry Parnes and Jack Good achieved in the fifties represented the beginning of the British rock revolution. By today's standards their perception of rock 'n' roll may seem stagey and tame, but judged by the precepts of 1958 they were near radical visionaries. Parnes' involvement with Billy Fury can always be used as a defence of his rock 'n' roll credibility, but this is ultimately unnecessary and even tangential to the main argument. His real importance lay in his commitment to youth. There were no jugglers, comedians or old crooners lying behind the stars in his stable. The willingness to sign fledgling talent and promote the songwriting of British kids via his publishing company Youngstar Music presaged the youth explosion of the sixties. Even by that time, Parnes was still regarded as a spokesman for British teenagers and frequently articulated their feelings with confidence. In 1960, *Melody Maker* pondered: 'Will rock be going a year from now?' Parnes' reply indicated that the old ideals had not been wholly sacrificed in the search for wider acceptance: 'I will be bold enough as to say that rock will be going 10 years from today!'

Since Parnes spent so much of his early life nurturing the careers of young stars, it is perhaps appropriate to allow a couple of them the opportunity to provide some concluding comments on their former manager. Joe Brown provides a grudging but realistic appraisal:

> You could say a lot of things about Larry Parnes but, looking back, I thought he was good for me. He did feel responsible for his boys. But perhaps he knew that if he wasn't responsible for them, he wouldn't have them. His strengths were that he was a shrewd bloke. I could be bitter . . . but there's no point. He was one of the top managers of all time. There's no disputing it.

Marty Wilde was far more analytical and revelatory in his summation:

> I think he made the right moves. With hindsight, it's easy to criticize but I think Parnes was one of the greatest managers this country has ever produced. He was better than Epstein in my opinion. I think his strengths and weaknesses were bound together, in that he would go one way and there was no turning back. Sometimes he'd make a *faux pas*, but he had this great knack of being positive. He was always considered to be right. Everything he said *had* to be right, which is what a good manager should feel.

During the seventies, Parnes owned various theatres and briefly returned to management in a different sphere, looking after the affairs of world-champion ice skater, John Currie. However, he still remembered his old stars. Marty Wilde recalls a gig at a

Dagenham working men's club in the seventies which was momentarily disrupted when Larry arrived unexpectedly in a gleaming
Rolls Royce, driven by a chauffeur dressed in black. The incident
reinforced Marty's conviction about his ex-manager's importance
in rock history:

> My wife and I travelled with Larry all over the world and we never
> ceased to be amazed. He could create scenes. Larry did it all himself.
> He had the courage and belief to see it through. I've seen the greatest
> managers and knowing what I know now, they must be very lonely
> people. You have to have a special kind of courage and you're bound
> to make mistakes, especially when you've got an ego which a manager
> like Larry has to have. I'm sure in some ways it could be levelled at
> Parnes that he destroyed various sections of rock 'n' roll, but, by God,
> he *made* other sections. He brought the whole British scene to life.

The epoch-making achievements of Parnes during the late fifties
are barely reconcilable with the resigned, nonchalant attitude
betrayed by the Great Provider today. Larry's listlessness and
apparent lack of ambition were revealed in his final words during
our interview: 'At the moment I don't want to get heavily involved
in any project. And I don't look to the future. I live for the present.'
Such comments are a reminder of how time erodes the passion of
youth. Here is a figure whose entrepreneurial power was capable of
changing the lives of an entire generation but whose reluctance to
accept that godhead irrevocably altered the course of British
popular music. Yet, his departure from pop music was uncannily
well timed and perhaps the present *laissez-faire* attitude betrayed in
his asides reflects the dilemma of choosing between history and
self-preservation.

Creative management effectively began for publicist Ken Pitt one Thursday afternoon in 1954. While working in the Albemarle Street office that he rented from bandleader Ted Heath, Pitt was distracted by the distant melodious sound of a ballad singer. When he investigated the commotion, his eyes feasted on a remarkable scene in the street below:

> There was this extremely attractive mediterranean boy who sang through a megaphone, and he had a one-legged 'bottler' who collected the money. This fellow was stomping around on a wooden leg like something out of *Treasure Island*. Another person was playing a French accordian. I was impressed by the effect that the singer had on the girls, who were hanging out of windows throwing money at him!

Although Pitt briefly commented on the megaphone marvel to Ted Heath, no immediate action was taken about his future. That situation changed abruptly one afternoon when Ken walked out of the building and felt the pain of a shower of coins raining down on his head from the windows above: the enthusiasm of the girls had evidently not waned. Pitt recovered his poise momentarily but soon became incensed when he noticed that a stray coin had smashed the lens of his glasses. Angrily, he accosted the singer demanding, 'Why don't you bloody well go to the next street?' To his great surprise the young man merely replied with an inane grin. Realizing the humour of the situation, Ken soon wilted and allowed himself to be inveigled into a long conversation. It quickly transpired that the youngster had deliberately chosen to play in Albemarle Street in the hope of being discovered by Heath and transformed into a star. Pitt had already heard enough to usher him into his office. Could this be the rough diamond that he had always dreamt of discovering? While pondering this, Pitt was suddenly overcome by an obnoxious odour emanating from the unusual boy. Upon further enquiry, Ken learned that he had unwittingly stumbled on a genuine Romany whose home was the notorious gypsy camp in Cooke's Meadow, St Mary Cray, Kent. The one-legged 'bottler' was an elder brother and the accordian player an uncle. That strange smell turned out to be hedgehog oil which the singer used as a surrogate Brylcreem to grease his jet-black hair. Ken's head was still spinning as the youngster recalled many dark, dank nights during which he had survived on a diet of hedgehog meat, roots and berries. As a publicist Pitt did not need to be told that the boy's gypsy origins, eating habits and unconventional appearance were worth their weight in gold. Within days, an elaborate career plan was mapped out for Pitt's first *bona fide* creation.

The grooming process that transformed Daniel Puccessi into singing star Danny Purches was achieved with minimum effort. A series of publicity photos were taken, each aimed at a specific audience and age group. First, there was the profile of the romantic, Latin lover, perfectly turned out and ready to seduce. For the younger fans Danny was stripped to the waist and positioned with legs slightly apart revealing an impressively padded crotch. In other photographs he could be seen flexing his muscles and showing off bulging biceps, for unlike most teenage heroes Purches was a genuine hunk. Some of the photos were daringly macho for the early fifties and in order not to offend the moral majority Pitt persuaded his protégé to wear a large dangling crucifix around his neck. Every single angle had been covered, including the possibility of winning a substantial amount of Roman Catholic support!

Purches's prospects were strengthened when Pitt introduced him to Hyman Zahl of the all-powerful Fosters Agency. On the strength of this connection alone EMI was pleased to negotiate a recording deal. Radio exposure followed with *In Town Tonight* and soon the press were alerted. The *Daily Mirror* decided to give Purches the full treatment. When their photographer arrived at Pitt's office, however, he was disappointed to discover that the gypsy boy was not wearing his famous earring. Ken thought quickly, removed his key ring and attached it to Danny's ear-lobe. The following day Purches was splattered across the pages of the *Daily Mirror* under the heading 'Gypsy Boy Signs £10 000 Recording Contract'. In reality, the figure was only a fraction of that sum, but everyone agreed that it would be a better headline if EMI's generosity was exaggerated.

Purches looked a good bet for success following his grand launching and Pitt was confident that he would emerge as an accomplished live performer. His stage show was quite elaborate for the time, including a full-scale caravan and gypsy fire, both of which enhanced his romantic repertoire. Within a relatively short period of time, Purches was topping the bills at Moss Empire theatres throughout the country. Implicit in his rise, however, were the seeds of his own downfall. Purches was not a Fleet Street hype but a genuine gypsy whose philosophy of life differed markedly from all those around him in the music business. Pitt became increasingly concerned when Danny's extended family began appearing at stage doors looking for hand-outs. However, he soon learned that Danny felt a moral duty to protect the welfare of his 18 brothers and sisters. After years of sharing all his worldly possessions, poverty and prosperity were as one. In an attempt to protect his artiste's interests, Pitt shared a bank account with Purches and arranged for him to withdraw small amounts of pocket money to cover everyday expenses, but the wily gypsy still managed to spend over the limit. Eventually, Danny's carefree attitude cost him his career. When he offended the imperious Hyman Zahl and lost the support of Fosters, Pitt knew the boy had sealed his fate.

Before long, Purches's 'unprofessional' conduct was the talk of Tin Pan Alley and Pitt was frequently called upon to defend his charge's reputation. One golden rule of show business was that the artiste never appeared in the theatre bar when the patrons were present. Danny, of course, couldn't resist the temptation. He was also seen frequently in the company of attractive dancing girls which was frowned upon by eagle-eyed theatre managers. Although these transgressions seem laughable today, they were sufficiently serious to ruffle the conservative show business élite of the fifties who privately denounced Purches for failing to control his animal instincts.

In spite of the gross overspending and attendant indulgences, Pitt managed to accrue a sizeable reserve for his boy, but such efforts ultimately proved worthless. Purches became embarrassed by Pitt's husbandry and complained that it was unmanly to have a manager controlling his finances. Like many gypsies, Purches was a compulsive spendthrift for whom the word investment was meaningless. Reluctantly, Ken handed over several thousand pounds and watched helplessly as Purches blew it all in the space of a month. Suddenly, all his sisters were seen wearing beaver-lined coats and Danny was the toast of the camp fire. Pitt's tenuous hold of the management reins was finally broken when Danny became involved with the singing duo the Mackell Sisters. His relationship with Pat Mackell eventually led to marriage, which many hoped would curb his excesses. With the best of intentions Pat set about trying to reform the untameable Danny. Suddenly, Purches was playing down his gypsy background and aiming for a straight career in cabaret. Pitt argued that the Romany roots were his greatest asset and must be retained at all costs, but the gypsy boy ignored his manager's guidance. Far from succeeding as a cabaret star, Purches spent his twilight years singing in strip clubs before eventually retiring from the business. It was a sad ending to a promising career but for Pitt the experience of managing such a wildcat would later prove invaluable.

For the next few years Pitt continued to work as a publicist for a diverse series of singing stars, jazz musicians and comedians of international repute. His first brush with rock 'n' roll came with Jerry Lee Lewis's infamous 'child bride' tour of 1958. It was a publicist's nightmare, for the whole of Fleet Street was united in its attempt to destroy the reputation of this barbarian who had married his 13-year-old cousin. Pitt worked overtime, even equipping young Myra Lewis with a bible in order to remind the world of Jerry's religious background. The tour was an unmitigated disaster, but Lewis was sufficiently impressed with Pitt's valiant efforts to employ him on subsequent visits. The loss of Purches and the savaging of Lewis must have made Pitt wonder whether he was born under an unlucky star, but he looked with optimism towards the new decade.

It was as late as 1963 before Ken became involved in the management of a pop group. Following the recommendation of a friend he visited the Hambrough Tavern, Southall and was greatly impressed by an R & B octet, the Mann Hugg Blues Brothers. Pitt told their South African leader that he should dispose of his brass section and streamline the group to a five-piece. A management deal was completed and following a lengthy residency at the Marquee the newly-christened Manfred Mann were signed to EMI and assigned to producer John Burgess who played an important role throughout their recording career. When the influential television programme *Ready Steady Go* adopted their third single '5-4-3-2-1' as its theme tune, a chain of chart hits commenced which continued almost uninterrupted until the end of the decade.

The Manfreds thrived on tension and conflict and proved extremely difficult to manage. Their image was also suspect, neither emulating the smart-suited Beatles nor the fashionably outrageous Stones. With their Marks & Spencer's black roll-neck sweaters, beards and thick rimmed glasses, the group looked more like disgruntled college beatniks than pop stars. On the credit side, they were unquestionably one of the first 'intellectual' groups and it was widely reported that singer Paul Jones had studied at Oxford and came from an upper-middle-class family that included in its ranks a Royal Navy officer and a member of the clergy. Jones even boasted a political consciousness, distributing Labour Party leaflets and singing at CND rallies in Trafalgar Square. He was also boyishly good-looking and soon emerged as a pin-up hero in striking contrast to his fellow Manfreds. Pitt, who had originally dismissed Jones as a poor singer, was amazed by his transformation into a vocalist of poise and grace:

Paul Jones turned out to be magnificent. He improved so rapidly and got great enjoyment from performing; each day he'd learn something new. He would always go out beforehand and size up a stage to see whether there were any props he could use. He was very inventive and his movements were superb.

Unfortunately, not everyone appreciated Jones' increasingly central role in the group. Pitt claims that Manfred was irritated by the attention being lauded upon the singer and this manifested itself in a series of ego clashes that were to continue unabated until Jones departed from the group in 1966. Pitt himself was ousted the previous year. Evidently, the 25 per cent cut he had negotiated was now regarded as too high, even though it incorporated office expenses and publicity fees. Pitt perceived the split as financially expedient:

> I think Manfred suddenly wanted too much. It's a human failing. There was an atmosphere in the band and it had been there for some time: it was always Manfred. Manfred was neurotic and he was also an anarchist and neurotic anarchists are difficult to cope with. I had a deal whereby if they didn't earn any money then I got nothing and if they earned a million I did very nicely. So I worked like mad, but then Manfred began to resent what I was getting.

The Manfreds survived Pitt's departure and do not seem to have been seriously disrupted by the split. Nevertheless, Pitt's contribution should not be underestimated. He shared the group's enthusiasm for the music of Bob Dylan and his close association with Albert Grossman ensured that their interest was sustained and rewarded. Dylan even visited the group at the Marquee and reputedly informed the press that they were the most accomplished interpreters of his material. The ideas that Pitt had implanted bore fruit in successive years, but he was forced to look further afield for new talent.

1965 was not a particularly happy year for Ken Pitt. Having lost the Manfreds he was able to concentrate attention on two other up-and-coming groups, the Mark Leeman Five and Dave Antony's Moods. Leeman was an exciting singer in the Paul Jones mould, but whatever plans Pitt had for the boy ended when his protégé was killed in a car crash. In his sadness Ken turned to Bournemouth-based Dave Antony's Moods, and for a time they seemed likely candidates for success. Their lively act proved a big hit in hip London clubs such as the Cromwellian, but middling record sales left them branded as an average support act.

It was Dave Antony who introduced Ken to solo singer Goldie, lately estranged from her backing group, the Gingerbreads. Pitt was confident that he could establish the American singer alongside such homegrown talent as Dusty Springfield, Cilla Black, Sandie Shaw and Lulu. For several months all went well, but by early 1966 the fates had once again turned against Pitt and Goldie abruptly departed:

> We went out one night to the Cromwellian and she said 'I want to go home!' London was very tame for her; she came from Brooklyn and missed the Jewish New York ambience. When I went to see her there and met her mother, I realized why she was homesick.

Fortunately, by the time Goldie returned to Brooklyn, Pitt had netted a new chart act thanks to an enterprising co-management deal.

It was towards the end of 1965 that Dave Nicolson first entered Ken's life. Nicolson was a typical sixties whizz kid dabbling on the fringes of the music business. While working at the EMI press office, he harboured dreams of establishing himself as a manager/producer in the Andrew Oldham/Larry Page mould. After advertising for groups in *New Musical Express*, he plucked lead singer Peter Smith from the Beat Formula Three and launched him as Crispian St Peters. Nicolson was no fool. He signed the bemused Crispian to a 10-year management and production contract, borrowed money and set up his own label, the Decca licensed Cash Records. The name was delightfully ironic for Nicolson had little cash and his company consisted of little more than a ream of headed notepaper. He secured a further loan from Danny Betesh of Kennedy Street Enterprises, but after two flop singles ('At This Moment' and 'No No No') his benefactors quickly lost interest. The final financial port of call was Kenneth Pitt.

Nicolson desperately needed £120 to record Crispian's third single, a cover of We Five's American hit 'You Were On My Mind'. In return for a 50 per cent share of any profits, Ken proffered the sum, though he expressed little confidence in Crispian's star potential. He had virtually written off the single when Nicolson returned with an extremely well-produced record. 'You Were On My Mind' foundered in the Christmas rush, but was revitalized in early 1966 and began to sell in prodigious quantities.

With a potential star in his pocket, Nicolson sought to strengthen his management concerns and generously offered Pitt a 33 per cent interest in Crispian. The next move was to create a sensation in the pop press using Crispian's ingenuousness as bait. *New Musical Express* journalist Norrie Drummond could hardly believe his ears when this upstart newcomer to the charts arrogantly asserted: 'I've written about 80 songs and they're of a better class than most Beatles' songs'. Revelling in his imaginary role as the new Colonel Tom Parker of pop, Nicolson proudly butted in: 'This boy is going to be Presley all over again'. Indignant at being branded a mere copyist, Crispian retorted: 'Better than Presley. I'm going to make Presley look like the Statue of Liberty . . . I am sexier than Dave Berry and more exciting than Tom Jones . . . And the Beatles are past it'. Today, such comments would be mildly amusing but in January 1966 such arrogance was deemed almost blasphemous. The following week *New Musical Express* was bombarded with phone calls and irate letters denouncing Crispian as a presumptuous, big-headed, talentless nonentity. Many claimed he would be forgotten within a year. They weren't far wrong.

Crispian had all the makings of a one-hit-wonder, but Pitt and Nicolson procured a successful follow up, 'The Pied Piper', which went Top 5 on both sides of the Atlantic. Tours of Australia and the United States brought further success but Crispian was constantly hounded as the man who had claimed he was bigger than Elvis and the Beatles combined. In reality, St Peters was an average singer, totally lacking the charisma of those artistes he had so blithely dismissed. Pitt recalls the boy's artistic shortcomings:

> Crispian couldn't project. He thought he could just amble on to the stage and sing a song as if he was at home in his bedroom. But that way you don't sell records or get people to see you in concert again.

When the next single, 'Changes', flopped, Crispian was thrust from Fortune's Wheel. Several attempts were made to salvage his career and his managers even pushed him as a country 'n' western singer, a role better suited to his singing style. For the general public, however, he remained the insufferably arrogant young pop star who claimed he would be a god but rapidly fell into obscurity. One year after his first chart success, Crispian scored a belated US Top 40 entry with 'You Were On My Mind', but by then he was ancient history. Psychological pressures blighted any lingering hopes of a comeback, as Pitt reveals:

> His problem was his illness. I didn't realize it at first. We then found that this was the only reason we could find for his behaviour. One tends to be a little antagonistic and blame him but then I don't know what it's like to be schizophrenic. Unfortunately, he became something of a joke figure, which was very sad.

Even today, the memory of those days is still a painful subject for the ill-starred St Peters, as Nicolson testifies:

> He's still bitter about 'You Were On My Mind'. He wrote to me not
> long ago saying, 'You forced me to record that song!' He's now very
> unhappy about that period of his life . . . He's got a very powerful
> imagination that overrules him at times. He feels that some sort of
> curse has been put on him by that record. 'You Were On My Mind'
> has the line, 'I got wounds to bind'. For some reason that line sticks in
> his mind and it's something that haunts him still . . . It's very strange.

The Pitt/Nicolson amalgam lasted long enough to influence the
career of another aspiring new act — the Truth. Frank Aeillo and
Steve Gold were two young singers who had taken their group title
from Ray Charles' 'Tell The Truth'. In early 1966, they became
involved with a young entrepreneur named Jeff Cooper who steered
them to chart success with a cover of the Beatles' 'Girl'. After
seeing them supporting Crispian St Peters an enthusiastic Nicolson
approached Cooper who was happy to sell the group's contract in
order to spend more time attending to his Sterling/Cooper jeans
empire. Both Pitt and Nicolson were impressed by the Truth's
stage act, but in spite of continued success on the live circuit that
all-important follow up to 'Girl' proved elusive. In his search for a
hit Nicolson was adventurous enough to ignore the ageing songwriters of Tin Pan Alley and sought assistance from his contemporaries. The Truth covered Ray Davies's 'I Go To Sleep' and Reg
Presley's 'Jingle Jangle', but neither the Kink nor the Trogg could
provide the easy road to the charts that Lennon and McCartney
had previously ensured. Eventually, the Truth persuaded Nicolson
to buy back Pitt's share of the management on the grounds that he
was too straitlaced for them. No further successes followed.

By mid-1966 Pitt was determined to discover a new, original act
with sufficient potential for achieving international stardom. Since
the days of Danny Purches, he had dreamed of developing the
career of a rough diamond and in the wake of the beat boom there
were innumerable young kids convinced that they were the new
Bob Dylan or Elvis Presley. Pitt was adamant that a carefully
tutored artiste could transcend the limitations of the fashion-
conscious pop world and succeed in a number of related fields. In
later years he was lampooned for suggesting that the time was right
for the emergence of the new Tommy Steele, but that name
expressed only a minimal aspect of Pitt's overall vision. What Pitt
desired was an artiste of similar potential who was different enough
to capture the public's imagination. The ideal applicant would be a
charismatic singer, songwriter, actor and musician, capable of

adopting a variety of roles and exploiting all areas of show business. Remarkably, the perfect candidate had been within Pitt's orbit for the previous nine months.

Pitt had first heard about David Bowie in September 1965 when a manager named Ralph Horton phoned his office requesting financial support. It transpired that Horton was Bowie's second manager and the artiste had already cut three failed singles under the name David Jones. The singer hardly sounded like a world-beater but Ralph was convinced of his potential as a song-and-dance man. Pitt politely suggested that the name Jones should be dropped and several weeks later he was informed that the boy had been rechristened David Bowie. Unfortunately, due to a bookful of commitments, Pitt was unable to pursue the Bowie case for the remainder of the year. Horton was too extravagant to wait patiently so he temporarily abandoned Pitt in favour of other benefactors.

When Horton next contacted Ken Pitt in April 1966, his tone was as confident as ever. Bowie now had television experience, a chart hit[1] and a new record, 'Do Anything You Say', released only days before. In short, he was already on the threshold of stardom and all Horton required were the talents and business acumen of an established manager to provide that all-important final push. Pitt expressed enthusiasm and finally agreed to see this much-touted singing star play a Sunday afternoon concert at the Marquee. Ken recalls an amazing set of self-penned songs, R & B standards and, most surprisingly, a dramatic rendition of 'You'll Never Walk Alone'. As the show reached its climax, the bespectacled entrepreneur closed his eyes and imagined the boy performing for a full house at one of the world's largest venues. He was transfixed.

During a subsequent meeting at Horton's Warwick Square flat, a verbal agreement was concluded between the two managers by which Ken agreed to take on the administrative work load, leaving Ralph free to concentrate on Bowie's gigging schedule. Rather uncharacteristically, Pitt neglected to commit these agreements to paper immediately, and this would cause some consternation in later months. Within days of allying himself to Horton, Ken discovered that his partner was an incurable spendthrift whose profligacy seemingly had no bounds. Soon, Pitt was besieged by creditors ranging from the GPO to car hire firms and even Bowie's own record company. Amazingly, Pye Records had obtained judgement against Horton for failing to pay for a small number of

---

[1] The desperate Horton had in fact borrowed £250 which was used to hype 'Can't Help Thinking About Me' into the *Melody Maker* chart at number 34. The disc was conspicuous by its absence from the *Record Retailer* Top 50.

the artiste's records. Pitt immediately smoothed things over with Pye managing director, Louis Benjamin, but these constant administrative and financial problems severely tested his patience.

The early summer of 1966 was not a particularly auspicious period in Bowie's history. Another Pye single, 'I Dig Everything' had failed and finances were tight. Ken had arranged for Maurice Hatton of Mithras Films to see Bowie at the Marquee in the hope of gaining him a part in a short musical film. Hatton was impressed and several ideas were thrashed out but it was all pie in the sky. Undeterred by this disappointment, Pitt set about securing Bowie a new recording contract, this time with Deram, a subsidiary label of Decca that was about to be launched as a haven for promising young talent. In order to alleviate financial worries, Pitt also turned his attention to publishing. Negotiations commenced with David Platz of Essex Music who proffered an advance of £1000, a figure that Pitt felt could be bettered by an American publishing company.

On 8 November, Pitt embarked on an American/Australian tour with Crispian St Peters and this allowed him sufficient time to negotiate with New York publishers and lawyers on behalf of Bowie. Following a series of meetings, Pitt finally secured a world-wide publishing deal offering a $10 000 advance, with a guarantee of a further $20 000 to be paid during the next three years. Ken neglected to cable Horton or Bowie about this piece of good fortune, preferring to wait until the contracts were actually in his hands. This was probably sound business sense since Pitt was in a dangerous position, having still not signed a management agreement with Horton. In the event of any dispute between the parties the lack of a written document would leave Pitt little hope of receiving full compensation for the time, effort and money he had already pumped into Bowie's career. Unfortunately, during Pitt's absence Horton had re-assumed administrative control and made a disastrous decision that was to have far-reaching effects. Upon returning to England, Ken was shattered to learn that his partner had accepted an offer from David Platz of Essex Music for an advance of £500, precisely half the figure previously negotiated. Poor Horton felt that he had made a sound decision at a time when hard cash was needed. For Pitt, the loss of the American publishing deal was a devastating blow and it would require all his tenacity to sustain David's livelihood during the next couple of years.

Ken Pitt's strategy for 1967 was to bury the mistakes of the previous year and start from scratch. David's Deram debut received a favourable response though one perceptive reviewer felt obliged to point out the vocal similarities to Anthony Newley and added that the flip side, 'The London Boys', was a stronger cut. All this

was true and much has been made of the contention that it was Ken
Pitt who promoted the Newley image and suppressed the provocative flip side. In fact, it was the record company that made this
decision, supported by Bowie himself who evidently preferred
'Rubber Band'. Contrary to popular belief, Pitt was actually concerned about the Newley comparisons, particularly as his wish was
for Bowie to emerge as a unique and individual artiste.

Dismissing the Newley fixation as a passing phase, Pitt turned
his attention to more pressing matters. Still smarting from the
publishing fiasco and concerned about the lack of a binding
management contract, he was forced to consider his future as
Horton's partner. Conflicting loyalties, however, prevented
decisive action. Eventually, it was Bowie who solved this political
impasse:

> David phoned me one day and said: 'I'm very worried about Ralph'.
> He was concerned about the debts and felt that Ralph was a good
> friend and would tear up the contract that David had with him. He
> went to see him and I think Ralph was rather relieved because the next
> day he phoned me and said: 'I'm going to finish with David'. To his
> credit, he's never bothered me since.

Indeed, Horton virtually disappeared from the music business
overnight. In many respects, he was a classic example of the
flamboyant but flawed manager — a breed that proliferated in the
mid-sixties pop world. Horton had supported Bowie through some
bad times, and his remarkable enthusiasm and braggadocio had
extracted money from wealthy benefactors who really should have
known better. He was also acutely aware of the importance of
image and carefully groomed many of the musicians in his circle,
not least Bowie himself. For all the bluster, however, Ralph could
neither transform himself nor Bowie into the millionaire of his
dreams. The price of his Epsteinian extravagance had been all too
noticeable in the escalating debts that refused to subside.

It was not until 25 April 1967 that Pitt officially had the
contracts signed by which he was legally appointed David Bowie's
manager. In the meantime, a second Deram single appeared in the
form of 'The Laughing Gnome', an unashamed comedy workout
complete with Newley phraseology. It was certainly a dangerous
move for Bowie and had it charted he would probably have been
dismissed as a one-hit-wonder novelty singer in the vein of Napoleon
XIV or Whistling Jack Smith. Surprisingly, Ken Pitt does not
regard this embarrassing single as an error of judgement:

Nothing he ever did was a mistake. This is late 1970s criticism . . .
Nobody was aghast in 1967. You must put it in the context of the time.
It was right for the time. David is a highly inventive writer and he does
have a sense of humour. It was just another facet of David's personality.

The failure of 'The Laughing Gnome' at least enabled Pitt to push
Bowie's debut album as a serious work worthy of critical attention.
Several good reviews were forthcoming, but without the back-up
of a quality hit single sales were negligible.

With Pitt providing food, money and shelter, Bowie was able
to continue with his sometimes over-ambitious projects, but
occasionally these extra-curricular interests bore fruit. After
enrolling in Lindsay Kemp's mime classes, for example, Bowie
made a surprise appearance in several performances of *Pierrot In
Turquoise*. This flirtation with mime contributed to his store of
knowledge and would later encourage him to think in terms of
fusing theatre and rock. In retrospect, one can see that Bowie was
very much ahead of the pack in branching out from pop music.
Had he been an established pop star, the publicity generated by his
superficial involvements in theatre and film would have been
invaluable. Unfortunately, Bowie was at best a cult figure and until
he achieved substantial commercial success, the music press would
remain uninterested in his other activities. This was the major flaw
in Pitt's plan of action. He had the power to influence and direct
Bowie's butterfly mind but there could be no immediate financial
gain from such a policy without the elusive yet essential hit single
which alone would inevitably focus attention on his artiste's many
talents.

Pitt's commitment to Bowie was seemingly limitless, so perhaps
it was not too surprising that the superstar elect moved into his
Manchester Street flat. This allowed Ken to spend even more time
educating the singer and introducing him to cultural pursuits
previously outside his experience.

Following the commercial failure of another promising single,
'Love You Till Tuesday', Pitt engaged in a long war of attrition
with Decca. He bombarded the record company with letters complaining about the lack of promotion on Bowie's discs and even
suggested that they drop him from the label rather than continue in
a half-hearted fashion. When Bowie's next two singles were rejected
as 'unsuitable', Pitt announced that he was taking his star elsewhere.
Within twenty-four hours he was knocking on the doors of Apple
— the Beatles' enterprising record label for the development of
new talent. Much to Bowie's disappointment, however, a terse

rejection letter was all that Pitt received for his efforts. It would be over a year before another record contract was signed.

In spite of all his flop records, Bowie was still earning a reasonable working wage and with support from an over-protective father and manager there was little chance of him starving. Nevertheless, Pitt was sufficiently concerned about his protégé's finances to suggest a stab at cabaret. For any serious young singer/songwriter such an artistic compromise would have been unthinkable, but Pitt's vision of Bowie as an all-round entertainer was broad enough to encompass even this unlikely area. In the event, David's attitude remained ambivalent. Occasionally, he was fired with enthusiasm for the idea, while at other times he seemed to regard it as demeaning. Pitt had the foresight to sweeten the pill by encouraging Bowie to perform a set consisting of a mixture of his own songs, sprinkled with a few Beatles covers. The cabaret concept reached the audition stage but went no further. It was probably just as well. According to Pitt, the well-known agent Harry Dawson was overwhelmed by Bowie's performance and following the Astor Club audition he reputedly exclaimed: 'It's a marvellous act, but where can I book it? It's too good'. It is difficult to imagine how an act can possibly be 'too good' and when I finally found Harry, he was frank enough to admit that he had actually dismissed Bowie as a no-hoper:

> I turned around to Ken and said, 'Let him have a good day job — he's never going to get anywhere'. That was my judgement of David Bowie. Ken said, 'You're out of your mind. I'm going to make him an international star'. Bowie basically did impressions at the time. I couldn't see it.

Indeed, it suddenly seemed that the only person who was convinced of Bowie's talent was the ever-optimistic Kenneth Pitt.

It is difficult to determine precisely when Bowie began to lose faith in his manager, but the first signs of a possible change of heart occurred when he left the Manchester Street flat to move in with his girlfriend, Hermione Farthingale. Together they formed an acoustic group named Turquoise, which later became Feathers. It was an appropriate name, for their music was decidedly lightweight and their earnings virtually non-existent. Bowie's adoption of a pseudo-hippie lifestyle was characteristically half-hearted and when his money ran low he was more than willing to suffer the indignity of appearing in a Lyons Maid ice-cream commercial. Nevertheless, peer-group pressure had placed the star elect in an extremely uncomfortable position. He knew that Pitt represented security, order and direction in his life, but the new friends he was acquiring clearly disapproved of such a father figure. The hippie movement had been nurtured on the mid-sixties catchphrase 'never trust anyone over 30' and Pitt was not the kind of man who could lie about his age. Although Bowie was a long way from seriously considering the termination of his management contract with Pitt, the seeds of discontent had already been sown. Confused feelings about his possible career development seem to have thrust the singer into a series of ephemeral ventures. Feathers dissolved before it had time to develop and David's relationship with Hermione ended shortly afterwards. Suddenly, the singer seemed confused, dejected and unwilling to forge ahead with Pitt's carefully structured career plans.

Pitt wisely chose not to interfere in Bowie's artistic decisions but voiced concern about the amount of time he was frittering away on counter-culture pursuits. Ken had shared David's life long enough to understand the psychology of the performer and realized that without a major long term project to spark his interest there was always the danger of a descent into inertia:

> David had bouts of laziness and I would get a little sharp with him from time to time. Yet the moment he got interested in a particular scheme he outran everybody else. But he had to be turned on and fired with enthusiasm.

Clearly, Bowie no longer felt enthusiasm for the old ideal of becoming an accomplished all-round entertainer. However, the alternative lifestyle offered by hippie friends and folk singers seemed even less likely to enable him to achieve long-lasting success in the music business. Pitt decided that Bowie urgently required to work on a major project before all momentum was permanently lost. In financing the projected television film *Love You Till Tuesday* Pitt seemed to be proving beyond doubt that he was the major catalyst in Bowie's performing life. His investment was not only a magnanimous gesture, but a dangerous gamble involving several thousand pounds' expenditure. Ultimately, his gesture of commitment proved only partly successful. The much hoped-for screening on a major network never took place and this prevented Bowie from ingratiating himself with television and film producers as Pitt had intended. On the credit side, the filming had encouraged Bowie to write several new songs, one of which, 'Space Oddity', was particularly impressive.

For a time, Pitt remained firmly in the driving seat but his power was gradually eroded due to the intervention of two

Americans — Calvin Mark Lee and Mary Angela Barnett. These latest acquaintances of Bowie had provided the connection through which Pitt negotiated a deal with Mercury Records. As the months passed their influence grew stronger, but Pitt still hoped that the old order could be restored if 'Space Oddity' charted as a single. With the American moon launch imminent, the topical value of the single was undeniable and Pitt invested all his efforts in ensuring its success. He even employed the services of a chart-hyper, an uncharacteristic action, which underlined the extent of his desperation and determination. Weeks passed, but the expected chart breakthrough failed to materialize. Deflated by the poor sales, Bowie embarked on a Continental jaunt, appearing in two song festivals in Italy and Malta. Upon returning to England with his manager, Bowie received some disturbing news that made the fate of 'Space Oddity' seem irrelevant by comparison.

Haywood Stenton Jones had always been a delicate figure, but his sudden death from a lung infection came as a terrible shock to his son. Jones had diligently guided David's career over the years, ensuring that he received the best professional advice and never fell into financial difficulties. His demise was also a serious blow to Pitt who had established a close and trusting relationship with Bowie's family since signing the artiste in 1967. Without Jones's sobering influence it would prove increasingly difficult for Pitt to convince Bowie that he was acting in his best interests. Of course, Jones's death might have enabled Ken to adopt a more paternalistic role, but instead Bowie turned to his newer friends for moral support. In September, less than one month after his father's death, 'Space Oddity' belatedly stormed the charts, peaking at number 5. This long-awaited breakthrough would have been the cause of tumultuous celebration in earlier days but Bowie was now an older, somewhat sadder figure. While the disc was scaling the charts he moved into a flat in Beckenham housed in a grand Edwardian building named Haddon Hall. There he lived with Angela Barnett, producer Tony Visconti and a host of visiting rock musicians and counter-culture flag-wavers. Pitt was forced to watch from a distance as his rising star went through a tortuous period of reassessment:

> The disillusionment didn't really start until after the success of 'Space Oddity' . . . I've always noted that artistes are nice people until they achieve their aims and become stars. David eventually got what he wanted, but it drove him to the depths of despair. A little bit of it was affectation, I admit. The putting down of the single and pretending he wasn't a pop star and hating all these people wanting to take his photograph. But you must remember he was living with this rather

pseudo-hippie commune. They had a great influence on him; they were very anti-success, anti-hit record, anti-pop star. He'd go home at nights to that. It was a strange dichotomy.

For the final six months of his association with David Bowie, Pitt seems to have been singlehandedly fighting the inhabitants of Haddon Hall. He now admits, 'David became unmanageable. I was manager in name only'. The breakdown between artiste and manager resulted in organizational chaos. Prior to a prestigious Bowie concert at London's Purcell Room, Pitt was abruptly relieved of publicity duties by David's new aide, Calvin Mark Lee. The confusion caused the media to stay away in droves and Bowie was incensed. After that concert Calvin was seldom seen in Bowie's circle, but Pitt did not particularly benefit from this turn of events. The second David Bowie album had just been released and was largely ignored, much to the disappointment of its creator. While Pitt encouraged Bowie to take advantage of his recent single success by working even harder, the disillusioned star returned to his Haddon Hall sanctuary.

Pitt could have been forgiven for abandoning Bowie to his own devices, but instead he pushed ahead with a number of new strategies. The most intriguing of these was persuading Bowie to be interviewed by the gay magazine *Jeremy*. In 1969, it was an adventurous and potentially dangerous move to ally an artiste with the gay movement, but Pitt felt that Bowie's career prospects could be enhanced by tacitly supporting such a cause:

> It was the turning point in the whole Bowie campaign. I probably put too much value on *Jeremy* and its readers. It wasn't a very good magazine, but one worked on the assumption that it was read by some very important people in the business. I didn't know what would happen, whether it would bring down on David all the calumny that the devil could muster . . . But it was important, especially when you consider what's happened since with Boy George, Frankie Goes To Hollywood and Marilyn.

Three years after the *Jeremy* interview Pitt's pioneering publicity work reached fruition when Bowie stunned the rock world by confessing to *Melody Maker* that he was bisexual. Surprisingly, Pitt could never make up his mind about the nature of Bowie's sexuality:

> David had this aura. He would sometimes come into a room looking like a ravishingly beautiful girl, then, 10 minutes later, he'd be a 'Gor blimey' yobbo. He would turn the cockney persona on and off. He did

a whole interview in cockney once. Of course, he was always surrounded by gay people and got on with them very well. But I really
didn't know for certain until I read *Melody Maker*. Frankly, I wasn't
quite sure then.

While Bowie remained in relative seclusion, Pitt continued with
his dream of establishing the artiste as a straight actor. There was
talk of casting David in an adaptation of Sir Walter Scott's *The Fair
Maid of Perth* and plans were also underway for film director Tony
Palmer to produce a Bowie documentary. Strangely, the one area
that remained unexploited was the most obvious of all. As Christmas
loomed the patient public still awaited a follow up to 'Space Oddity'.
   In many respects, the delay in releasing a new single was not
surprising. Deciding upon a successor to 'Space Oddity' was no
easy task and much was at stake. Eventually, almost six months
after his last single had charted, Bowie selected 'The Prettiest
Star', a non-gimmicky record that flopped. Although Pitt objected
to its release, it is debatable whether an alternative choice would
have proven chartworthy. The problem lay in the nature of 'Space
Oddity', a self-contained statement that offered little possibility of
a follow up along similar lines. Producer Tony Visconti had spotted
the danger prior to its release and refused to be associated with the
disc. In spite of its hit potential, 'Space Oddity' had all the hallmarks
of a one-off novelty record. The timing of its release persuaded
many people that it had been written to cash in on the American
moon launch. Significantly, one month before 'Space Oddity'
charted, an American duo, Zager and Evans, hit the top of the UK
and US charts with the futuristic 'In The Year 2525'. Thematically,
there were superficial similarities between the songs, each dealing
with possible future events and containing a pat moral. For Bowie
to be placed alongside Zager and Evans in the public's consciousness
was far from ideal. They were quintessential one-hit-wonders, and
following the enormous success of 'In The Year 2525' slipped back
into the netherworld from where they had mysteriously emerged.
In the autumn of 1969 it was by no means certain that Bowie would
avoid the same fate. Even Pitt was forced to concede that in the
public's eye Bowie had been overshadowed by his own creation —
the enigmatic Major Tom.
   From Pitt's point of view, the ghosts of Haddon Hall remained
the invisible force in Bowie's life and any lingering hopes of winning
back the impressionable star were irrevocably destroyed when he
married his *âme damnée*, Mary Angela Barnett. David and Angela
went on to become Beckenham's answer to John and Yoko, but
even today Pitt sees the marriage as a form of artistic castration:

Angela coming on the scene was the worst thing that ever happened to David Bowie. She would probably argue that she helped his career. In actual fact, she held it back. She turned out to be the division between David and me. I think she put him back at least two years. Her attitude towards life and other people didn't help him a great deal. I think she was the destroyer.

Following his marriage, Bowie became extremely capricious and seemingly unable to reconcile the Haddon Hall notions of artistic integrity with the common man's desire for an easy living. Pitt was unwittingly cast in the role of the devil's advocate and his willingness to procure Bowie steady work in television commercials was frowned upon. The fact that Bowie himself had requested such employment was apparently irrelevant. When Pitt booked a series of live performances Bowie again reversed previous instructions and complained that his manager was preventing the group from forging ahead with studio work. Given such inconsistencies, it was no great shock when the star phoned one afternoon to announce that he wanted to manage himself. Without fully articulating his fears, Bowie had evidently lost confidence in Pitt's managerial style and suddenly felt he needed a radically different approach. His disenchantment was probably a product of the times, for by the end of the sixties many artistes were searching for specialized business managers rather than the traditional Tin Pan Alley entrepreneurs who had often emerged as creative guiding forces in their clients' lives. Bowie took his problem to Olaf Wyper, General Manager of Philips, who swiftly washed his hands of the entire business but provided the artiste with the names of several lawyers, one of whom was willing to branch out into rock management.

Tony De Fries was the complete antithesis of Ken Pitt: arrogant, ruthless and aggressive in business dealings, he represented an attitude that was thoroughly distasteful to his quiet, urbane rival. Pitt recalls his feelings upon first meeting De Fries:

I was most alarmed when he came to see me. He wasn't a manager. He was working as a litigation clerk at a firm of solicitors, one of whose clients was Olaf Wyper . . . He had no qualifications to manage anybody. David was still a close friend of mine and I wouldn't have taken him to court, but I didn't want this man cashing in on my investment. I'd seen the likes of Tony De Fries many a time. I tried to alert David to my worst fears but it didn't seem to sink in.

On the contrary, Bowie was evidently smitten by the idea of being represented by such a high-powered lawyer. In De Fries he had found his own version of Allen Klein, an alchemist who could apparently transform Mercury albums into gold.

Pitt's response to De Fries was to request £2000 compensation, an absurdly low figure in view of the work and money he had previously pumped into Bowie's career. Instead, De Fries fobbed him off with promises of a possible percentage of Bowie's future earnings. Pitt sat tight and strengthened his position by enforcing a clause in the Essex Music contract which ensured that any royalties due were payable initially to his company. De Fries later contested this arrangement, Essex froze the assets and a court case ensued. Pitt eventually settled with Bowie, but by that time De Fries was no longer managing the seventies superstar. Even from a distance, however, De Fries was an imposing figure whose influence could not be underestimated, as Pitt found to his cost:

> I was awarded £15 000 plus costs and De Fries tried to stop it. He said that David had no right to apportion any of the monies. But that couldn't work. It just delayed it for a long time. De Fries was fighting for his life. It would have gone on forever if he'd had his way.

Tony De Fries has always been a controversial figure so it is hardly surprising that his involvement in the Bowie saga still produces markedly ambivalent responses from different sources in the music business. His well-publicized achievements and dollar earnings during Bowie's RCA years have inevitably overshadowed Pitt's quiet industry and commitment during the late sixties. The extent to which De Fries profited from his predecessor's groundwork cannot be calculated but Pitt clearly feels that his reputation was often hyped by the early seventies music press:

> In the *Melody Maker* there was a two-page article on De Fries where they used the cliché 'De Fries' masterstroke was taking Bowie away and not making him available to the press . . .' Bullshit! Do you know how many times that's been used during the past 50 years? Masterstroke?! It was an elementary stroke . . . Who do you think pointed Bowie into those somewhat 'unconventional' channels? He lived in my flat for two years and what eventually happened to David was all part of a plan that I had formed. The plan had nothing to do with Tony De Fries.

In spite of Pitt's objections few would argue that De Fries was responsible for breaking Bowie internationally. Yet the litigation clerk's entrepreneurial strategies are still derided by his elder adversary:

De Fries was a disaster. Is anybody better off for what De Fries has done? He managed *himself* very well. David didn't have money then. When *Hunky Dory* was on the charts and the name Bowie was quite big he was living in Oakley Street. He and Angela came back one night and found the door padlocked. Things were so bad that Zowie had to go up to Aberdeen to his nanny's parents to ensure he got fed. He didn't take David Bowie over for the same reasons I did. Think about that and you've got the answer to the whole story.

Unfortunately, the plot still leaves several unanswered questions. Would Bowie have achieved megastardom without the consuming ambition of De Fries? Were De Fries' strategies devised to strengthen his position in anticipation of Bowie's eventual defection? Would their business relationship have improved if De Fries had given his artiste a larger slice of the cake? Since De Fries was exiled from Bowie's court such questions have continued to multiply and, as a result, his historical importance in terms of rock management has been reduced considerably. History has been kinder to Pitt and in recent years his career has been placed in a clearer perspective. During the early seventies he was ridiculed as the manager who wanted to transform the embryonic Ziggy Stardust into a neo-Tommy Steele. Pitt's claim that Bowie was an all-round entertainer seemed an absurd conceit characteristic of a dinosaur mentality hopelessly entrenched in the outmoded philosophies of fifties rock 'n' roll. However, Bowie's increasing involvement in film and theatre work in recent years has left the nagging suspicion that Pitt's vision may have been largely correct. Had he chosen a more radical analogy than Tommy Steele, mythologizing Bowie critics might have hailed him a sage. Instead, his reputation remains that of a solicitous soul, strangely out of place in the rapacious rock music business.

The loss of Bowie at the end of the sixties effectively closed Pitt's career in pop management. Like many of his sixties contemporaries, he became disillusioned with the American-styled business manager favoured by many new artistes. He was also weary of young acts demanding financial support but refusing to accept advice on career development. Not wishing to become either a full-time accountant or a sugar daddy, Pitt gracefully bowed out. Before making that decision, however, he briefly represented Tony Dangerfield, one of the more durable performers of the previous decade. Ironically, Tony remembers Pitt not as the creative ideas man of the Bowie days but as a hard-nosed negotiator, eager to score points off cautious record companies:

Ken was a very good organizer and highly efficient in negotiation, but I felt he could no longer see potential and break down walls. He was purely an office man; with a rock manager you need something more. I think he burnt himself out with David. He put so many ideas into him. He must have been disillusioned when he didn't get the cream. If I wanted advice on contracts today I'd go to Ken, but I wouldn't sign him as personal manager. Ken was too much of a gentleman, a pro. He couldn't stand inefficiency and the business is rife with it. It must have been difficult for Ken to deal with such people.

Pitt's old partner Dave Nicolson concurs with Dangerfield's viewpoint:

Ken was honest, truthful and reliable. He was also very straight, both in the business sense and his attitude. I'm sure with Crispian St Peters he would have advised against making a statement like, 'I will be bigger than the Beatles'. He sobered up a lot of ideas I had which were quite crazy.

This emphasis on Pitt's sober and gentlemanly nature has often been made and may be the key to his lack of millionaire success. Bowie has seldom commented on Pitt but one of his asides reiterates Dangerfield and Nicolson's main point: 'He is a very nice man. I like him very much, but that's not enough in this business'.

By his colleagues' reckoning, Pitt lacked the ruthlessness and aggression of an aspiring mogul. Even in the seventies he regarded diplomacy and integrity as the hallmarks of good management and refused to surrender to the demands of cynical young artistes. Instead, he acted as a consultant to visiting American and Continental stars, just as he had done 20 years before. Looking back over his career he admits that his greatest weakness was a lack of effective communication with his acts:

Artistes always want to know what you're doing for them. If I'm guilty of anything it was sitting in my office being very busy while the artiste was at home biting his fingernails. This often happened. When they poured their hearts out, I listened but made no comment. They didn't realize I'd heard it all before, knew the problems and how to handle them. I knew David Bowie was going to be one of the biggest acts in the world, but I couldn't get it across to him with any emotion.

In analysing the strengths or weaknesses of Kenneth Pitt as a manager it is difficult to ignore an apparent streak of ill luck that runs through his career. Danny Purches, the untameable gypsy boy, could not control his urge to spend every penny he earned; Manfred grew money-conscious; Crispian St Peters suffered psychological problems; Goldie fell victim to homesickness; Dangerfield arrived too late and, worst of all, David Bowie abandoned Pitt after achieving his first hit. Perhaps a more politically shrewd entrepreneur might have averted some of the above turns of fortune, but not all of them. Ultimately, one is left with the question 'Was rock management the most suitable occupation for Pitt?' His younger contemporary, Simon Napier-Bell, clearly thinks not:

> Ken Pitt was almost the epitome of the indulgent, all on the side of the artiste manager and Tony De Fries was the opposite. In both cases there you don't have what I would call the professional 'music business' manager. Neither has been substantially successful on a continuous basis with rock acts or continued with them. That isn't condemning them in terms of strengths or weaknesses. They just don't seem to have found their métier in rock management.

It should be added, however, that very few sixties managers were dedicated to rock management *per se*, and even fewer could sustain an interest over a long period. While admitting that no contemporary rock group would tolerate his ideas for more than a couple of hours, Pitt does not consider his unfulfilled dreams as evidence of failure. Indeed, he compares himself favourably with any of his multi-millionaire contemporaries, and for his contribution to Bowie's career development alone, Pitt deserves a special place in the history of rock management.

Reg Calvert never spoke much about his early career. He was always too busy thinking up crazy stunts, discovering new hobbies and administering the affairs of his latest singing discovery to dwell on the past. For his artistes, Calvert filled so many roles and demonstrated skills in such diverse areas that it seemed impossible to pin him down. Farmer, vet, laboratory assistant, graphic artist, photographer, mechanic — Reg would turn his hand to almost anything and never fail to amaze his impressionable teenage protégés. Behind the chirpy jack of all trades persona, however, there was a history of hard struggle that had taken Calvert far away from his poor Yorkshire background to the relative luxury of a small house in Southampton. Along the way, he had worked in a printing firm and played alto saxophone in dance bands, supplementing his income through various outrageous schemes. At one stage, he even made considerable money from the middle name he shared with a leading firm of jam-makers. Only Reginald 'Hartley' Calvert would have had the nerve to sell his own jam with a Hartley label stuck impudently on the jar! From feeding the public new jam in old jars, Calvert moved to a far more lucrative business venture — the copying of pop stars.

The rock 'n' roll revolution of the late fifties had a profound effect on Calvert, who had always been searching for new and exciting ways to exploit his creative and organizational abilities. In the ground floor of his premises in Southampton he opened a record shop, The Band Box, and simultaneously promoted rock 'n' roll shows at dance halls throughout the area. His initial efforts were so successful that he extended his operation and soon found himself in need of local groups to fill his halls. At this point, Calvert effectively became a pop manager and during the next few years would build a school of pop stars, closely following the blueprint set by the greatest British rock 'n' roll entrepreneur of the era, Larry Parnes.

Many miles away in Southall, London, a group of teenagers were sitting in a coffee bar, The Spiral Steps. Among them was a vivacious youngster named David Hurren whose good looks prompted the proprietor to enquire: 'Are you a pop singer?' Hurren laughed, explaining that he had never sung outside of his bathroom. The star-spotting proprietor shrugged his shoulders but advised Hurren to pay a visit to the Boat House in Kew where a group called the Statesiders were searching for a guest singer.

Hurren arrived at the club and soon found himself onstage singing a shaky but passable version of Craig Douglas's 'Only 16'. His presence did not go unnoticed by another group in attendance who immediately stepped in with a firm offer of work. Within 24 hours, Hurren was onstage at the Ivy Leaf working man's club in West Drayton singing a swiftly rehearsed rendition of 'The Shape I'm In'. His backing group, the Rebel Rousers, were impressed enough to take the kid on the road and, for a time, he became their permanent guest singer. Many gigs followed until one evening the group arrived at Staines Town Hall for a performance booked by Calvert, who took one look at them and immediately lined up a series of shows on the South Coast. It was all done with typical fifties autonomy and lack of pretension; the group accepted the work, asked no questions, signed no contracts, jumped in a van, arrived in town, played, copped some pocket money and returned home. Eventually, the Rebel Rousers found other employment but Hurren decided to throw in his lot with Calvert who arranged further tours with another staunch rock 'n' roll outfit, Vince Taylor and the Playboys. By this stage, Calvert had a sizeable number of artistes booked on a regular basis and from these he was able to select a body of musicians for long-term employment.

In 1959, David Hurren became the first fully-fledged member of Calvert's academy of pop and was thereby given a new name — Danny Storm. Following his stints with the Rebel Rousers and Playboys, he moved to Southampton where Reg formed his backing group, the Strollers. Throughout this period, Calvert groomed the teenager until he was transformed into a replica of Cliff Richard. His quiffed fair hair and sideburns were carefully dyed black and hundreds of posed photographs were shot until Calvert was satisfied with the results. Soon, giant posters began appearing outside many South Coast dance halls bearing the stark message: 'This artiste will be appearing here tonight'. Startled teenagers looked closely at the face on the poster and convinced themselves that the mystery star was indeed the chart-topping Cliff Richard. Not surprisingly, all the venues sold out of tickets long before the artiste hit town. Calvert's strategy was brilliant in its simplicity and even more audacious than his Hartley jam spoof.

On the night of the performance Danny Storm would sit patiently in his dressing room while Calvert teased and incited the audience with his unrelenting patter. By the time the singer took the stage their excitement and hungry anticipation had made the spectators almost uncontrollable. Even here, nothing was left to chance. As the curtain slowly ascended, Calvert's evangelical rhetoric was drowned by the incessant screams of hundreds of teenage girls. There, before their eyes, was a figure in semi-darkness, the spotlight trained tantalizingly at his feet. Although nobody could see his features clearly, the distorted vocal sounded remarkably like Cliff Richard singing through a wall of screams. The few sceptics in the audience were never given a chance to test their doubts, for Storm's performance was inevitably brief. After a couple of numbers ecstatic fans would clamour on to the stage, forcing the bouncers to whisk the fragile star into the wings and through the exit door where Calvert lay waiting in a revved-up van. Immediately, Danny would be taken to the next town to witness further pandemonium. Often, Calvert squeezed in three performances a night, eventually covering the entire South Coast circuit. It would be many months before the mystery star was allowed to appear under his own name.

In many ways Danny Storm was a perfect candidate for short-term exploitation. Shy, acquiescent and still finding his feet in the hurly burly world of pop, he had little time to reflect on his earnings: 'I wasn't interested in money. I haven't got a clue what I was paid or what I was supposed to be paid. Reg just gave me money when I needed it.'

Fortunately for Danny, Calvert was neither greedy nor unscrupulous and treated his artistes fairly throughout their years in his employ. Storm feels that Calvert, and his wife Dorothy, were unusually protective towards him, and always ensured that he was kept out of trouble:

> Reg did more than enough for me. I wasn't any good. I was a good-looking bloke as a youngster, but I couldn't really sing. But, during those years, I learned to do a good show and earn money. Up until 1964, I had everything I wanted. Reg was the greatest, a smashing bloke. Sometimes I used to think, 'The guy's a maniac!' but you couldn't help admiring him. It was a great period. Reg never did me rotten. I've got nothing but respect for him. And Dorothy especially. She was like a mother to me.

The manic side of Reg's personality that Storm describes manifested itself in a series of colourful incidents over the years. One evening, Danny, Reg and Playboys' drummer, John Watson, were driving home to Southampton when a herd of deer ran across their path. Suddenly, Reg leaped from the back of the car clutching a .22 rifle and shot one of the stags. Danny and John stood in open-mouthed astonishment as Calvert began jumping up and down exclaiming excitedly: 'I killed one! I killed one!' When the trio approached the carcass, however, they were saddened to discover that Reg had unwittingly killed a pregnant doe. Ever resourceful, the chastened Calvert dramatically demonstrated hitherto unforeseen skills as a veterinary surgeon and attempted to save the offspring. The delivery was inevitably abortive, but Reg soon perked up with a new idea. The doe was hoisted on to the car and driven to a remote spot where the trio built a fire and feasted themselves on venison. It was typical of Calvert to transform a boring drive into a scene reminiscent of the days of Robin Hood and his Merry Men.

Calvert's lust for excitement and hatred of dull routine were reflected in his attitude towards his fledgling stars. Even after Danny Storm was revealed to the world, Calvert insisted that he retain the mystique that had been so carefully nurtured during his nights as the ghost of Cliff Richard. The over-friendly pop star was ordered to act aloof and not talk to anybody onstage or off. Often, he would be locked in his dressing room to ensure that the image remained inviolate. According to Storm, Calvert's strategy paid dividends and a strong female following increased at each successive performance.

Having established Danny Storm as a local attraction, Calvert felt ready to launch another xeroxed star. This time the prototype model was Buddy Holly and the copyist a lanky singer-guitarist called Buddy Britten. With his backing group, the Regents, Britten was a formidable co-starring attraction and stayed on Calvert's books for several years. Many touring rock 'n' roll stars noted the sensation that Calvert was causing in and around Southampton and were tempted to join his troupe. For a brief period, Calvert netted no less a personage than Rory Blackwell, who had the historical distinction of forming the first ever rock 'n' roll group in Britain. Reg immediately decided that it was time for Blackwell to enter the record books once more. With great pride, Calvert informed the local media that his protégé would attempt to break the world record for non-stop drumming! Southern Television covered the event, providing Calvert's other acts with some useful publicity in the process. After seven days, the exhausted Blackwell emerged as world champion and attendances at Calvert's dance halls reached a new peak. Rory moved on, but his departure was not a severe blow to Reg who proceeded with plans to create a bizarre parallel universe of regional pop. The rock 'n' rolling blond bombshell Mike West (backed by his Silhouettes) was added to the ranks, alongside the attractive Carol Lane. Calvert even created his own version of *Oh Boy*'s diminutive black singer Cuddly Dudley in the person of 17-year-old Cuthbert Fender, who was rechristened Baby Bubbley.

In spite of Calvert's growing reputation as an impresario, he was not without rivals. An influential promoter named Bob Potter also had a strong interest in Southampton rock and soon attracted rival acts such as Keith Kelly, Smokey Dean, Eddie Sex and Danny Hunter. At first, there was friendly rivalry, but when the groups began appearing at the same venues all hell broke loose. A long-running feud developed between the two camps and the results were often farcical. While one group blitzed a small town with posters another would tarnish them with the dreaded word 'cancelled'. The warfare reached new levels of intensity when the rival factions began deflating each other's tyres and pouring sand, sugar and flour into their enemies' petrol tanks. Providing facilities for a stable of artistes was exhausting enough without these additional problems, so it came as little surprise when Calvert announced he was moving his operation from Southampton to a new area.

With the money he had accumulated over the years, Reg bought Clifton Hall, a once opulent stately home in Rugby. In these lavish surroundings he was able to accommodate all the groups and singers in his employ and still have enough room to fulfil his family obligations. Clifton Hall was a fantasy kingdom ruled by one of the most eccentric figures in pop history. For many of the artistes, it seemed a teenage paradise, a refuge from the dingy digs of humourless landlords whose sole pleasure seemed to come from curbing the late-night revelries of their drunken tenants. Calvert allowed them a new-found freedom and encouraged their pop star fantasies with a succession of novel ideas and schemes each more bizarre than its predecessor.

All the musicians who stayed at Clifton Hall have fond and amusing memories of those days. Mike West remembers arriving at the grounds and walking the quarter-mile pathway from the main gate to the mansion door. There, a beaming Reg escorted him to the servants' quarters where all the musicians lay waiting like bemused characters from a Dickens novel. Looking around, West noticed several crates of milk piled on top of one another and wondered who these could be for. Reg answered his question by flinging open a cupboard door to reveal dozens of packets of cornflakes. The astonished West was then handed a packet with a bottle of milk and told 'That's your breakfast for the week!' It became a long-running joke that many of the undomesticated kids of Clifton Hall lived on cornflakes. Most of the artistes slept in a large dormitory in bunk beds filled with straw. Storm, Britten and West were occasionally allowed their own cubicles on the tenuous grounds that they were 'stars'! Reg tried to enforce only two house rules: artistes were instructed never to enter his quarters unless they were specifically invited, but that command was often broken in the early hours of the morning when the groups returned from various gigs in a state of ravenous hunger. Although some satisfied themselves with their cornflakes and bread and jam, the more confident youths would risk incurring Dorothy's wrath by raiding the Calvert fridge. Reg's second taboo concerned any reference to the Clifton Hall ghost. In his previous house, Calvert had been plagued by a poltergeist and had even called in a parish priest to exorcize the spirit. Not surprisingly, wild rumours of ghostly happenings at Clifton Hall were rife among the groups, especially when they drove up the moonlit driveway at two in the morning. The worst offender was probably Buddy Britten whose girlfriend was extremely interested in spiritualism and filled his head with strange tales of black magic and psychic phenomena. Reg actively discouraged such conversations which merely provoked his more mischievous protégés to fabricate more spooky stories. On more than one occasion, Reg left a room in a huff growling 'There's no ghost here!' However, visiting musicians always noted the solitary light in Calvert's quarters that burned throughout the night.

In spite of his many commitments at Clifton Hall, Calvert found time to visit television producers in the hope of securing a break for one of his protégés. Eventually he found a willing listener in Jack Good, a producer who shared his manic enthusiasm and love of innovation. Good was the godfather of televised rock 'n' roll in Britain, having produced such programmes as 6.5. Special, Oh Boy and Boy Meets Girls. His latest rock 'n' roll extravaganza, Wham!!, was scheduled to begin a three-month run on 30 April 1960 and Good was searching for new talent. Calvert knew only two things about Jack Good — he favoured the Larry Parnes school of pop and was instrumental in launching the career of Cliff Richard. As the principal of a rock 'n' roll academy that included a Cliff clone, Calvert, for once, had a head start over his staid London rivals. Danny Storm was granted an audition.

The news was greeted with great enthusiasm at Clifton Hall, but on the day of the audition Calvert and his protégé were at loggerheads over the choice of material. Storm was intent on performing one of his current stage numbers while his manager insisted he sing the Cliff Richard-influenced songs of earlier days. Although Storm attempted to rebel, he was finally bludgeoned into submission by his red-faced manager who ordered: 'You must do these songs!' Danny followed instructions and sheepishly went through the motions. Jack Good seemed impressed, but later criticized Storm in print as a Cliff Richard copyist. Nothing came of the all-important audition. For once, Calvert had misjudged the situation and failed to remember that Good was a seeker of innovation rather than flattering imitation. Nevertheless, an important contact had been made and since the producer and manager shared such similar personality traits, a return engagement in the near future seemed a distinct possibility. Calvert's hopes died on 18 June 1960, however, when *Wham!!* was discontinued and Good's reign as television rock 'n' roll supremo effectively ended. Disappointed, Reg returned to his favourite role as impresario and waited patiently for further opportunities.

The idea of a pop finishing school housed in a grand old stately home eventually attracted a sizeable degree of media interest. Pathe News, whose newsreels were once shown in virtually every cinema in the country, despatched a production team to Clifton Hall in order to shoot a short documentary. The producer decided to take full advantage of the expansive grounds and include a sequence featuring one of Calvert's artistes riding a horse. Poor Danny Storm, one of the least experienced horsemen in rock history, was chosen to play the part. While the imaginative producer was conjuring up visions of wealthy aristocratic huntsmen in the form of working-class pop stars, Storm's ebullient steed was charging towards the film cameras and threatening to destroy their equipment. After scattering the entire film crew, the unruly beast ground to an abrupt halt and threw its terrified rider into the air. Storm fell awkwardly and one side of his face was badly bruised and grotesquely swollen. In order to disguise his injuries, the embarrassed star was shot in profile throughout the remaining sequences.

Although the Pathe Pictorial reached a national audience, a far more important programme, from Calvert's point of view, had been broadcast on local television. An inspired producer had contacted Larry Parnes and secured his cooperation as guest commentator on a programme featuring the work of his provincial rival. Larry was less than complimentary about Calvert's clones, though he did not brand him a copyist as the producer had hoped:

> That programme was all wrong. They said he was trying to copy me and my stable of stars, but I thought it was unfair to Reg Calvert. I think he was just trying to do something in the business and earn a living.

Parnes was somewhat taken aback to be confronted by Calvert after the show. Fortunately, the Yorkshireman was good-humoured and unconcerned about Larry's superficial criticisms. The friendly rapport they established that day later enabled Calvert to book several of Parnes' acts for his Midlands dance halls, including Billy

Fury and Joe Brown. The irrepressible Brown lasted only one night at Clifton Hall; screams of blue murder were heard when he discovered a nest of bugs in his straw mattress. Scooping up a handful of insects, Joe placed them in an envelope which he mailed to Larry Parnes! Occupants of Calvert's 'star' cubicles were generally more fortunate and visiting Americans, including Jerry Lee Lewis, had no qualms about bedding in an old-fashioned English stately home. Indeed, several of Calvert's musicians recall a memorable party lasting until daybreak during which 'The Killer' treated them to some of his wildcat piano playing, followed by an exhibition of American pool.

The party atmosphere at Clifton Hall invariably extended into the centre of Rugby whenever the groups played there. Every Sunday night, the local cinema screened a horror double bill and during the intermission the audience would be treated to a live spectacular featuring one of Calvert's top acts. Soon, attendances virtually doubled and every Sunday night the 'Full House' sign told its own story. Calvert's complete troupe were also brought into play every Wednesday and Saturday night at Rugby's Benn Memorial Hall. At times, it was difficult to determine who was the star of the evening — Danny Storm, Buddy Britten or Calvert himself. Reg never referred to his shows as dances, they were always 'party nights' and each evening offered something unique. The concept of a bland, workmanlike performance was inconceivable to Calvert, who would pull out every showbiz trick in the book to ensure that the halls remained constantly packed. Between sets, Reg would emerge and inaugurate some crazy competition off the top of his head. 'A prize for the prettiest girl in the hall' he would cry as teams of youngsters bounded on stage to the shouts of their friends. Party hats would be issued to the competitors and often Reg would produce some white mice from his pocket which would run over their bodies causing hysterical screams and general mayhem. Reg would then announce that the mice had scrambled into someone's trousers and the entire hall would be in an uproar as the participants wriggled their backsides and desperately tried to cover their embarrassment. The prizes offered to these brave contestants were invariably bizarre and usually resulted in a finale that brought the house down. From the wings, Reg would emerge with a piglet which would be presented to the lucky winner. The frightened animal would, of course, escape, causing more pandemonium as Reg went off in hot pursuit crying: 'Look at the pig! Look at the pig!' A 'catch the piglet' contest might then ensue with more embarrassment for the hapless winner. Before long, Clifton Hall began to resemble a menagerie, as Calvert became more and more engrossed in his showmanship. One musician discovered an odd-looking box in the rehearsal room and upon lifting the lid was amazed to observe several writhing pythons. He was even more astonished when Reg revealed, quite casually, 'They're prizes for tonight's show'.

Of all the animals that passed through the gates of Clifton Hall, the most remarkable was Dorothy's monkey. The animal had been bought by Reg as a present for his daughter, Susan, but it spent most of its time perched on his wife's shoulder. Reg was determined that the monkey should be taught hundreds of tricks, but his efforts as an animal trainer were not entirely successful. The beast took an instant dislike to its master, and every time Reg approached Dorothy, the monkey would attempt to scratch his eyes out. The musicians thought this was hilarious, but Calvert soon shut them up by incorporating the monkey into their performances. It was rather disconcerting to be blasting out a rock 'n' roll classic while the audience's eyes were following the antics of a monkey. The incorrigible animal would climb up stage curtains and sometimes swing from the rafters while trying to play a guitar. After frequently having their act stolen by the chimp, the groups would pile into their smoky, claustrophobic, cramp-inducing van and suffer the stench of monkey urine as the animal leered at them knowingly throughout the seemingly endless journey back to Clifton Hall.

By 1961, Calvert was known throughout the Midlands rock 'n' roll circuit as one of the nuttiest impresarios ever to set foot on a stage. Screaming Lord Sutch, who guested on many of Calvert's early shows and later came under his wing, maintains that his showmanship could forestall any disaster, including group illnesses and cancellations:

> Reg Calvert was a genius. He was like a carnival man; he'd get a show on the road from nothing. He was unflappable, that's what I loved about the man. Even if a band didn't turn up, Reg could play a few records, talk to the audience, keep them happy and before they knew it, everybody went home satisfied. And he gave the boys a great environment to write and create. He was the perfect manager.

Another of Calvert's early disciples was Stuart Colman, who had moved to Rugby as an apprentice draughtsman at the Associated Electrical Industries factory. Stuck in a small town, Colman attended one of the shows half expecting to see some boring below-average groups playing sub-standard rock 'n' roll. Instead, he was pleasantly surprised:

> The quality of the Reg Calvert bands was fantastic. Incredible. I'd

never seen such a standard. They were better than the London bands. Reg used to rehearse the backsides off them at Clifton Hall. At one time, Buddy Britten and the Regents were second to none. Danny Storm and the Strollers, and Mike West and the Silhouettes were always good. They *had* to be to keep playing those venues over and over again.

The consistently packed halls and low overheads enabled Calvert to accumulate a considerable amount of money and this was put to good use at Clifton Hall. A recording studio was built on the premises in order to allow the groups to rehearse their material and record demos of any songs they particularly liked. Reg loved tinkering with electronic equipment and spent lavishly on film projectors and other paraphernalia. Mike West remembers Dorothy Calvert recoiling from one of her husband's spendthrift expeditions and confiding: 'I don't know what I'm going to do with him. He's just spent £2000 in London today'. The new equipment was used for 'experimental work' which included a promotional film of Tanya Day 'The Turkish Towel Girl', a singing sensation from Cannock, who bore a strong resemblance to actress Julie Christie. Calvert also filmed another girl, Tracy Martin (Clifton Hall's answer to Brenda Lee) but progressed little further in promoting these ideas. At one stage, he was planning to outflank his London rivals by filming all his groups and sending promotional clips to foreign impresarios, thereby securing lucrative engagements in top continental clubs. Many of these concepts were both ingenious and prophetic, but all too often Calvert overreached himself and was continually distracted by the everyday problems involved in running Clifton Hall and organizing his dances.

While Calvert's cavalcade of stars were causing a commotion in the Midlands, their prospects as potential national celebrities were not so bright. Clifton Hall was a long way from Tin Pan Alley so Calvert tended to be dismissed as a provincial by insular record company A & R representatives. Significantly, the same fate later befell a forlorn Brian Epstein, which speaks volumes about the conservatism of the British record industry during the early sixties. Any great desire to break down the walls of record company apathy was further hampered by the lackadaisical attitude of some of the Clifton Hall groups whose lust for fame had already been sated on the Midlands ballroom circuit. What Calvert needed was inspiration and flair from his artistes in order to fuel his over-fertile imagination.

The necessary push came unexpectedly one afternoon when Danny Storm announced that he had written a song. After listening to a couple of verses, Reg jumped up and exclaimed, 'Right, let's record it!' Storm cut an impressive demo in the recording studio at Clifton Hall which Calvert immediately took to Pye. The reaction was surprisingly favourable but the cautious A & R executives insisted on seeing the artiste in live action before any further discussion could take place. Calvert invited them to an obscure club in Totton, Warwickshire, the remoteness of which ensured that Storm would be afforded a hero's welcome. Prior to their arrival, Storm had stirred up the already partisan audience to a fever pitch. When Ian Ralfini and Peter Prince of Pye arrived at the club they witnessed extraordinary scenes. Excited fans clambered towards the stage as if Elvis Presley himself had suddenly decided to descend on Totton. Not only that, but they were all wearing Danny Storm rosettes which Calvert had slyly distributed earlier in the evening. The A & R men nodded with satisfaction and arranged for Storm to record his composition for release on their Piccadilly label. 'Honest I Do', a standard early sixties ballad, reached the Top 50 in April 1962 and continued to sell steadily over a longer period of time thanks to consistent plugging on the top-rated BBC radio programme *Two Way Family Favourites*. With solo singers dominating the charts, Storm had a reasonable chance of consolidating his initial success. But it was not to be.

Danny Storm's attempts to control his recorded output proved as abortive as his failed rebellion against Calvert during the *Wham!!* audition two years before. The powers at Pye insisted that Danny continue to record bland ballads and he was given a ludicrous 72 hours to write a follow up. They even had the audacity to suggest that he re-interpret the melody line of 'Lavender Blue' and throw in some new lyrics. His plea to be allowed to record one of his own rock 'n' roll compositions fell on deaf ears and even Reg supported the unadventurous 'boy next door' image propagated by the record company. Reluctantly, Storm complied with their requests, thereby sealing his fate as a one-hit-wonder.

Calvert's business dealings with record companies would later produce markedly conflicting responses from his artistes, though Storm had no complaints and was pleased to accept the 1d. per disc royalty deal that was offered. This figure may seem remarkably small, but for a soloist it was quite reasonable for the period. Indeed, Storm was arguably much better off than, for example, the Beatles, who were forced to split the pitiful 1d. per record royalty rate four ways. Even two years later, a successful group such as the Nashville Teens were issuing records for a royalty rate as low as seven-eighths of a penny to be split *six* ways! And there are far worse tales than these in the contractual history of rock. Of course, the majority of Storm's royalties came from songwriting. Rather uncharacteristically, however, Calvert insisted on receiving a co-writing credit in return for promoting Storm's discs. This undoubtedly harsh arrangement could have proven costly to Storm had he been more successful and would have netted his manager a disproportionate amount of his overall royalties. In the event, most of these considerations were to prove academic since the majority of Danny's royalty earnings barely covered his living expenses at Clifton Hall.

The success of 'Honest I Do' enabled Storm to fill Midlands halls for the rest of his performing life. Indeed, he became something of a local superstar among Midlands girls and was frequently mobbed: 'They'd tear you apart and bring up their knickers for you to sign. I used to think they were mad.' Irate boyfriends resented Storm's sex appeal and on one date, as far away as Banbury, Oxfordshire, he was set upon by a group of thugs known as the 'Swallow Gang'. The following day, the back page of the *Daily Sketch* announced 'Swallow Gang Attack Star!' Amazingly, the case even went to court, much to the satisfaction of Storm's publicity-seeking manager.

In order to prevent further disturbances at his halls, Calvert increased his 'team' of bouncers to 20 strong and equipped them with 'gas guns'. The gas gun, a pencil-shaped instrument loaded with ammonia, had first been introduced to Calvert by one of his groups following a trip abroad. Although technically illegal in England, the gun was generally available in countries such as Germany where it proved a popular form of protection against assault. Reg was as fascinated by the instrument as a wilful schoolboy with his first air gun. According to Storm and others, Reg didn't think twice about using the gun: 'He wanted them to fire at the slightest provocation. It was in his character. He wanted all the tear gas going up.' However, Reg's intent was never to cause violence but to prevent it as quickly and effectively as possible. And yet, he also wanted to create an absolute sensation. Calvert's dream was to open a newspaper and read that his groups were now so popular that they had caused unprecedented scenes of fan mania requiring the use of tear gas to control demented teenagers. Sadly, the gas gun was destined not to bring publicity to the groups but to Calvert himself.

The success of Danny Storm spurred on the other groups in Calvert's stable whose performances continued to improve. Mike West's competence was undeniable while Buddy Britten and the Regents underwent a radical transformation after temporarily moving to Germany and playing the Star Club, Hamburg. Suddenly, the old Buddy Holly standards were replaced by such

R & B numbers as 'Money', 'Tricky Dicky' and 'If You Gotta Make A Fool Of Somebody'. It was an uneasy and not entirely successful transition but at least Britten was trying to progress. The fourth member of Calvert's original school was not so lucky. Baby Bubbley, the ebullient teenage dynamo, suddenly began to act strangely. Danny Storm, his room-mate during the period, recalls the youngster suffering violent headaches which frequently prevented him from performing. After several weeks of often intense pain, Bubbley abruptly packed his belongings and returned to his home in East London. His final words to a puzzled Danny Storm were both plaintive and revealing: 'I've had enough. I'm going home to my mum.' Within a month Clifton Hall was silenced by the almost unbelievable news that Cuthbert Fender, their own Baby Bubbley, was dead. Cause of tragedy — brain haemorrhage.

During his final days at Clifton Hall, Bubbley had been backed by another of Calvert's discoveries — Gulliver's Travels. The group had actually been formed solely for appearances on a Midlands television show featuring Janice Nicholls, the famous teenage record reviewer of ATV's *Thank Your Lucky Stars*. At the time, Janice was dating singer Brian Mecham, who was recommended for the job along with a couple of Nuneaton musicians. The fourth member of the group was Tony Dangerfield. Gulliver's Travels were classic Calvert material with their thigh-high boots and black and white peroxide hair. When he first approached them, however, the group were in disarray. They had split with Brian Mecham, severed connections with Janice Nicholls' management and, rather tentatively, appointed Dangerfield as the new front man. Reg was unconcerned about such ructions, however, and accepted the group on their visual image alone. Over the next 12 months they rehearsed almost daily and gradually established themselves as a local attraction. Tony Dangerfield recalls this period with great nostalgia:

> We were very loud and totally outrageous. Reg liked us. We worked consistently and were very popular on his circuit. We used to get mobbed, pulled from the stage — the whole bit. I remember once he booked the Searchers. The kids were still trying to drag me off the stage when they were trying to come on!

Characteristically, Reg loved to witness the fan mania and after every performance he would reward the battle-torn Dangerfield with a new shirt. Gulliver's Travels eventually won a recording contract, but were hampered by the shock departure of Tony Dangerfield, who went on to join the Savages.

While the Clifton Hall groups continued to multiply, their

bombastic manager revealed increasing signs of eccentricity, bordering on the dangerous. In spite of a couple of near-fatal car crashes, Reg still drove too fast and on more than one occasion frightened the life out of Tony Dangerfield. Calvert was even more dangerous around 5 November when his activities resembled those of a mad scientist intent on blowing up the world. As Guy Fawkes night approached, Calvert would be locked away in his laboratory, experimenting with various types of gunpowder in order to add sparkle to the Clifton Hall fireworks display. He made no secret of the fact that his ambition was to create the biggest firework ever made. One evening, however, the groups were startled by the sound of loud cries coming from the laboratory. Suddenly, Calvert emerged screaming, his hair ablaze and his skin horribly burned. Fortunately, the burns turned out to be superficial but his face remained disfigured for several weeks after. Amazingly, Calvert continued his work, using a safety mask to prevent further facial injuries. The great Calvert banger was eventually completed and detonated in a metal dustbin. According to Tony Dangerfield, the explosion blew a hole in the ground 4 feet deep and 8 feet wide.

In spite of his injuries, Reg continued to celebrate Guy Fawkes night in his own inimitable style. The boys were instructed to dig two parallel trenches, approximately 60 feet apart, and build a huge bonfire between the dividing lines. They were then assembled into two separate units and ordered to take their places in the trenches. What then ensued can best be described as a 'firework fight'. In order to make the spectacle more exciting, Reg introduced home-made bazookas constructed from cardboard tubes and old drainpipes. His musicians stared in amazement as he explained, in great detail, the most effective way to fire rockets at each other. Eventually, this crazy reconstruction of World War I got underway and, predictably, the only person to receive any injury was Reg. One of the rockets had lodged itself in a bazooka and backfired, badly burning Calvert's arm. A cease-fire was called while the self-styled general inspected the injury, surrounded by his concerned platoon. Suddenly, Calvert emerged from the trench, walked over to the bonfire and thrust the offending arm into the flames. A horrified Mike West ran over to assist his manager, while the other musicians exchanged puzzled looks. When West enquired what the hell Reg was doing, his mentor merely turned round and with a knowing smile uttered the unforgettable words: 'I'm burning the burn!' Mike knew better than to question his manager's logic so returned to his trench armed with a revolutionary, indeed inflammatory, theory concerning the treatment of first-degree burns.

Christmas at Clifton Hall also brought its more bizarre moments. While the musicians were preparing for festivities, Calvert's thoughts wandered to the subject of food. Predictably, his speculations led to further strange happenings as Mike West remembers:

> We had a turkey and one day Reg said: 'We're going to have it for Christmas'. So we said, 'Ah, Reg, he's a pet . . .' 'No, it doesn't matter; we'll kill him'. So Buddy Britten volunteered to do it with a scythe. He was chasing the turkey around with this scythe and it kept ducking. In the end, Reg wrung its neck. 'That's the way you do it' . . . He did have a sick sense of humour.

Danny Storm also recalls Buddy Britten 'running around like a fairy' trying to kill the already half-decapitated fowl, while Reg and the others stood laughing. In spite of such anecdotes, none of the musicians regarded Calvert as a cruel person. The turkey was doomed to be slaughtered anyway, but even here Reg could not resist transforming an everyday farmyard event into a mini-sensation. This tendency towards sensationalism and self-dramatization would one day backfire in tragic circumstances.

By 1963, Clifton Hall was still progressing as a pop finishing school and seemed more popular than ever. In order to add variety to his shows, Calvert put together a new group of musicians and named them the Clifton All Stars. Several months later, they became the Fortunes. Although they later established themselves as a close-harmony vocal group, the original Fortunes were a far more eclectic unit capable of playing virtually any style of music. Often, Reg would appear onstage in the middle of their set and challenge the audience to participate in another competition: 'Name any tune and if the Fortunes can't play it, you win five shillings'. The group were already so well-rehearsed and self-confident that Calvert's silver coins remained deep in his pockets. Like many of the other groups at Clifton Hall, the Fortunes were encouraged initially to rely heavily on image and produce a spectacle that would ensure a full house whenever they played. Calvert found a willing disciple in the Fortunes' madcap saxophonist, Tony Britnall, whose antics included climbing up curtains and chasing girls across the stage. Another of his stunts was to appear naked in a bath tub while playing the saxophone. Reg adored these occasional lapses into slapstick humour for they always brought out his finest moments as a compere. Once a crowd had reached a certain level of excitement, there was no stopping Calvert. He would instruct his groups to play a dance number and regiment the audience into several long lines, while expertly coordinating their movements like some modern day square-dance caller. Stuart Colman recalls being amazed by the sight of over 400 kids swaying to the sounds of a Hully Gully rhythm while Reg guided them across the dance floor. These were probably his happiest moments, more satisfying than the money, the record contracts or the national success that he was destined to achieve over the next two years.

In spite of Clifton Hall's growing reputation, not all the artistes were satisfied. Mike West eventually grew weary of the Midlands circuit and returned to London in search of brighter prospects. His timing could not have been worse for agents and managers were now united in the belief that Liverpool was the centre of the universe. The Beatles boom seriously hampered West's chances, particularly as his repertoire remained hopelessly entrenched in good old fifties rock 'n' roll. Like a hound without a home, West returned to his once celebrated haunt — the Two Is coffee bar in Old Compton Street. Gone were the days when sharp-suited Denmark Street spivs scoured the precinct in search of the latest ingenuous, knee-trembling adonis. Yet West elected to remain there, ever hopeful that some former contact might lead him to greener pastures.

One evening, a manager did enter the coffee bar, but it was Reg Calvert. The beaming smile and gleeful look in Calvert's eye was enough to convince West that this was no social call. After finishing work, Mike was whisked across to a local restaurant and during dinner was told: 'You're going to be Robbie Hood'. Calvert had already formed a group called Robbie Hood and his Merry Men, but the lead singer had quit, and now he was anxious to develop the project. West agreed to return to Clifton Hall and accepted his lincoln-green outfit with a smile of resignation. His new backing group, the Merry Men, looked equally colourful in their boots, feathered hats, and jerkins made from old sacks with green sleeves sewn on. Reg even insisted that they each wear different coloured tights, preferably bright red, blue or yellow. The Robbie Hood image remained popular, and soon West was busy recording demos at Clifton Hall while Calvert plotted his next move.

During 1963, Danny Storm, Buddy Britten and Robbie Hood were each recording for a major label, but no hits materialized. Mike West suspects that this was no coincidence:

Reg had a funny attitude about record contracts. He didn't want to get his artistes too well known in case they'd move out of his circle and work elsewhere, so he wouldn't do a lot of promotional work. To get a record out was just a bonus. He could then put up a poster saying 'Pye Recording Artiste — Danny Storm' or 'Decca Recording Artiste —

Robbie Hood'. As long as his halls were full and the kids were happy, he was satisfied.

Other artistes in Calvert's stable do not support West's theory. Tony Dangerfield, for example, left Reg at one stage to work for Joe Meek and later returned disillusioned. Far from being possessive and criticizing the legendary producer, Calvert advised Dangerfield that such an association would benefit his long-term career. On another occasion, it was rumoured that Brian Epstein was interested in Dangerfield and, once more, Calvert showed every willingness to release the boy. Such memories are sufficient to convince Tony Dangerfield that Calvert was totally committed to his artistes. He argues convincingly that West probably underestimated his manager's conviction:

> Who's to say Reg wasn't just being polite? He probably pushed a lot more than they thought. A manager can only push so much. The most viable proposition he had on his books were the Fortunes — and he broke them.

The Fortunes' later success may qualify much of West's criticisms but he remains perplexed by several strange episodes. At one point Mike auditioned successfully for a part in *Fings Ain't What They Used To Be,* but he and Reg were warned not to reveal this news until the producer had gone through the formalities of hearing the remaining hopefuls. According to West, Calvert immediately phoned the *New Musical Express* who duly placed the information in their gossip column, the *Alley Cat.* The producer was allegedly so furious and embarrassed by the incident that West's name was struck off his list. Even during his time as Robbie Hood, West noted many occasions when Calvert's stubbornness proved counter-productive:

> Reg used to bungle things, but whether he did it on purpose, I don't know. He upset Buddy Britten no end of times with his record company. In the end Buddy didn't want him to negotiate and said, 'I'll do it myself', which he did towards the end . . . Reg messed up about five different recording contracts for me. He wouldn't agree to their terms. He was very pigheaded that way. He'd just say, 'No!' He would try and squeeze more money from standard contracts . . . Once, the company wanted to sign the Merry Men to do their own record. To me, to get somebody else on record who was working for you was great. But he just turned around, point blank, and said, 'No, you can't have them'.

West admits that he was mystified by many of Calvert's eccentric actions and thinks that record company officials probably felt the same way:

> Once, we went out to dinner with producer Peter Sullivan, whom I'd known from the Johnny Kidd days, and Reg was stuffing himself with smoked salmon in front of him. Peter said, 'The man's got atrocious manners but, never mind Mike, he's an eccentric millionaire. He's prepared to spend money and that's all that really matters to us as a record company.' But he upset Peter. Reg had this knack of upsetting people . . . He had an outlook on life that he was *right*. And who could argue with him? He was successful as an impresario and he was filling his halls every night and making a fortune.

Once more, West's account conflicts with the testimonies of many other musicians at Clifton Hall who regarded Calvert as a brilliant spokesman. Even the self-mythologizing Screaming Lord Sutch admitted that Reg was one of the most persuasive and friendly people he ever met in the music business: 'He was a great talker and had people eating out of his hand. He could get people to help him and they'd do it for nothing. They would just get caught up in the excitement.'

Although these conflicting statements seem irreconcilable, Sutch feels that West may simply have failed to grasp Calvert's particular strategy in negotiating with record companies. Far from being a 'bungler', Sutch insists that Reg was years ahead of his time:

> A lot of artistes in those days were conned. Calvert knew that money wasn't forthcoming from record companies and agencies. He used to see people that were 'stars' backstage and they were eating fish and chips! When Reg got a record deal he naturally fought for higher royalties. He'd already invested a lot of money in his acts. Some of them he'd been keeping at his house for several years. He wasn't just some guy off the street. He was a hard man with the record companies and that made him a very modern manager.

Sutch's eloquent defence was supported by many of the other acts and even West conceded that his manager was always extremely generous. That he would deliberately sabotage their careers in order to keep them at Clifton Hall seems neither logical nor convincing. Perhaps the lack of originality among many of his artistes may best explain why their recording careers were generally unsuccessful.

The early months of 1963 saw Calvert at an important cross-roads. He had already achieved great success in the Midlands and although his artistes were far from chart regulars they all had record contracts. Indeed, his singers were arguably no less success-ful than the second division stars of the great Larry Parnes. With Vince Eager, Johnny Gentle, Dickie Pride and Duffy Power all falling by the wayside, Calvert could hardly expect his own copyists to be scaling the charts. In order to strengthen his position, Calvert joined forces with an aspiring London agent.

Terry King had first entered the music business in 1956 when he opened a jazz club. Within four years, he had moved into agency and publishing work, though apart from the celebrated weight-lifter/singer Ricky Wayne, his artistes were all jazzers. What Calvert offered was a ready-made school of pop musicians eager and willing to infiltrate the clubs and halls that King had marked out as his own. The partnership proved beneficial to both parties and gave Terry the opportunity to observe 'the most inventive stunt-man of the period'. King was constantly amazed by Calvert's imaginative creations and even testifies to the existence of a short-lived group who bore the unlikely name Freddie Flicker and his Knicker Flickers. In an attempt to gain the infamous Mr Flicker some cheap publicity Calvert informed the media that a mystery singer would be giving away pound-notes to the public outside the Bullring in Birmingham. Flicker was duly armed with 250 one-pound-notes and despatched to Birmingham where television cameras were at the ready. Although the media took the bait, Calvert had underestimated the suspicious nature of the Birmingham shoppers, most of whom ignored Flicker and refused to accept the money he thrust into their hands. By late afternoon, the camera crew had abandoned Flicker who was still trying to convince an unbelieving world that his notes were genuine. Calvert was undaunted by this setback, for he had already discovered another walking publicity machine in the form of his old friend Screaming Lord Sutch.

David Sutch had been associated with Calvert since 1961 and was already well known as the original wild man of British rock 'n' roll. Years before the Pretty Things or the Stones, Sutch had grown outrageously long hair and was infamous for his lunatic habits which included incessant screaming and chasing people around while wearing Viking chieftain buffalo horns. His gigs were no less bizarre. Gasps of mock horror could be heard as several pall-bearers emerged from the back of a dance hall carrying a coffin containing the body of Sutch. Once onstage, the corpse would come to life and subject the audience to a repertoire of bloodcurdling songs acted out in gruesome detail. For a time, the Sunday papers chronicled his every outrage, but as more ghoulish rockers came to the fore, his horrific antics became decidedly passé. Returning to Clifton Hall, Sutch sought the advice of the one person whose flair for publicity matched his own. David explained to Calvert that he was tired of being dismissed as a half-witted caveman freak and wanted to counteract this publicity with something crazy but positive. Between them, they concocted the idea of entering Sutch as a parliamentary candidate for the National Teenage Party, with a manifesto that demanded the introduction of commercial radio, the lowering of the voting age from 21 to 18 and the abolition of the 11-plus. Given the whimsical nature of the campaign some of the issues proved ironically prophetic.

Sutch's political aspirations would probably have been forgotten within hours were it not for one brilliant idea. In order to gain maximum publicity, Calvert convinced his protégé to stand against Conservative Angus Maude at Stratford-Upon-Avon. This was no ordinary constituency for it had previously been held by John Profumo, the Secretary of State for War who had recently resigned after being named in a sex scandal. The fact that Profumo had first denied these allegations in Parliament and later admitted to misleading the Commons cast a dark cloud over the integrity of Britain's aristocratic politicians. Calvert seized the moment to introduce the anti-heroic, working-class rock 'n' roll caveman as a worthy candidate for such an election. It was a magnificent spoof, better than Freddie Flicker, Cliff Richard replicas or Hartley jam fraud. Here was the bane of the Sunday press proclaiming that he could set a better example for youth than a Cabinet Minister. Calvert pulled out all the stops, designing posters, organizing political meetings and putting on free concerts. He even coined Sutch's dual campaign cries: 'Vote for the ghoul, he's no fool' and 'Parliament will be screaming when Lord Sutch is elected'. The press loved every aspect of the Sutch campaign and even *The Times* featured the wildman on its front page. The biggest joke of the summer ended with Sutch's Teenage Party polling 209 votes from the adult population of Stratford. Although Sutch later attempted a series of political campaigns, including a well-publicized stand against Harold Wilson, he never matched the sensationalism caused by Calvert in Stratford-Upon-Avon.

The publicity resulting from Sutch's election campaign haunted Calvert for several months. One whimsical notion had produced front page news for weeks on end, and now suddenly he was back in the insular world of Clifton Hall, organizing gigs and marshalling groups on a small scale. What he craved was the tension and excitement produced by a major happening, and soon this became a near obsession. Although he was still spending time developing the careers of acts such as the Fortunes, many late hours would be lost contemplating more elaborate ventures. In Sutch, he had found the perfect vehicle for his more bizarre ideas and the eccentric pop star proved more than willing to execute them. The main problem was that neither party could think up a stunt even remotely as newsworthy as their electioneering fiasco. Yet, Calvert refused to abandon his strange dreams. Often, he would seem uncharacteristically gloomy, sitting in a chair lost in thought, then suddenly he'd jump up excitedly and dance around the room in jubilation over some short-lived, ill-conceived notion. Once his mind became fixed on a particular idea, Calvert's energy was inexhaustible and his enthusiasm irresistible. His flamboyant gestures and bombastic tone imprisoned the imaginations of enraptured listeners who would unwittingly argue through the night before staggering off to bed in a state of exhaustion. Even there they could not escape the manic enthusiasm of their manager who would be hammering on their doors two hours later with a completely new set of ideas. After many months and endless hours of discussion, the next 'Calvert concept' came unexpectedly one evening during a conversation with Sutch about his failed recording career. The self-styled king of horror rock 'n' roll was annoyed that the BBC Light Programme had failed to broadcast such cultural landmarks as 'Jack The Ripper', 'I'm A Hog For You Baby' and 'Monster In Black Tights'. During his rant, he suggested that it might be possible to get airplay on the recently-launched pirate radio station, Caroline. At that point, Reg fell from his chair. The broad smile on his face suggested that an idea was forming. A big idea.

Radio Caroline was the brainchild of Ronan O'Rahilly, a 23-year-old Irishman, whose entrepreneurial ambitions had already been partly realized when he ran the celebrated Scene Club in Great Windmill Street. A favourite watering place for the pop élite, the Scene had demonstrated through its bustling clientele the enormous untapped potential that lay in giving teenagers what they wanted. O'Rahilly soon discovered their constant need to hear new, loud pop records, a craving that British radio had steadfastly refused to satisfy. With his wealthy Irish background, Ronan had the power, the means and the imagination to spark a revolution that would ultimately transform the face of British radio. With a Dutch passenger ferry armed with expensive broadcasting equipment, O'Rahilly launched Britain's first pop pirate radio ship on Easter Saturday 1964. With typical self-conscious sixties optimism he had named the vessel after the daughter of America's recently assassinated president, John F. Kennedy.

Calvert's mind was not concerned with grand symbols of American achievement but instead centred on a rather lower and more basic species of mankind in the form of Screaming Lord Sutch. As with everything else in his life, Calvert would achieve his aims in microcosm. O'Rahilly could have his Kennedy-inspired passenger ferry, Reg would make do with Sutch and a fishing boat. The full implications of Calvert's idea were still being assimilated by Sutch as his mentor feverishly ran around pulling out car batteries and transmitters and attaching them to a turntable. After an experimental broadcast in a field, Calvert made a deal with a local fisherman who agreed to hire out his boat every afternoon. On the strength of this minimal organization, Reg informed the local and national press that a new pirate station was to be launched — Radio Sutch. Incredibly, the entire operation had been completed so quickly that Sutch set sail on 27 May, only a week after Radio Caroline began broadcasting.

The majority of press representatives who attended Radio Sutch's launching probably suspected that the whole affair was a publicity stunt, but they also knew that the Calvert/Sutch amalgam guaranteed good copy and a laugh a minute for anyone caught up in the fun. They were not to be disappointed. Eager journalists anxious to talk to Sutch found it impossible to stand upright in the boat and provoked howls of laughter as they slipped on fish scales and landed ignominiously on their backsides. As the vessel pulled away from the harbour, spectators observed the full magnificence of this picturesque comedy. There was Sutch, dressed in a purple velvet cape and bright blue trousers menacingly waving a cutlass as his leopard-skinned crew clung desperately to the rigging. Cheers could be heard as the skull and crossbones flew rebelliously in the wind, undaunted by the police presence nearby. Calvert spoke optimistically about the future of the station, unaware that his customary rhetoric contained not one word of exaggeration.

Radio Sutch provided Calvert with enough ideas to transform its potential into something greater than anyone could have imagined. At first, the station seemed doomed to last but a few days. Fishermen were instructed by their insurance companies that no cover could be guaranteed for their boats while in the hands of a pop pirate. What looked like the end of another Calvert publicity stunt took a strange twist when the Army were informed that Sutch had moved into an abandoned, derelict gun tower at Shivering Sands, off the Essex coast. The fort stood on long poles 117 feet high and was joined together by catwalks. Although well within the three-mile limit its remoteness ensured that any attempted eviction would prove difficult and time-consuming. So, for five months, Radio Sutch could be heard over a 50-mile radius, broadcasting at erratic hours from the early afternoon till two in the morning. Soon, the station degenerated into an embarrassing joke and served mainly as a vehicle to promote the more obscure groups at Clifton Hall. Most of the 'disc jockeys', including Danny Storm and Calvert himself, were unaccomplished broadcasters and sounded stilted on the air. Initially, however, there were some good ideas and a couple of surprise successes. Calvert's 13-year-old daughter, Elaine, compered her own show, *Candy's Pop Shop*, which was generally well-liked. By contrast, the post-midnight slot included 'saucy readings' from *Lady Chatterley's Lover* which inevitably produced some much-needed publicity. After several months, however, the novelty appeared to be wearing thin. Sutch admits that he had become a mere figurehead and was spending much time abroad while the station limped on in his absence. Bored disc jockeys no longer bothered to introduce records and would often play entire albums rather than structuring a varied programme. In spite of this lackadaisical attitude, Radio Sutch remained on the air and its prospects were strengthened by some unexpected publicity.

The authorities had been tardy in dealing with the Radio Sutch fiasco, but eventually the Navy intervened and sent a gunboat to Shivering Sands to remove the pirates. Calvert acted quickly and informed the media which turned out in force. The pirates were ordered to leave the gun tower and warned that serious action would be taken if they refused. Sutch called their bluff and, much to the delight of the assembled journalists, defied them to do their worst. After radioing its superiors for further instructions, the gunboat abruptly pulled up anchor and sailed away without a further word. Excited newshounds rushed to the nearest telephones to provide their editors with a story that combined comedy and human interest. The following day the newspaper headlines said it all — 'Lord Sutch Turns Back The Navy!'

The thorny issue of who should take action against Radio Sutch swiftly became an official embarrassment. The responsibility passed from the Navy to the Army who immediately buried the question in a quagmire of legal complexity. Seizing upon this bureaucratic interwrangling, Calvert announced that Radio Sutch had assumed territorial rights and instructed Queen's Counsel to entangle the authorities still further in their self-created web of confusion and uncertainty. The strategy proved so successful that Calvert decided to take his ambitions to their furthest extreme. The energy, imagination and vision that had produced the Clifton Hall academy was now directed towards an even loftier goal — the development of a pirate radio station so powerful that it might one day topple the Caroline monolith.

In September 1964, Reg took the first step towards fulfilling his dream when he purchased Radio Sutch from his protégé for £5000. He knew it would take several years before the station achieved its full potential, but, given the government's amenable attitude, time hardly seemed the major problem. With two transmitters, the renamed Radio City — 'The Tower of Power' — slowly etched its way into the history books. Soon, local advertisers were buying time on the air and Reg even persuaded a US religious organization to invest in six hours a week.

While Rugby fell under the threat of eternal damnation from fire-and-brimstone evangelists, the future of the Clifton Hall academy became a matter of equally burning speculation. With his increased commitments at Radio City, Calvert had less time than ever to deal with his groups, whose over-reliance on his managerial guidance closed their ears to contemporary musical undercurrents which threatened their very existence. While Merseybeat groups infiltrated the charts in increasingly marauding numbers, Calvert was advising the rock 'n' rolling Robbie Hood to include 'Dashing Away With A Smoothing Iron' into his already archaic set. Why Calvert failed to exploit the beat boom during its zenith remains *the* great mystery of his managerial career. As a hardened expert in the art of xeroxing, Reg could easily have recruited a veritable tribe of groups and transformed them into Beatle clones. Recreating Merseybeat in the Midlands could have been undertaken at any time between 1963 and 1965, yet, for some inexplicable reason, Calvert went against his nature and stuck with the old order. This error might have been understandable in an old-fashioned Tin Pan Alley manager, but Calvert was on the dance floors every night and must have been aware of his audiences' needs. Incredibly, he had even booked the Beatles and the Merseybeats early in their careers and witnessed the phenomenon firsthand. Moreover, Reg had many interests in Birmingham and could have signed the cream of the city's groups long before Tony Secunda arrived to lure the Moody Blues and the Move to London. Instead, he rebelled against prevailing fashions and dismissed the beat group scene as a transient trend.

Calvert's fatal attraction for Radio City ensured that the once-thriving pop school fell into decline. Danny Storm had been the first to leave, playing his final gig at Dartford Town Hall on New Year's Day 1964. Buddy Britten had moved on after an argument with Reg, leaving Mike West as the sole survivor from the fifties. Characteristically, Reg's reaction to the prevailing ennui was to regiment his depleted forces for a belated chart assault.

While many Merseybeat groups came and went during the 1963-4 period, Calvert continued to groom the Fortunes who eventually emerged as a smart-suited innocuous close-harmony unit. They looked distinctly unfashionable and soft alongside their new wave contemporaries, but Calvert was convinced that he could break them. They had already achieved a near hit with 'Caroline' which had been chosen as a theme tune by the radio station of the same name. That amusing irony was noted by Calvert who confided to his remaining artistes that he would one day infiltrate the other pirate stations and blitz the entire country with their recordings! In the meantime, he had to be content with plugging the Fortunes subsequent discs on Radio City and hoping for a lull in the all-consuming beat group domination of the charts.

Calvert's breakthrough came in July 1965 when the Fortunes' 'You've Got Your Troubles' climbed confidently to number 2 in the UK charts and also hit the American Top 10. Unfortunately, Reg also had troubles of his own that prevented any tumultuous celebration of his artistes' good fortune. The problem began early in September when he decided to commandeer a nearby gun fort four miles from Shivering Sands. This expansionist policy was the first stage of a long-term strategy designed to increase the broadcasting strength of the Tower of Power. Unfortunately, Calvert's plans were threatened by Roy Bates, a Southend businessman who intended to take the fort as a base for his own pirate station, Essex Radio. The ensuing conflict was reminiscent of the swashbuckling days of old, with Calvert cast in the role of Long John Silver. Undeterred by Bates, Reg landed on the Knock John Tower armed with £3000 worth of radio equipment. He met little resistance from the feeble duo representing Radio Essex who were swiftly expelled to nearby Whitstable. When Bates heard that his men had been forcibly removed he immediately retaliated with a counterattack that ended with the unfortunate Radio City crew suffering exile on Shivering Sands. It was a remarkable spectacle, seemingly outside the jurisdiction of the police who were reluctant to involve themselves in a pirate war. Eventually, Calvert conceded defeat and agreed to surrender the fort to his rival. However, this would not be the last occasion that Reg became involved in such a dispute and his next encounter was destined to end in tragedy.

Although the Fortunes' hit run continued with another UK/US success, 'Here It Comes Again', they were not without their problems. Their success largely depended on Tin Pan Alley song-smiths and although the group attempted to compose their own material, the results were unimpressive. They were further hampered by the loss of lead singer Glen Dale, who decided to pursue a solo career, though he remained under Calvert's aegis. In spite of these setbacks, the group retained a life-preserving asset — they were classic easy-listening MOR performers who, in times of crisis, could always look forward to rich pickings on the cabaret circuit. The technique was habitual. Again and again, Calvert sustained the flagging careers of artistes whose musical invention seemed long dead. His cavalcade developed a showband mentality which kept them on the road for years while once fashionable pop stars waited dejectedly for their telephones to ring and found themselves all but forgotten by once enthusiastic agents. The legend of Clifton Hall lived on and even Tony Dangerfield, who had left Calvert for Joe Meek, found he could return to past glories as though nothing had changed: 'I was screwing birds left, right and centre. I had money in my pockets, which a lot of bands didn't. I worked five to six nights every week. I got mobbed. We had everything we wanted.' Although Calvert undoubtedly made a financial killing on this thriving dance-hall circuit, his willingness to support little-known groups showed an altruistic streak unusual in pop managers. Terry King was amazed that his partner sought no management commission from David Sutch and impishly admitted: 'I wouldn't have done 90 per cent of the things that Reg freely did for his artistes'.

Clearly, Calvert was driven not by financial need or artistic aspiration, but love of novelty, excitement and sensationalism. Significantly, he ignored all the major movements in rock music during the mid-sixties; the beat boom, R & B, folk rock, the protest movement — all were deemed irrelevant in his scheme of things. Instead, he gambled on novelty and visual appeal to attract an audience. Reg came to despise the multitude of faceless beat groups with their standard suits and monotonous line-ups of three guitarists and a drummer. Always, he demanded something different. At one stage, he even threatened to build a revolving pulpit specially for rock drummers. Bored by their traditional anonymity, Calvert's idea was to place their drumkits upside down in the air and force them to play on their backs so that the audience could see as well as hear every beat. Like many of his inventive ideas, this was never implemented. The pressure of organizing gigs and administering the affairs of Radio City left little time for playful indulgences. Yet, Reg still managed to spot local talent to add to his depleting stable and towards the end of 1965 signed the

Liberators. Earlier in the year they had released an unsuccessful single on Stateside produced by the legendary Shel Talmy. Like many promising Midlands musicians they'd received their shot at fame and looked destined for the scrap heap. Calvert intervened, bought them garish multi-coloured clothes and relaunched them as Pinkerton's Assorted Colours. This unusual stress on colour was reflected in their early publicity stunts, which included polluting the fountains of Trafalgar Square with various shades of dye. Calvert's typically madcap idea ended with a big feature in the daily papers the following morning. What caught most people's imagination, however, was Pinkerton's use of several unusual instruments, including a kazoo and auto-harp. The latter was used to great effect in promotional photographs and could be heard distinctly on their Decca debut, 'Mirror Mirror'.

In earlier days, Calvert would have relied entirely on gimmicks and publicity stunts to break his acts, but by 1966 corruption was rife in the pop industry, and hard cash provided the easiest route to success. A former member of Pinkerton's Assorted Colours remembers how 'Mirror Mirror' achieved its Top 10 placing: 'The single broke via City and Caroline and a few well-placed pound notes. Reg bought the record into the lower half of the charts and it took off from there.'

Calvert's chart successes brought him a new reputation almost overnight. Suddenly, he was no longer the eccentric provincial but an important businessman whose assets included several promising groups and a thriving radio station. The ever-vigilant Phil Solomon noted Calvert's rise with interest and towards the end of 1965 press reports indicated that their two stables were poised to amalgamate.[1] The proposed merger failed to occur, however, and by February 1966, Solomon and Calvert were at war. A dispute arose after Solomon learned that Calvert was booking out a bogus offshoot of Them, a group that had been in his stable since 1964. Calvert attempted to outflank his rival by registering the xeroxed Them as a limited company, thus preventing Solomon from using the title. It was a crazy but highly imaginative strategy that might well have confused a less experienced entrepreneur. However, Calvert had completely underestimated Solomon's tenacity for within a week the Irish manager had transformed two little-known Birmingham groups into Fortunes Ltd and Pinkerton's Assorted Colours Ltd.

---

[1] Phil Solomon was a formidable mid-sixties entrepreneur who specialized in Irish acts. Despite his power in the industry he has been consistently ignored by rock historians. I have already dealt with his managerial career at some length in chapters 2–4 of *Van Morrison: Portrait Of The Artist*.

He also informed Sir Edward Lewis that he now owned the names of Calvert's hit groups and demanded that the Decca chairman delete all their records forthwith.

It was an absurd situation but Solomon clearly had the upper hand. His influence at Decca was far greater than Calvert's and, in fairness, he had only acted in retaliation. Calvert was hoist with his own petard. The great copyist could only sit back helplessly as his own groups were xeroxed before his eyes. Eventually, Calvert agreed to back down, just as he had done in his disputes with Bob Potter and Roy Bates. The registered names were forgotten and the rightful groups continued in their rightful stables.

The February dispute with Solomon was a disastrous error on Calvert's part for during the same month his adversary became a director of Radio Caroline and would soon assume complete control of the station's programming. An alliance with Solomon would therefore have placed Calvert in an extremely powerful position and enabled his artistes to reach a further eight million listeners. Of course, it was still possible that some reciprocal arrangement regarding airplay might be achieved between the two managers at some future date. In the meantime, Reg continued to work alone, spending even more time developing Radio City which was already broadcasting to an audience of three million.

The economic strength of Radio City was greatly enhanced by the Labour Party's stance on the pirate radio issue during early 1966. Although ideologically opposed to the pirates, the government had been uncharacteristically tardy in finalizing legislation. The impending spring election undoubtedly served to weaken their resolve for it was widely known that young voters were extremely concerned about the fate of the pirates. The man at the centre of the issue was the unfortunate Postmaster General, Anthony Wedgewood Benn, who soon found himself trapped between the political hammer and the public anvil. During parliamentary sessions he provided only tentative answers regarding the thorny issue of piracy and admitted that his enquiries were not yet complete. When the attacks became more vigorous and the questions more pertinent, Mr Benn was forced to fend off his opponents with convoluted political rhetoric: 'It is tempting to deny but by denying you tend to confirm what you don't deny, and then by confirming and denying what you have announced before you have decided.' Even during the broadcasting debate in the House of Commons, pirate radio was relegated to a secondary issue and brushed aside somewhat flippantly by the Postmaster General: 'Really, what are the pirates but hulks with big masts, carrying microphones, gramophones and seasick disc jockeys?'.

Calvert had good cause to dispute Mr Benn's pronouncement. The station he had bought for £5000 had now increased in value by an incredible 4000 per cent in under two years. Meanwhile, the Fortunes had charted again and Pinkerton's Assorted Colours were bubbling under. Money was literally pouring into Calvert's bank account and his standard of living improved accordingly. The same musicians who had eaten bread and jam at Clifton Hall invariably stood in silent awe upon seeing the magnificent thick pile carpets and chandeliers that adorned Calvert's palatial London office. No longer the provincial hick, he now had a fashionable and expensive flat in classy Wigmore Street. After years of hard struggle, Calvert had at last secured the entrepreneurial power that, combined with his brilliant invention and organizational ability, promised a future of unparalleled and incalculable achievement. The strange and dramatic events of June 1966 were destined to transmogrify that vision of supreme personal attainment into one of pop music's most profound tragedies.

Since the beginning of 1966, Calvert had been at a mental crossroads. Although he was outwitting the government and making a fortune from Radio City it was clear that at some time the station would be closed. Rather than fight to the bitter end, Reg was shrewd enough to consider selling his major asset while its value was still as high as £200 000. Having reached the limits of his success in radio, it was perhaps time to move on. Already, he was negotiating the purchase of a submarine in order to pioneer pirate television from outside territorial waters. This, Reg argued, would be his most fantastic coup to date. Such an ambitious venture obviously required a large capital outlay, so, reluctantly, Reg decided to dangle Radio City in front of the extended jaws of his ravenous rivals. He first approached Project Atlanta, a limb of the powerful Radio Atlanta, which had amalgamated with Caroline in 1964. Atlanta's head man was to prove a formidable opponent.

Major Oliver Smedley was a most unlikely pirate whose public school education and monied background contrasted sharply with that of the Yorkshire pop parvenu who appeared at his Dean Street office one cold afternoon. Yet, beneath Smedley's conservative upper-class gloss there lurked a character whose exploits and diverse interests reflected the renaissance man quality that Calvert so admired. The Major's military history was particularly impressive: during service in the Royal Artillery he had been wounded twice and was later awarded the Military Cross for bravery. After leaving the Army a hero, Smedley sought new excitement in politics and as a member of the Liberal Party Executive fought four elections, including two campaigns against R.A. Butler. By the mid-sixties, he had established himself as a wealthy and powerful figure in the entertainment world with related interests in companies dealing with pirate radio, instruments, breweries, fruit farming and a distillery. Like Calvert, he preferred to keep several irons in the fire but he was clever enough to remove them all when his entrepreneurial nose sensed imminent conflagration. In spite of his negotiating skill and business acumen, the proposed takeover of Radio City failed to materialize. However, during the discussions, Smedley had handed over a radio transmitter to Calvert, which, he later claimed, was worth £10 000. According to Dorothy Calvert, however, the transmitter was obsolete, and had never been used for broadcasting. Indeed, she stressed that it would have cost thousands of pounds to make it serviceable. Whether worthless or extremely valuable, Smedley expected future remuneration for the transmitter which was duly taken to the gun fort on Shivering Sands.

By mid-June, Calvert had found another potential buyer for Radio City and this time the deal looked certain to proceed. The interested party was an American firm, whose UK representative was Philip Birch, head of Radio London. When Smedley heard about this deal he apparently became worried about the fate of his transmitter, for which he had yet to receive payment. However, the involvement of Radio London in the affair had more important implications which could not have gone unnoticed elsewhere. The annexing of Radio City to the London organization would have boosted Big L's listening figures by several million and represented an important victory over other rival stations, most notably Radio Caroline.

On 18 June, the telephone rang in a council house in Gravesend. The enormous hand that lifted the receiver belonged to 17-stone 'Big Alf' Bullen, a burly docker whose forte was providing cheaprate gangs to work on ships. The caller instructed Bullen to recruit a party of men at short notice and assemble late the following evening at Gravesend Pier. When the gang arrived they were met by a distinguished lady and gentleman and herded into a tug boat. 'Big Alf' was taken aside and informed that their mission was to invade and seize control of the Shivering Sands fort.

On 20 June, at 3 a.m., the crew of Radio City were sound asleep in their quarters, unaware that their station had been boarded by 17 strong-arm men. By the time the alarm was raised, the fort had already fallen to the invaders and Calvert's seven subdued seamen could only look on helplessly as a mysterious man and woman removed the crystals from their transmitter. Nor was this the end of the affair. The boarders were instructed to hold the fort for an indeterminable period while their employers returned to shore. Several hours later, bewildered listeners vainly attempted to tune their transistor dials to the Radio City frequency, but the Tower of Power remained ominously silent. Meanwhile, two clandestine figures, a former Major and a theatrical impresario, drove towards the country home of Philip Birch and requested his presence at an important meeting in London later that morning.

Many miles away, the shell-shocked owner of Radio City was still putting together the pieces of this confusing puzzle. By mid-morning, Calvert learned of the proposed meeting between Philip Birch and Major Oliver Smedley and wasted no time in scuttling towards Project Atlanta's office in the heart of Soho. Many thoughts must have flashed through his brain as he hurried along Dean Street, but uppermost was an absolute conviction that Radio City be restored to its rightful owner. Certainly, any weakness on his part would only serve to strengthen Smedley's confidence and enable him to force a wedge between the proposed City/London deal. By the time Calvert reached Project Atlanta's office, he was in a state of near hysteria. If the musicians at Clifton Hall had attended the meeting, they would probably have interpreted Reg's words as typical manic hyperbole but to outsiders and potential enemies, the effect was extremely unnerving. Nobody will ever know for certain whether Reg genuinely lost his temper or chose this moment to indulge in some over-emotional acting. Most likely, it was a combination of the two. Certainly, Calvert had every right to be angry, especially when he learned the terms that Smedley was offering in return for a truce. While the Major later claimed that his primary aim was to retrieve the alleged £10 000 transmitter, his actions clearly indicated that this was not his sole purpose. With Radio City in his hands and the transmitter crystals in his pocket, Smedley was undoubtedly in a very strong bargaining position and showed no hesitation in flexing his muscles. His justification concerning the Robin Hood-style retrieval of the transmitter was now virtually irrelevant. Smedley desired something much greater — a share in the profits of Radio City. Only under these terms would he remove the boarders and return the transmitter crystals. In many ways, this was an extraordinary proposition guaranteed to bring out the worst in Calvert. A half share in Radio City was worth an estimated £100 000, precisely ten times the figure Smedley himself had calculated as the value of his precious transmitter. Not surprisingly, both Birch and Calvert rejected his offer, and the former described the meeting as being both 'high-handed' and bordering on 'blackmail'. Calvert was more careful with his words which, as the meeting progressed, became increasingly disturbing.

The role that Calvert assumed during the Project Atlanta meeting sounded like a cross between Al Capone and Dr Frankenstein. He began by actually thanking those responsible for the boarding party since they had given him the opportunity to have some fun. With a sinister grin he added, 'I will have them screaming to come off'. Continuing in this vein, Calvert described himself as an expert in explosives and poison gas and confided that he had recently made a startling discovery. While experimenting in his laboratory, he had accidently discovered a new nerve gas, derived from ammonia. Calvert boasted that he had already used the gas on several animals and was extremely interested to discover what effect it might have on human beings. Since the gas was heavier than air it could drift down on Shivering Sands and was therefore an excellent method of aerial attack. Reg added that he would personally lob gas shells on the Radio City tower and, if necessary, exterminate every one of the invaders. The assembled company were still recovering from this remarkable outburst when Calvert suddenly changed tack. Perhaps realizing that his Frankensteinian self-portrayal might seem somewhat far-fetched, he abruptly transformed into a character straight out of an American gangster movie. Now he was the pathological hood who had muscled in on dance halls and could command the best fighters in the country. There was more than an element of truth in this assertion for Reg had a sizeable team of bouncers, all of them equipped with tear gas pistols. As if suddenly remembering this fact, he dramatically pulled out his own gas gun, adding ominously that he always carried the instrument in case of trouble. Horace Leggett, a shareholder in Project Atlanta who attended the meeting, found it 'difficult to decide whether the whole thing was a colossal bluff or whether he was as ruthless as he made out to be'. Evidently, Major Smedley had the same forebodings as the controversial meeting drew to a close. With the situation unresolved, all that remained were the echoed threats of death and destruction from a desperate and seemingly deranged man.

Having failed to secure a deal with Radio London, Smedley sought to strengthen his position by amalgamating with another radio station. He phoned disc jockey Mike Raven, whom he had known from the Radio Atlanta days, and asked him to set up a meeting with Ted Allbeury, the head of Radio 390. Since City and 390 were only several miles apart Smedley figured that both stations could be combined and strengthened. With a higher advertising rate than City and a listening audience in excess of two-and-a-half million, 390 was a formidable and perfectly-situated companion.

Smedley's expansionist policy suggested, most forcibly, that he now regarded Radio City as his own property. Whatever else, he had certainly moved a long way from merely worrying about the loss of his radio transmitter.

Calvert, meanwhile, spent the night working out a plan of action. In spite of his threats, he decided not to take the law into his own hands but wisely went to the police the following morning and reported the raid on his fort. This eminently logical and clear-headed decision met with a cold response from Scotland Yard who felt powerless to investigate the complaint because of the fort's peculiar position. The apparent inertia of the authorities in the face of an illegal and highly dangerous act forced Calvert to deal with the matter in his own way. Unwittingly, the police had exacerbated a situation already bordering on anarchy.

Following his trip to Scotland Yard, Calvert attempted to bluff his way out of the impending crisis. He rang Project Atlanta and informed Smedley's secretary, Pamela Thorburn, that he intended to visit the fort and warn the boarders that the police had their photographs and were preparing to arrest them. According to Thorburn, he punctuated his message with threats ending with the ominous 'I will kill them all'. These strangely conflicting boasts of personal vengeance and police intervention sounded typical of Reg's manic confusion. However, later that afternoon, Calvert sent another message which was phoned through by his secretary, Mrs Wildman. Pamela Thorburn transcribed the words on a piece of notepaper which she later passed to Major Smedley. The message read: 'The situation is getting dangerous'.

On the evening of 21 June, Calvert elected to visit Smedley's home in Saffron Walden. It was not untypical of Reg to overcome the intense emotion of brick wall boardroom politics by confronting his opponent alone and thrashing out a solution to their problems in a frank but amiable manner. Prior to his departure, Reg admitted to his wife that he was concerned about the safety of his men, but showed no signs of agitation or anger. In normal circumstances, he would have undertaken the journey alone, but his arm was still sore following an injection for a holiday trip to Gibralter, so he enlisted a colleague to drive. At 9 p.m., they set out on the last mission of Reg Calvert's life.

During the 60-minute drive, Calvert had time to reflect on the events of the last few days and place them in a new perspective. With the welfare of his Radio City crew uppermost in his mind, he was faced with the dauntingly insoluble dilemma: aggression or appeasement? Was he willing to meekly surrender half the profits of the empire that he had singlehandedly built during the past two years? What tactic could possibly succeed in convincing the powerful Major Smedley to withdraw his outrageous demands? Were physical intimidation and violence the only methods left to protect his interests? He was not a ruthless man and had always carefully avoided personal vendettas and unnecessary confrontation, consistently backing down to powerful rivals such as Bob Potter, Phil Solomon and Roy Bates. But was this diplomacy a strength or weakness? Perhaps Reg recognized his old self as too soft and became angered by his past deference. That anger could easily have turned into malice and redirected itself at the figure whose meddling threatened to destroy his future plans. But it is equally likely that other ideas captured his imagination. Recalling the recent confrontation at Project Atlanta he no doubt remembered the uneasy faces of Horace Leggett and Philip Birch as his tirade against Smedley and the Radio City invaders reached its explosive peak. Perhaps the Major had also been moved by the violent rhetoric, and beneath his composed exterior was a worried man. If so, the subsequent threatening phone call and note may have weakened his resolve. Perhaps the physical presence of Reg on his doorstep might convince the Major to reconsider his plans. Then again, maybe it required something more dramatic — a scene so frightening that even the unflappable Smedley would be left distraught and outmanœuvred. If Calvert was thinking along these lines then he may have concluded that the Al Capone persona was his most effective weapon . . . At this point speculation must end. In the next few minutes Reg Calvert either completely lost self-control and became a violent maniac or brilliantly acted out his last and most tragic performance.

It was 10 p.m. when Calvert's Ford Zodiac pulled up in a narrow lane next to Smedley's seventeenth-century thatched cottage. Accompanied by his driver, Arnold, Reg hammered loudly on the door, which was answered by Smedley's secretary cum housekeeper, Pamela Thorburn. Her astonishment at seeing Calvert quickly turned to fear as he brushed her aside and forced his way into the house. Within seconds, a scuffle had broken out in the hallway, as Thorburn vainly attempted to forestall Calvert's progress to the sitting room. The driver, meanwhile, became alarmed and ran upstairs to warn Smedley. The Major was nowhere to be seen. In fact, he had already left by the back door and was instructing a neighbour to ring the police. By this time, the luckless Arnold was back in the hall and in a state of agitation. Rather than intervening in the struggle between Thorburn and Calvert, he rushed out of the house to seek assistance. Pamela was still arguing with Reg in the sitting room and made a brave attempt to dial 999, but before she had even reached the first digit the phone was wrenched from its socket and she was shoved away. As she went careering through an open bathroom door, Calvert was loudly exclaiming: 'I'm a desperate man. I don't care what happens to me and I am going to get him alive or dead'. Amazingly, the irrepressible Pamela Thorburn came bursting forth from the bathroom and attempted to do further battle with Reg who thrust her aside with the telephone handset. Her loyalty and protective attitude towards her employer might seem somewhat extreme, but she later admitted there was considerable attachment between herself and Smedley and that they 'sometimes shared a bed'. What happened next is a matter of burning conjecture. Thorburn claimed that Calvert was acting like a raving maniac and had held an 18-inch bronze statuette close to her head. 'I literally thought I was within a split second of losing my life', she later confessed. Whether Reg intended to use the instrument will never be known. Certainly, some damage had already been done to the house; the phone had been disconnected and a heavy marble bust of Napoleon thrown to the ground and smashed. While Ms Thorburn cowered for cover, Smedley entered the room, produced a shotgun and fired directly at Calvert. Arnold had got no further than the driveway when he heard the shot and immediately rushed back into the house. He saw Smedley still holding the gun, while Calvert staggered forwards from the sitting room to the hall and finally fell dead near the front door. Still reeling from the shock, Arnold ran across to a nearby cottage, only to discover a concerned figure still trying to telephone the police on behalf of Smedley. The entire tragedy had occurred within a matter of minutes.

About 15 minutes after the shooting, Detective Superintendent George Brown arrived and wasted no time in interviewing the witnesses. Smedley told the police:

> I knew it must have been him. He had threatened to do me harm and kill me and all the others . . . I knew he came here to kill me, I could see he was mad, and I knew he carried arms. I had no choice but to fire. I did not think of aiming at his legs. I just fired.

As he was led away, Smedley looked down at the corpse and remarked: 'Silly boy, silly boy. I was warned the situation was getting dangerous.'

It was 4 a.m. when Dorothy was woken with news of her husband's death. She was immediately driven to Saffron Walden and interviewed by several officers, following which she spent the night in the lounge of a local hotel. Bravely, she agreed to appear on television the following evening and announced that Radio City would continue to run under her control. Meanwhile Detective Superintendent Brown visited Shivering Sands in order to complete his inquiries. Following this, the police left the fort, still in the hands of the illegal boarders. It was an incredible decision in view of the seriousness of recent events.

While the boarders sat tight, scores of journalists besieged the fort but were warned off by the intimidating figure of Big Alf. Even Mrs Calvert had received a threat following her television appearance and was advised not to visit Shivering Sands. There was no doubt that the boarding party meant business. It was soon learned that the crew were equipped with oxy-acetylene burners with which they intended to repel boarders. They even threatened to destroy the 240 foot transmitting mast, causing thousands of pounds worth of damage. In the event of a counter invasion, they were ready to cut the catwalks which would effectively maroon the seven strong Radio City crew in their quarters. Amazingly, the authorities still did nothing.

While Dorothy Calvert instructed lawyers to issue proceedings against the boarders, her plight was taken up by no less a personage than Sir Alan Herbert, Chairman of the British Copyright Council. In a damning speech against the government's inertia, he declared:

> Ministers seem to be speechless as well as paralysed. For many months the British Copyright Council has been urging the Government to turn the pirates off as trespassers. Now, with two hostile gangs aboard, the need is urgent. There may be violence, even a death, and Ministers will be responsible. They should send the Navy at once.

These words were met by further ministerial silence.

The attitude of the authorities towards the boarders indicated that they were unimpeachable. Yet at 9 p.m. on 26 June, an extraordinary incident occurred. Without a word of explanation, Big Alf and his crew left Radio City, just as mysteriously as they had arrived. Having tenaciously held the fort for a full week and secured their position, even in the face of threats and violent death, they abruptly abandoned the entire enterprise. Smedley, meanwhile, was led from Brixton Prison to Saffron Walden for a preliminary hearing on a charge of murder. During the brief hearing a number of witnesses took the stand including Dorothy Black (the theatrical impresario), Horace Leggett, Pamela Thorburn and Detective Superintendent George Brown. Following the submissions, the defending solicitor, Mr Gower, opined that the sanctity and security of the Major's home had been violated and, in a tone of aristocratic indignation, announced that the defendant was completely innocent of the charge: 'It is abundantly clear that Smedley acted in self-defence of himself and Miss Thorburn. It may be old-fashioned, but it is the law of our country that an Englishman's home is his castle.'

After a 50-minute deliberation the Chairman of Magistrates concluded that 'no reasonable jury could convict on a charge of murder'. Smedley was duly committed to Chelmsford Assizes and requested to reappear on 11 October to face a charge of manslaughter.

Ironically, the two-day trial of Major Oliver Smedley was even shorter than the preliminary hearing. The verdict was never in any doubt and it took the jury less than 60 seconds to deliver a unanimous 'Not Guilty'. Major William Oliver Smedley walked from the courtroom a free man and delivered a noble tribute to his unfortunate victim:

> I feel no elation, and there will be no celebration. The whole affair has been such a tragedy. It is an appalling wastage of a brilliant man's life. Reg Calvert was the sort of man I regarded highly, who had found his way up through his own efforts.

This magnanimous epitaph was not sufficient to save Calvert's already tarnished reputation. The truth was he had damned himself. His theatrical display at the Project Atlanta meeting and subsequent violent behaviour at Smedley's home provided sufficient justification for retaliation and prompted Mr Justice Stevenson to conclude: 'He was quite clearly a very angry and very uncontrolled man'. Even the driver who accompanied Reg to the cottage admitted that he was 'flabbergasted' by what had occurred. With lurid tales of nerve gas, ammonia pistols, animal experiments and bomb threats, the press and public were left in little doubt about the apparently evil nature of the deceased.

Of course, Reg Calvert was not on trial so there was little opportunity to present a well-rounded, authentic portrayal of the man. Instead, the world was left with a distorted image based on the strange events of those last two days of his life. If only Reg's business associates or artistes had been allowed to take the stand they would have told the jury about the *real* Reg Calvert. The following testimonials indicate the gap between the violent maniac of media notoriety and the true nature of the man.

Terry King, business associate:

If anything people described Reg as an absent minded professor. In all the years I knew him I never saw him raise a hand to anybody. I never really heard him raise his voice except when getting a point across. I think the whole description about gas bombs being dropped is farcical . . . Anyone who knew Reg Calvert would not say that he was violent in any way.

Danny Storm, pop star:

Reg's death shocked me although I always imagined him to end up a multi-millionaire or in prison. He was that type of man — a different type of man . . . When I read the newspapers I just thought, 'The man has completely changed' because that's not how he was . . . And I knew him for seven years. I never heard Reg swear and I never saw him lose his temper. He would always turn away.

Stuart Colman, former member of Pinkerton's Assorted Colours:

When he died we were playing in Yorkshire. We were on the best money we'd ever seen: £1000 a week. We were stunned when we heard the news. We made enquiries straight away because we didn't believe any of it; we felt it was a fabrication. There was a lot that never came to the fore. We were pretty disgusted by it. It left a bad taste. There was a lot of crookedness going on that was far beyond Reg's capabilities or background.

Screaming Lord Sutch, singer and parliamentary candidate:

I was totally shocked because he wasn't a violent man. I never saw him punch or kick anybody . . . He was a talker. There were hecklers at my election campaign and Reg even handled them . . . He was a jolly guy blown away by a gun. It seems unbelievable.

It is ironic and amazing that amid all the great hustlers and strong-arm managers of fifties and sixties pop, Calvert should be the one whose life was ended by a bullet. Several of his musicians suspect that there was some unexplained conspiracy surrounding his death, but this seems unlikely. Certainly, there may have been more powerful hands manipulating the Atlanta/City dispute for their own advantage, but the cold facts of Calvert's killing can hardly be disputed. Apart from Smedley and Pamela Thorburn's statements there were corroborative testimonies from Reg's driver and the man in the adjoining cottage. Calvert's outburst at the Project Atlanta meeting was also witnessed by several people, including Philip Birch, who was firmly on his side during the dispute. The real mystery of Calvert's death lies in his own actions rather than those of others. The psychological pressures of the dispute and the realization of what was at stake may have pushed him into a corner from which he felt the only escape was threats and violence. Plausible as this seems, however, it is my belief that Reg Calvert was killed in the midst of an emotional outburst, largely self-generated to frighten his adversary into surrender. Like some demented method actor, Calvert created his own Hamlet and finally transformed pop piracy into a modern day revenge tragedy. In the aftermath of Calvert's death, the popular press propagated rumours of bitter disputes and pirate wars involving important and influential figures in the City. Bribery, corruption and blackmail suddenly became synonymous with the once happy-go-lucky radio pirates and this inevitably encouraged the government to clamp down. Following the publication of the Marine Offences Bill, Rochford Magistrates decreed that Shivering Sands was within territorial waters and fined Mrs Calvert £100. Disillusioned, Dorothy left the pop world and opened an antiques business.

Meanwhile, Calvert's original artistes struggled on, most of them receiving managerial guidance from the Terry King Agency. The publicity surrounding Reg's death did little to help their progress. Stuart Colman maintains that the Calvert stigma prevented Pinkerton's Assorted Colours from obtaining bookings at many important venues. They went through a lean patch, abbreviated their name to Pinkerton's Colours, then Pinkerton and finally metamorphosed into the Flying Machine. Surprisingly, in the summer of 1969, they achieved a one-off Top 5 US hit with 'Smile A Little Smile For Me'. The song went on to sell two-and-a-half million copies. As Colman noted, 'Reg would have been proud of that. America was something he wanted to aim for'.

The Fortunes also went through a dry period chartwise but like Pinkerton's unexpectedly came back with such hits as 'Freedom Come, Freedom Go' and 'Storm In A Tea Cup'. They also cracked the US charts for the third time in 1971 with 'Here Comes That Rainy Day Feeling Again'. These belated successes suggest Calvert's vision may not have been as blinkered as it seemed in 1965. Although he failed to create or discover even one great rock group, nearly all the artistes with whom he was associated managed to continue working long after their contemporaries had retired. Even today, the Fortunes and Pinkerton's Assorted Colours are still touring on the timeless cabaret circuit, Tony Dangerfield plays in various London groups, and Screaming Lord Sutch alternates between playing with the Savages and laying siege to the House of Commons as the founder of the Monster Raving Looney Party.

The longevity of Calvert's minor artistes is a tribute to his skills as a manager, but even more remarkable is their continued devotion to his memory. Every person I interviewed concluded that at the time of his death, Calvert was poised to emerge as one of the most important entrepreneurs of the era. Many claimed he would eventually have built an empire the equal of Robert Stigwood's. Screaming Lord Sutch's vision of that future was just one of many testimonies:

> If Reg was alive today he would be heavily involved in video. Just as he had a school of musicians, he'd have a school of people making the best videos. He would have been a master of costume, directing and picking songs with good stories. He would have been a multi-millionaire by now. I really believe that. He would have done it through radio, pirate television and films.

Ultimately, Reg Calvert emerges as a paradoxical figure in the history of rock management. A master of novelty, invention and far-sightedness, he was also a blatant copyist who stubbornly ignored the all-consuming early sixties beat boom. At times the epitome of provincial stolidity, he also achieved national fame with the development of Radio City. Like Larry Parnes, he built a self-contained stable of pop stars, but preferred to exploit them in dance halls rather than theatres. He retained a provincially altruistic artistes-orientated outlook reminiscent of early Brian Epstein, yet revealed aggressive expansionist policies similar to Phil Solomon. Finally, in common with Andrew Oldham, Larry Page, Kit Lambert and Tony Secunda, he was a born sensationalist with a flair for publicity more bizarre than any of his rivals. By 1966, he had established himself as a new force in the music industry with sufficient money, power and vision to transform imaginative ideas into surprisingly lucrative ventures. The great tragedy was that such a man, all his achievements still before him, should die needlessly and uncommemorated. Precisely what lay ahead we will never know, but when Major William Oliver Smedley shot Reginald Calvert he undoubtedly robbed pop music management of its finest inventor and most spectacular showman.

Like many of his contemporaries, Peter Walsh's entry into the fabulous world of pop management was totally fortuitous. Raised in Mottram, a small town just outside Manchester, he led a settled, if unexciting, life, working in his parents' greengrocer business. One summer, he visited Eire for a month's holiday and was so charmed by the country that he remained there for five years. A Dublin greengrocer by trade, Walsh spent most of his free time promoting dances and soon discovered that there was easy money to be made. The rock 'n' roll era was just beginning, so most of Walsh's business revolved around ceili bands and dance orchestras. However, he also imported several notable jazz players for lengthy Irish tours, and their bohemianism prepared him for the liberalism of the succeeding decade. The swinging sixties began prematurely for Walsh in 1958, at the Olympia Ballroom, Waterford, where he was first introduced to cannabis. A touring jazz troupe had been smoking reefers in a nearby guest house prior to their performance, safe in the knowledge that the drug's distinctive aroma could not possibly alert the suspicions of the innocent local gardai. When Peter entered their bedroom, he was virtually overpowered by the haze and uttered the classic words: 'My God, what sort of cigarettes are you smoking?' Apparently, the musicians had a great evening, though it was not until several years later that Walsh identified the name of their mirth-inducing substance. Such was the innocence of the fifties.

By the end of the decade, Walsh had been wooed back to England, not by jazz musicians or rock 'n' rollers, but the musical director of a dance orchestra. Eric Winstone had recently lost his manager to a television company, but following a successful Irish tour discovered a replacement in the loquacious greengrocer, who was more than willing to accept a £20-a-week wage for his services. Their partnership continued for nearly two-and-a-half years, during which Winstone established himself as musical director for Southern Television. One of the programmes Eric worked on was *Homegrown*, which served as a forum for local performers. One group particularly impressed Walsh and when they won the contest he decided to leave Winstone and take over their management.

The Brook Brothers were accomplished and versatile enough to win a recording contract with the recently established Top Rank label. Their A & R manager, Dick Rowe, had previously met Walsh when he was in competition with Phil Solomon for the management of a promising ceili band. Walsh lost that contest, but won the sympathy of Rowe, who would later prove an extremely important ally in a far more crucial game of brinkmanship. Rowe produced and recorded the Brook Brothers who foundered disastrously with a cover of the Everly Brothers' 'Cathy's Clown'. A brief tie-up with an American quartet, the Brothers Four, also proved unsuccessful and when Top Rank closed and Rowe returned to Decca, the duo found themselves without a label. Fortunately, their career was saved by a young sergeant in the Guards.

Tony Hatch had a most unusual arrangement with Top Rank Records. Every afternoon, the soldier was allowed to leave his barracks in order to work as a freelance musical arranger with the record company. When that source of income evaporated Hatch negotiated a similar arrangement with Pye and offered his old clients, the Brook Brothers, a fresh start. Under the young sergeant's direction, the duo recorded two successive Top 20 hits, 'Warpaint' and 'Ain't Gonna Wash For A Week'. Walsh, meanwhile, concentrated on promotion and through his friendship with producer Jimmy Grant, secured them a regular monthly slot on the influential radio programme, *Saturday Club*. The duo proved solid but unspectacular and struggled on with minor hits such as 'He's Old Enough To Know Better', 'Welcome Home Baby' and 'Trouble Is My Middle Name'. Walsh claims that the younger brother was a reasonably talented songwriter whose progress was held in check by the commercial dictates that Tin Pan Alley imposed in the days before Lennon and McCartney. The duo were eventually thwarted by the elder brother's decision to settle down to married life and reduce touring commitments. Walsh later guided them into cabaret and remained their manager until as late as 1966, by which time they were an anachronism and had virtually ceased recording. Nevertheless, they served Walsh well over the years, and the sprinkling of hits ensured that he had record company clout long before the all-important beat group explosion.

The Tony Hatch/Pye set up also brought Walsh into contact with his second pop group, the Kestrels. Hailing from Bristol, the group was a West Country equivalent of the Viscounts, specializing in close harmonies and boasting an impressive stage act, ideal for cabaret. In the pre-Beatles era, they were highly regarded and unlike most groups strengthened themselves through line-up changes. Eventually, their ranks included such pop notables as Roger Greenaway, Roger Cook and Tony Burrows. In effect, they were a walking Tin Pan Alley confectionery shop and it came as little surprise when they branched out into songwriting and session work. Cook and Greenaway wrote a number of hits for artistes ranging from the Fortunes to Andy Williams and, for a brief period, rechristened themselves David and Jonathan, under which guise they scored with a cover of Lennon and McCartney's 'Michelle' followed by their own 'Lovers Of The World Unite'. Tony Burrows, meanwhile, ended up as the session man of 1970 when he found himself singing in no less than three Top 10 groups during the same month — Edison Lighthouse, White Plains and the Brotherhood Of Man. Yet, for all this candy pop ingenuity, the fledgling Kestrels had proven less than the sum of their parts. Although Walsh had failed to reap the full fruits of his investment, it was clear that he was on the right track. Groups, rather than singers, would remain his speciality.

Unlike most managers of the early sixties, Walsh was not caught napping by the beat boom. Although his involvement with dance orchestras and jazz ensembles suggested otherwise, Peter's real forte lay in the exploitation of commercial pop. Long before the arrival of the Beatles in London, he had accidentally stumbled upon one of the first wave of sixties British beat groups. From that point onwards, his standing as a first division pop manager was assured.

Brian Poole and the Tremilos (later the Tremeloes) had first introduced the Dagenham Sound to the Friends Meeting House in Barking at the end of the fifties. Soon after, they won a talent contest at the Ilford Palais and elected to turn professional. Poole was a devotee of American music, particularly early Tamla Motown and, somewhat contrastingly, Buddy Holly and the Crickets. The group's note perfect repertoire of Holly standards won them a series of gigs at various US air bases, and they wisely invested their profits in expensive Fender guitars. In further imitation of their hero, Buddy Holly, Poole wore horn-rimmed spectacles filled with plain glass! From American air camps, the boys moved to Butlin's Holiday Camp in Ayr, Scotland, where they remained for a year.

The Butlin's apprenticeship may not have been as glamorous and gruelling as the Beatles' wild nights in Hamburg, but Poole and his colleagues emerged as one of the most professional groups of the era. When Walsh auditioned them, he was astonished by their slick repertoire and immediately offered a contract. Initially, the boys were reluctant to sign with the manager of the famous Brook Brothers for fear that they might be overshadowed by the hit duo. Walsh, however, proved irresistible. He offered the Tremeloes fame beyond their wildest dreams, then dragged them outside into the street where his Riley car was parked. Pointing at the vehicle, Walsh announced: 'This will become a Jaguar and you'll have flash cars too if you sign with me'. Although it sounded like Lucifer tempting Christ on the Mount, they signed. Walsh only took a 10 per cent management commission, a comparatively low figure for the early sixties. In later years, the remuneration increased to 15 per cent by mutual consent, and when Walsh finally established a thriving agency, a 25 per cent cut was agreed upon. It says much for the Tremeloes' faith in Walsh that he was able to increase his commission *after* they had become famous. Although the group had no record contract, Walsh secured work in abundance, including a tour with Gary US Bonds during which they were employed to sing backing vocals while sitting behind the stage!

The next stage in the career of Brian Poole and the Tremeloes has been one of the most documented events in pop history. It all began when John Creman, a Barking optician and Tremeloes fan, introduced Brian to one of his patients, Mike Smith. When Poole learned that Smith worked in the A & R department of Decca Records, he convinced the young producer to grant the Tremeloes an audition. On 1 January 1962, the group drove across to Decca's studios, unaware that Smith had just routined a rival combo from Liverpool known as the Beatles. Dick Rowe forced Smith to choose between the groups, and the Tremeloes emerged triumphant. Brian Poole adds a missing perspective to a well-worn tale:

> They chose us because we were London based, it's true. But nobody has ever revealed the real reason why they turned the Beatles down. The Beatles were doing R & B whereas our style was almost like punk, very fast and furious. We were dashing things out as quickly as we could whereas they had a very steady beat. And Decca wanted a front singer. They told us that we were doing a type of music that was about to be popular. We weren't writing our own stuff though; they should have spotted that.

Even if fate had taken a different course and Mike Smith had chosen the Beatles, it is unlikely that Brian Poole and the Tremeloes would have been rejected outright. Peter Walsh was already placing great pressure on Dick Rowe and the A & R head could seldom resist the lure of a convincing manager. Walsh explains his philosophy of management:

> I always felt that the artistes created themselves. It was my job to package it together in a businesslike way and sell it to the highest bidder. I always felt that if you were a good salesman, you could sell *anything*. It didn't matter whether you were selling a can of beans, a tin of potatoes or a musical group. I was a wheeler-dealer and based my philosophy on selling the right product at the right time.

Walsh's early forays into pop management rapidly encouraged exploitation in other areas. Retaining his interests in promotion, he teamed up with agents Tito Burns and Danny Betesh and struck lucky with the Beatles' first bill-topping tour. Walsh and Betesh flew over to the States and successfully negotiated for Roy Orbison, though Peter was concerned about his lack of pin-up potential: 'When we saw his photograph we insisted that there be a clause in the contract stipulating that he would not do any television before our tour because he was so ugly. It was all pretty, pretty boys at the time!' Walsh's luck continued when Brian Epstein persuaded Betesh to add Gerry and the Pacemakers to the tour. By the time the itinerary had been set both the Beatles and Gerry and the Pacemakers were topping the charts, ensuring the three impresarios an unexpected financial killing:

> Everybody was Beatle crazy. Brian eventually said that the Beatles' price should go up so we paid them £1350. That was for the Beatles *and* Gerry and the Pacemakers . . . At that time Johnny Hamp, who was in charge of Granada theatres, wouldn't let us charge 10 shillings for top seats; we had to keep it at 9/6d. Of course, the rest is history. We started at the Adelphi, Slough and sold out every concert, straight through 21 nights.

By the end of the Beatles' tour, Walsh was so prosperous that he immediately went out and bought his first Jaguar.

Within months of that famous Beatles tour, Brian Poole and the Tremeloes scored their first UK hit with a cover of the Isley Brothers' 'Twist And Shout'. According to Poole, the group was unaware that the Beatles had already recorded the song on their first album and were about to release it as the title track of an EP. Upon learning this alarming news, they attempted to cancel the release, but Decca insisted they were too late. In another of those uncanny parallels in pop history, the two groups again crossed swords on the same day. The split sales were unfortunate, but Brian Poole and the Tremeloes still managed to take the disc into the Top 5.

The chart breakthrough enabled Walsh to flex his managerial muscles, as Poole remembers:

> Behind the scenes Peter worked very hard. He kept his promise to us. He got us the right gigs, television and the front page of almost every paper. We seemed to get more publicity than the Beatles in those very early days. Peter had a lot of influence and he'd do things the *right* way. He'd take producers to lunch and get to know them as friends.

We were very impressed. He was a great manager.

Walsh's sales patter even persuaded producer Vicki Wickham to allow the boys to launch the first edition of *Ready Steady Go*, backed by no less than 50 dancers!

For the next single, Poole chose to cover the Contours' US hit 'Do You Love Me', which went all the way to number 1. Amazingly, this produced another weird parallel with the Beatles' history. For when the boys heard about their chart-topper they were in the middle of a UK tour with Roy Orbison. For the second time in 1963, the Big O surrendered his headlining status to the beat kings of the moment. Brian was grateful for such magnanimity and even more pleased when Orbison offered them one of his old songs. 'Candy Man' gave them another hit early the following year. In the meantime, 'Do You Love Me' was topping the charts in 16 different countries, but surprisingly there was no breakthrough in America. The Stateside failure of Brian Poole and the Tremeloes has always seemed one of those unsolved mysteries in pop, for they were at the forefront of the beat boom, with an astute manager and strong commercial material. Admittedly, many of the songs were cover versions, but this did not prevent the Dave Clark Five from taking 'Do You Love Me' into the US charts eight months later. Peter Walsh explains how this anomaly occurred:

> Unfortunately, Decca owned a company in America called London Records. There was a little fat guy there, the head of overseas products, who said it would never be a hit. When I flew over, we were number 1 here and he still said: 'You're wasting your time, Peter, it'll never be a hit and we can't put it out' . . . So we never really got the support of the record company in America. All their sales people were into Mantovani.

Although Walsh signed with a prolific US publisher, even he could not break down the walls of corporate apathy.

Walsh recruited Buddy Holly's former mentor, Norman Petty, to play piano on what became two further smashes, 'Someone, Someone' and 'The Three Bells', but, by 1965, the group's popularity had waned and they seemed embarrassingly dated alongside such new wave R & B acts as the Rolling Stones, the Animals, the Kinks, Manfred Mann and the Yardbirds. Sensing a crisis, the group elected to split into two factions for an experimental period. According to Walsh, Poole saw himself as a *nouveau* Tom Jones and decided to record big ballads with an orchestra, while the Tremeloes preferred straightforward pop. Neither faction achieved any record success during 1966 and although they still played together on live dates, the set up was no longer productive. A final split occurred at the end of the year, leaving Poole the loser. He made a fatal stab at cabaret before retiring to the family butcher business and later resurfacing with a record/publishing company.

The Tremeloes' decision to stick with mainstream pop and update their image with longer hair and trendier clothes eventually paid off. Within weeks of Poole's official departure they broke through with their third single, 'Here Comes My Baby'. A number 1 followed with 'Silence Is Golden' and suddenly the Tremeloes found themselves churning out an almost non-stop series of commercial hits for the next three years. In many respects, their struggle was the perfect vindication of Walsh's general philosophy that non-complicated, easy-listening pop will always be in demand, whatever the prevailing fashion. Unfortunately, the Tremeloes ignored the lessons of their own history and broke away from Tin Pan Alley songsmiths in order to write their own material. '(Call Me) Number One' was unexpectedly impressive and just missed the top spot, seemingly confirming that a more ambitious approach could still reap commercial rewards. It was a happy delusion that led to over-confidence and a ludicrous miscalculation of their public standing. The Tremeloes effectively committed pop hari-kari by proclaiming to the press that their previous singles were rubbish churned out for morons. Walsh must have buried his head in his hands in despair and suppressed laughter as the boys boasted, 'We're going heavy!' Their much publicized progressive album, *Master*, failed to attract a new audience and left them looking very foolish. Ironically, this abortive attempt to establish themselves as 'serious' artistes merely precipitated their descent into cabaret.

Like many of his major early sixties contemporaries, Walsh spent much time building up his own agency, Starlite Artists. At one stage, he employed that wayward journeyman, Robert Stigwood, who later found more lucrative employment with Brian Epstein's NEMS Enterprises, before setting up his own agency. During the same period, Walsh decided to expand Starlite by pooling his resources with Terry King for a six-month period. At that time, the agencies seemed well matched for neither had current hit artistes. Starlite boasted the Tremeloes and Brian Poole, neither of whom had charted for 18 months; King, still recovering from the death of his former partner, Reg Calvert, controlled Pinkerton's Assorted Colours and the Fortunes, whose hits had ceased 11 months before. None of the acts seemed likely to re-emerge as world beaters at the time, so the proposed amalgamation appeared mutually beneficial. Unfortunately, there was some disagreement over the distribution of shares, so it was suggested that whoever secured the greater volume of business would take the biggest slice of the cake. After six months, however, King decided not to renew their contract, much to Walsh's regret. It was a further two years before Starlite reached its peak, controlling the bookings of such chart acts as Fleetwood Mac and Love Affair.

Walsh's next chart act was a Glasgow group that had been playing to packed clubs throughout Scotland. Dean Ford and the Gaylords were typical of the Walsh school of pop — simple, unpretentious and irresistibly commercial. Peter persuaded them to move to London and change their name to Marmalade. Soon, they were signed to CBS, the Tremeloes' label, and cracked the charts in May 1968 with 'Lovin' Things'. An opportunist cover of Lennon and McCartney's 'Ob-La-Di, Ob-La-Da' reached number 1 several months later and the hits continued virtually non-stop for four more years. After several successes at CBS, Walsh negotiated a deal with Decca, via Dick Rowe, and pulled off a large advance. Marmalade's fortunes dwindled during the early seventies, but they left the world with some saucy touring tales in the Sunday newspapers. Later in the decade, Walsh resuscitated the group for cabaret and, like the Tremeloes, they went on to become ghostly figures trapped in a pop netherworld where old hits still ring true. Both groups appear to have learned from Walsh the valuable lesson that nostalgia equals commodity.

In spite of his successes as a manager and agent, Walsh never forgot those Irish dances back in the fifties. His early days as a hustling promoter might well have persuaded him to expand his organization along the lines of Kennedy Street Enterprises, but this never occurred. Yet, he could still remember that first Beatles' bill-topping tour and claim a certain talent as an astute impresario. Towards the end of the sixties he again attempted to place his name in the history books by pulling off a near impossible promotional feat. After touring the Beatles, there was only one name in pop that could inspire a greater sense of achievement. Peter Walsh set off for America determined to become known as the man who brought Elvis Presley to Britain. His plan was straightforward and persuasive. He would offer Colonel Tom Parker a flat fee of one million dollars for two appearances in Europe. Even by Parker's standards, this was a phenomenal amount of money.

When Peter arrived at the famous Las Vegas International Hotel, he was amused to discover that the Colonel had commandeered the entire fourth floor of the establishment as his office and suite. Upon entering the hallowed lair, Walsh bespied the ageing starmaker, surrounded by a dozen ferociously alert subordinates, armed with boards, sheets and pens. Parker eyed his visitor as if summing up the man, then pointedly enquired: 'You're one of our friends from England. What can I do for you?' Without flinching, Walsh got straight to the point: 'I'd be interested in doing two concerts with Elvis in Europe'. The Colonel smiled. It was clear that he had heard that request many times before. Leaning back in his chair, he remarked as casually as possible: 'Well, there's a lot of people who want to do that. What sort of money are you talking about, son?' Ignoring the paternal condescension, Walsh retorted: 'I would be prepared to pay you a million dollars for two concerts, one in London and one in Europe, at venues of your own choice'. The Colonel seemed neither surprised nor impressed by the offer. 'Right', he said, 'that's very good . . . take a note of that'. A dozen pens scribbled down the information as Walsh waited for an answer. But this was not the Colonel's way. All Walsh received was a polite, but curt dismissal: 'We'll be in touch with you, Mr Walsh, if we decide to come to Europe'. The formal tone indicated that the interview was over. For an offer of one million dollars, Walsh had been granted an audience of less than 60-seconds duration. He never heard another word. On the plane back to England, Peter allowed himself a smile while considering a final irony. The failure to secure Elvis, it seemed, was no great disaster:

> After I'd seen Presley I wouldn't have given £100 000 for a show because he was one of the worst artistes I ever saw perform. He was very poor. It was like Bill Haley — once you'd seen him, that was it!

The meeting with the legendary Colonel was excellent psychological preparation for a more rigorous encounter following his return to England. Suddenly, Walsh found himself in direct conflict with a manager whose wrath it was not wise to incur. He had offended the mighty Don Arden. In the past, Arden had encountered problems with other managers, and now history was repeating itself. The drama began during a *Top Of The Pops* appearance when one of Walsh's assistants approached the Move about a possible change of management. When Arden learned of this invitation he was understandably furious. He had already expended much effort in persuading potential poachers to stay away from his groups. On one occasion, the proprietorial Arden had actually hung a manager from a fourth-floor window while lecturing him on the subject of entrepreneurial etiquette. Another frightening scene had occurred during his tenure with Amen Corner when a deadly rival was scared out of his wits by a posse of Arden's hirelings, casually brandishing sawn-off shotguns. Although Walsh was a powerful and respected pro with a good track record, this did not prevent

Arden from once again taking drastic action. Peter recalls the eventful day when Don Arden and his men paid a surprise visit:

> He didn't hang anybody out of a window in my office. He just came in and beat up a guy that was working with me called Clifford Davis, who was then managing Fleetwood Mac. He beat him up in this chair actually! When I say 'beat him up' I mean he slapped him around the face a little and threatened what he would do if he didn't lay off the Move . . . I don't know why he came around when he did. I was out at lunch, fortunately, so he got Davis and gave him a going over. When I came back it had all finished.

Walsh was incredibly lucky to have missed the drama. He later re-upholstered the famous chair in order to remove some cigarette burns. After considering Don's threats, he decided to inform the police about the incident and this proved sufficient to prevent further trouble, as Peter explains:

> I got police protection against him . . . In fact, if anything, Don Arden was my protector because the police warned him, and this came from very high up at Scotland Yard, that if anything happened to me, he would be dragged in *immediately* and whether it was him or not, he would be charged. We got his accusations and what he was going to do to me on tape. So he never did anything at all. He was warned off in a big way, a very big way, because I had a lot of muscle at Scotland Yard . . . He doesn't speak to me anymore, but he's very wealthy now.

Following all the commotion, Arden eventually decided to sell the Move's contract to Walsh. It was hardly the bargain of the year for the group were entering a tricky transitional period. Ace Kefford had just left following a nervous breakdown and there was intense disagreement among other members concerning image and musical style. Guitarist Trevor Burton was intent on retaining the rebel image pioneered by their original manager, Tony Secunda, while drummer Bev Bevan favoured a less controversial stance. Walsh left them to their own devices but was grateful when they reverted to quality commercial pop. 'Blackberry Way' and 'Curly' restored them to the charts in a big way, but Burton dismissed the songs as lightweight pop and left in disillusionment, later rejoining his former mentor, Tony Secunda, to form the ill-fated supergroup Balls. Walsh, meanwhile, persuaded the remaining members to venture into cabaret in order to maintain a regular income. It proved a disastrous move. Relations within the group worsened and, following an embarrassing fracas at a Sheffield nightclub, lead singer Carl Wayne quit in disgust. Disillusioned, the group abandoned the supper club circuit and sought a release from Walsh. As if to prove nothing is ever predictable in the topsy-turvy world of pop management, the Move ended their days back with Don Arden.

The loss of the Move at the end of the sixties appeared to symbolize Walsh's desertion from pop management in favour of broader record company activities. His doors were still open to old pop favourites, however, and, rather fittingly, he managed the Troggs for a couple of years during the early seventies. Walsh kept them in constant work, arranging several foreign tours to supplement their income. Nothing startling came from their partnership however, except the notorious 'Troggs Tapes', a bootleg recording of an abortive session, consisting mainly of a stream of indecent four-letter words. Unlike their previous association with manager Larry Page, the Troggs left Walsh on reasonably good terms.

In surveying Walsh's career, it is not difficult to categorize him in the history of pop management. He emerged between the eras of Parnes and Epstein, an interregnum during which many ambitious businessmen infiltrated the pop scene as managers, impresarios or publishers. Like Don Arden and Phil Solomon, Walsh was first and foremost a business manager, lacking the creativity of the younger breed of charismatic entrepreneur that flourished during Epstein's reign. Compared to Page, Oldham, Napier-Bell and Secunda, Walsh seemed old fashioned in some respects, but this was advantageous to a certain type of artiste. Peter never fell victim to his own ego or sought vicarious fame through his chart acts. Realizing his limitations in the creative sphere, he made business acumen the most distinctive feature of his managerial style. There was never any question of his acts maturing into 'serious artistes' for he never saw pop music as art and steered clear of temperamental prima donnas. This lack of pretension made him perfectly suited to hard-working, no-nonsense pop groups. It was no coincidence that the Brook Brothers, the Tremeloes and the Marmalade all continued touring years after the hits had dried up. Walsh never fed their egos, so there was never any real sense of paradise lost.

The number of people whose careers in pop management began and ended with the sixties is staggering, and Walsh places himself amongst them, though he did enjoy further chart success in the early seventies with novelty pop outfit, Kenny. Like the best of his contemporaries, Walsh remains active in the music business and harbours no delusions about the past. He does not pretend that he masterminded his own exit from pop management and regards the possibility of a comeback in that sphere as an unlikely occurrence:

Management left me. I can't communicate. I'd love to have a couple of acts now. And I really think I could contribute something because I've still got my wherewithall for negotiating. But, unfortunately, the acts today want a manager who's with them 24 hours a day. My type of management went out in the seventies when accountants and solicitors took over.

In England during World War II many kids were transported from major English cities to the safer confines of the countryside. The tougher youngsters regarded the exercise as a great adventure and felt themselves impervious to the dangers of falling bombs. More rebellious youths pointedly refused to be evacuated and in their brash naïveté seemed not to understand the full meaning of mutilation and death. One such kid was Don Arden. Aggressive, confident and fiercely independent, Arden invariably went his own way and refused to knuckle down to anybody. By the age of 13, he had already dropped out of school and launched himself into a show business apprenticeship, later remembered as '20 years of rough and tumble'. It was certainly an exciting period which Arden embraced with all the enthusiasm of a starstruck kid who had run off to join a travelling circus. During a seemingly endless series of tours and revues, he developed his craft as a stand-up comic, singer and impresario. At 16, he was entertaining troops before finally being drafted himself. As soon as the war ended he was back in vaudeville — the classic hard-headed hungry young trouper.

Arden spent most of the fifties working the boards as a singer/comedian. Given his later reputation as a strong-arm man, it seems strange to imagine Don as a comic. Yet, even one of his later adversaries, Peter Walsh, remembers him as 'a tremendously funny man'. Arden had ambition and drive in abundance but lacked the necessary diplomacy to ingratiate himself with influential show business moguls. His uncompromising aggression and short temper alienated so many important contacts that eventually he decided to branch out from performing into promotion. He began modestly, organizing Hebrew folk song contests before putting together his own shows.

By the late fifties, Arden had found his niche. As a master of ceremonies, he could still sing, crack jokes and keep audiences happy while his star attractions lay waiting in the wings. During 1959 he compered Gene Vincent's first British tour and his organizational abilities ensured that the shows were a tremendous success. When Vincent decided to move to England, Arden agreed to assume managerial responsibilities, an arrangement not without its administrative headaches. Gene was a brilliant but erratic performer, subject to tempestuous outbursts brought on by alcoholism. His unruly behaviour upset many promoters and theatre managers, resulting in a gradual decline in earnings and drawing power. Ever resilient, Arden kept the American in constant work, frequently sending him out on Continental jaunts. He even attempted to cure Vincent's alcoholism, installing him in a Harley Street clinic where he was put to sleep and fed intravenously for several days. The 'cure' proved ineffectual, however, and Vincent's alcoholism continued to worsen. He frequently railed against old friends and grew increasingly disillusioned about the state of his career. At one point, he even pulled a knife on Arden, but his manager was unfazed and advised the distraught Virginian wildcat to pull himself together. Shortly afterwards, Vincent saw a psychiatrist but there was no quick and easy cure for his self-destructive tendencies. As time passed, he became more resentful towards Arden and they eventually parted amid much acrimony in 1965. In later years, Arden still felt outstanding moral debts were owed by Vincent and his men made pertinent enquiries at selected box offices during the American's final UK tour in 1971. Vincent's caustic response to his former manager was effectively summed up in the words 'How's that, Mr Arden!' at the end of a song titled 'Our Souls', irreverently sung as 'arseholes'.

By the mid-sixties, Arden had reached a crucial stage in his career. He had promoted many successful package tours involving a number of American acts such as Jerry Lee Lewis, Little Richard and Sam Cooke, but his progress in this area was thwarted by the dramatic emergence of the Beatles and their ilk. Suddenly, American stars were passé and as the beat boom reached its peak, attendance figures at Arden's concerts revealed a noticeable slump. After losing approximately £100 000 in a disastrous 10-week run, Arden abandoned his fifties rock 'n' roll stars and set out in search of young pop groups. His first involvement in the beat group scene came through Mike Jeffrey, manager of the Newcastle-based Animals. Jeffrey, a notorious hustler and shady operator, was looking for an influential agent to get his group work in the South. Arden brought them to London and secured a residency at the fashionable Scene club. The Animals went down a storm and Arden immediately became their full-time agent, ensuring that he had sole rights to promote them worldwide. He also claims responsibility for recruiting producer Mickie Most, who proved instrumental in setting in motion the Animals' rise to international fame. Following the transatlantic chart-topper 'House Of The Rising Sun', Arden made substantial profits from promoting the Animals, but their association was relatively short lived. A dispute arose with Jeffrey and rather than involve himself in protracted legal action, Arden sold his rights to other parties. Jeffrey's own managerial career was relatively short lived. Several years later, he died in mysterious circumstances following a plane explosion. The body was never recovered.

By this stage, Arden realized that pop group management could prove extremely lucrative, and he wasted no time in signing the Nashville Teens. The Weybridge sextet had already undergone a gruelling apprenticeship at Hamburg's all-night Star Club and emerged as one of the most exciting groups of their day. Soon they were snapped up by Decca in a deal which offered seven-eighths of a penny for every record sold. While this meagre figure might have been acceptable for a solo singer, a group split meant that in order for each member to earn a modest £1000, the disc would have to sell 1 600 000 copies! Of course, such abysmal recording deals were far from rare in the sixties. Even the Beatles had been signed on a one penny per record basis, though their royalty was successfully renegotiated after they charted. The Nashville Teens were not so lucky. They peaked with their first single, 'Tobacco Road' (number 6 UK; number 14 US). A downward spiral followed with 'Google Eye' (number 10); 'Find My Way Back Home' (number 34); 'This Little Bird' (number 38) and 'The Hard Way' (number 45). Although the group worked with some excellent producers, including Mickie Most, Andrew Oldham and Shel Talmy, they never quite managed to transform the power of their live performances on to vinyl. In strictly monetary terms, however, chart success was a largely irrelevant issue to the Nashville Teens. Even if they had achieved a string of number ones, the financial rewards would have been negligible. This can be demonstrated by a close analysis of the sales figures relating to their first three singles:

'Tobacco Road' UK sales: 200 000 @ 7/8d = £ 725. 10s. 5d.
'Tobacco Road' US sales: 600 000 @ 7/8d = £2187. 1s. 0d.
'Google Eye'   UK sales: 100 000 @ 7/8d = £ 364. 1s. 2d.
'Find My Way
   Back Home' UK sales: 65 000 @ 7/8d = £ 237. 1s. 7d.

This grand total of £3513. 14s. 2d meant that each member could reasonably expect a paltry £585. 12s. 4d. for three successive chart singles, including two in the Top 10! Teens' vocalist Ramon Phillips maintains that the group lost track of their royalty payments and did not fully understand various contractual clauses. At one stage they employed Arden's solicitor David Jacobs to look into their business affairs, but midway through his research he was found hanged.

Like many sixties artistes, Ray Phillips perceives his recording career as a comedy of errors:

The Decca deal was one of the big mistakes. They were a big label but they signed up so many bands that we had no personal attention. We didn't release any original material, which went against us. Anything we had was just slammed on a B-side. The direction of the group was never determined . . . We never knew where we were going.

The Teens' erratic career was further hampered by the unwieldy size of the group. All too often, six members meant six different points of view. What they needed was inspired leadership, but although Arden was firm, he seldom had time to discuss their long-term prospects.

Arden's main contribution to the Nashville Teens was keeping them in work constantly throughout their career. Ray Phillips remembers their gigging schedule with a mixture of pride and amusement:

We were working every night. The only money we really made was from gigging. We used to look at the gig list to see if we had a free day that month . . . The management opted for getting us as many gigs as possible rather than spreading us a bit more thinly and building up the image. I think the top money then was about £350 – £400. That was good money. We got that on a lot of gigs. But with publicity there was never anything instigated from the office . . . It was hit-and-miss all the time.

Arden's success on the live circuit was reinforced by the awesome presence of a former wrestler turned booking agent, Peter Grant. Working for Arden provided valuable experience which Grant later used to formidable effect in guiding Led Zeppelin to seventies superstardom.

Superstardom would never be a word synonymous with the Nashville Teens. Instead, they became a workmanlike road group, struggling on through changing musical fashions, personneal upheavals and the disillusionment of observing lesser talent succeed in their place. In spite of the Teens' intense gigging schedule, Arden occasionally found difficulty releasing sufficient funds to cover their various expenses. Ray Phillips recalls how Arden's severe budgeting frequently frustrated the group:

We had to go up and barter for the money. If we were owed a grand he'd say, 'Would you settle for £600?' We'd be sitting in the office waiting for some money to get to a gig. He'd keep us waiting till the banks closed. 'Oh, I've got no money now. I've got some here — would you settle for that?' Little did you know, that's it — you were paid off.

Although the group grudgingly accepted the 'bartering system' as a method of payment, pianist John Hawken insisted on challenging Arden's absolute authority. Prior to a performance in Manchester, he arranged to collect £120 from his manager's Carnaby Street office, but, upon arrival, he was handed a cheque for £20. Overcome by reckless indignation, Hawken raised his voice in complaint and demanded the full sum in no uncertain terms. Arden was evidently astounded by his impudent outburst. Incensed, he leapt from his chair, seized Hawken by the throat and pinned him against the wall. Staring directly into his eyes, Arden screamed: 'I have the strength of 10 men in these hands'. Feeling the pressure of Arden's fingers on his neck, young Hawken realized that this was no idle boast. Within seconds, the agitated Arden had dragged the musician towards his office window, two floors above ground level, and exclaimed wickedly: 'You're going over, John, you're going over'. Fortunately, Hawken managed to free himself from his manager's grip and fled from his office in a distraught state. Suffice to say, Hawken learned the hard way that a manager of Arden's stature always demands respect.

In the aftermath of their brief success, the Nashville Teens continued working with Arden, always hoping to re-establish their old reputation. As Ray Phillips now admits, it was not to be:

> Working does increase your popularity, but we were doing nothing for the future. There was no help from the management end to get us back. We just kept working and working until we faded away . . . We tried changing management and agency and we came up against a few brick walls. They'd had a phone call saying, 'You will not!' It was a dog-in-a-manger attitude really. 'We can't do anything with you, but nobody else can have you either!' It just saddened me that because of mismanagement and the bookings not coming in anymore, it had to fade away . . . I suppose it was inevitable in the end.

The fact that Arden kept the group on his books long after they were a lucrative proposition was some consolation and he would no doubt argue that without his involvement their life span would have been considerably shorter. Under the terms of their management contract he received one third of their gross receipts from live performances, so there was every incentive to sustain their flagging career. Although their business relationship was never ideal, there was no animosity forthcoming from the group when they finally left their long-time manager. In retrospect, Phillips portrays Arden as a highly successful business manager whose main deficiency was a lack of creative input: 'I got on well with Don Arden. I liked Don.

But he couldn't *manage* a band. He couldn't inject ideas . . . He was
into buying and selling rather than making. The Teens needed
guidance and direction.'

Phillips continued with the group and, remarkably, still leads
them today. Over the years, he has watched the original members
gradually drift away, the saddest departure being Art Sharp who
quit in 1972. Overweight and unemployed, Art was given a lifeline
by his former manager who offered him a job as a booker for Jet
Records. It was poetic justice.

The minimal chart success of the Nashville Teens did not
impede Arden's progress as a pop manager. One of his employees,
Ian Samwell, had spotted a young 'mod' group and persuaded
Arden to audition them. Although the Small Faces had already
attracted the interest of Who manager, Kit Lambert, lead singer
Steve Marriot evidently preferred Arden, having previously known
his son, David, at acting school. Prior to their all-important
audition, the Small Faces had been involved in a brawl which
culminated in Marriot receiving a bottle in the face and guitarist
Ronnie Lane being struck across the head with an iron bar.
Fortunately, Arden was not the type of manager easily put off by
the sight of bruises and stitches. On the contrary, he was much
taken by their roughhouse street credibility and charmed by their
cockney cheekiness. An agreement was immediately drafted and
the Small Faces signed to Arden's Contemporary Records management and production company. Their debut disc, 'Whatcha Gonna
Do About It', an in-house composition/production by Samwell,
was an instant smash hit, which came as no surprise to Arden, who
had craftily hyped the disc into the charts. His fraternization with
chart fixers lasted two years and involved an outlay of several
thousand pounds.[1] Arden recalls his manipulative tactics with
some pride:

> I knew that for certain sums, any record I was associated with could be
> elevated to the charts. It got to be a habit. I paid out anything from
> £150 to £500 a week to people who manipulated the charts and who in

[1] Arden's breakdown of 'hyping' expenses, taken from a written statement, was as
follows: £5500 paid to two individuals to buy Contemporary's records from shops in
order to boost the number of apparent sales to the public; £2750 paid to chart fixers
to hype Contemporary's records into the hit parade and between £5000 and £6000
for extensive airplay on Radio Caroline. The chart manipulation was executed by a
certain Tony Martin, who had successfully infiltrated the advertising department of
the *New Musical Express* and had the lower regions of the chart at his fingertips.
Apart from his successes with the Small Faces, Martin hyped, among others, the
Jimi Hendrix Experience's 'Hey Joe' for manager Mike Jeffrey and Track label
licenser Kit Lambert, and David Bowie's 'Space Oddity' for Kenneth Pitt.

turn shared the cash with people organizing other charts so as to ensure they tallied . . . Neat little swindle, wasn't it? Of course, the Small Faces had no idea what went on.

Indeed, the Small Faces were totally naïve and showed little interest in their manager's business dealings until it was too late. Much has been made of the Small Faces' problems with Arden, who has been criticized frequently for keeping the group on a £20-a-week wage. His detractors rarely acknowledge that he also cocooned the boys in pop star luxury. An expensive flat was purchased for the group in Pimlico, including a full-time maid and an attendant chauffeur complete with a Mark 10 Jaguar. Arden even opened accounts for the group at most of London's fashionable boutiques where they squandered a small fortune on whatever garments took their fleeting fancy. Arden has always regarded these extravagances as evidence of his affection for the lads: '. . . . just to prove that the Al Capone of the pop world has a soft spot, let me tell you I felt these kids should have at least one year of enjoying the very best in life'. Unfortunately, such unbridled freedom merely exacerbated the group's spendthrift indulgences, and they were soon brought down to earth with a resounding bump.

For one awful moment in late 1965, the Small Faces looked like following the downward path of the Nashville Teens. A line-up change, preceded by the failure of their second single, 'I Got Mine', suggested they were unable to thrive without the benefit of a hyped hit. Arden responded to the crisis by recruiting hit songwriters Kenny Lynch and Mort Shuman, whose 'Sha-La-La-La-Lee' brought Top 3 glory in early 1966. From that point onwards, Arden treated the act like fledgling superstars, adamantly refusing support spots and dragging them off the set of *Thank Your Lucky Stars* when they were allocated only one showstopper. This confidence was reinforced by another Top 10 hit, 'Hey Girl', and completely vindicated by the awesome chart-topper 'All Or Nothing', which Arden himself produced.

The Small Faces could have conquered the world, but for their yobbish behaviour. Instead, British impresarios grew cool towards them and the final indignity occurred when they were banned from *Top Of The Pops* after Marriot insulted producer Johnnie Stewart. Although Arden admired their brashness, he was understandably perplexed by their self-destructive streak and inexplicably carefree attitude towards their career.

As 1966 wore on it became blatantly obvious that there was a growing rift between Arden and his number one act. Prompted by their concerned parents, the group began to take a closer look at their financial state. With no accounts forthcoming from Arden and a history of extravagant spending behind them, the Small Faces were unsure whether they were millionaires or paupers. Eventually, the parents decided to pay Arden a visit and demand an explanation. For some reason, they never quite got round to talking about money. Arden fended off such questions by expressing his deep concern about the boys' drug-taking habits. Not surprisingly, the parents were up in arms and left Arden's Carnaby Street office convinced that their children were hardened addicts. According to Ronnie Lane it took a great deal of persuasion to convince them otherwise. On another occasion, Lane himself visited Arden to discuss money matters but his confidence was shattered upon being introduced to one of Don's assistants, a certain 'Mad Tom'. Arden alone was an imposing figure, but the selected heavies that hung around his office suggested that any criticisms of the man would best be left unuttered. Following a group meeting, the boys decided to employ an independent lawyer and accountant to sort out their financial affairs. Battlelines were being drawn.

The Small Faces would probably have remained under Arden's aegis but for their concern over unaccounted revenue. News of their disenchantment spread through the back lanes of Tin Pan Alley, but Don convinced himself that all would be well. His countenance grimly altered when he heard a rumour that one of Robert Stigwood's associates had expressed an interest in the group. Inflamed by proprietorial zeal and a sense that some unwritten code of entrepreneurial etiquette had been transgressed, Arden decided to teach the unfortunate Stigwood a lesson that he would never forget. Marshalling his forces, Arden enacted a remarkable scene which will live forever in the folk-lore of sixties pop management:

> I had to stop these overtures — and quickly. I contacted two well-muscled friends and hired two more equally huge toughs. And we went along to nail this impresario to his chair with fright. There was a large ornate ashtray on his desk. I picked it up and smashed it down with such force that the desk cracked — giving a good impression of a man wild with rage. My friends and I had carefully rehearsed our next move. I pretended to go berserk, lifted the impresario bodily from his chair, dragged him on to the balcony and held him so he was looking down to the pavement four floors below. I asked my friends if I should drop him or forgive him. In unison they shouted: 'Drop him'. He went rigid with shock and I thought he might have a heart attack. Immediately, I dragged him back into the room and warned him never to interfere with my groups again.

The shaken Stigwood, who had never personally contacted the Small Faces, took heed of Arden's advice, as did many other figures in the pop world.

By this time, however, the Small Faces were soliciting interest elsewhere in the hope of acquiring a better deal. As Steve Marriot explained, 'All it took to get away was money'. Unfortunately, nobody was willing to risk signing them for fear of being hung from an open window or worse. However, one manager who almost got involved was the eloquent Simon Napier-Bell, an entrepreneur whose background and demeanour contrasted sharply with that of Arden. Simon recalls the fateful day that the Small Faces arrived at his office and placed him in a compromising position:

> I sat and thought, 'I'd love to manage the Small Faces — but what can I do? He's only got to know they're in my office and he's going to be around trying to get me'. I wouldn't even have let them in the office. It's just that I opened the door and they were sitting outside in reception . . . I got them in quick before someone walked by and saw them. Then I thought, 'How do I get out of this?'

Napier-Bell could have ushered them out of the building but he was not particularly happy about the possible repercussions if Arden heard of their visit. Not wishing to be branded a poacher, Simon eventually phoned the mighty Arden and confessed the truth. Don was on the point of screaming abuse at the innocent Napier-Bell, but was eventually calmed down sufficiently to listen to an intriguing proposition:

> I said, 'Sooner or later it won't work out for you, Don, but I've got a super idea. Why don't they sign to me with your full knowledge, I'll manage them and you'll get half the commission? That way you don't lose everything, they're happy, I'm happy and the business goes on'. And he said, 'Fuckin' hell, Simon, you and me, we're the only honest ones left in the business, aren't we?'

For a moment, Napier-Bell deluded himself that Arden might be an easy-going partner whose truculence could be kept in check. While musing on this, he suddenly realized that the Small Faces had yet to be consulted on the purported agreement. Without thinking, he blurted out, 'Hang on Don, they haven't agreed to sign it yet!' The indignant Arden jokingly suggested that if they didn't he would come over and try and sort things out. Suddenly, Napier-Bell had this horrible vision of Arden bursting into his office and unwittingly terrifying half the street. Realizing the vast incompatibilities in their respective management techniques, Simon quickly made some excuses and talked his way back out of the deal. He has never regretted that decision.

The growing rift between the Small Faces and Don Arden reached crisis point in October 1966. With some justification, Don had voiced concern about the group's lack of motivation in failing to record a follow up to their number 1 hit, 'All Or Nothing'. In the mid-sixties, it was extremely dangerous for an aspiring group to leave long gaps between singles and Arden knew that unless the Small Faces released a single by November they would miss the lucrative Christmas market. In order to placate their manager, the boys had sent a rough demo to the office and promised to complete the recording at the earliest opportunity. However, one night, while driving to a gig, they switched on their car radio only to be greeted by the strains of their new single, 'My Mind's Eye'. Although the recording was far from poor and climbed to number 4 in the charts, the group bitterly resented Decca's decision to release the song. By Christmas, Arden and the boys had terminated their relationship. During the succeeding months, the Small Faces moved on to Harold Davison, Robert Wace and Andrew Oldham, respectively. Clearly, their problems were far from over.

Although Arden had sold the Faces' agency contract for a reputed £12 000, his company still owed the group royalty payments in respect of record sales. Retrieving those sums was to prove extremely difficult. An intriguing dispute ensued during which Arden demonstrated his predilection for drawn-out court proceedings. During the summer of 1967 an action was brought against Arden's Contemporary Records for an amount of royalties due to the Small Faces. On receipt of the order, dated 9 June 1967, an account was filed which revealed that £4023. 7s. was owed to the group. Several months later, on 11 October 1967, the Small Faces obtained judgement in their favour and Counsel for Arden stated in Court that his company had sufficient funds available to pay the debt. Having battled for nearly a year, it seemed as though the group had won a hard-earned victory against their former manager. Unfortunately, the Small Faces had underestimated Arden's tenacity and, within a week, their premature celebrations came to an abrupt end. On 16 October, Arden's solicitors, M.A. Jacobs & Sons, wrote to the Small Faces' legal advisers stating '. . . with regard to the judgement which you have obtained against our Clients, our Clients are not in a position to meet this fully and in one payment. Therefore, they would suggest that they should discharge the debt by instalments of £250 per month . . .' Of course, this meant that the group would not receive their full

£4023. 7s. until as late as January 1969. Reluctantly, they accepted this instalment plan, but after proffering £500, Contemporary Records suddenly ceased payment. The Small Faces were left with no option but to petition for the winding up of Arden's company and an order was duly granted on 5 February 1968. Amazingly, it was not until February 1977, approximately 10 years after payment was due, that the group finally recovered the full sum of £4023. 7s. Arden's mastery of litigation was to remain a constant throughout his future managerial career.

The loss of a major group such as the Small Faces might have proved a severe blow to a minor-league manager, but Arden always ensured he had acts in reserve. His strength lay in the success of his agency, Galaxy Entertainments, which booked over a hundred groups in its heyday including the Nashville Teens, the Applejacks, the Action, Neil Christian, the Fairytale and the Skatellites. In his role as starmaker, Arden carefully chose to manage those acts whom he felt had the strongest chance of achieving success. His decisions were generally sound, but raw talent and strong potential could not always be translated into stardom. One promising group that failed to prosper under Arden's regime was the Attack, featuring David O'List, who later achieved success in the Nice. Arden had great hopes for the boys but in spite of some impressive singles, including a cover of 'Hi Ho Silver Lining', the desired breakthrough proved elusive.

While awaiting the emergence of a new act to rival the chart feats of the Small Faces, Arden temporarily revived his own singing career. He was probably influenced by the dramatic rise in sales of ballad material in the UK during the first half of 1967. With Tom Jones, Engelbert Humperdinck, Vince Hill, Frank Sinatra and even Harry Secombe all scoring massive hits Arden must have felt that he stood an outside chance. He even hired a well-known 'promoter' to exploit the sales of his single, investing £250 in the process. 'Sunrise Sunset', released on Decca, failed to chart, though it is doubtful whether many people expected to see Arden on *Top Of The Pops*. Don later boasted that the single sold approximately 27 000 copies, though if such a figure is accurate, it is surprising that he decided not to release further material. Perhaps he was distracted by the formidable hit machine which fell into his hands in 1967.

When Arden took over the management of Amen Corner from agent Ron King, they had already achieved some chart success. Don was intent on continuing their hit run and it was bizarre to witness how uncannily their career paralleled that of the Small Faces. Lead singer, Andy Fairweather-Low quickly emerged as a pin-up hero in the same manner as his predecessor, Steve Marriot; both singers hit the headlines by collapsing during rehearsals for important television programmes; both groups failed to crack the US market while managed by Arden; both were involved in disputes with their mentor; both prompted Arden to threaten a potential poacher; both left him and signed to Andrew Oldham's Immediate label. For Amen Corner, 1967-8 was a tremendously exciting and frequently frustrating period which they will never forget. Signing to Arden appeared to guarantee drama and intrigue and under his tutelage they served the equivalent of a university course in the politics of the pop world. By the summer of 1968 they had notched up four hits, 'Gin House', 'World Of Broken Hearts', 'Bend Me Shape Me' and 'High In The Sky' and were regarded by the media as a cut above the average pop group. What the press did not reveal was the intense power struggle that served as a backdrop to this group's short career. Guns, threats of physical violence and even a proposed assassination were just some of the happenings during Arden's term of management.

Events reached a head when Don learned the by now familiar tale that his group were searching for new management and had been approached by certain individuals. On this occasion, however, Arden found himself up against a consortium of wealthy and influential figures backed by a powerful pop music entrepreneur. The aims of the consortium have never been made clear, though Arden suggests that they may have regarded themselves as an independent trade union in search of better deals for pop artistes. However, the involvement of the mysterious pop mogul implies that their prime motive may have been to pressurize Arden into surrendering his more important assets. The first signs of trouble occurred when an intermediary of the consortium phoned Arden and suggested that he might release Amen Corner from their management contract. Arden's reply was characteristically blunt and intimidating:

> I warned him that committing suicide might be better than causing trouble for me . . . The story was that £3000 had been put up to get me 'fixed'. I know full well that it is possible to hire someone to maim or kill for a few thousand pounds. But this time I was scared because there was talk of getting at me through my one weakness — my family.

Arden has always been strongly protective of his family, so it is not surprising to learn that he acted quickly. Three bodyguards were employed for a three-figure sum to provide round-the-clock protection for Arden's wife and children while a counter-plot was being hatched. Don then hired a further six bodyguards and briefed them of his plans for frightening off the consortium. Their focus of attention was a patsy whom Don suspected had some connections with the consortium and seemed the single weakest pawn in their richly-funded Mafia-style vendetta. In broad daylight, Arden's henchmen set out to his mews flat armed with sawn-off shotguns and revolvers. When the potential victim saw these thugs from his upper window, he screamed his lungs out. Having terrified this character out of his wits, the heavies casually returned to their car and drove away. Arden had presented his visiting card and effectively persuaded the consortium that it would be folly to risk taking this dispute to its logical extreme. Of course, Arden's intimidatory retaliation was itself a dangerous ploy which might have backfired on him in various ways. Indeed, during the aftermath of this incident, he was contacted by a senior police officer investigating complaints concerning guns. It took all of Arden's rhetoric and cunning to persuade the police that their informant was a crank.

In spite of flexing his muscles, Arden could not retain the confidence of Amen Corner who left him for another manager shortly afterwards. There was much talk in the press about Don taking legal action to retain his interests in the group, though nothing came of it. Arden later claimed that he had sold Amen Corner's contract for a profit of £50 000.

The employment of minders and persuaders and the frequent disputes with managers and artistes soon earned Don Arden the title 'the Al Capone of Pop'. An absurd rumour spread that he had been appointed by the Mafia to supervise their activities in London. Amused by the anxiety this caused in certain quarters, Don actively perpetuated the myth by refusing to comment on the matter. The notorious reputation he acquired in the late sixties may have alarmed some of his acts, but many others were flattered by their association with such a powerful entrepreneur. Such was evidently the case with Skip Bifferty, another of Arden's rare failures. During the early stages of their career, the group harboured ambitions of achieving overnight success. However, the grinding toll of endless one-nighters that Arden so favoured frustrated and disillusioned them. Arden was less than impressed by their seeming lack of commitment and endurance:

> They weren't tough enough to make it . . . They wanted to become stars, but just when we got them from £10 to £100 a night, they went to pieces. They seemed to forget that nothing comes easy, you've got to

work for what you get. They had no staying power, no patience and they wouldn't accept guidance. And artistes have to cooperate with me.

Skip Bifferty not only refused to cooperate with Arden, but actively sought to terminate their management contract, a course of action guaranteed to inflame their mentor's wrath. Following a disagreement, they spent most of their time outside London, unsure of what to do next. Frightened and emotionally intimidated, they confessed their worst fears to Beckenham police and were advised by Detective Inspector John MacNamara to report any threats, unexpected visits or disturbances. Shortly afterwards, two cars pulled up outside their house and they were confronted by several thugs brandishing firearms and threatening dire consequences. Wisely, they telephoned MacNamara and after a lengthy chase one of the cars was stopped in London's Tottenham Court Road. Several offensive weapons were discovered in the vehicle and the heavies were duly charged. It was another astonishing episode in the career of an Arden group who found themselves hopelessly out of depth in their dealings with the all-powerful Al Capone of Pop.

It was inevitable that Arden would one day become involved with an already highly-established group and, rather fittingly, his choice was the controversial Move. When Arden first entered their lives, the group were in a transitional state, having still not recovered from their first year as pop stars. The Move had created more short-term controversy than any of their contemporaries, bar the Rolling Stones. In many respects, they were the brainchild of manager Tony Secunda, one of the great sensationalists of the sixties. Tony appeared to thrive on the chaos that the Move created and during his stay with them he masterminded their public image in a series of outrageous publicity stunts and instant happenings that took the pop world by storm. Secunda played upon the media's ever-present fascination with scandal and used stock shock tactics involving nudity, drugs and violence. Strippers were employed to add spice to live performances and Secunda even had a publicity shot taken of the group signing a contract on the bare back of model Liz Wilson. During that session, the group were decked out in thirties mobster-style suits, a clear suggestion of their violent image. Even their gigs included orchestrated acts of aggression such as smashing television sets or demolishing American cars. Although the group were not involved in any drug busts and probably preferred pints to pot, the papers still managed to point out supposed LSD influences in such songs as 'Night Of Fear' and 'I Can Hear The Grass Grow'.

As a publicist and creative force, Secunda seemed peerless and successfully navigated the Move through a series of different images and musical styles, but his lust for sensation inevitably brought about his downfall. When he promoted the Move's 'Flowers In The Rain' with a scandalous cartoon postcard of Harold Wilson, the British Prime Minister successfully sued for libel. As a result, the Move were forced to surrender their royalties from the disc to a charity of Mr Wilson's choice. The loss of earnings annoyed their songwriter Roy Wood and considerably weakened Secunda's position.

When the Move elected to appoint Don Arden as their new agent, Secunda bitterly opposed the motion and forced them to choose between himself and his elder rival. Eventually, they took on Don, but the decision was far from unanimous and almost split the group. Bass guitarist Chris 'Ace' Kefford was already on the way out having been reduced to a nervous wreck during the previous 18 months. Trevor Burton switched from guitar to bass and lasted several months more, but his relationship with drummer Bev Bevan gradually deteriorated. The Move were clearly in disarray and the failure of their fifth single, 'Wild Tiger Woman' only made matters worse. Arden needed their full support in order to revitalize their career, yet they remained strangely uncommitted. One might have assumed that Don could at least rest easy in the knowledge that no manager would dare attempt to usurp him. Remarkably, however, some managers chose to ignore the tales of sawn-off shotguns and were not frightened by the possibility of being hung from a fourth-floor window. Like the Small Faces and Amen Corner before them, the Move soon found themselves in the centre of an entrepreneurial feud, this time involving Arden and Peter Walsh. The violence, threats and subsequent police intervention resulting from that escapade are documented in the previous chapter. Suffice to say, Arden eventually sold the Move's contract but won them back the following year. It was a fascinating power game that ended in another legal wrangle, but for Arden this particular struggle would later reap rich rewards.

For a time it seemed that Arden had inherited a dying group, but he always retained faith in the Move, who struggled on as a trio, with Roy Wood as lead vocalist. Having flirted with acid rock, pop art, flower-power and psychedelia, they next emerged as a heavy metal band with 'Brontosaurus' and 'When Alice Comes Down To The Farm'. Wood even adopted a startling new image and appeared like a tribal warrior with multi-coloured backcombed hair and a painted face. For some critics Wood's theatrics smacked of desperation but, in reality, the Move were already formulating new plans, punctuated by the arrival of singer- composer-guitarist Jeff

Lynne. Soon, there was talk of an offshoot group whose grandiose music required oboes, violins and cellos as well as standard rock instrumentation. Although Arden was initially sceptical about such a radical move away from the pop mainstream, Wood and Lynne's enthusiasm remained unquenchable.

The grandly-named Electric Light Orchestra was finally launched in early 1972 and Arden booked an impressive tour, spending lavishly on billboard and trade announcements. After 18 months of preparation, however, the group was still not ready and the tour was postponed. When they eventually made an uneasy debut at the Fox and Greyhound, Croydon, the audience merely registered perplexity and Arden expressed concern about the over-ambitious nature of the project. ELO stuck to their guns, however, even as the final Move single, 'California Man', climbed into the Top 10.

By the winter of 1972, the creative teamwork that had launched ELO was replaced by infighting and rivalry between Roy Wood and Jeff Lynne. The bickering culminated in the departure of Wood, who went on to form Wizzard. Arden prophetically described the split as 'the best thing that could have happened to ELO'. During the next year, both groups stormed the charts, but it was Wizzard that won the psychological battle for supremacy with two number 1s, 'See My Baby Jive' and 'Angel Fingers'. The prolific Wood even found time to score solo hits with 'Dear Elaine' and the brilliant Brian Wilson/Neil Sedaka/Phil Spector tribute, 'Forever'. Suddenly, Arden was poised to reach a new peak in his managerial career.

Arden was confident that both groups would be world-beaters, but Wood proved too restless to stick with an easy formula. During the next few years he abandoned pure pop in favour of such fleeting fancies as rock 'n' roll revivalism and classical jazz-rock experimentation. In spite of his obvious brilliance as a singles specialist, he has not registered a chart entry since 1975. Ironically, it was the less adventurous ELO that ultimately fulfilled Arden's ambitions by establishing themselves as consistent hit-makers throughout the decade. By the mid-seventies they had achieved remarkable success on the US stadium circuit and sold millions of albums worldwide. Throughout this period, their relationship with Arden remained exemplary and his paternalistic guidance played a major part in ensuring their long-term popularity.

While ELO thrived under Arden's aegis, singing star Lynsey De Paul suffered contrasting fortunes which were to end in bitterness, tears and near suicide. Their relationship began amicably enough in May 1973 when her previous manager/agent Harold

Davison fell ill. Arden recommended himself as a replacement and De Paul was pleased to sign a three-year management and initial one-year recording contract with his company, Dartbill, on 6 April 1974. Under the terms of the agreement, Dartbill promised to pay a signatory advance of £12 500, to be followed by £7500 six months later. For the first year all went well and by 6 March 1974 Dartbill had exercised its option to extend the agreements for a further year. This required them to pay a £10 000 renewal advance to be followed by a further £10 000 within six months. By this stage, Arden's company had invested £30 000 in Lynsey De Paul's recording career and, confident of her future success, they decided to extend the contract to its limit covering the tax year 6 April 1976 to 5 April 1977. By a letter dated 23 June 1975, it was agreed that two payments of £12 500 became due on 21 March 1976 and 21 September 1976, respectively.

In the autumn of 1975, Lynsey had to meet certain financial obligations and found herself in need of the £10 000 due on 6 September. Accordingly, in November she visited Arden's house in Wimbledon to seek payment of the overdue amount. Lynsey later said she felt apprehensive about visiting Arden because of his notoriously aggressive reputation but, strangely, such fears had not prevented her from signing with him in the first place. Given her uneasiness, it was doubly odd that she chose to attend their meeting unaccompanied. On one level, the visit proved extremely successful, for Lynsey left clutching a cheque for £10 000. Yet she also felt frightened, upset and intimidated by what she perceived as Arden's unfriendliness towards her. Precisely what prompted Arden's tetchiness remains unclear; he could hardly have justifiably begrudged paying the singer her advance since at the time of the visit she was in the Top 10 with one of her biggest hits, 'No Honestly'. Whether the events of winter 1975 constituted a misunderstanding or a genuine rift between the parties remains debatable, but there is no doubt that their business relationship subsequently suffered. Once a manager and artiste lose confidence in each other, the effects are always problematic and this has seldom been better illustrated than in the battle royal between Arden and De Paul.

The spring of 1976 was a disastrous period in De Paul's professional career. A potentially triumphant season at the London Palladium was soured by financial wrangling and the release of her next album was delayed due to disagreements between Arden and AIR Studios. To make matters worse, the £12 500 payable on 21 March 1976 was now ominously overdue. Recoiling from these crises, Lynsey sought legal advice and instructed solicitors to threaten Dartbill with a termination of contract notice if payment was not promptly issued. The money was received in September 1976, but De Paul took exception to the six-month delay. Disillusioned, she decided to break free from Arden and by proceedings instituted in the Chancery Division of the High Court of Justice, a writ was issued against Dartbill on 10 November 1976. Predictably, Arden's company chose to contest the issue, thereby setting the scene for another protracted legal argument.[1]

The fight between De Paul and Arden dragged on throughout 1977. Although she had a strong case, Lynsey was dealing with a man for whom contractual litigation had become second nature. The protagonists were unevenly matched in High Court experience and as the solicitors' bills mounted it was De Paul who felt most vulnerable. Her career took a slight upward turn when she represented Britain in the Eurovision Song Contest, duetting with Mike Moran on 'Rock Bottom'. Even here, however, success was tinged with disappointment and, in chart terms, the single fared worse than any UK Eurovision entry for 11 years. Intentionally or not, the words of 'Rock Bottom' reflected accurately the state of Lynsey's artistic career. As the year wore on, the young singer was physically, emotionally and psychologically devastated by the seemingly never-ending struggle to defeat Arden in the courts. As a result of her anxiety, she was unable to sleep and even collapsed on two occasions in 1977. The pressure of work and constant worry caused her hair to fall out to such an extent that her scalp became visible at the back of her head. At times, she even considered the possibility of ending it all and had to seek help from psychiatrist R.D. Laing. No wonder she looks back at the Arden years with regret: 'It was a time in my life that I'll never forget and I'll never forgive him. And if anybody was near suicide, and if ever I was near, it was then, because it was awful.'

It was not until October 1978 that Arden and De Paul finally reached terms of settlement and terminated their contracts. How-

---

[1]Arden's company, Dartbill, had been fighting a similar action in the High Court exactly 12 months before against Ann O'Dell's group, Chopyn. Under the terms of an agreement in late 1974, Dartbill had arranged to pay the group all costs in making sound recordings, plus £10 000 and specified royalties following the delivery of their album *Grand Slam*. Dartbill failed to pay the amounts due on receipt of the mastertape and in October 1975 Chopyn brought High Court proceedings claiming £14 411.35 plus £10 000 and damages for breach of contract. On 1 November judgement was given in their favour to the tune of £15 218.52 (representing £10 909.27 recording costs and £3000 for breach of contract, plus interest). Arden's company gave notice of appeal and the following August the parties agreed on a settlement by which Dartbill paid £10 000 plus legal costs.

ever, as part of the settlement Dartbill retained world rights of
recordings made under the agreements, including unreleased
masters. As Lynsey later remarked, 'I'm still not free.'

While De Paul scored her pyrrhic victory, ELO were enjoying
the positive aspects of Arden's management. Million-selling albums
and stadium concerts were par for the course as Don took their
earnings skyward. He frequently toured with the group, who
leaned heavily on his vast experience as an impresario and promoter.
While testifying to Arden's hard-working efficiency, drummer Bev
Bevan remembered one occasion when his manager's fierce temper
caused unforeseen problems. During an ELO gig in Italy, Arden
was accosted backstage by a stocky individual who proceeded to
raise his voice and point at the concert platform. Arden ignored his
ranting and continued conversing with a member of his party.
Indignant at such treatment, the agitated Italian poked Arden in
the chest with his finger, hoping to attract his attention. Such an
irreverent gesture was guaranteed to unleash the entrepreneur's
aggressive streak, and without considering the consequences he
lifted the mystery man up by his lapels, shook him violently and
threw him aside. Don then returned to his interrupted conversation, unaware that he had just humiliated the local Chief of Police
who had been attempting to stop the show for fear of a riot. A riot of
a different kind almost ensued when Arden was surrounded by
police officers and escorted to the local nick, following which he
was ordered to appear in court. Luckily, the boys bailed him out
and immediately booked him on a flight home before any further
trouble occurred. Arden left claiming a moral points victory.

By the late seventies, Arden had established himself as one of
the most successful entrepreneurs in the music business with an
international record label, Jet. His son, David, helped run the
affairs of the UK company while daughter Sharon served an equally
tough apprenticeship on the road looking after ELO and others.
Flamboyant, outspoken, garrulous and high-living, Sharon shared
many of her father's personality traits and was no stranger to the
excesses of road life, which included loud parties, food fights and
hotel room demolishing. Her 'rock 'n' roll' lifestyle was welcomed
by ELO and applauded by her greatest admirer, Ozzy Osbourne.

Osbourne had re-signed with Don Arden as a solo artiste after
splitting from heavy metal group Black Sabbath in 1980. At the
time, he described Jet as 'one big happy family' and before long he
joined the dynasty by marrying Sharon Arden. Unfortunately, his
wife and father-in-law had a falling-out which resulted in Sharon
taking Ozzy to Epic Records where he has since built a steady
career under her sole management. What sounds like a 'happy ever

after' tale has been marred somewhat by the sporadic and puzzling lawsuits that have plagued Osbourne since splitting from Arden. The most bizarre of these was served backstage at Live Aid after Ozzy had appeared briefly onstage with his old friends from Black Sabbath. The writ alleged that Osbourne was attempting to reform the original group as a performing unit and actively discouraging them from associating with their former manager. Ozzy was astonished by the implications of the legal document and could be heard fulminating: 'If Don thinks I'm going back to Black Sabbath, he must be crazy!' Clearly, with a solo career in bloom, the last thing he envisaged was a Sabbath revival. Osbourne still seems unsure whether Arden is genuinely aggrieved or merely playing some clever game. Who can fathom this entrepreneur who never forgets or forgives past transgressions and appears to regard management contracts as eternally binding?

For many, Arden remains the most notorious manager in the history of British pop music, justifiably feared by enemies and associates for his unbridled aggression. Such a heavy reputation has frequently proven advantageous since any manager, agent or promoter attempting to rip off or delay payment to the man knows that it will probably create more trouble than profit. Of course, such a controversial character is always likely to invite unwanted scrutiny and in 1979 Arden found himself under investigation by the BBC's watchdog programme *Checkpoint*. Roger Cook's team made some damning comments on Arden's business methods which greatly upset the man. Faced by Cook's relentless questioning, Arden became increasingly evasive and frequently appeared bamboozled by the sheer weight of the accusations levelled against him. He swore at Cook, conjured up spurious rumours of homosexuality, and even threatened, on air, to break the neck of any person found tailing him! It was a remarkable and chilling confrontation.

Understandably, the most provocative and unflinching attacks on Arden came from his old adversary Lynsey De Paul who concluded: 'He's caused a lot of pain to a lot of people and he shouldn't get away with it . . . and I hope he rots in hell!' Arden's retort to her catalogue of accusations was a tight-lipped aside: 'Lynsey De Paul has a personal vendetta against me.' In the wake of the programme, many news-hunting neutrals hoped that Arden would re-open the debate in the High Court, but he resisted the temptation, thereby robbing us of several new chapters in the annals of British pop music.

There was one final footnote to the Arden/BBC extravaganza which neither party had anticipated. One of Don's sixties groups, the Nashville Teens, took advantage of his plight in order to promote a comeback single, 'Midnight', which they cheekily dedicated to the man. Extending the ironic gesture still further, they embarked on a 'Be Nice to Don Arden' tour and even offered to play a benefit concert for the beleaguered rock mogul. It was a delightful spoof and a pleasing reminder that after all the financial disputes, harsh criticisms and bitterness, this hard-working, stoical group had somehow retained its sense of humour.

Don Arden assumed a lower profile in the eighties, leading to speculation that he had mellowed with passing years. It was a happy delusion broken by newspaper headlines in 1985 and 1986 suggesting that he was in more trouble than ever.

On 19 March 1986, David Arden appeared at the Old Bailey charged with carrying out his father's instructions to blackmail and imprison Harshad Patel, an accountant who rose to power in the Jet organization to become Don's partner. Patel had fallen out with Arden, who accused him of extorting company funds in excess of $100 000. It was not a vast sum by Arden's financial standards, but rather than pursuing his allegations through the courts, Don allegedly decided to take the law into his own hands using strong-arm methods. One evening, Don and David Arden, accompanied by two thugs, allegedly held Patel captive for over 24 hours. During his long ordeal, the unfortunate accountant was verbally abused by Arden Snr, who at one point allegedly flew into a rage and threw a cup of coffee over his victim. In an earlier hearing, it was suggested that Patel had been 'beaten up' and forced to sign a letter of credit for £69 000. Evidently, Arden had not bargained upon Patel's indignation and willingness to contact the police about the incident. In the past, Don's intimidatory tactics had attracted enquiries from the police, but these allegations were arguably the most serious yet, and, if proven, would almost certainly place Arden behind bars.

The Old Bailey trial ended with Arden's son, David, being sentenced to two years' imprisonment, albeit with one suspended. Meanwhile, Arden Snr remained in Los Angeles awaiting his fate. In open court, it was confidently stated that Arden would be brought back to England at the earliest opportunity to face these charges. An extradition order followed and, 20 months after his son's incarceration, Arden arrived at the Old Bailey for one of the most dramatic court cases in pop history.

Don Arden was arrested in the US in late 1985 and prior to extradition proceedings voluntarily returned to the UK where he was charged under his family name, Harry Levy, on two separate counts of false imprisonment and blackmail. During November 1987, the Old Bailey heard a staggering series of accusations from

Harshad Patel, Arden's former book-keeper/accountant. Patel explained that Arden suspected him of misappropriating funds from Jet Records and during a stormy meeting in November 1983 allegedly attacked him with a hatstand, pulled a gun from his briefcase and threatened: 'I'm going to shoot you'. The accountant was then dispossessed of several post-dated cheques and car keys before being unceremoniously sacked. He claims Arden demanded 'substantial compensation' for the supposed fraudulency and threatened to recruit Mafia associates to take care of matters. The perturbed Patel returned to England, but further trouble followed.

On 7 December 1983 at 1 a.m., Patel was asleep at his house in Harrow when an American heavy named Charlie Holbrook allegedly smashed down his front door and threatened to split his head open unless he accompanied him immediately to Arden's Wimbledon home. There, Patel was supposedly interrogated by the son of a leading New York Mafia boss and physically assaulted by Arden, resulting in superficial injuries including a fractured rib. Following his alleged night of captivity, Patel claims he was taken to Arden's accountants and persuaded to sign a bank draft for £69 132.37. That, he assumed, was the end of the matter. Two months later, however, Arden discovered further irregularities. On 14 February 1984, Patel claims he received a second visit from Charlie. This time he was taken to Arden's office in Portland Place and supposedly held prisoner for over 24 hours, a period in which he claims to have been attacked by Arden, punched in the face and stomach, showered with coffee and water, consistently hit over the head with a 16 oz. paperweight, suffered danger from various flying missiles including an ashtray, prevented from leaving his seat or going to the lavatory for agonizing spells in excess of 14 hours, and threatened with the possibility of being beaten with a baseball bat and chained up and done away with, along with his parents. The alleged presence of another Mafia persuader and the suggestion that David Arden alluded to Muslims chopping off the hands of thieves completed the accountant's grim scenario. Eventually, Patel claims, he was released, bloodied and bruised, and warned that he must repay a further £10 000 compensation to Arden within one month. Soon afterwards, Patel contacted solicitors and police intervention followed.

During the two-week trial, Arden strenuously denied Patel's allegations, flew in several star witnesses from the States and focussed considerable attention on a separate civil action concerning Patel's alleged fraudulency of Jet. On 19 November 1987, a jury of eight men and three women found Arden 'Not Guilty' on all charges. At the age of 62, his character remains unblemished by a criminal record.

Born in 1934 at a private nursing home in Liverpool, Brian was the eldest child of Harry and Queenie Epstein, a wealthy Jewish couple whose assets included a thriving furniture shop and the recently acquired North End Road Music Stores (NEMS). Cosseted by a proud and over-protective mother, Brian showed every sign of developing into a precocious school boy, but his academic progress was mediocre. Expelled from Liverpool College for 'inattention and being below standard', the troubled pupil fared little better at the other six schools he attended prior to his thirteenth birthday. After failing the dreaded Common Entrance Examination, Epstein found himself barred from Britain's top public schools and was extremely fortunate to be admitted to Wrekin College. At 15, he left that prestigious institution without a single academic qualification. Such a disgrace was small beer in comparison to his next bombshell. The tutors at Wrekin shared Harry Epstein's shock and dismay upon learning that his eldest son intended to make his fortune as a dress-designer. The idea was dismissed as unmanly and under pressure from his father, Brian meekly surrendered his independence and returned home to serve an apprenticeship in the family business.

Whatever dreams he harboured at public school were quickly displaced by the relentless tedium of everyday work. Fortunately, this also had beneficial effects. Submitting to his fate as a £5-a-week furniture salesman, Brian's industry and efficiency surprised both himself and his father. His greatest enjoyment came from enforcing his tastes on unsuspecting members of the public. For the first time in his life, people listened attentively to his views and respected his opinions. On 9 December 1952, however, a letter arrived that disrupted this happy state of affairs. Brian had been conscripted for two years of national service.

Private Epstein proved a hopeless soldier, regressing immediately to the ineptitude that characterized his school life. He was quickly dismissed as potential officer material and assigned a clerical job in the Royal Army Service Corps at Albany Barracks, Regent's Park. The sense of failure produced by his subordinate military role encouraged Brian to bolster his self-image by frequenting West End clubs and dressing more smartly than his superiors. When he returned to barracks one evening in a bowler hat and pinstripe suit, several guards mistook him for a superior, but the orderly was not so unobservant and, enraged by Epstein's presumptuousness, hauled him up before the disciplinary committee on a charge of impersonating an officer. With his nerves in tatters, he was sent to the barracks doctor who was concerned enough to seek assistance from an army psychiatrist. After listening patiently to Epstein's life story, several more specialist opinions were required before it was agreed that the hapless private should be honourably discharged. The euphemism 'medical grounds' subtly understated sexual predilections that would have rendered the soldier subject to prosecution under British law in the fifties.

Predictably, Brian returned home once more to the family business. Contentment soon led to impatience, however, and his parents suffered another shock when their son abruptly announced that he intended to pursue an acting career. After three short terms at London's Royal Academy of Dramatic Art, he returned home disillusioned. The Epstein business was now expanding and Brian dutifully took over the record department of their new NEMS store in Liverpool. He worked diligently and before long NEMS was established as one of the most important record departments in the North.

By the end of the fifties Epstein seemed a settled, successful shopkeeper, but his personal life was riddled with anxiety and guilt. He enjoyed female company and even dated one of his employees, Rita Harris, who was attracted by his aristocratic looks and sophistication. Brian kept the relationship secret, fearing that his family would not approve of his association with a working-class, Roman Catholic girl. More than anything, he was searching for a stable relationship and a chance to bury the memory of previously unsuccessful liaisons. Often, they would sit in his car talking until 5 a.m., but the dawn brought no answers to the doubts and fears that plagued the wealthy provincial bachelor. Rita soon learned that it was not merely her background and religion that threatened their future:

> He said no one was really happy but one should aim to be reasonably content. I knew he wanted to get married but he didn't think he would make a good husband. He admitted he was a homosexual and talked about it frequently. It used to make him very depressed. He hated himself for it. He never remembered being any other way.

When their relationship petered out, Epstein was left to mull over the more negative homosexual aspects of his life and his disquietude was only partially alleviated by a long summer holiday in Spain.

Following his return, Epstein became slightly bored with the smooth-running record shop he had so masterfully created. He needed a new challenge that would fully utilize his entrepreneurial flair. But where could this be found? The answer arrived at approximately 3 p.m. on Saturday 28 October 1961 when an 18-year-old customer named Raymond Jones asked for a record called 'My Bonnie'. Epstein scoured his singles shelf with a pessimistic and puzzled expression until the wry teenager remarked impatiently: 'It's by a group called the Beatles. *You* won't have heard of them'.

Raymond Jones was correct. The conservative young businessman in his smart suit was blissfully unaware of the phenomenon around him. Upon further investigation, this fussy shopkeeper, who prided himself on his ability to predict public taste, realized the extent of his ignorance. His female employees were very familiar with the four young musicians who crowded into the shop on wet afternoons to listen to the latest pop singles. Epstein had even rebuked his staff for wasting time aimlessly chatting to these scruffy, uncouth boys. Brian could forgive himself for only half remembering such a superficial incident, but his face reddened when he learned that the group had featured frequently in advertisements and articles in the local music magazine *Mersey Beat*; not only did NEMS sell the paper, but Epstein penned a regular column in its pages. His embarrassment was complete upon being informed that the Beatles played regularly at a club less than 200 yards from his premises. Suddenly, Epstein recognized the chasm between himself and his customers. He knew absolutely nothing about the local music scene. For the sake of his own edification, not to mention that of Raymond Jones, the pernickety proprietor decided to find out more about these Beatles and their obscure recording.

When Brian Epstein first entered the Cavern Club in Mathew Street, his immediate reaction was to take flight and run. The cellar was dark, dank and dreary, it smelt to high heaven and the condensation from the walls was matched only by the sweat-drenched teenagers who writhed in ecstacy to the deafening sound of an almost non-stop beat. Slinking into the shadows, Brian peered through the smoky haze and focused his eyes on the centre stage. What the 27-year-old middle-class Sibelius man saw was scarcely believable. The entertainers seemed oblivious to any notion of stage decorum. Between songs they smoked, ate and generally took a mischievous delight in insulting members of the audience. Yet there was a genuine rawness and ineffable quality in their unrestrained performance that appealed even to Brian's cultivated taste. The hypnotic beat of the music combined with their leather-

clad sexuality drew him closer to the stage and even the embarrassment of hearing his name announced over the blaring PA could not
persuade him to retreat. Eventually he was introduced to George
Harrison, who curtly inquired 'What brings Mr Epstein here?' It
was a pertinent question that provoked no definite answer beyond
the confession of a vague desire to glean some information about
their mysterious recording. The single was played by disc jockey
Bob Wooler while the four Beatles explained their origins, revealing
along the way that they had cut the disc during a residency in
Hamburg. The lead singer was Tony Sheridan and the record label
Polydor. Brian was unimpressed by the recording but fascinated
by the group and after listening to their afternoon set invited them
to his office the following month. Precisely what he had in mind
remained a mystery, both to the Beatles and himself.

In the weeks prior to their meeting, Brian endeavoured to
discover something about managing artistes, but his enquiries in
the trade proved unrewarding. He also sought people who knew
the Beatles, including their previous manager, Allan Williams,
who understandably hadn't a good word to say about them. The
Epsteins' solicitor, Rex Makin, was equally unenthusiastic about
Brian's plans while his father dismissed the idea as little better than
dress-designing. The universal apathy that he encountered must
have plagued Epstein on the fateful afternoon of their proposed
meeting. John Lennon was not only late but had obviously been
drinking, and the others were even tardier. Brian, a stickler for
punctuality, was horrified by their blasé attitude but continued
with his vague plan. The latecomers were told that their only hope
of success in the music business depended on the efforts of a
professional manager. Epstein was willing, but required their full
support. After receiving assurances that a management tie-up
would not mean a change in musical style, the Beatles accepted the
offer.

Epstein was remarkably confident about his abilities as a
manager and assumed that a major record deal could be easily
secured. He boasted incautiously that the leading record companies
would be falling over themselves in their attempts to sign an act
associated with the brains behind the great disc emporium of the
North. Brian was soon to discover that the politics of A & R were as
alien to his sphere of reference as beat groups and cellar clubs had
been two months before. Initially, however, his efforts looked
promising and after winning the support of journalist Tony Barrow,
the way was clear for a confrontation with Decca's A & R manager
Dick Rowe. Overburdened by administrative duties, Rowe
despatched his assistant Mike Smith to assess the potential of the

group. It was the least that he could do to appease the pushy head of the sales department. Fortunately, Smith was impressed enough by the Beatles to recommend an audition at Decca's West Hampstead studios. The date chosen was New Year's Day 1962.

Prior to the great day, the ever-presumptuous Brian insisted that he knew precisely the type of songs that would please the discerning Decca A & R executives. Against their better judgement, the Beatles were cajoled into selecting a disproportionate number of cover versions for their all-important audition. On the wintry morning of 1 January, the population of London was still recovering from the excesses of the previous evening as the four Beatles set out for their crucial appointment. Nervous yet excited, they mentally recapitulated the 60-minute repertoire which included only three Lennon/McCartney originals: 'Hello Little Girl', 'Like Dreamers Do' and 'Love Of The Loved'. Their performance that morning was tentative and rather tame in comparison to the excitement that Smith had witnessed at the Cavern. Nevertheless, he voiced his mild approval which was sufficient to convince the starry-eyed Epstein that the record deal was signed, sealed and delivered. Unbeknown to Brian, however, Smith auditioned another group later that afternoon and their performance made the Beatles sound second rate.

The following day, Mike walked into Dick Rowe's office and proudly announced that he had discovered two hit groups in one day. His superior was understandably sceptical and after hearing the tapes and discovering the respective merits of each group, he forced Smith to choose between them. It was no contest.

Brian Poole and the Tremeloes not only played better than the Beatles but were near neighbours to Mike, thereby saving travelling expenses and administrative hassles. Rowe was momentarily satisfied with the decision, but later that day a slight doubt gnawed in his mind. Meticulous to the last, Dick decided to take a day off and visit Liverpool 'just to make sure'. He had already heard how Epstein had entertained his assistant with a lavish meal before escorting him to the Cavern. Rowe wanted none of this. As an old pro, his policy was always to take a group by surprise rather than unwittingly encouraging them to put on a grand show.

It was pelting down with rain as Dick took a taxi from his hotel and asked the driver to head for the Cavern in Mathew Street. Upon arrival, Rowe was dismayed to discover a crowd of people between himself and the cellar entrance. Everybody was jostling to try and get out of the rain and after being pushed and shoved, Rowe left in a huff. By now, the last thing he wanted was to stand around looking at a pop group: he was soaked. Only months afterwards did

Dick realize his error:

> The fundamental thing I missed was all those people trying to get into
> the Cavern who couldn't. If it hadn't been so wet I'd have thought
> 'Something's going on here that's interesting. All these kids aren't
> trying to get in here for no good reason'.

While the Beatles reached the climax of their set, the all-powerful
A & R head was already sitting on a train bound for London,
feeling cross and rather foolish.

When Brian learned that the Beatles had been rejected by
Decca he was furious beyond words and immediately phoned the
A & R department to demand a *post mortem*. Although Rowe had
already dismissed the audition as 'amateurish' and 'dreadful' he
admired Epstein's persistence and agreed to a meeting. One thing
that impressed him above anything else was a charismatic manager.
He had previously worked closely with the great Larry Parnes and
signed most of his stable on the strength of the impresario's entrepreneurial reputation alone. Later in his career, figures like Philip
Solomon also frequently proved more important in the decision-
making than even the artiste under consideration. Since abandoning
the Beatles, Rowe had met Brian Poole and the Tremeloes' manager,
Peter Walsh, a born rhetorician who had already achieved chart
success with the Brook Brothers. If the pushy Liverpudlian manager
was the equal of Walsh, Rowe argued, then the decision concerning
the Beatles could be reversed. Even as he waited for Epstein to
arrive, Dick repeated to himself the famous words of his boss Sir
Edward Lewis: 'Don't turn anything down because you're short on
budget'.

Over lunch, Rowe and colleague Sidney Beecher Stevens listened
patiently as Epstein reiterated the merits of his great discovery.
The Decca executives quickly concluded that the Liverpudlian was
living on hopeless dreams and empty rhetoric. At one stage, he
even had the audacity to suggest that the Beatles would be bigger
than Elvis Presley. Rowe could tolerate such hyperbole from Larry
Parnes, but found himself increasingly irritated by Epstein's
insufferable pomposity and condescending demeanour:

> It's very difficult for me to say a nice word about Epstein. I just didn't
> like him. He was too conscious of the fact that he'd been well educated
> and fancied himself as a gent . . . It's unfortunate that I didn't get on
> with the person I should have got on with the most.

In an attempt to assuage the sales department, Epstein was passed on to Tony Meehan who was then working at Decca as a freelance producer. Brian found Meehan even less enthusiastic than Rowe and felt indignant about being asked to pay £100 to hire a studio for a further recording session. Exasperated by their indifference, Epstein stormed out of Decca as though he were rehearsing a scene from a Shakespeare play. Although he didn't actually say 'I'll be revenged on the whole pack of you', those were undoubtedly his sentiments. Years later, he took that revenge by crediting Rowe with the immortal words, 'Groups of guitarists are on the way out'. The former Decca executive always maintained that this was a malicious fabrication.

Epstein soon discovered that Rowe was not the only Doubting Thomas in the record industry. Pye, Philips, Columbia, HMV and Oriole all rejected the Beatles without even bothering to request an audition. Whenever Brian returned from a business expedition to London, he would be greeted by four hopeful faces at Lime Street Station. Together, they would retire to a nearby cafe where their humiliated and frustrated manager would pour out his latest sorrowful tale. Although the boys remained optimistic, it was difficult to ignore the discrepancies between Epstein's wild promises and the reality of consistent rejection. One evening, Brian confessed that he was running out of record companies to approach. A sullen silence ensued, broken by Lennon's caustic rejoinder: 'Try Embassy'. Embassy, the cut-price label owned by Woolworths, specialized in bland xeroxed cover versions of current hits. It would seem a most suitable resting place for a group that had failed a Decca audition largely due to their manager's propensity for non-original material.

Epstein's tardiness in securing a record deal did not diminish his administrative ability in other areas. Under his tutelage, the Beatles became a more professional outfit, no longer eating or horsing around onstage and even playing a carefully-rehearsed repertoire. Conversely, Brian was not immune to their influence and during the evenings took to wearing a black turtleneck sweater and leather jacket. His forlorn attempt to become one of the lads backfired, and he retired hurt upon learning that Lennon and the others had been secretly laughing at him. Characteristically, he took his revenge soon after by persuading them to replace their black leather gear with smart grey lounge suits. Lennon was not amused. But in the battle over the Beatles' image, Epstein's force-fulness was irresistible.

By the spring of 1962, the Beatles were still without a record contract and even a much-heralded return to Hamburg was blighted by news of the tragic death of their former bassist Stuart Sutcliffe.

Epstein, meanwhile, embarked on another trip to London, and on this occasion met with an incredible series of lucky breaks. His first stop was at the HMV shop in Oxford Street where he arranged for the Decca audition tape to be transferred to an acetate disc. Ted Huntley, the engineer responsible for the operation, was mildly impressed by the tape and referred Epstein to retail manager Kenneth Boast. In his exuberance, Brian adopted his usual pompous tone and informed Boast that the tapes represented a landmark in the history of British pop music. Kenneth accepted the hyperbole with a knowing smile but remained remarkably courteous to his NEMS counterpart. The stream of superlatives ended with Brian being ushered upstairs to meet Syd Coleman, head of EMI's Ardmore and Beechwood publishing company. The Liverpudlian was still in a daze as Coleman casually offered to publish two of the songs and arranged a further appointment with George Martin, who ran the A & R department at EMI's Parlophone Records. Epstein breathed a sigh of relief. Parlophone was one of the few record labels in the country that he had not approached.

George Martin was the perfect A & R executive from Brian's point of view. As a parvenu, he respected the wealthy middle classes and had even developed a posh newsreader's voice that belied his relatively poor origins. Far from being offended by this arrogant young manager who pontificated at length about the virtues of his artistes, Martin actually admired his air of superiority. It soon transpired that Martin knew very little about pop groups, having previously specialized in comedy records. Brian couldn't believe his luck. Instead of showing him the door, the producer listened to the acetate and passed some guarded but complimentary comments on the music. Martin was at a stage in his career where he urgently required a fresh challenge so it seemed quite logical to move from Peter Sellers to the 'best of cellars'. The Beatles were granted an audition.

When they arrived at EMI's Abbey Road studios on 6 June 1962, the group were pleasantly surprised to meet a genial, well-mannered producer who took an obvious interest in their work. Even the usually acerbic John Lennon was completely overawed upon learning that George Martin had worked closely with his heroes the Goons. The rapport they established that day was to prove extremely important in influencing the producer's final decision. Initially, Martin intended to select one member as leader, in imitation of Cliff Richard and the Shadows. He veered towards Paul McCartney, but felt reluctant to relegate Lennon for fear of destroying the group's equilibrium. Ironically, the rivalry between Lennon and McCartney ensured that the Beatles remained a democratic unit.

No firm decision was made on the day of the audition, but Brian remained hopeful that a deal would be forthcoming. Martin's only negative comment concerned the drumming of Peter Best, and it was agreed that a session player would take his place in the studio. This was common procedure in early sixties pop, most producers preferring technically accomplished drummers such as Bobby Graham, Clem Cattini and Andy White. What George Martin did not realize was that Paul McCartney and George Harrison were anxious to oust Best from the group in favour of Ringo Starr. Pete lacked the zany, fun-loving personality of the other Beatles, preferring to cultivate the mean, moody magnificence of a James Dean. His evident maturity and reliability often made his fellow Beatles seem childish by comparison. He was also better looking than any of them and boasted a formidable female fan following which must have irked the competitive McCartney. Brian had noted the underlying friction but dismissed the bitchy comments as petty rivalry. The objections of George Martin, however, provided Paul and George with strong ammunition that even Epstein could not ignore.

While Pete Best's future hung in the balance Brian received word from George Martin concerning the proposed record deal. Parlophone agreed to sign the Beatles to a one-year contract offering a royalty of one penny per single record sold, as well as retaining a four-year option with annual increments of 25 per cent. Epstein accepted the contract gladly and has been much criticized since for his lack of business acumen. In truth, the deal was fairly standard for an unknown group in 1962. Record companies failed to distinguish between soloists and groups in their computation and it was to the Beatles' disadvantage that they evenly distributed their royalties. They would have received no more or less if they had been Paul McCartney backed by three hired musicians. While it is probably true that Epstein would have signed virtually anything at this stage, the fact remains that he could actually have fared worse with several other companies.

News of the Parlophone deal was not revealed to Pete Best, though Brian still hoped to retain his place in the group. He knew that the drummer was a valuable asset and attempted to persuade the boys that his presence onstage would benefit the act. Epstein had also not forgotten the close friendship that existed between Best and roadie Neil Aspinall. If Aspinall quit in sympathy it might take months to find a suitable replacement. Throughout this unseemly episode, Brian accepted the argument that Best's drumming was below standard. The great irony, however, was that many

Liverpool musicians regarded Best as one of the finest drummers on the circuit. If Epstein had been fully aware of Peter's popularity among musicians and fans he might have fought harder in his defence, but once Lennon joined the anti-Best lobby, there was no point in further prevarication. On 16 August, Brian performed his management duties by informing the dejected drummer that he was an ex-Beatle.

By October 1962, Epstein was at last ready to sign a management agreement with the Beatles. A previous makeshift contract had been drawn up earlier in the year but Epstein had deliberately avoided signing the document until his new company, NEMS Enterprises, had been formed. Under the terms of the agreement Brian was allowed 25 per cent commission, a figure he maintained for all future signings. Even as the ink was drying on that contract, the controversy surrounding Pete Best's departure continued to rage. Although Aspinall agreed to remain with the Beatles, the fans of the dethroned drummer were not so easily appeased. On the streets outside NEMS and the Cavern, pickets waved banners and incessantly chanted 'Pete For Ever — Ringo Never' and other slogans of solidarity. Eventually, the frustrated fans turned on their former heroes and the youngest Beatle, George Harrison, received a punch in the face. Following the incident, Epstein feared for his own safety and refused to attend their Cavern performances unless the proprietor, Ray McFall, provided a bodyguard.

George was still sporting a black eye when the Beatles entered Abbey Road studios to cut their debut single, 'Love Me Do'. Exactly one month later, the single entered the charts and to everyone's joy climbed into the Top 20. The fact that the record charted within seven days of release lends some credence to the popular rumour that Epstein ordered 10 000 pre-release copies on behalf of NEMS. However, Brian always denied this during his lifetime, and his recently deceased brother Clive also told me that the story was preposterous:

> I am able to confirm with confidence that this is untrue. My father was very involved in the business then and neither he nor myself at any time were going to risk these thousands of records which have been suggested as part of the stock or part of the hype . . . It's absolute rubbish! Invoices and statements went through the office and every cheque was either signed by my father or myself. Something like that would obviously have been noticed. Even then, 10 000 records would have cost £3000.

The chart success of 'Love Me Do' was not reflected in the sheet-music sales, so Epstein refused to renew his publishing contract with Ardmore and Beechwood. Ever grandiloquent, he had set his heart on signing the Beatles to Hill and Range, primarily because they published the songs of Elvis Presley in the UK. George Martin was more realistic and advised Epstein to seek a smaller, hungry publisher who would have the time and personal commitment to fight for the artiste. His candidate was Lee Sheridan, better known as Dick James, a dance-band singer and fifties chart star who had recently set up his own publishing company. Martin approached James initially and met with a favourable response; the publisher even presented him with a suitable demo for the Beatles' next recording.

'How Do You Do It', composed by Mitch Murray, had already been rejected by Adam Faith, but James felt that it was a palpable hit. Martin was even more enthusiastic but, to his dismay, the Beatles rejected the song outright. Although he bullied the group into recording a demo, the final product was so lacklustre that the ever-amenable producer agreed to record a Lennon and McCartney song in its place. The result was 'Please Please Me', an irresistibly commercial composition that Martin prophesied as a number 1.

The news that 'How Do You Do It' had been rejected by the Beatles did not dissuade Dick James from seeing Brian Epstein. On the morning of their appointment the Fates smiled on the singing music publisher to his lasting benefit. Brian had a prior engagement with one of James's rivals who was so tardy that the Liverpudlian stormed out of his waiting room in a huff. By the time he arrived at Dick's office Brian was still seething, but recovered his poise upon learning that not all music publishers overslept.

James listened attentively to the demo of 'Please Please Me' and immediately offered to publish the song. Epstein was still cautious about surrendering the Beatles' publishing to a virtual unknown and candidly enquired about James's standing in the industry. Dick smiled, picked up the phone and, within two minutes, secured the Beatles a starring spot on the prestigious television pop programme *Thank Your Lucky Stars*. Brian was flabbergasted and remained in a daze as James outlined an extraordinary proposition. Rather than creaming off the customary 10 per cent retail price of sheet music and 50 per cent royalties from broadcasting and cover versions, James suggested the formation of Northern Songs, a separate company that would deal exclusively with Lennon and McCartney compositions. The offer proposed was a straight 50/50 split: half to Dick James and his business partner Charles Emmanuel Silver; 20 per cent each to Lennon and McCartney, and 10 per cent to Epstein. From this, James's parent company would take a 10 per cent commission. It was an extremely clever deal for the period, virtually assuring that James and the Beatles were inextricably linked. Brian was so astonished by James's apparent altruism that all he could say was 'Why are you doing this for us?' Why, indeed. It seems that James, even at this early stage, was astute enough to realize the songwriting potential of Lennon and McCartney and his willingness to look beyond the limited horizons of the collecting agencies that masqueraded as song publishers would shortly transform him into a millionaire.

Dick James was not the only Beatles prophet of 1962. The renowned impresario, Arthur Howes, had booked the boys as support for Frank Ifield, the most popular singer of the year whose singles 'I Remember You' and 'Lovesick Blues' dominated the number 1 spot for over three months. The Beatles were clearly out of their depth playing before such a current chart celebrity and the audience reaction ranged from polite indifference to genuine hostility. In spite of this, Howes saw something that he liked and secured an option on future shows. Epstein now had a record company, producer, publisher and promoter and a minor hit record. Few realized that he also had a second group.

Although Epstein's relationship with the Beatles has been variously described as a vocation, a religious experience and a sexual fantasy, it is important to place such romantic notions in perspective. Few would deny that Brian was anything but obsessed with the Beatles, but that did not curtail his managerial ambitions. Many small-time pop managers were monogamous and dared not sign any other artistes for fear of upsetting their one insecure and spoilt star. In spite of his emotional involvement with the Beatles, Brian never adhered to such rules, always perceiving himself as a potential pop mogul with a string of artistes at his command. Long before the release of 'Love Me Do' he had signed the second biggest act on the Liverpool circuit, Gerry and the Pacemakers.

Unlike the Beatles, Gerry and the Pacemakers were essentially a one-man group built around the small but dynamic Gerry Marsden, whose permanent grin and vivacious personality ensured a sizeable fan following. After three years playing youth clubs and small dance halls the group had gone fully professional in the autumn of 1961 and, like the Beatles, appeared regularly in Hamburg clubs. The decadent Germanic lifestyle was not reflected in their image, however, and for those who contend that Epstein's propensity for signing pop groups was due to some 'rough trade' sexual fantasy then his involvement with Marsden only months later provides a much-overlooked contradiction. When Brian first saw the group they were wearing clean white shirts, ties and immaculately tailored royal blue blazers complete with shining gold buttons and red handkerchiefs neatly tucked into their breast pockets. Like members of some exclusive club, they even wore special crests bearing the group initials 'G/P' inscribed in a gothic flourish. For a former would-be dress-designer, their off-beat uniform was almost as amusing and interesting as their music. Yet nothing could be further removed from the sexually-arousing, tight-fitting leather jackets and trousers favoured by his previous discoveries. Compared to John Lennon, Gerry Marsden was a cuddly teddybear. The contrasting visual images underline the important point that Epstein's motives for entering pop management were complex. The reductive criticism that crassly seeks to interpret the Liverpudlian's every move as sexually motivated invariably distracts attention from his purely entrepreneurial endeavours. Even while the Beatles were auditioning for George Martin, Gerry and the Pacemakers lay waiting in the wings, ready and available to exploit their success.

Learning from past errors, Epstein waited for the right psychological moment before presenting his second discovery to capricious A & R executives. After 'Love Me Do' reached the chart, Martin was invited to a Pacemakers gig on 12 December at the Majestic Ballroom in Birkenhead. Following a second audition at EMI Studios, the group were signed to the prestigious Columbia label, much to the envy of their Parlophone colleagues. Martin found Gerry Marsden even easier to work with than Lennon and McCartney and was pleased when the artiste felt no qualms about recording the twice rejected 'How Do You Do It' as a first single. Much to George's satisfaction, the song was immediately incorporated into the group's live repertoire. Meanwhile, Epstein was scouring the Cavern for more potential recording stars and his name became linked with several artistes including Tommy Quigley, the Four Jays and Billy Kramer and the Coasters. Far from clinging to the Beatles, Epstein seemed determined to expand his interests. One Top 20 hit had transformed the Liverpudlian into a potential Larry Parnes. As 1962 ended, Epstein confidently predicted further chart successes and drank a toast to the continued development of NEMS Enterprises.

On 12 January 1963, the Beatles appeared on *Thank Your Lucky Stars* and were seen by a record-breaking six million viewers. The gods had smiled on them again by stage managing the severest winter blizzards of the century, thereby ensuring that normally peripatetic teenagers were forced to remain at home huddled around their television sets. The promotion generated record sales to such an extent that the Beatles were soon challenging their recent rival,

Frank Ifield, for the coveted number 1 spot. On 22 February *Record Retailer* revealed that Ifield's 'The Wayward Wind' was still top; *Melody Maker* disagreed and placed 'Please Please Me' in first place; the most influential chart of all, *New Musical Express*, refused to settle the argument and showed *both* discs at number 1. That week was a crucial turning point in pop history, signalling the imminent overthrow of the solo singer in favour of an unstoppable torrent of Mersey talent. By the end of the year, the Beatles would have three further number ones, each more spectacular than its predecessor. Nor were they alone. Stablemates, Gerry and the Pacemakers soon found themselves in the incredible position of observing their first three releases reach number 1, a feat unsurpassed in British chart history until the advent of Frankie Goes To Hollywood in 1984. Brian himself had secured the magical treble by selecting 'You'll Never Walk Alone', a ballad from Rodgers and Hammerstein's musical *Carousel*. In the midst of the beat boom it was a dangerous but courageous third release, fully demonstrating Epstein's determination to show off his protégés as versatile and multi-talented performers.

Epstein's third hit-makers were appropriately named the Big Three. They were the loudest, most aggressive and visually exciting group playing the Liverpool circuit and boasted an impressive following, particularly among other musicians. Yet they only scored two minor hits, Ritchie Barrett's R & B classic 'Some Other Guy' and the innocuous Mitch Murray composition 'By The Way'. An inability to capture the full excitement of their live performance on vinyl merely reinforced their already noticeable self-destructive tendencies. Epstein attempted to tame this Merseyside version of the Rolling Stones, but they refused to be disciplined and soon fell apart, leaving respected drummer Johnny Hutchinson as the sole surviving original member. Brian dumped them in despair before the year was out.

Within a month of the Big Three's initial chart entry, Epstein's third major artiste was heading for the top. Billy Kramer and the Coasters had already achieved great amateur success playing such clubs as the Cavern and the Iron Door, as well as supporting the Beatles on several occasions. When they achieved third place in the influential *Mersey Beat* poll, Epstein decided to play the starmaker. At the time, Billy's career was overseen by an elderly gentleman named Edward Knibbs who was magnanimous enough to surrender his protégé for a £50 fee. Kramer recalls being invited to a Liverpool restaurant by Knibbs where Epstein blurted out his proposal, much to the astonishment of the fledgling star. Billy's backing group, the Coasters, lacked the confidence to turn professional, so

Epstein recruited a Manchester combo, the Dakotas, who agreed to a deal on condition that Kramer smartened himself up. In order to maintain a mutual independence the billing read Billy Kramer 'with' as opposed to 'and' the Dakotas. With a middle initial supplied by John Lennon and a new group, Kramer was promptly presented to George Martin as Brian's latest discovery. Amazingly, the EMI producer totally dismissed Kramer as a no-hoper with a terrible voice. It was a surprisingly myopic decision which left Brian flabbergasted. Billy's voice, for all its technical imperfections, was arguably the most distinctive of any Liverpool artiste, a view shared by John Lennon. Under pressure from Epstein, the ever-amenable George Martin agreed to record the lad, whose pedigree was confirmed by the end of the year with a trio of smash hits penned by Lennon and McCartney: 'Do You Want To Know A Secret?', 'Bad To Me' and 'I'll Keep You Satisfied'. Such was his popularity that even the Dakotas cashed in with a minor instrumental hit, 'The Cruel Sea'. The spectacular rise of Billy J. Kramer appeared to confirm Epstein's svengali touch. For Brian, Billy was an unpolished jewel, whose physical attraction even surpassed that of his beloved Beatles. In moments of managerial pride he began referring to the boy as 'the best-looking singer in the world'.

Early successes convinced Epstein that half the Cavern could be accommodated in the British Top 20. He tentatively approached a number of groups, including Kingsize Taylor and the Dominoes and the Swinging Blue Jeans, each of whom rejected his advances. The Merseybeats showed a keen interest but soon abandoned Brian following a ridiculous argument over his refusal to purchase Beatle-style suits. The Fourmost (formerly the Four Jays) proved equally elusive, but were finally won over to NEMS after witnessing the chart achievements of Gerry, Billy J. and the Big Three. Their decision to turn professional was soon rewarded with two Lennon/McCartney hits 'Hello Little Girl' and 'I'm In Love'.

Having broken through with a series of male artistes, Epstein emulated his illustrious predecessor, Larry Parnes, by adding a filly to the NEMS stable. Priscilla White was a typist who supplemented her income by working part-time as the Cavern's cloakroom attendant. Occasionally, she would appear on stage as guest singer with such local groups as Rory Storm and the Hurricanes, the Big Three and Kingsize Taylor and the Dominoes. The quality of her voice was defined in local parlance by that most condescending of epithets, 'Cavern Screamer'. Brian had first met this orange-haired chanteuse when she sang a couple of numbers with the Beatles at the Majestic Ballroom, Birkenhead. Although he initially dismissed her as a well-meaning amateur, a subsequent appearance at

Liverpool's Blue Angel Club revealed hitherto unforeseen talents. No mere screamer, Priscilla was equally adept at singing ballads and displayed a remarkably mature understanding of audience psychology, expertly introducing an ingratiating humour between songs that disarmed even her most hard-hearted critics. Epstein was rapidly captivated by her charm and total lack of pretension. When he first asked her if she had ever considered turning professional, she giggled 'Who'd have me?' It was a self-effacing rejoinder, for 'Swinging Cilla' had been hotly pursued by several so-called managers, none of whom were taken seriously. Her father, a burly docker, was blessed with a healthy cynicism and overprotective nature that prevented his Cilla from falling into the clutches of any would-be svengali. Brian was not deterred by such an imposing figure, having already dealt successfully with Paul McCartney's sceptical father and John Lennon's uproarious Aunt Mimi. Like his predecessors, White was won over by Epstein's diplomacy and grace, aided by a fortunate coincidence. He had once bought a piano from NEMS stores that proved an excellent instrument. Evidently, this confirmed the integrity and professionalism of the Epstein family.

Prior to signing with NEMS, Priscilla was informed that her stage name would henceforth be Cilla Black, a colour more accurately describing her soulful wailing. While Epstein confidently plotted her future, an unusual incident occurred which he later remembered as one of the most frightening experiences of his life. During the early hours of an insomnious night, the phone rang unexpectedly in Brian's home; upon lifting the receiver he was confronted with an ominous threat: 'Keep off Cilla White, Epstein. She doesn't need your management. She's signed with friends of mine'. This was a blatant lie, as Cilla confirmed the following day, but Brian was still worried, especially when a different caller issued the same menacing warning at 2 a.m. the next morning. Eventually, Epstein overcame his timidity and met the aggressor with such cold disdain that the threats weakened and finally ceased. Whether the caller was a crank or a genuinely jealous rival was never ascertained.

Recovering his poise, Brian introduced Cilla to George Martin and arranged for her to record a Lennon/McCartney song taken from the much maligned Decca audition tape. The poignant 'Love Of The Loved' was transformed into a dramatic ballad with a powerful vocal, typical of a 'Cavern Screamer'. It was more than enough to provide Epstein with his sixth chart act of 1963.

The spree of NEMS signings that year was the most spectacular managerial coup since Larry Parnes' celebrated monthly discoveries of 1959. Unlike Larry, however, Epstein seemed capable of transforming virtually all his artistes into prodigious hit-makers. Only two of his first battalion of signings failed to chart. The Remo Four, whose uninspired releases included such old chestnuts as 'Peter Gunn' and 'Sally Go Round The Roses' languished in permanent obscurity, outflanked by their more adventurous Liverpool contemporaries. Tommy Quigley (later renamed Quickly) fared little better. He was originally 'discovered' in true Larry Parnes fashion at a talent contest prior to a Beatles gig in Widnes the previous year. Quickly was presented with the by now obligatory Lennon/McCartney composition, but even the Beatle association could not disguise the fact that 'Tip Of My Tongue' was a poor song which deserved to flop. Another of his discs bore the remarkably astute advice, 'You Might As Well Forget Him'. Brian, of course, could not, and continued to extol his talents to smiling but sceptical journalists. Like his fellow Pye recording artistes, the Remo Four, Quickly never really recovered from his poor start and in spite of scraping a belated chart entry with Hank Thompson's 'Wild Side Of Life', the freckle-faced youth remained an anachronism in the age of the beat group.

By the end of 1963, Brian Epstein was able to look back at a year in which his artistes had dominated the hit parade with an incredible 9 number ones, spanning 32 weeks at the top. No manager in British pop history has ever achieved comparable chart supremacy. The accomplishment was even more remarkable when one considers the professional inexperience of Epstein and the acts under his tutelage. It was not surprising that British journalists turned to Brian and repeated the question that had launched Gerry Marsden's career: 'How Do You Do It?' Brian smiled and said nothing. Beneath his cool persona, he was as excited and perplexed by the Liverpool explosion as almost every other person in the country.

A number of theories have been put forward to explain the phenomenon known as 'Beatlemania', yet so much remains elusive because it was born of a series of factors — demographic, political, sociological, musical and managerial. The post-war baby boom had created a disproportionately large number of young people who were not only crying out for greater independence but had the money to indulge their adolescent whims. Britain and America had already been subdued by the rock 'n' roll explosion of the fifties, but Tin Pan Alley quickly recovered lost ground, exploiting and trivializing trends until traditional show business once again called the tune.

By the end of 1962, British teenagers were musically undernourished and greedy for any form of new excitement. The Beatles arrived at the perfect psychological moment, spearheading a working-class assault on music, fashion and the peripheral arts. Their rise coincided with the fall of a Conservative Cabinet Minister and emancipation from straitlaced Tory British life. Everything had been perfectly scripted. Even their early development as song-writers and musicians seemed uncannily consistent, almost as if the releases were designed to chronicle an ever-growing talent. And for once the public responded to these small steps of artistic progression with gradually ascending record sales. After seven weeks at number 1 with 'From Me To You', the Beatles produced the strident, wailing 'She Loves You', a rocker with a magical catchphrase ('Yeah Yeah Yeah') that was echoed in newspaper headlines when-ever their name was mentioned. 'She Loves You' did not merely repeat its predecessor's chart-topping longevity: it actually defied gravity. It hit number 1, went down, then returned to the top, seven weeks later. Eventually, the Beatles themselves removed this refluent disc with another of their own songs, creating further pandemonium in the process. With advance orders of one million, 'I Want To Hold Your Hand' entered the charts at number 1, the first disc to achieve this distinction since Cliff Richard's 'The Young Ones'. For the next two-and-a-half years *every* Beatles single entered the hit parade at number 1, establishing them as the most consistent chart-toppers of all time.[1]

The onslaught of Beatlemania in Britain did not distract Epstein from seeking larger markets abroad. He was determined to break NEMS acts in the States and in November 1963 embarked on a fateful visit accompanied by Billy J. Kramer. At that stage, British pop singers were regarded as little more than a joke, and even Larry Parnes had failed to convince US record companies that his boys were anything other than second-rate Elvis clones. Brian's acts seemed equally doomed, for their singles had already been licensed to such obscure labels as Vee Jay, Imperial and Laurie.

---

[1] A note on chart statistics. In recent years, there has been a growing tendency among lazy rock writers to follow the gospel according to *The Guinness Book Of Hit Singles*, an excellent, assiduously documented work free from the multitudinous errors that usually blight such voluminous undertakings. Unfortunately, over-reliance on this fine book has resulted in virtually every journalist, broadcaster and encyclopaedist accepting the charts used by the *Guinness* compilers as though none other existed. It should be noted, however, that the *Music Week* (previously *Record Retailer*) chart widely used today for such programmes as *Top Of The Pops* and the BBC Top 40 had no such credibility during the sixties, before the advent of independent compilers such as BMRB and Gallup. In those days, *Record Retailer* was an extremely dull chart with abnormally low entries, ironically similar to those of the weekly music press today. It was rated no higher and, in many respects, considerably lower than the other charts of the period with the relatively poor-selling *Record Mirror* as its major media outlet. By contrast, *New Musical Express*

Even the blockbusting 'She Loves You' had been rejected by Capitol, forcing George Martin to surrender the disc to Swan. Epstein's Stateside campaign therefore seemed doomed to failure yet, against the odds, he persuaded Capitol to release 'I Want To Hold Your Hand'. Even more surprisingly, he arranged an ambitious American launch for the Beatles at the prestigious Carnegie Hall. The man behind the scheme was Sid Bernstein, one of the few New York promoters who actually bothered to read British newspapers. Another key figure who showed more than a superficial interest in Beatlemania was the celebrated Ed Sullivan, whose CBS television show was the American equivalent of *Sunday Night At The London Palladium*. Sullivan had witnessed the Beatles phenomenon first hand during a recent European trip and was amused enough to offer the boys a novelty spot in his show early in the New Year. Brian was horrified at such a suggestion and immediately insisted on top billing. After much haggling, Sullivan agreed to the proposal but acquired the group's services at bargain basement prices. It was a peculiar arrangement, typical of Epstein's management during this period. In strictly monetary terms, the deal was lousy, but Brian was astute enough to balance a feeble profit against the enormous publicity that such an appearance might create nationwide. More important than profit or publicity, however, was the Beatles' dignity. In a world of chancers and spivvy profiteers, Epstein continued to act as though his artistes were British nobility. As he left America, the cultivated Liverpudlian felt satisfied with his efforts: Gerry and Billy J. had been booked for a couple of television pop shows; Capitol agreed to release 'I Want To Hold Your Hand', and the Beatles were set for a New York concert and headlining appearance on the Ed Sullivan Show. The gods had smiled again, though the chances of recreating Beatlemania in America remained about a million to one. In Britain,

---

boasted licensees as diverse as the *Daily Mail* and Radio Luxembourg, which used the chart for its own widely broadcast Top 20. Even the *People* preferred the *Melody Maker* chart to the dullard *Record Retailer* whose charts always appeared before the weekly sales receipts were calculated over the normal seven-day period. The latter not only failed to place 'Please Please Me' and Billy J. Kramer's 'Do You Want To Know A Secret' at number 1, but showed a perverse interpretation of record sales, claiming, among other things, that no records entered number 1 from 1963 till the end of the sixties apart from the Beatles' 'Get Back'. Yet in virtually every other chart, pre-release orders inevitably resulted in instant Beatles number 1s and *New Musical Express* showed that the Rolling Stones achieved the same feat with 'Little Red Rooster'. Significantly, there was a big news feature in *New Musical Express* when the Beatles actually *failed* to enter the chart at number 1 with 'Paperback Writer', so traditional had become their supremacy.

Today, *Music Week*, with its computerized compiling system, is rightly regarded

a weary press and disillusioned youth had turned to the Beatles for light relief in the depressing aftermath of a sordid political sex scandal, but no comparable mood existed in the New World. Yet, within a week of Epstein's homecoming, an entire nation was plunged into a long period of mourning. On 22 November John Fitzgerald Kennedy had been assassinated.

Meanwhile, back in London, Brian was gradually adapting to a new set of business values. The press had severely criticized him for overpricing the Beatles, yet rival entrepreneurs felt he was soft and naïve. For Epstein, the name of the game was making as much money for himself and his artistes without appearing greedy or unscrupulous. Other managers boasted of their stinging percentages and financial coups, but Brian always felt that was bad PR. Even when the *Daily Mirror* described the Beatles as 'Four frenzied Little Lord Fauntleroys who are earning £5000 a week', Epstein stated that the figure was exaggerated and should have read £1000. For all his financial foibles, the Liverpudlian remained independent, refusing the advances of more powerful entrepreneurs intent on swallowing up NEMS. Although he was later accused of provincial-mindedness in his business dealings and aspirations, the ability to transform a family business into a multi-million pound organization was no small feat. The fact that this was achieved with the assistance of a dedicated team of employees, many retained from the Liverpool days, was equally remarkable. Epstein insisted on loyalty from his colleagues and chose junior staff with the care of a politician. The NEMS team respected Brian and were extremely tolerant of his caprices and occasional fits of bad temper. It must have been extremely tempting to recruit an entrepreneurial high-flier during the early days of Beatlemania, but Brian was wise enough to realize that such a move could effectively destroy the smooth running of NEMS and divide loyalties. Although Epstein was reluctant to

---

as *the* chart specializing in dramatically high entries, precisely the opposite of its sixties *Record Retailer* counterpart. For the sake of consistency of form the *Guinness* compilers should have stuck with the *New Musical Express* chart until the arrival of BMRB at the end of the sixties. The only real reason for selecting the boring *Record Retailer* as a source was that it happened to be the first chart to include a Top 50. To add fuel to my argument, the omnipotent BBC was also sceptical of *Record Retailer* and during the sixties compiled a national chart based on combined statistics from all four weekly music papers. As far as I am aware, the nationally broadcast *Top of the Pops/Pick of the Pops* charts of the sixties have never been printed in any book but my memory confirms that virtually all Beatles records from mid/late '63 to mid '66 entered at number 1. In retrospect, the combination of all four charts by the BBC probably resulted in greater accuracy since the hyping of all four would have been beyond any single chart-fixer. Only once did the four chart system create a real anomaly: in 1968, *Top of the Pops* listed three records at number 1 *simultaneously*!

surrender his interests to powerful businessmen, he still managed to employ some notable personalities. His choice of press officers, for example, brilliantly complemented the Beatles' ever-changing public image. In the Cavern days, there was the tough, part-time hustler, Andrew Oldham; the Liverpool to London route was smoothed over by a freelance journalist, Tony Barrow; the Royal Variety performances and Palladium spectaculars ushered in a sophisticated former Royal Navy lieutenant commander, Brian Sommerville; finally, there was the eccentric, sentimental, laid-back, quest-seeking Derek Taylor who, like Brian, loved the Beatles as though they were his own children.

The strength and independence of NEMS ensured that the Beatles had few administrative problems during the Epstein era. They were protected from disruptive wheeler-dealers and encouraged to concentrate on their music while Brian held the financial reins. Scrupulously fair in his dealings, Epstein even allowed them a 10 per cent interest in NEMS, almost as though they were members of his own family. While many of their contemporaries lost their hard-earned money through poor investments or ill-advised largess, the Beatles were always protected from themselves. Their stern Czech accountant, Dr Strach, ensured that their money was safely banked and discouraged ridiculous extravagances. Similarly, the road managers, such as Neil Aspinall and Mal Evans, were solid, no-nonsense Liverpudlians. Without this back-up, the group might so easily have fallen victim to their own egos and wallowed in the darker areas of stardom. Instead, they survived the intense pressures of Beatlemania and continued to thrive artistically, which was a great tribute to their manager's organizational abilities.

In spite of his qualities, Epstein's importance during this period has often been severely denigrated. Some commentators have suggested that his managerial involvement after 'Love Me Do' was superfluous and may have hindered the Beatles as a creative and financial enterprise. Such a view seems harsh, if not perverse, yet it is not difficult to pinpoint Epstein's deficiencies. Unlike later figures such as Oldham or Page, his creative input in the studio was largely non-existent. Once, during the recording of *With The Beatles*, Brian had attempted to make his presence felt by criticizing the vocal line on Paul's version of 'Till There Was You'. The surly John Lennon immediately intervened and curtly defined his own conception of the manager/artiste relationship: 'We'll make the records. You just go on counting your percentages.' That may well have been the most ironic comment Lennon ever uttered, for Epstein had just made the greatest blunder of his managerial career by failing to attend to those all-important percentages.

It was after the Beatles' celebrated appearance on *Sunday Night At The London Palladium* that the question of merchandising reared its ugly head. Suddenly, NEMS was besieged with offers to manufacture Beatles goods ranging from badges, wigs, jackets and boots to aprons, scrapbooks, plastic guitars and pillowcases. The ferocity of the competition surprised even Brian who initially dismissed this avalanche of requests as an attempt to make a quick killing in the Christmas market. Eventually, he agreed to endorse certain products on condition that they were of the highest quality. These included the famous Beatle jacket and the 'official' Beatle sweater, on postal offer via their British fan club. It soon became clear, however, that the demand for Beatle-related products was no mere Christmas fad and manufacturers redoubled their efforts to obtain licences, bombarding NEMS with every product imaginable. It was a nightmare which became worse when Brian learned that several unscrupulous companies were manufacturing unauthorized goods, boldly using the Beatles moniker. In desperation he sought legal advice, employing the services of one of the most experienced and prestigious firms in show business. M.A. Jacobs of Pall Mall boasted a regalia of star clients, including Laurence Harvey, Judy Garland, Marlene Dietrich, Diana Dors and Liberace. The senior partner, David Jacobs, was already a minor celebrity, having won substantial damages for Liberace in his widely publicized libel action against the *Daily Mirror*. More importantly, from Brian's point of view, Jacobs also represented Larry Parnes and Don Arden; their involvement confirmed what Epstein had already heard elsewhere — Jacobs was the best.

After considering various ideas, Jacobs advised his client to employ a separate company to administer the merchandising worldwide. He recommended the services of Nicky Byrne, a fashionable young entrepreneur who once managed the Condor Club, where Tommy Steele had been discovered by John Kennedy in 1956. Having played a bit part in the career of Britain's first rock 'n' roller, Byrne was poised to enter the history books once again. Ironically, he was initially diffident about Epstein's supposed lack of business acumen. The involvement of Jacobs, however, ensured that a deal was hammered out. Byrne and five colleagues duly formed a merchandising company called Stramsact, plus an American subsidiary Seltaeb (Beatles spelt backwards). At this point, of course, nobody was interested in marketing Beatles goods in the United States and it was assumed that Byrne's company would function as a collection agency dealing in negligible sums. An agreement was drawn up between Stramsact, Seltaeb and NEMS and, rather uncharacteristically, Epstein allowed his solicitor to approve and sign the document independent of his eagle eye. For once, Brian had overcome his punctilious nature and answered those critics who were always castigating him for failing to delegate on important matters. When Byrne arrived at the offices of M.A. Jacobs he had no idea what constituted a fair percentage for his efforts, so suggested an absurd 90 per cent expecting the solicitor to barter towards a more reasonable figure. Amazingly, Jacobs agreed to these terms without argument, even making the ludicrous conclusion that 10 per cent was better than nothing. Jacobs' blunder was nothing less than extraordinary and would cost Epstein and the Beatles an incredible sum. Historically, Epstein's reputation as a business manager had been destroyed not by his own hand, but that of a trusted 'expert' adviser.

While the Beatles prepared for an important series of appearances at the Olympia Theatre, Paris, in January 1964, their manager was in a state of mild depression. By his own admission, Brian's life was 'in an awful mess'. The pressures of top-flight management, the wheeling and dealing, constant travelling and solicitations from film corporations and merchandising companies had insidiously worn down his spirits. His personal life was full of emotional inadequacies and though these had been partly submerged in the workaholic atmosphere engendered by Beatlemania, Brian was now questioning the relevance and purpose of his passion. For all his Herculean efforts the Beatles seemed distant, autonomous and sometimes unwittingly hurtful. Lennon's sarcasm was more cutting than ever; McCartney remained aloof and awkward; Harrison voiced concern over money and even the phlegmatic Ringo had suddenly proved tetchy and rebellious prior to the French trip. Epstein's ambiguous feelings about his relationship with the group were dramatically brought home to him during an interview with Derek Taylor when he was asked the pertinent question: 'Will you ever sell the Beatles?' Weeks earlier, Brian would have laughed at such a notion but on this particular day his disillusionment was such that he paused and averted his eyes in embarrassment. Sensing a scoop, Taylor piled on the pressure and like an interrogating police officer demanded: 'Look me in the eye and say you'll *never* sell the Beatles.' For all his conviction and fondness for the boys, Brian could not reply. His bamboozlement was no mere affectation for, unknown to Taylor and the Beatles, he was seriously considering an offer of £150 000 from a rival agency for a 50 per cent interest in NEMS.

The temptations of unburdening his work load seemed irresistible, yet Brian felt uneasy about sharing his crown. Eventually, he turned to the Beatles, desperately hoping for a show of loyalty but secretly fearing that they would blithely accept the proposed merger. In the circumstances, Lennon's response was not entirely unpredictable. He dismissed Brian and the proposal in two earthy words. Never had his brusqueness been so welcome as in that unintended display of fidelity. If Lennon's words were comforting, the reaction of McCartney seemed nothing less than astonishing. The Beatle whom Brian regarded as his most severe critic was not only appalled by the suggestion, but threatened to break up the group rather than lose his manager. Epstein was overwhelmed. Their words confirmed his belief that the relationship between them was infinitely more important than a signature on a contract.

Epstein's re-assessment of his managerial role was perfectly timed as the early months of 1964 required unwavering commitment. Even while the Paris trip foundered amid a series of apathetic concert reviews, news reached the Beatles that 'I Want To Hold Your Hand' was number 1 in the States. The record had broken via regional airplay and, sensing a sensation, Capitol quintupled the allocated number of pressings. A staggering one million copies had been sold, much to Brian's amazement. By the time the group arrived in America, a new wilder form of Beatlemania had been incited by frenzied, garrulous disc jockeys intent on out-hyping their rivals. The Beatles' airport reception was a graphic display of fan hysteria, unparalleled in pop history; the concerts in Washington and New York's Carnegie Hall were sell-outs; the Ed Sullivan appearances were seen by an unbelievable 75 million viewers. Amid the chaos, Epstein smiled like a Cheshire cat, coolly rejecting astronomical sums and amazing his new friend, Sid Bernstein, by turning down an offer to play Madison Square Garden. The only man in New York with a broader smile than Brian was another Englishman, Nicky Byrne. Since the Beatles' arrival he had been inundated with requests to issue licences for every product that the American merchandising mentality could conceive. One firm even succeeded in marketing cans of Beatle breath and made substantial profits in the process. Epstein was initially overwhelmed by Byrne's efforts but when he finally realized the percentages accruing to Seltaeb, his joy turned to horror. The lost sums that Brian could not stomach to calculate were revealed in the pages of the *Wall Street Journal*. According to their report, teenage Americans would spend over $50 million on Beatles goods before the end of 1964, while the world market was estimated at approximately £40 million.

Epstein's folly was brought home to him every time he saw Nicky Byrne whose lavish lifestyle was a major talking point in New York business and social circles. To his credit, Brian reacted quickly and, before the summer, persuaded Byrne to increase

NEMS' share of the profits to 46 per cent.[1] Unfortunately, relations between the parties continued to deteriorate and before long the merchandising millions were buried in a bog of legal complexity. NEMS sued Seltaeb for allegedly neglecting to pay all the royalties owed to them; Byrne's partners issued a lawsuit against their president for allegedly squandering Seltaeb funds on personal luxuries; Byrne sued NEMS for breach of contract and damages to the tune of $5 million. The dispute effectively alienated the major department stores Woolworths and Penneys resulting in the cancellation of orders conservatively estimated at $78 million. The dispute dragged on for three years during which a $5 million judgement was awarded against NEMS for failing to appear in court. The judgement was later overruled and Byrne finally settled for a pay-off of less than $100 000. In an attempt to atone for Jacobs' original error, Epstein contributed the legal expenses from his personal income.

The Seltaeb dispute was the one black mark in an otherwise vintage Epstein year. The Beatles had eclipsed their British success with American record sales and chart achievements that defied the imagination. In April, *Billboard* showed the group holding the first five places in the chart with records on four different labels: 'Can't Buy Me Love' (Capitol); 'Twist And Shout' (Tollie); 'She Loves You' (Swan); 'I Want To Hold Your Hand' (Capitol); and 'Please Please Me' (Vee Jay). In Canada, the phenomenon was even more pronounced with nine Beatles singles hogging the Top 10! A return trip to the States in August saw the group performing at sports arenas throughout the country. The celebrated Hollywood Bowl concert was another important landmark in pop history, ushering in the era of stadium rock when live rock 'n' roll music became synonymous with absurd amounts of money. Once again, Epstein had helped to radically alter the direction of rock music.

For the Beatles, these latest triumphs meant freedom from the financial restraints of the previous year. Their star status in Britain showed no sign of declining and, between American trips, further critical acclaim was forthcoming with the release of their first film *A Hard Day's Night*. In retrospect, the deal Brian secured was far from ideal. Producer Walter Shenson recalls that United Artists

---

[1] Most Beatles commentators maintain that this was still peanuts. It is worth noting, however, that Seltaeb successfully held out for an impressive 15 per cent of the retail price of most products. Therefore, with the revised NEMS/Seltaeb contract, Epstein was receiving approximately 7 per cent of the retail price value. Even the great Colonel Tom Parker, generally regarded as the most astute business manager in rock history, was receiving no more than 8 per cent of the retail price of goods during Elvis's merchandising heyday.

were willing to offer Epstein 25 per cent commission, but he pushed them no higher than 7½ per cent. The contract included an option on the next two Beatles films, as well as granting Shenson sole rights to the movie after 15 years. In fairness, the deal had been finalized long before any sign of an American breakthrough and, once again, there was no precedent to guide Brian in his calculations. Up until that time, most British films based on pop stars were poorly received, low-budget potboilers, and the amount invested by United Artists suggested that this tradition was not about to be broken. By the end of 1964, Epstein learned the hard way never to underestimate *anything* connected with the Beatles.

The Beatles' invasion of America did not prevent Epstein from fulfilling his managerial duties to other NEMS artistes. Gerry and the Pacemakers almost achieved a fourth consecutive chart-topper with the Marsden penned 'I'm The One', and throughout 1964 retained their place on the next rung down from the Beatles. They had their own equivalent of Northern Songs in the Dick James-inspired Pacermusic and although Marsden never progressed as a hit composer, his early efforts, including 'Don't Let The Sun Catch You Crying' and 'Ferry Cross The Mersey', showed considerable promise. When Gerry and the Pacemakers broke in America with a string of Top 20 hits there could be little doubt that Epstein's early promotional work had paid surprisingly impressive dividends.

Billy J. Kramer also scored a trio of American hits in 1964 and consolidated his home position with another number 1, 'Little Children'. Against his manager's wishes, Billy had insisted on recording the Pomus/Shuman composition rather than following form with another Beatles song. Brian was amused and visibly proud that his shyest protégé should rebel so successfully. However, even Kramer could not reject a follow up as perfectly tailored to his style as 'From A Window' though, surprisingly, the song failed to challenge strongly for number 1.

With the number of new pop groups appearing in the charts during 1964, it was clear that Mersey beat was no longer the only road to success. Manchester, Birmingham, London, Newcastle and other major cities were providing their own chart-topping groups, many specializing in R & B rather than the primitive backbeat so favoured by Liverpudlians. Although Gerry and Billy J. looked secure, their chart positions belied the speed with which public taste was changing. Epstein's other hit act, the Fourmost, had scored again with 'A Little Loving' but were struggling vainly for chart survival by the end of 1964. More alarmingly, the new non-Liverpool NEMS acts lacked the charisma and appeal of their predecessors and revealed the first signs of Epstein's waywardness. Cliff Bennett and the Rebel Rousers were solid enough to score a Top 10 hit with 'One Way Love' and later charted with McCartney's 'Got To Get You Into My Life', yet they could not match the image and style of their flashier contemporaries. Sounds Incorporated were essentially a session group though even they prospered briefly under Epstein's tutelage with a couple of minor hits including 'The Spartans' and 'Spanish Harlem'. By contrast, the Ruskies from Devon proved a complete commercial flop, lacking even the promotional push from NEMS. The case of Michael Haslam was even stranger. Brian had originally discovered the 24-year-old Lancashire tanner singing heart-rending ballads in a Bolton pub and immediately decided to play the svengali. Haslam fared even worse than Tommy Quickly, though, in fairness to Epstein, he was probably regarded as a long shot for chart success. In truth, Epstein was anxious to cover any new trend that might temporarily dislodge his beat groups, and the re-emergence of the solo singer always seemed likely.

Significantly, with the exception of the Beatles, Brian's most successful act of 1964 was a former Cavern Screamer turned dramatic balladeer. What he could not do with Michael Haslam or Tommy Quickly, Brian achieved with that giggly cloakroom girl whose awkward persona could not mask an inner talent. Cilla Black has been described as Epstein's one *bona fide* 'creation' but, paradoxically, his influence upon her image was always superficial. He may have helped choose her dresses, advised on make-up and complimented new hair-styles, but this feminine solicitude was held in check by a stronger desire to retain her innocence. Epstein immediately recognized that the true lasting charm of Cilla lay in the gauche, unsophisticated girl-next-door image that a less astute manager would have attempted to alter. There was nothing remotely pretentious about Cilla Black and though she was patronized for her broad scouse accent and homely manner, these were the very features that endeared her to the British public. Epstein's recognition and exploitation of that appeal was his great achievement rather than any elaborate grooming process, which would probably have failed in any case. His determination to extend Cilla's appeal was expertly executed with a much-publicized season at the London Palladium, followed by appearances in pantomime and gradual experience in other areas of traditional show business. He also took a strong interest in her recording career and, even with the pressures of Beatlemania, still found time to search for a suitable 'Cilla song' while touring the States. When he heard Dionne Warwick's 'Anyone Who Had A Heart' Brian immediately knew it was a guaranteed hit and informed George Martin of his intentions. Unfortunately, Martin concluded that the number would be better suited to Shirley Bassey, an idea that horrified Epstein. Rather than arguing with the temperamental Liverpudlian, George agreed to record the ballad with Cilla and within weeks she was number 1. Once again, Brian was proven right.

Press interest in Cilla proved unusually strong for she was the first girl singer to reach number 1 since the precocious Helen Shapiro back in 1961. The burning question of the day was whether Cilla could continue to thrive in the midst of an all-male beat group explosion. Another number 1 with the heavily orchestrated 'You're My World' rendered the question superfluous. Cilla deserved a hat trick of number 1s with the poignant Lennon/McCartney waltz-time tearjerker 'It's For You' but, like Kramer's 'From A Window', the song just reached the Top 10. 1964 ended with a cover of the Righteous Brothers' 'You've Lost That Lovin' Feelin'' and it says much for her popularity that Cilla's version challenged the Spector produced original for number 1 early the following year. For Brian, Cilla's emphatic breakthrough provided almost as much joy and satisfaction as the Beatles' US success. His achievements were now threefold: with the Beatles he had helped to create the greatest pop phenomenon of all time; with Gerry, Billy J. and others he had, at least in chart terms, surpassed Larry Parnes as a discoverer of raw talent; finally, with Cilla, he had found an all-round entertainer whose success enabled him to infiltrate more conservative show business circles.

Following the record-breaking achievements of 1964, Brian and the Beatles must have wondered whether the New Year had anything new to offer. Remarkably, the answer was yes. Fleet Street editors searched desperately for suitable headlines to convey the seemingly unbelievable news that the Beatles were to be granted Membership of the Most Excellent Order of the British Empire. Ageing colonels and indignant war veterans responded predictably by returning their medals in protest against the government's profane apotheosis of Beatlemania. The remainder of the population, by now accustomed to the concessionary show business awards in the Honours List, applauded the good sense of their Queen and Prime Minister. Few, however, noted the questionable omission of the tenacious tycoon behind the phenomenon. Surprisingly, it was Princess Margaret who uttered the pertinent and unwittingly eyebrow-raising statement: 'I think MBE must stand for Mr Brian Epstein.'

For the Beatles, an audience with the Queen could only be matched by a meeting with the King. This was arranged later in the

year when Elvis Presley played host to the Beatles at a rented house
in Los Angeles. Prior to that memorable encounter, Brian was
entertained by his fifties American counterpart, the cigar-smoking,
hard-headed, former fairground barker whose personality and
background contrasted so markedly with his own. When Colonel
Tom Parker learned about the NEMS set up he recoiled in amazement: 'I have only Elvis and he takes up all my time. How do you
do it?' Beneath the Colonel's perplexity, there lurked the lingering
criticism that Epstein was a fool for wasting precious time and
energy on lesser beings when he had already captured the gods.

Perhaps it was coincidence, but after the Parker meeting Brian
became less involved with his subsidiary artistes. He moved from
his main offices to an annexe in Stafford Street where he intended
to concentrate almost exclusively on the Beatles. With trusted
aides like Peter Brown and Geoffrey Ellis now based in London,
Brian felt confident about delegating on important matters. In
truth, he had little choice for NEMS had never stopped growing
and the work load was proving unbearable. For the press and
public, this was far from apparent. On the contrary, the sudden
decline of Gerry and Billy J. as hit acts and the chart absence of
Cilla, who was working on her token film *Work Is A Four Letter
Word*, suggested that NEMS was contracting. Brian, however,
lacked the ruthlessness of a hatchet man and could never cut away
the fat that was spreading around NEMS. By the end of 1965, the
company still controlled the affairs of those half-remembered acts
that the impetuous svengali had signed years before. The Ruskies,
the Remo Four and Tommy Quickly still pricked the conscience of
their manager sufficiently to remain a permanent fixture on his
books. Indeed, they were soon joined by the school of 1965 signings,
another bunch of young hopefuls. There were the Moody Blues,
recently departed from their charismatic manager, Tony Secunda,
and desperately searching for a record to revive their ailing chart
fortunes. In former days, Brian might well have conjured up
another 'Go Now', but the time and energy required to relaunch
the Moodies could never be found. Folk group the Silkie were a
John Lennon discovery and he produced and wrote their minor hit
Beatles' cover 'You've Got To Hide Your Love Away'. When John
moved on to more important matters the Silkie took their place in
the wasteland alongside the Ruskies and their ilk. Lennon was also
responsible for encouraging Epstein to sign Paddy, Klaus and
Gibson, a Liverpool group featuring his old friend from Hamburg,
Klaus Voormann. Brian bought out their managers, Tony Stratton-
Smith and Don Paul, but in spite of a string of singles releases
nothing happened. An almost identical fate befell Southend group

the Paramounts, who were already in decline when NEMS took up their contract. Eventually, they split and lead vocalist Gary Brooker went on to form the million-selling Procol Harum. Although several of these signings showed promise, they were essentially artistes out of time, requiring radical changes beyond the execution of their new, overworked manager. At the end of 1965, Epstein's expansionism reached new boundaries when NEMS swallowed up the Vic Lewis Agency, thereby gaining control of bookings for Matt Monro and Donovan, as well as British representation for Tony Bennett, Herb Alpert, Pat Boone, Trini Lopez, Roger Miller, Johnny Mathis and the Supremes.

Epstein's determination to spend more time on the Beatles foundered after his move to Stafford Street. His personal life was a mess, worsened by an increasing dependence on drugs. Barbiturates and amphetamines were the fuel by which he functioned but the artificial stimulation he borrowed was inevitably repaid with bouts of mild depression. His insomnia encouraged an active night-life which led inexorably to the gambling casino, where he was renowned for losing large sums of money. Often, he would appear at Stafford Street late the following afternoon having missed a call from one of the Beatles. It was a far cry from his earlier years when, according to his brother, he never gambled and was noted for his punctuality and efficiency. His nocturnal existence caused little consternation as yet, for Brian had a remarkable propensity for disguising his excesses. Occasionally, however, his self-control would snap, causing an explosive temper tantrum over some trivial incident. During a US tour the faithful Derek Taylor resigned in indignation following an unwarranted verbal attack from Brian. On another occasion, Pan Am Airways suffered the Liverpudlian's petulancy after refusing to weigh his baggage (the fact that his late arrival had caused the problem was apparently irrelevant). As he sat snugly and smugly in his first-class cabin, the autocratic idol-maker wrote a message on some notepaper which was handed to a stewardess. The note read: 'Brian Epstein will never fly Pan American again'. By the time the plane reached Kennedy Airport several worried and obsequious Pan Am representatives were waiting to apologize.

By 1966 the Beatles were more independent than ever. Their music had progressed way beyond the point where Epstein could make any relevant criticisms. Yet, he still insisted that they should perform their increasingly complex arrangements before vast audiences of screaming fans. The group resented touring, but for Brian it provided a fleeting opportunity to play the old svengali role. On this occasion, however, a series of catastrophes ensured that the Beatles would never set foot on a stage again. After a nostalgic visit to Hamburg, the group met with their first scare in Tokyo. Upon arrival, they were informed that a powerful group of militant reactionary students objected to their proposed performance at Budokan as an offence against Japanese culture. The warnings sounded absurd, but Japanese officials confided that several death threats had already been received and there was no doubt that the Beatles' lives were in some danger. In order to avoid the possibility of an international incident, the government mounted a massive security operation that left the Beatles feeling more frightened than secure. The performances passed without incident, but the harrowing experience left them wondering whether money could compensate for such intense pressure.

The next leg of the tour brought them to the Philippines. Prior to their performance in Manila, the wife of President Ferdinand Marcos despatched an invitation requesting their presence at a palace party. Brian politely declined the invitation but, unfortunately, the reply arrived too late to forestall the elaborate party preparations. Unaware of the likely repercussions, Brian stubbornly refused to reconsider, even after the British Ambassador had intervened with a special plea. Although the Beatles' concert at the Rizal Stadium was well received, subsequent television reports unleashed national fury by condemning the group for their unfriendliness and ingratitude. Ever-protective, Brian rushed to the television station and attempted to broadcast a convincing explanation and sincere apology. Unfortunately, his words were rendered inaudible by heavy static and the message was not properly conveyed. The following morning the newspaper headline 'Beatles Snub President' confirmed that the group was in great mortal danger. The thriller in Manila ended with a near riot during which the group were kicked, punched and verbally abused by angry, patriotic citizens. Lennon was particularly annoyed by the incident and hinted that he might never tour again. Epstein, meanwhile, was riddled with feelings of guilt for needlessly having endangered his boys' lives. Nor was this the last dramatic episode in this most bizarre series of events.

It seemed as though the Fates were systematically plotting the destruction of the once-invincible entrepreneur. Within weeks of the Manila incident, Brian received news that Beatles records were being ceremoniously burned in the redneck Southern states of America. Overnight, the group had become the objects of a witch hunt unparalleled in pop history. The cause of the furore was to be located in an interview John Lennon had given to the *Evening Standard* several months before. During a discussion on the spiritual impoverishment of the modern age, John had casually remarked: 'Christianity will go. It will go. It will vanish and shrink. I needn't argue about that. I'm right and I will be proved right. We are more popular than Jesus now. I don't know which will go first — rock 'n' roll or Christianity'. Such blasphemy went unnoticed in Britain, but when John's words were reprinted in the inappropriate setting of an American teenzine, all hell broke loose. Death threats, ritual burning of Beatles records, the shearing of teenagers' hair and a massed campaign by members of the Ku Klux Klan were just some of the highlights. With a major US tour looming, Brian was justifiably mortified. He flew to America at the earliest opportunity and in a fit of near panic threatened to cancel the tour, even if it meant forking out a million dollars of his own money. Eventually, Nat Weiss persuaded him to arrange a press conference in order to explain the 'misunderstanding'. After considerable arm-twisting, John Lennon agreed to meet his media aggressors and under some duress apologized to all god-fearing Americans. His retraction assuaged the moral majority but the lunatic fringe was still seething. For the first time in their history, the Beatles were no longer heroes in America. Amid the screaming fans, there were some hostile faces, an ever-present reminder that it took just one unbalanced religious fanatic armed with a handgun to end the Beatles legend. During a concert in Memphis, the group was harangued by Ku Klux Klansmen and mid-way through their short set, a firecracker exploded on the stage. The Beatles were visibly shaken by the incident and Epstein was still suffering palpitations as they set out for the next date.

In Cincinnati, an open-air concert was postponed at the eleventh hour when rain literally stopped play. Thousands of frantic teenagers were forced to restrain their Beatlemania until the rescheduled performance the following day. Back at their hotel, the tension caused McCartney to throw up. By the time they reached Candlestick Park, San Francisco, on 29 August, Brian knew that the Beatles were finished as a performing group. He also realized that his special relationship with the boys would never be the same without the spirit of camaraderie produced by life on the road. Ironically, the nightmare tour ended with Epstein missing the group's final performance. Even while they waved their audience goodbye, Brian was anxiously trying to placate a predatory former boyfriend who had stolen his briefcase and was threatening to reveal the contents to the press. This Pandora's box included a phial of pills and some correspondence allegedly implicating Brian in a homosexual liaison; the possible repercussions of the publicity were almost too horrible to contemplate. Not long after this incident,

Epstein attempted suicide, leaving a bedside note that summed up the futility of his present existence: 'This is all too much and I can't take anymore'.

The effects of homosexuality on Brian's life and work have provoked considerable comment. In almost every Beatles biography lurid tales of illicit liaisons are pinpointed as the key to Epstein's despair, drug use and escapist nocturnal existence. Although these conclusions may well be correct, they invariably tend to present Epstein in doomed isolation, almost as though he were a furtive, solitary, social outcast. Yet Brian was merely one of many epicure pop managers from the period and quite a number of his show business friends and associates shared his sexual preferences. Since most of these figures are still alive, their personal lives have never received the public scrutiny to which the hapless Beatles manager has been subjected. Suffice to say, they too risked their public reputation as well as the violence and blackmail threats that make Epstein's existence sound so sordid and exceptional. Judged within the context of that insular homosexual show business community, Epstein was far from unique except perhaps in the degree of introspection to which he subjected himself. Whether his private hell was any worse than that of his apparently more stable contemporaries remains a pertinent question.

While the Beatles spent the winter of 1966 pursuing individual interests, Brian thought long and hard about his future. He seemed determined to prove that there was life beyond the Fab Four and buried himself in a series of distracting and largely unprofitable ventures. Ever since 1964, he had dreamed of combining his twin interests in pop and theatre. That year, he had booked a series of groups at the Prince of Wales Theatre, Piccadilly Circus, but poor attendances resulted in staggering losses. Undeterred, he then involved himself in the proposed construction of a theatre and recording studio in the unlikely area of Bromley, Kent. His partner in the scheme, disc jockey Brian Matthew, claims that the project foundered due to objections from 'enemies on the local council'. The following year, Epstein bought the fashionable Savile Theatre in Shaftesbury Avenue and announced his intention of alternating serious drama with Sunday pop shows. The first production under Brian's ownership was the London première of James Baldwin's *The Amen Corner* which gained considerable publicity, but mixed reviews. It was the pop concerts, however, that attracted the bright young things from Chelsea whom Brian so loved to have under his spell. Generally, the acts reflected Epstein's eclectic tastes and personal whims: Chuck Berry, Fats Domino, the Four Tops, the Fourmost, Julie Felix and Cream. Fashionable London descended upon the Savile in droves and sat like obedient subjects gazing up at the magisterial young entrepreneur in the Royal Box. Often, a Beatle would be seated alongside Brian, which was reason enough for him to suffer the financial losses incurred by his importation of highly paid American artistes. For a time, Brian enjoyed the fame and glory, but his ego was bruised following an incident during Chuck Berry's appearance in early 1967. Two excited teenagers climbed on to the stage during the climax of his performance, prompting officials to lower the curtain prematurely. Hundreds of disappointed fans mounted a demonstration and heaped verbal abuse on Epstein, still seated in the Royal Box. Brian was acutely embarrassed and furious beyond words. His wrath descended on the unfortunate House Manager, Michael Bullock, who was immediately dismissed. This childish tantrum later backfired on Epstein when the National Association of Television and Kine Employees called their members out on strike over the 'irresponsible attack' on the hapless House Manager. Another happy dream had ended in disappointment and frustration.

Epstein's surge of creativity continued in ever-puzzling detours, including the sponsorship of an Anglo-Spanish bullfighter, Henry Higgins. Brian even attempted to persuade Billy J. Kramer to embark on an acting career, but the poor boy was petrified at the thought: 'I felt if I was uptight about appearing on *Ready Steady Go* and miming to records, what chance did I have in the acting field?' Instead, Billy continued singing with the Dakotas, eagerly awaiting the following year when his NEMS contract could be renegotiated. Although Brian had been neglecting Billy's career of late, both parties were looking forward to a relaunch following the new contract. Kramer claims that Epstein promised a new backing group, fresh material and a more contemporary image, but any long-term commitments seemed less likely for NEMS was rapidly losing its image as a highly-personalized family business.

The multifarious activities of NEMS had long since ceased to absorb Epstein, who privately expressed a desire to be rid of the company, retaining interests only in the Beatles and Cilla Black. Several wealthy entrepreneurs had already expressed interest in acquiring NEMS, but the exclusion of the Beatles quickly put paid to any serious offers. It soon transpired, however, that even if Epstein could not secure a firm eight-figure offer he was still willing to surrender his empire for a far smaller sum, given the right terms. The man whom Brian finally decided to offer a 51 per cent controlling interest in his company seemed a strangely inappropriate choice for such a prestigious position.

Robert Stigwood was an Australian adventurer who had settled in England and set up a theatrical agency. When one of his clients, John Leyton, hit number 1 with 'Johnny Remember Me', Stigwood branched out into management. Soon, he was into music publishing, concert promotion and independent record production, emulating the entrepreneurial expansionism of vintage Larry Parnes. Unfortunately, his inexperience and over-ambitious streak proved his undoing, and eventually Stigwood plummetted into bankruptcy. In spite of his disastrous history, Epstein was impressed by Stigwood's great flair and imagination. Such was his faith in Stigwood and his new partner, ex-city financier David Shaw, that Brian offered them a controlling interest in NEMS for the astonishingly low figure of £500 000. In spite of all his recent setbacks, the tenacious Australian knew his luck had returned.

Although the Stigwood deal suggested otherwise, Epstein was still in control of his business faculties at the beginning of 1967. In January, he renegotiated the Beatles' recording deal with EMI, wisely rejecting a nine-year contract for fear that the group might stop recording and find themselves trapped in a situation where they owed the record company product but were unable to deliver. Instead, a five-year contract was concluded requiring the completion of a number of songs which the Beatles could easily deliver long before the allocated deadline. Brian was even more pushy on the thorny question of the Beatles' royalty rate, and secured a deal revolutionary for the period. In Britain, the group's remuneration was raised to 10 per cent on singles and albums, rising to 15 per cent on sales in excess of 10 000 and 30 000 respectively. In America, the rising royalty rate was increased to a staggering 17½ per cent. Even EMI director Leonard Wood was moved to remark, 'It was a stiff deal'.

While the Beatles released their finest double A-side, 'Strawberry Fields Forever'/'Penny Lane', and forged ahead with work on the epoch-making *Sgt Pepper's Lonely Hearts Club Band*, Brian was still devising new management strategies. In April, he flew to America and arranged an extraordinary meeting at New York's Waldorf Hotel attended by himself, Robert Stigwood, Sid Bernstein and Nat Weiss. Brian had already formed Nemperor Artistes with Nat to supervise the activities of NEMS artistes in America and was now hoping to create a transatlantic quadruplicate management structure. Stigwood had recently brought the Bee Gees and Cream to NEMS while Weiss had found the million-selling Cyrkle. All that was required from Bernstein was the Rascals and Blues Project, in return for which Brian would throw in all his artistes bar the Beatles. After some consideration, Bernstein turned down this remarkable offer. His reasoning may seem astonishing today, but at that point few of the NEMS artistes were world-beaters and their potential looked uncertain to the cautious American.

In spite of his grand designs, Brian was struggling against an increasing drug habit that threatened to propel him into a nervous breakdown. For a time, he seemed in control of his self-abused body, but the lethal combination of uppers and downers was shortly to take its toll. By the time Brian left America, he was in poor psychological shape. On the way to the airport he became extremely morbid and insisted that the plane was destined to crash. According to Weiss and Brown, Epstein was habitually making dramatic predictions, many of which had an unfortunate tendency of proving correct. Before boarding the plane, Brian passed a note to Weiss which read: 'Brown paper jackets for *Sgt Pepper's Lonely Hearts Club Band*'. The message reveals a great deal about Epstein. Here he was, his life flashing before his eyes and all he could focus on was the remote fear that the Beatles might be sued for including a montage of famous personalities on their album jacket. Even on the brink of a nervous breakdown, his devotion to the Fab Four was all-consuming.

Within a month of returning to London, Brian entered a private clinic in Putney. Doctors diagnosed his condition as a combination of depression, stress and physical exhaustion, aggravated by insomnia. Brian had become a modern day Henry IV, riddled with anxiety about the future of his realm and unable to enjoy the soothing sleep granted to even the poorest of his subjects. Eventually, he was drugged into a week-long sleep and fed intravenously. The treatment was partially successful, but could not rid Brian of negative thoughts about his future as Beatles manager. Their contract was due to end within four months and all discussion on the matter had been diplomatically avoided. In Brian's mind, this was reason enough to suspect the worst. Rather fittingly, he confided his fears to the monarch whose golden reign had preceded his own. Like a father confessor, Larry Parnes sat at his bedside, offering spiritual comfort and guidance:

> Brian was very ill. He told me that the contract was coming to an end and he understood the boys were going to leave him because another man was taking over. My answer to Brian was, 'I could never see the boys leaving you. Ever. I think you're depressed over nothing.'

After leaving the clinic, Brian managed to place his worries in a clearer perspective. In his own mind, his most severe critic was Paul McCartney, yet for all their past differences, many noted that they had drawn closer during recent months. When Paul was pilloried by the media for admitting that he had taken LSD, Brian stepped forward and risked his own reputation by supporting the remarks of his artiste. Interviewed in *Queen*, he invoked a counter-culture vision of hippy utopianism: 'There is a new mood in the country and it has originated through hallucinatory drugs. I am wholeheartedly on its side.' It was a selfless but reckless remark that unleashed a torrent of criticism from every conceivable quarter. Newspaper editors, church leaders, public shareholders of Northern Songs and even MPs in the House of Commons voiced concern over Epstein's 'irresponsible' remarks, yet neither he nor the Beatles were subjected to police harassment. In truth, the most serious threat to his future as Beatles' manager came less from misguided statements to the press than the excessive lifestyle that had already taken its toll on his health and led to two suicide attempts.

By July 1967, the physical and psychological pressures that threatened to wreck Brian's career were alleviated by the tragic news of his father's death. Suddenly, his own depression was rendered inconsequential in comparison to his mother's bereavement and he showed no hesitation in offering moral support. Shortly after the funeral, Brian wrote a revealing letter to Nat Weiss:

> I'm coming to New York on 2 September. I'd have come earlier but my father's passing has given me the added responsibility of mother. The week of *Shiva* is up tonight and I feel a bit strange. Probably good for me in a way; time to think and note that at least now I'm really needed by mother. Also time to note that the unworldly Jewish circle of my parents' and brother's friends is not so bad. Provincial maybe, but warm, sincere and basic.

The contemplative tone could not disguise Brian's determination to put his life in order and a programme of reform was undertaken upon his return to London. With Queenie by his side, Brian suddenly seemed capable of working a normal 9 to 5 office day and no longer whiled away the early hours in gaming casinos or all-night clubs. Duties that he had previously shirked were attended to with a solicitude reminiscent of the old Brian. He successfully reconciled his differences with Cilla Black, who had been far from enamoured with Stigwood and somewhat alienated by her manager's protestations in favour of LSD. There were strong rumours that she intended to leave NEMS, but her will dissolved when Brian begged her to stay. Suddenly, he was organizing her affairs with real gusto, even insisting that she take a well-earned holiday. With svengali punctiliousness, he appeared unexpectedly on the day of her departure and while ushering her into an empty railway carriage announced that she would be soon appearing in a major television series. Cilla was astonished. Brian had always dissuaded her from considering television work, but now he felt that the time was right. His decision was to prove remarkably astute for the following spring *The Cilla Black Show* received critical plaudits and, soon after, its star was named Television Personality of the Year.

The extent of Epstein's spiritual revival was further revealed in a series of interviews with *Melody Maker*'s Mike Hennessey. Gone was the furtive, guilt-ridden depressive so often characterized by Beatles biographers. Instead, Epstein emerged as uncharacteristically confident and forthright in his views and feelings. His argument in favour of legalizing marijuana was presented persuasively, without resorting to hippy proselytizing. On that old bugbear LSD, Brian conceded that he had taken a calculated risk in experimenting with the drug but added, 'I think LSD helped me to know myself better and I think it helped me to become less bad-tempered'. Even more surprisingly, Brian himself brought up the subject of homosexuality and championed the forthcoming 1967 reform bill: 'Isn't it silly that we have had to wait all this time for the legislation to go through'. Other personal subjects were glossed over with considerable frankness; Brian confessed that he would probably never marry; that he had contemplated suicide 'but I think I've got over that period now', and admitted that his greatest fear was loneliness. Further clues of a growing self-realization were provided in occasional asides: 'I hope I'll never be lonely. Although, actually, one inflicts loneliness on oneself to a certain extent.' Inevitably, the questions eventually centred on Epstein's relationship with the Beatles, and the response was unambiguously positive:

> The manager-artiste relationship is one of mutual dependence and one of the most perfect relationships there has ever been, in my experience, is that which exists between the Beatles and myself. If I'd been domineering or dictatorial they would never have accepted me and it would all have gone wrong. You have to allow for freedom. You can easily be cut down to size in certain circumstances and you realize that humility is very important.

Indeed, Epstein spoke as though humility was a recently-discovered virtue and effectively summed up his managerial career in a few poignant words: 'I have done what I can and will continue to do so. People who criticize me may have a point and may be sincere — but it doesn't really matter what they say. I know I have done my best.'

The final chapter of Epstein's candid interview was run on 21

August. Once more, Brian stressed that his friendship with the
Beatles was still strong and revealed that they were intending to
produce a film version of *Sgt Pepper's Lonely Hearts Club Band*.[1]
One question that could not be avoided was the possible termination
of the Beatles' management contract in two months time. Far from
showing concern or slight doubt, Brian appeared almost blasé
about the subject:

> I don't think they mind how long I sign them for; a contract doesn't
> mean much unless you can work and be happy together. And I am
> certain that they would not agree to be managed by anyone else. Most
> of the time we think in the same direction anyway.

Interestingly, Clive Epstein confirms that Brian was thinking in
terms of continuing with the Beatles without a formal contract,
which would probably have meant a reduction in management
commission. He had, at least, assuaged his greatest fear that the
group would abandon him in favour of another high-powered
entrepreneur.

On 21 August, Queenie Epstein returned to Liverpool, leaving
Brian alone once more. Two days later he wrote an extremely
optimistic letter to Nat Weiss, expressing his enthusiasm for the
forthcoming American visit. Weiss was requested to arrange a
yachting trip in New York and ensure that a number of famous
friends were available to meet Brian during his East and West
Coast sojourns. Further enthusiasm was expressed for a proposed
visit to Toronto where the Beatles' manager intended to continue
his extra-curricular creative activities by hosting a series of television
variety shows. The letter ended with a chirpy positivism, suggesting
that Epstein's worst days were behind him: 'Till the 2nd, love,
flowers, bells, be happy and look forward to the future. With love,
Brian.' Four days later Brian Epstein was dead.

The Beatles and their manager had gone their separate ways on the
August Bank Holiday weekend. Accompanied by the Maharishi
Mahesh Yogi, the group and their entourage set off for Bangor,
North Wales, to attend a course in transcendental meditation

---

[1] The *Sgt Pepper's Lonely Hearts Club Band* film was never pursued by the Beatles.
Ironically, Robert Stigwood revived the idea over a decade later, casting the Bee
Gees in the central role. Epstein was probably turning in his grave, for he loathed
the Bee Gees and was particularly annoyed at the premature comparisons between
them and the Beatles during 1967. Unlike Stigwood's other cinematic efforts,
Sgt Pepper's was not a box-office success.

which would prompt the recently maligned McCartney to announce that he had given up drugs. Brian, meanwhile, decided to spend some time at his country house in Kingsley Hill. On the Friday evening, he entertained NEMS employees Peter Brown and Geoffrey Ellis, but their conversation was not scintillating enough to restrain his wanderlust and by the early hours of Saturday morning he was back in London. The following afternoon, Brian rang them and arranged to return to Kingsley Hill by train. He never arrived. By late Sunday morning his butler and maid were worried by their employer's non-appearance and apparent inability to answer the house intercom. A series of phone calls brought Epstein's personal assistants Alistair Taylor and Joanne Newfield to Chapel Street, but still there was an ominous silence behind the doors of Brian's bedroom. Soon after, a doctor arrived and the assembled company agreed to risk incurring Epstein's wrath by breaking down the doors. Inside, they discovered the body of their employer lying on his side surrounded by remnants of the previous morning's mail. The inquest, 12 days later, found that he had died from a cumulative overdose of the drug Carbitrol. He had become so used to administering sleep-inducing drugs into his tired body that sensible precautions regarding intake were not strictly followed. The coroner concluded the proceedings with a verdict of accidental death from 'incautious self-overdoses'.

Over the years several alternative theories have been put forward to explain Brian's death, the most common being suicide. However, Epstein's psychological upswing in the weeks prior to his death and the extremely optimistic letter to Nat Weiss of 23 August suggest otherwise. Philip Norman has posited a further theory that the pop mogul may have been the victim of foul play. Indeed, he goes as far as to connect Epstein's death with that of his solicitor, David Jacobs, who was found hanged the following year. Was it possible that both had been assassinated for their part in the Seltaeb fiasco which had inadvertently crippled many American financiers? It all sounds like a highly imaginative plot from a detective story, yet the number of people that believe these rumours is surprising and a little disconcerting. Even the sober-blooded Larry Parnes supports the foul play theory, though he does not connect Brian's death with the Seltaeb dispute. Parnes maintains that Brian unwittingly courted danger by hoarding ridiculously large sums of money in his house. Interestingly, Peter Brown has recently revealed that Epstein skimmed off thousands of dollars from Beatles concerts in 'paper-bag money', so it is not so unlikely that the entrepreneur would habitually continue to amass wads of bank notes later in his career. If the low-life characters that occasionally entered his orbit were aware of the existence of such sums then foul play was not out of the question. Intriguing as these theories are, however, there is no hard evidence available to contest the coroner's findings and an 'accidental overdose' remains the most likely cause of death.

The death of Epstein inevitably provoked speculation about the future of NEMS. Robert Stigwood still intended to exercise his option to buy the company, but met strong resistance from the Beatles and others. Under pressure, Clive Epstein decided that it would be politic to offer the Australian a golden handshake rather than suffer further internal company friction. Although Brian came to regret the recruitment of Stigwood to NEMS, Clive was sorry to see him leave:

> Naturally, I was disappointed that we couldn't keep Stigwood in the company after Brian died because I believe he had the flair and ability to make things move. But a lot of people were putting words in my ear. I knew the Beatles didn't really want Stigwood to be part of NEMS. But if you think about it, one of Brian's major contributions to NEMS was bringing Stigwood in. Just suppose where Stigwood might have taken NEMS if we hadn't extinguished that option — where he took himself.

When Stigwood left NEMS he was accompanied by the Bee Gees, Cream and the Foundations and, soon afterwards, set up his own organization, which achieved considerable success. The nomadic Australian later moved to America and stunned the world during the late seventies by transforming the anachronistic Bee Gees into one of popular music's biggest-selling acts. His involvement in films and musicals also produced phenomenal box-office receipts and album sales with *Grease* and *Saturday Night Fever*. It is no wonder that the younger Epstein muses on what might have been. Of course, the remarkable swings of fortune in Stigwood's career reveal the thin line between prosperity and bankruptcy. It is quite plausible that he might have been a failure had he stayed with NEMS, rather than the great Australian/American pop mogul.

The effect of Brian's death on the Beatles was long-range rather than short-term. At first, they were reduced to stasis by the shock and Lennon later admitted: 'I knew we were in trouble. I thought, "We've had it"'. The numbness soon passed, however, and the Beatles concluded that they no longer required a manager in the proprietorial sense; they decided to manage themselves. Initially, they enjoyed the challenge and found to their surprise that it was remarkably easy. What the Beatles were really experiencing, however, was the deceptive aftermath of Epstein's five-year tenure.

Like a famous football team that suddenly loses its inspirational coach, the Beatles played on for a season, still astonishing their fans and themselves by the high quality of their performance. Their confidence was such that they failed to realize the implications of the growing dissension between them or the vast amounts of money lost in overambitious idealistic ventures. Bereft of Epstein's vigilance, the Beatles fell victim to their own egos and demonstrated a profound fallibility as businessmen. The successive losses of NEMS and Northern Songs and the battle royal between Allen Klein and the Eastmans systematically demythologized the Beatles. Even in defeat, however, they were still capable of exerting influence on the future of British pop management. The publicity surrounding their association with Allen Klein was largely responsible for the unprecedented influx of accountants and solicitors into rock management during the late sixties and early seventies. Klein, at least, had flair, but most of his followers were dull and unimaginative. The downfall of the Fab Four coincided with the death of the charismatic manager, thereby ensuring that there would be no new Beatles or Rolling Stones during the seventies.

One question remains. Was Epstein the greatest manager in British pop history? The answer largely depends on what one considers the characteristics of great management. As a financier, Epstein was certainly flawed, though even here his faults have been greatly exaggerated. The 'poor' record and film royalties that he negotiated for the Beatles have frequently produced accusations of naïveté and provincial-mindedness. Judged in the context of his time, however, he was no worse than most other British pop managers and subject to the same lousy deals offered by the powers of the day. As he grew wiser in the business, Epstein became noticeably tougher, though he never fully exploited the Beatles' vast earning power. He could easily have involved them in dubious tax schemes and short-term financial investments, but he valued their reputation above everything else. In this respect, Epstein was a great manager for he understood that the Beatles were no ordinary run-of-the-mill pop group but an entertainment phenomenon. He protected them and their public from the corporate avarice that destroyed many lesser groups during his era. Thus, the world was saved from such horrors as cheap and nasty Beatles compilation albums, all of which would have increased their short-term income but undermined their status as a quality group. While Brian survived, the Beatles lived like kings, but never gave the impression that they were particularly interested in money. Such security came largely from the protective wall that their manager built around them.

It is unfortunate that Epstein has so frequently been judged by economic standards alone since, in comparison to the great American manager, Colonel Tom Parker, his financial coups inevitably seem tame. Yet, in other respects, his entrepreneurial vision almost equalled that of the old fairground huckster. Parker was famous for turning down offers of a million dollars for Elvis, but his reasoning was always that the boy was worth more. He was quite willing to pander to the lowest common denominator of taste by putting Elvis through a decade of bad movies, safe in the knowledge that he had secured a foolproof deal and financial killing. For all the dollar earnings, Elvis's sixties recordings and films are a sad reminder of unrealized potential. Parker was indisputably brilliant at marketing, publicity and every aspect of business negotiation, but Epstein was more successful at reconciling the art versus money dichotomy. Judged on percentage points alone, the Beatles' manager seems like a novice beside the Colonel, but it is not easy to put a price tag on the public respect and artistic reputation that Brian helped his protégés achieve. What scale can measure the dreams of a generation?

In historical terms, Epstein's reign initiated the creative managerial explosion of the mid-sixties. He was the great empire-builder of pop, whose expansionism even surpassed Larry Parnes. Epstein's phenomenal success during the 1963-4 period inspired a legion of younger, flashier swinging sixties tycoons who took the history of pop management into its next phase. Andrew Oldham, Larry Page, Simon Napier-Bell and others were not content to control their artistes' images and business affairs, but moved into the recording studio to produce their discs, thereby influencing the art as well as the artiste. The golden age of the charismatic pop manager coincided with Epstein's rise and would continue until the end of the sixties.

The unlikely rise of Lenny Davies from a luckless early school-leaver to one of Britain's most powerful pop entrepreneurs is one of the great success stories of the sixties. Born in Hayes, Middlesex, Davies followed the lead of most local working-class lads by joining the nearby EMI factory. There he worked as a packer, an unchallenging job that allowed the teenager to fantasize about more exotic lifestyles. By the time Elvis became a household name with 'Heartbreak Hotel', Davies's dreams of stardom were about to be tested. The ambitious youngster auditioned for EMI as a singer and to everyone's surprise, he passed. Seeking a more professional name for recording purposes, Lenny remembered Larry Parks, the star of *The Jolson Story*, and henceforth became known as Larry Page.

In spite of his youth, Page was canny enough not to be swept off his feet by a recording contract. Even after his debut disc was released, he continued working at the EMI factory, occasionally packing his own records as they whisked by on a conveyor belt. Page did not remain unknown for long. His fame spread thanks to the intervention of Jack Bentley, the renowned show business columnist of the *Sunday Mirror*. Larry recalls their first meeting with some amusement:

> He came up to me convinced that I was the best man at Tommy Steele's wedding [Steele was not yet married but the Press were anxious for a scoop]. He came down to see me at Reading and it was all very heavy — 'Now I know Tommy's married. I can either make or break you'. It scared the bloody pants off me because it was a real threat job. I said I knew nothing about it.

Bentley failed to get his Tommy Steele scoop, but he was kind enough to write a feature extolling the virtues of another young talent whom he dubbed 'Larry Page — the Teenage Rage'.

The Teenage Rage lived up to his name and before long his exploits were attracting considerable press coverage. The dearth of homegrown teenage talent in fifties Britain encouraged the media to latch on to any aspiring star capable of providing good copy. Pop stars were treated like adolescent gods whose virility seemed inextricably linked with their bachelorhood: the cardinal sin was marriage. Like several of his contemporaries, including Tommy Steele, Marty Wilde and Terry Dene, Page discovered that one human interest story could create greater attention than a number 1 hit. When Larry boldly announced his engagement to a young fan following a whirlwind eight-hour romance, the phone never stopped ringing. His marriage at Caxton Hall was attended by a posse of journalists and made front page news in the national press. The exposure was incredible. Even Mrs May Davies contributed to the drama by threatening to boycott the wedding on the grounds that the couple were too young. Naturally, she relented at the last minute. When the marriage later hit troubled waters Larry was in the news again, addressing full-scale press conferences for the most melodramatic pop star feature since the saga of Terry Dene and Edna Savage.

Apart from his marital status, the media displayed an inordinate interest in the colour of Larry's hair. 'What the hell was he doing appearing on stage with blue-rinsed locks?' was the big question of the day. Like many pop star images, it was the result of a happy accident. During rehearsals for a television show, the make-up department noticed that the floor lighting exaggerated the fairness of his hair, so he was dragged off for a dark tint. Following the show, Larry was due to appear at the Granada, Walthamstow, and his schedule was so tight that there was no time to rinse out the dye. Under the harsh theatre lights, the blue tint was accentuated and within hours of the show Larry's latest 'outrage' was a subject of great gossip among pop pundits. The press went as far as fabricating a feud between the blue-rinsed Larry Page and the orange-haired Wee Willie Harris. It was slapstick rock 'n' roll comedy at its best and the press loved it all.

In spite of all the media exposure, Larry failed to crack the charts with a sizeable hit. Like Vince Eager and the second battalion of Parnes' teen idols, Page appeared on a number of top-rated television and radio programmes but his recordings were generally unimpressive. Page was an anodyne rocker and monotone crooner whom Bruce Welch of the Shadows later described as 'the worst singer I ever heard in my life'. Larry admits that most of his discs were 'terrible', but there was one song that he was particularly pleased about recording before any of his rivals:

In those days you had no control over what you were doing. My producer said, 'I've found this song, "That'll Be The Day". It won't be released in this country because it's terrible. We're going to record it'. The backing was Geoff Love and his Orchestra and the Rita Williams Singers. It was the biggest load of crap you ever heard. But I was the first person in Britain to cover a Buddy Holly song and I had the opportunity of meeting him when he was over, which was great.

Unlike many of his contemporaneous teen idols, Page was astute enough to realize that his professional singing career would not survive the fifties. His manager, Maurice King, who later handled the Walker Brothers, was a tough professional, but unadventurous in comparison to Parnes. Page spent a lot of time in and around Denmark Street, where many small-time managers, not governed by Parnes' integrity, sought short-term profits from gauche teen idols:

> I never really found a manager who did the job for me. All the television I got myself, recording contracts, everything. I think managers were of the opinion that artistes were the enemy and that's how they should be treated. You could be sent out to buy a dozen suits from 'Mr X' and straightaway you'd have a hefty bill against your account. That seemed to be the way to work, to keep you in debt all the time. As long as you were in debt you were under the thumb.

Although Page was never fleeced, he made little money from singing and grew tired of hearing the phrase 'This is the glory!' as an excuse for poor pay. As the fifties wound to a close, Larry decided to retire from the pop business and moved to Wales where he managed a pub.

The former Teenage Rage rapidly became bored with the quiet life and was easily won back into the entertainment business by the garrulous Eric Morley of Mecca Enterprises. Mecca was busy converting dying cinemas and theatres into a network of ballrooms and Page was hired as a consultant manager. Essentially, his job was to select a suitable venue and spend three months working on a relaunch. If the results were profitable, Mecca poured further money into the scheme. Inevitably, Page found himself surrounded by young singers attempting to secure bookings at the ballroom and this precipitated his involvement in pop management. Word soon spread in music business circles that Page was establishing himself as a talent spotter with considerable flair and business acumen. Before long, his Coventry ballroom was besieged by several of the most influential producers, pop moguls and music publishers of the early sixties. Phil Solomon and Eddie Kassner virtually fell over each other in their attempts to entice the former pop star back to London. After considering a number of tempting offers, Larry decided to throw in his lot with music publisher Eddie Kassner. The decision was eminently logical. With Kassner spending most of his time in the States, Page was certain that the executive power of which he dreamed would not be diluted by the overbearing presence of an elder partner. A company named Denmark

Productions was formed, allowing Page to select and manage artistes in return for passing the publishing rights over to Kassner.

Before leaving Coventry, Page was responsible for launching several minor-league artistes, any one of whom might have hit the charts with better luck and the right song. Johnny B. Great (Johnny Goodison) was a club favourite who appeared on many major pop tours before emerging as a successful songwriter in the seventies, penning the Brotherhood of Man's 'United We Stand' and several minor hits. Shel Naylor recorded several tracks with producer Shel Talmy, including a vocal version of Dave Davies's 'One Fine Day', but it was not until 1972 that he finally hit the top as a member of Lieutenant Pigeon ('Mouldy Old Dough'). Perhaps Page's oddest discovery from this period was the Orchids, a trio of pre-pubescent Liverpool girls, who had to be seen to be believed. Their publicity photos made the most of their puppy fat, dour school uniforms and love of ice lollies. Shel Talmy pulled out all the stops in the studio in an attempt to establish the sound of these white underripe Ronettes, but the public refused to accept the bait.

Page named his girl group after Coventry's Orchid Ballroom, a venue where he frequently hosted talent contests in search of undiscovered stars. One hopeful candidate was an Irishman, fresh from the Bayswater Community Pioneer Band. Dick Hayes took on all-comers at Coventry and looked set for stardom when he won first prize in Page's knockout talent show — a five-year recording contract with Decca. After signing with Denmark Productions, Hayes underwent a name change and emerged as Little Lenny Davis. It was over 20 years later before he finally discovered that he had been named after his own manager! Page's attempt to recreate himself in microcosm was an extraordinary move, typical of a man who would later attempt to rewrite his own history. The rechristening was partly a private jest, but Hayes was never allowed to appreciate this irony as a successful artiste. After recording one single, 'Little Schoolgirl', and auditioning for Ready Steady Go, the career of Little Lenny Davis was all but forgotten. The follow up, 'Tomboy', was recorded as a demo but never released. Unfortunately, Page was far too busy concentrating on more important projects to spend time administering the career affairs of his young charge. It is not difficult to see why. By 1964, Hayes was a pop artiste out of time. His repertoire of ballads and old hits by Ricky Nelson, Cliff Richard, Pat Boone and Neil Sedaka seemed decidedly passé in the context of the all-consuming beat boom. Disappointed at missing his one chance of pop glory, Little Lenny Davis returned to Waterford where he cashed in on his 'recording artiste' status by forming the ironically titled Dick and the Decca. Eventually, he secured a job in a factory, thereby re-enacting his manager's career in chronological reverse.

Page, meanwhile, had found the pop group that would secure his reputation as one of the greatest managers of the mid-sixties. The Ravens were a north London pub group, lately discovered by a society gentleman, Robert Wace, who briefly sang with them before assuming management responsibilities. In partnership with a stockbroker friend, Grenville Collins, he secured the group several dates playing society functions, and then sought the services of an experienced music business specialist. That person was Larry Page, who agreed to take the group on for a 10 per cent management commission plus the placing rights on their musical compositions. The rechristened Kinks now had three managers with contrasting personalities, backgrounds and experience.[1] In one sense, this dilution of power offered the possibility of democratic leadership, but the individual parties would find it difficult to accept each other as equals.

The influence that Page exerted over the Kinks during 1964 was considerable. In an attempt to emulate the success of the anti-authoritarian Rolling Stones, Larry encouraged the boys to exude aggression and sexuality onstage, an image that was reinforced by their new name and a photo session in which they were shown in black leather shamelessly brandishing riding whips. The shock tactics proved effective and later in the year the group received considerable publicity following an appearance at Basildon New Town, Essex, where over a thousand teenagers invaded the Locarno Ballroom stage in an unexpected outbreak of fan hysteria. In the background, Page enjoyed his role as image consultant, eagerly instructing the boys to use their guitars as phallic symbols in order to exaggerate their 'kinkiness'.

Long before the Kinks' image had been formulated, Page paid particular attention to their all-important development as a musical group, pushing Ray Davies into the spotlight as a singer and songwriter. Long discussions ensued during which the fifties pop star lectured his young charge on the importance of simple, straightforward guitar riffs as a blueprint for hit success. Together, they worked on an instrumental number, 'Revenge', which served as a prototype for many of the musical ideas that followed. Davies continued to search for distinctive riffs, finally breaking through

---

[1] This notion of Page and Wace as mirror opposites was even reflected in the naming of their respective companies. Denmark Productions took its title from Denmark Street, the seedy Tin Pan Alley area of Soho where Page and Kassner rented offices. Wace and Collins registered their company as Boscobel Productions, after Boscobel Place in Knightsbridge where Robert was living.

with three massive sellers: 'You Really Got Me', 'All Day And All Of The Night' and 'Tired Of Waiting For You'. Within 12 months of Page's appointment, the Kinks were the third most successful pop group in Britain and their earnings had rocketed to an astonishing £90 000-a-year.

If the Kinks assimilated the creative ideas of Larry Page, then they also inherited his love of political intrigue. Most commentators have interpreted the group's general unruliness as a product of sibling rivalry, but surely it was much more than this. There is no evidence to suggest that the Ravens were ever troubled by violent conflict, but as soon as the Kinks were christened and the tripartite management agreement signed, tension increased and multiplied. The Davies brothers not only bickered among themselves, but frequently united in order to wage war on their scapegoat drummer. The much abused Mick Avory was both peacemaker and whipping boy, an unfortunate victim whose self-respect was somehow salvaged by the belief that his tolerance and humility alone could short-circuit impending group disasters. As roadie Sam Curtis percep-tively noted: 'You could insult him and treat him like dirt and it still didn't matter. He would just tolerate it.'

But to what extent were these rivalries within the group the product of a far greater conflict over which they had much less control? Robert Wace maintains that there were managerial differences of opinion as early as the first Kinks hit: 'Suddenly, everybody was jumping on the bandwagon. Larry Page jockeying for position . . . If we hadn't got rid of Larry Page, the Kinks would have been finished. It was either him or them.' Not surprisingly, Larry Page saw things differently and still argues that it was his colleagues who had a disconcerting influence on the Kinks: 'They saw the Hooray Henrys as money, as stability . . . but at the end of the day I was the only person in there with any musical knowledge who could have guided them.'

Predictably, the Kinks found it impossible to commit themselves to one master and those around them were equally divided in their loyalties. Their no-nonsense road manager tended to support the working-class Page, whereas their record producer clearly aligned himself with the Collins/Wace team. Shel Talmy had already felt the sting of rivalry in his relationship with the former Teenage Rage and remains convinced that Page was intent on usurping all his rivals at the earliest opportunity. Yet Page the aggressor was also the diplomat and the man responsible for persuading the group to continue working when their personal conflicts erupted in scarcely believable displays of stage violence. It is hardly surprising that the group was disorientated by the political turmoil. Their lives had become a theatrical drama, the theme of which was the absolute necessity to discover the villain of the piece. In the pop landscape, however, heroes and villains are often indistinguishable, and many managers are called upon to play both roles. The relationship between the Kinks and their management was destined to produce one of the most complex and intriguing examples of group dynamics ever seen in pop history.

The cold war between the managers was brilliantly reflected in the white heat of violent abuse that characterized and ultimately defined the Kinks. Page and Wace blame each other for many of the problems, yet fail to consider one important positive result of their dispute. For without the creative dynamic tension generated by the managerial skirmishes, it is doubtful whether the Kinks would have progressed much further than the north London pub circuit. Or, more accurately, if they had, their personality as a group structure would have been very different. It is possible that they would have been bland, ordinary and predictable, rather than original, self-destructive and delightfully dangerous. Ultimately, the Kinks' group personality must be defined not merely through the working-class image-mongering of Larry Page or the aristocratic stoicism of Wace and Collins, but the drama and tension created by these vastly conflicting visions. Page and Wace never exchanged blows because their rivalry was consistently relieved vicariously through the Kinks. In this respect alone, the Kinks were to Page and Collins/Wace what Avory was to the Davies brothers — an object of cathartic release from their personal and political confrontations.

The increasing hostility between Page and Collins/Wace was manifested in the physical and emotional state of the Kinks during early 1965. The group suffered illness, injury, exhaustion and unremitting internal friction. Although the rival parties were locked in separate dressing rooms, it was impossible to monitor their every move and one evening, after returning to their hotel, the drummer and younger brother set upon each other like mad dogs, leaving a trail of blood on the carpet. The gentle-natured Avory stormed off in a huff, unable to rationalize the love-hate relationship that had suddenly developed in the group. Road-manager Sam Curtis pinpointed the peculiar group dynamics:

It was the brothers against Mick . . . These guys could provoke the Pope! They didn't need anything. They would come down in the morning to go off on tour and when they'd see him they'd say, 'Morning cunt'. How would you feel? If somebody says that to you,

you just feel like going out on tour with them, don't you? But then, if he didn't he'd starve because he couldn't do anything else.

The constant bickering and petty violence that characterized the Kinks' behaviour offstage was finally made public on an eventful night at the Capitol Cinema, Cardiff, on 19 May 1965. Following their opening number, the incorrigible Dave Davies walked across to Avory for an exchange of insults, and then proceeded to demonstrate his boorishness by dismantling Mick's drum kit with a well-aimed kick. For the publicly humiliated Avory, this was the final straw. With the howls of cheering fans still ringing in his ears, he grabbed the nearest sharp object from the battered drum kit and gashed Dave across the side of the head. The guitarist collapsed in a heap and while his brother attended his bloody wound, the panic-stricken Avory fled from the theatre, eventually arriving at Page's door in London, still wearing his stage suit. It was not long before Larry learned the worst. The Kinks were finished. They had vowed never to play together again.

It speaks volumes for Larry's leadership that he was able to bludgeon the Kinks into fulfilling their commitments, which included a stamina-sapping American tour. Unfortunately, the US sojourn was dogged by disputes, poor organization and prima-donna displays by the irrepressible Ray Davies. By the time the Kinks bandwagon reached Los Angeles, the group's reputation as a professional unit was virtually non-existent. The last straw for Page was Ray's petulant refusal to appear onstage at the Hollywood Bowl. Although Larry's coaxing won the day, he could not stomach another self-destructive display from Davies and returned to London, leaving the group in the capable hands of their road manager, Sam Curtis.

The fact that Page had refused to play the 'gofer' was clearly an intolerable blow to the sensitive Davies ego. Enraged by Page's departure, he transferred his allegiance to the urbane Wace/Collins team. Robert Wace maintains that the decision was by no means unexpected:

> American tours are an eye-opener. If you manage young, temperamental artistes you've got to play the game by their rules. Larry's job was to talk them into honouring contracts. You can't just come back to Denmark Street and play the wheeler-dealer. I don't care what you say: *every* manager is a whipping boy. It's money geared to grief and aggravation, and that's the equation.

Page, of course, would never allow himself to be treated as a whipping boy by any artiste, no matter how successful. He refused to be a mere appendage to the Kinks and continued hawking their songs to other performers in the hope of establishing Davies as a name writer. The final threads of their once happy relationship were finally ripped apart one month later when Davies burst into a Sonny and Cher recording session and screamed at his manager: 'Get out of the studio. I don't want anything to do with you. Get out of my life.' If Davies assumed that the break with Page might be achieved with a minimum of pain, he was sorely mistaken. A three-year court case ensued between Denmark and Boscobel, which was finally ended in the Kinks' favour by the Appeal Committee of the House of Lords on 9 October 1968.[1] Even as he lowered the guillotine, Lord Justice Salmon spared some merciful words for the defeated Page: 'I think that almost anything a manager might do however harmless or trivial, could induce hatred and distrust in a group of highly temperamental, jealous and spoilt adolescents.' Ray Davies was less understanding and, two years later, damned all three of his managers in a back-stabbing satirical song, 'The Moneygoround'.

Page's animosity towards the Kinks inflamed his desire to discover an even bigger act. He had already half-heartedly launched a group called the Pickwicks but their theatrical garb and odd choice of material ('Apple Blossom Time') seemed embarrassingly passé. Far more interesting was the critically acclaimed Riot Squad, whose drummer, Mitch Mitchell, later went on to fame and fortune as a member of the Jimi Hendrix Experience. At that point, however, Mitch was more interested in acting than drumming, though his thespian ambitions did not extend far beyond child acting and a bit part in *Emergency Ward 10*. Although Page had faith in the Riot Squad, it was clear that they were destined to remain a fashionable club band rather than chart cracksmen. The *real* find, as far as Larry was concerned, was a group that he had already rejected — the Troggs.

Page first met the original Troggs in 1965, when they were hawking their demos around Denmark Street. Although Larry recognized their potential he was wary of incurring the jealousy of Ray Davies by spending time on a group whose material so closely resembled that of the Kinks. In a remarkable display of arrogance, Page told them to continue practising and come back in 12 months'

---

[1]Unfortunately, space restrictions preclude a complete analysis of the Denmark v. Boscobel action. Readers seeking further information are advised to consult contemporaneous law reports and chapters 5-8 of my previous book *The Kinks: The Sound And The Fury* (Elm Tree/Hamish Hamilton 1984).

time. Unfortunately, the group was not stable enough to follow his sound advice. Shortly after that meeting they split in half, leaving Dave Wright (vocals) and Reginald Ball (bass) as the surviving members. They inherited the group name, a sizeable amount of hire purchase musical equipment and the financial assistance of a small-time local businessman, Stanley Haydn Phillips. Coincidentally, another Andover group, Ten Foot Five, were suffering similar personnel upheavals and also found themselves reduced to a duo: Peter Staples (bass) and Chris Britton (lead guitar). Their manager, Lance Barrett, a former electrician turned entrepreneur, suggested that it would be an excellent idea if the two groups amalgamated. They now had two bassists, but no lead singer! Eventually, Reg Ball was shoved into the spotlight and encouraged to sing and, incredibly, this new bastardized line-up sounded infinitely better than either of its parent groups. With two managers fighting their case, the revitalized Troggs soon began writing their own material and decided to wage another assault on Tin Pan Alley. The obvious place to start was the Denmark Street office of the man who had cautiously rejected them several months before. Chris Britton remembers Larry's second confrontation with the boys from Andover:

> There he was confronted by four herberts full of enthusiasm and wanting to play him some songs. So we carted our equipment into the back office and he left us with a tape recorder and said, 'Get on with it!'

One week later, the Troggs were taken to Regent Sound to cut a single which Page licensed to CBS. Although 'Lost Girl' failed to chart, Larry was willing to persevere with the Troggs for two good reasons. Firstly, he had recently formed a new company, Page One, with the renowned music publisher Dick James, and both parties were anxious to develop new recording and songwriting talent. Secondly, Page was determined to show the Kinks, and the rest of the pop world, that he could easily transform another unknown group into a hit-making machine. The Troggs were chosen as the perfect instrument for Page's revenge.

On 1 February 1966, two years after officially signing the Kinks, Larry was appointed Troggs' manager for a term of five years. His 20 per cent management commission was a considerable improvement on the meagre 10 per cent offered by his previous clients. More importantly, the Troggs' managers, Lance Barrett and Stanley Haydn Phillips, were thrust into the background and agreed to a nominal 5 per cent cut, a figure staggeringly lower than the 30 per cent remuneration enjoyed by Wace and Collins. By this time, of course, Page was one of the most powerful entrepreneurs in the British music business, and like his great predecessor, Larry Parnes, strengthened his position by taking on an additional role as pop impresario. He had already arranged a successful series of concert appearances for Sonny and Cher and, early in 1966, he brought Bob Lind to Britain. At that time Lind was being widely publicized as 'the new Bob Dylan', having recently scored with 'Elusive Butterfly'. As the first post-protest singer-songwriter, Lind's flicker of fame was momentary, but, characteristically, Page took full advantage of the publicity and the short-term dividends were impressive.

Meanwhile, the search had begun for that all-important first Troggs hit. The group were determined to cut one of their own compositions 'With A Girl Like You', but Larry advised them to launch their campaign with a Stateside cover. A pile of demos arrived from New York and Page immediately pounced on the Lovin' Spoonful's 'Do You Believe In Magic?' as a certain hit. After further discussion, however, an even more obscure recording, 'Wild Thing', was selected as the next A-side.[1]

'Wild Thing' was destined to become one of the great garage group anthems of the mid-sixties and its playfully sexual but decidedly unthreatening macho tone proved perfectly suited to the Troggs' lead singer. Page was astute enough to realize that the group worked best under intense pressure and, incredibly, he recorded their first *two* singles in a few spare moments following a Larry Page Orchestra booking at Olympia Studios. Within weeks of that session the Troggs were astonished to find themselves proudly standing at number 2 in the charts.

Throughout this period, the Troggs had been signed to a probationary management and agency agreement and it was not until 26 May, several weeks after 'Wild Thing' had been released, that they officially committed themselves to Page One Records. The group surrendered copyright control of their recordings for a standard 20 per cent royalty deal. Lead singer, Reg Presley, is still bitter about this decision and feels that a higher percentage should have been offered due to the instant chart success of 'Wild Thing'. Page provides an alternative perspective: 'I'd say what a nice fellow

---

[1] Composer Chip Taylor told me that he wrote 'Wild Thing' as a novelty number for Jerry Branigan. After editing the song from 10 to three minutes it became a regional US hit for Jordan Christopher and the Wild Ones, much to Chip's initial embarrassment. That it reached Page at all, Taylor claims, was purely fortuitous: 'I asked them not to send it to *anybody*!'

I was to put a record out with no agreement before that and to spend money without a contract!'.

One advantage that the Troggs had over their rivals was the power of Dick James, whose status as the Beatles publisher' enabled Page One to secure substantially higher licensing fees than most of their contemporaries. Even Chris Britton now realizes that if the Troggs had pushed for a higher percentage Page One might have lost the necessary profit incentive to promote their recordings worldwide. As it was, Page ensured that this remuneration was substantially increased by composing many of the group's flip sides and album tracks, thereby gaining a share of the mechanical royalties. According to Britton, Larry was such a persuasive producer that the group felt powerless to veto any of his songs, and probably saw no good reason to increase their own productivity in order to compete with their mentor in the songwriting stakes. Their supplication towards Page was duly noted by the pop press, and as Keith Altham of *New Musical Express* observed: 'It's more noticeable with this group than any other that they have complete confidence in their manager and never make a move without consulting the office.'

In spite of all his power, Page was not infallible and shortly after the success of 'Wild Thing' he made a rare error. While searching for a suitable US outlet for the group, Page was approached by Sonny and Cher's managers, Charlie Greene and Brian Stone. They organized a re-recording of 'With A Girl Like You' at Pye Studios, employing session musicians to create a 'Tamla Motown feel', specifically aimed at the American market. The experiment proved interesting, but, eventually, everyone agreed that the hastily recorded Page version was superior. In what Larry now describes as 'one of the classic cock-ups of all time', Greene and Stone were allowed to take a master of 'Wild Thing' and 'With A Girl Like You' back to the States where they attempted to negotiate a deal with Atlantic. At that point, the transatlantic wires became crossed and, assuming that Greene and Stone had been turned down, Page openly finalized a deal with Mercury Records. By the summer, 'Wild Thing' was shooting up to number 1 in the US charts when suddenly the same record appeared on the Atco label. To make matters worse, the Atco flip side was 'With A Girl Like You', which had been scheduled as the follow up! Greene and Stone argued that there had been an unwritten agreement while Larry replied incredulously: 'But you don't release records on a verbal agreement anywhere in the world'. Eventually, the formidable lawyers of Dick James entered the fray and there was an out-of-court settlement. For the Troggs, however, the damage had already been done. The complex contractual arguments were beyond their understanding and interest at the time and even today they betray some confusion over 'the Atco business'. The lost sales resulting from this dispute proved sufficiently disconcerting to erode their confidence in the man who had taken them to the top.

For the remainder of 1966, however, Page remained in total control of the Troggs. His creative influence in the studio was matched only by a perennial flirtation with image building and publicity. When the Troggs had first appeared at his Denmark Street office, they were a fashion-designer's nightmare. Reg resembled a provincial mod; Britton was dressed like a beatnik; Ronnie looked like a fifties rocker and Pete Staples clearly hadn't decided which youth subculture deserved his allegiance. Page's first move, in true Parnes tradition, was to subtly alter a couple of their surnames in order to add a hint of sexuality. Reginald Maurice Ball was rechristened Reg Presley and Ronald James Bullis emerged as Ronnie Bond.[1] The next stage of the grooming process took place at Carnaby Street's Take Six, where proprietor Sid Brent decked them out in the garish striped suits that later became their visual trademark. Page knew that all the coaching in christendom could not change their country yokel accents and innate naïveté, so instead he chose to highlight their provincial homeliness. In contrast to the degenerate yobbish image that Andrew Oldham foisted on the Rolling Stones, Page pupilled the Troggs in Victorian politeness. Whenever a woman entered the room, the group would stand to attention; they responded to questions with such forgotten epithets as 'please' and 'thank you'. Following their manager's instructions to the letter, they refused to be drawn on any political or religious issue and were seldom heard swearing in public. Chris Britton recalls Page's image-consciousness with great amusement:

> He had this thing about making us change into our suits! It certainly worked. At airports we always got whisked through customs. Around that time there was anti-group propaganda and Larry wanted to make a statement divorcing us from that scene.

In effect, Page wanted the best of both images — the wild and the innocent. Onstage, the Troggs were anything but demure and polite, and exuded an overt and sometimes comic sexuality that frequently resulted in female fan hysteria. Jealous boyfriends and

---

[1] Page credits journalist Keith Altham for suggesting the Presley name. It was hoped that Elvis fans might react in some way.

thuggish jack-the-lads also caused considerable problems during those early months of fame. In Belfast, drummer Ronnie Bond, was thrown from the stage while at other gigs Staples was knocked out and Presley suffered a lacerated face. Page may well have exaggerated these incidents for the benefit of the sensation-seeking music press but he was noticeably quick in despatching three bodyguards to protect his boys for the duration of their summer tour. Larry's energy and industry during this period ensured that the Troggs' bandwagon kept rolling. While the group topped the US charts, Page somehow found time to marry his secretary, Aileen Hampson, record a couple of Troggs EPs and sell the rights to several Reg Presley compositions. While on his honeymoon, Page dutifully plotted a two-part invasion of Europe and considered various offers for Stateside tours. By now, the group was working nightly and their earnings had increased from £670 to £4000 a month. That glorious summer ended with the Troggs' 'With A Girl Like You' at number 1 in the UK charts.

In interviews of the period, the Troggs claimed their success was 'like a dream, like it was happening to someone else'. Their disorientation was not merely the result of sudden fame, for the Troggs had become unwitting pawns in a more elaborate drama beyond their understanding. Page had not simply established another hit group, but exploited the pop market in order to take revenge on the treacherous Kinks. The Troggs' flirtation with fashion and violent fan hysteria insidiously caricatured the dramatic events of the Kinks' career in a parodic manner that greatly appealed to Page's sense of humour. The biggest joke of all was that his country yokels from Andover were outselling and outmanœuvring the Muswell Hill brigade as a chart act.

The winter of 1966 was a period of expansion for Page One enterprises and Larry signed a number of artistes including several best-selling Continental acts. On 30 September, Page One released the first single under its own logo, appropriately the Troggs' 'I Can't Control Myself', one of the most humorously suggestive songs of the era. The sexual overtones were largely ignored by British radio, but the group were not so lucky in Australia where the single was banned from the airwaves and blacklisted by retailers.

The mild controversy surrounding 'I Can't Control Myself' only served to reinforce the Troggs' popularity and by December 1966, their earnings had risen to £5000 a month. Their golden year ended with that ultimate accolade, a *Ready Steady Go* spectacular, devoted entirely to their music. As if to comment on the group's recent gruelling schedule, Presley collapsed from exhaustion while recording the show.

During the early months of 1967, Page negotiated the changing fashions in pop music with characteristic astuteness. The Troggs were encouraged to record a Chip Taylor ballad, 'Any Way That You Want Me', in complete contrast to their previous raucous singles. Another Top 5 hit proved that Page still had his finger on the pulse. By March, the group's gross earnings had risen to £7000-a-month and they were indisputably one of the biggest draws on the British concert circuit. Suddenly, Page seemed invincible, though with so many diverse interests, there remained the extremely remote possibility that he might eventually over-reach himself.

After spending a year enjoying themselves and soaking up public adulation, the Troggs became increasingly inward looking and concerned about the power that they had vested in Larry Page. In spite of their continued success, they suddenly began to question the decisions of their manager/producer. The Top 20 success of the somewhat unimaginative 'Give It To Me' could not disguise the fact that rather than promoting new ideas, Page was falling back on the old 'safety first' hit formula. In 1965, he had displayed a similar lack of adventure in objecting to the Kinks' innovative 'See My Friend', a single that heralded the emergence of raga rock the following year. Chris Britton recalls the initial symptoms of change in the manager/artiste relationship:

> There was a lack of confidence in Larry's production by that stage. I think he was getting fed up with us being too interested in what was going on. He was great when he had total control of the musical direction, but as soon as we wanted to force our own opinion somewhat it made the management side of things a bit edgy.

The proposed follow up single, 'M'Lady', was also a source of disagreement between the parties, but the Troggs managed to persuade Page to delete the disc at the eleventh hour. It was replaced by the more atmospheric 'Night Of The Long Grass', a brave departure from their previous work, which provided yet another Top 20 hit. Page's willingness to accede to the Troggs' artistic demands on this matter indicated a growing maturity in their working relationship which should have augured well for the future. Unfortunately, Larry chose to loosen his control over the group at precisely the moment when they were most susceptible to the silver tongues of his rivals.

In March, Larry appointed Harvey/Block Associates as the Troggs' booking agents, a decision that he later regretted. The new agents quickly learned that the group still harboured certain misgivings about Page and were particularly upset that they had never been allowed to tour the States. Before long, Harvey/Block were approached by the equally disgruntled Lance Barrett and Stanley Phillips who suggested the possibility of terminating the management agreement with Page. For the second time in his career Larry was about to cross swords with a rival management team.

The Troggs' attitude towards Page throughout this period remained curiously ambivalent. Although, in private, they voiced concern about the extent of his influence, they were still firmly under his spell. Page's appetite for publicity was insatiable and the Troggs willingly lent themselves to all his schemes, as Britton wryly recalls:

> Larry would get ideas off the top of his head in five minutes flat and have us running around like blue-arse flies doing them. He wanted our names in the papers as much as possible. If we happened to be in an area where somebody needed a boutique, fête or record shop opened, we were loaded into a car and taken there.

At one point, Larry even interrupted the training sessions of the great world heavyweight champion Muhammed Ali in order to photograph him sparring with the group. Page's most magnificent manipulation of the press, however, occurred in April 1967 when it was announced that Chris Britton was leaving the Troggs.

In the mid-sixties, the fragmentation of a major pop group was always front page news in the music press and Britton's reasons for leaving were far more exciting than that standard euphemism 'musical differences'. The Troggs' lead guitarist was supposedly sick of the long-haired, drug-taking image associated with rock groups and his intentions were to spearhead a moral crusade to clean up the pop world! For three weeks, the story dominated the pages of *New Musical Express* like a long-running pop soap opera. By week two, Page had found a suitable replacement for Britton in the form of former Trogg Dave Wright, who was then playing in another Page One outfit, the Loot. However, it then transpired that Wright's playing was not compatible with the Troggs' sound, so Page drove to Andover in order to confront Britton. The third instalment of this gripping saga saw Page threatening his lead guitarist with a lawsuit for breach of contract. Eventually, Britton decided to face up to his responsibilities and returned to the Troggs just before they set out on their next tour. Every lover of garage group pop breathed a sigh of relief when they heard of this happy ending.

Although the 'Britton Leaving?' vignette has since become part

TOP LEFT: Kenneth Pitt auctioning a pair of his protégé's boots at a 1980 David Bowie convention.

TOP RIGHT: Larry Parnes (1957), the Great Provider of British rock 'n' Roll.

BOTTOM: Reg Calvert (left) in the grounds of his Clifton Hall pop academy with Robbie Hood (Mike West).

TOP: Don Arden (1979), the most feared manager in British pop history.
BOTTOM: Peter Walsh (1976), who sold pop groups like 'cans of beans'.

ABOVE: Brian Epstein, ironically prophesying the Beatles' 1966 American Bible backlash.

LEFT: Gordon Mills — pop star, hit songwriter, producer, record company mogul and multi-millionaire manager.

ABOVE: Larry Page (1966). 'I never screwed anybody'.

TOP RIGHT: Andrew Oldham — the manic Phil Spector was one of several self-mythologizing personas.

TOP LEFT: Harvey Lisberg, who temporarily abandoned pop management in favour of snooker players.

BOTTOM: Ken Howard and Alan Blaikley (1976). 'We never wanted to manage anybody'.

TOP LEFT: Tony Stratton-Smith (Mr Charisma) at his managerial peak in the early seventies.

TOP RIGHT: Simon Napier-Bell (1966), the face of a chart-topping songwriter and dilettante manager.

BOTTOM: Tam Paton at his Little Kellerstain home prior to his great downfall.

ABOVE: Malcolm McLaren displaying his strange fascination for tartan.

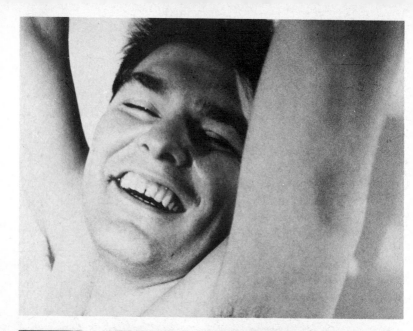

TOP: Stevo: 'Everything I do people will say is insane'.
BOTTOM: Rob Gretton (1982), manager of Joy Division and New Order.

of pop folk-lore, it is intriguing to learn that the entire incident was a deliberate hoax perpetrated by a grand master of sensationalism. Two decades later, Chris Britton reveals the truth and provides an interesting insight into the Page psychology:

> I used to suffer from migraines and was prescribed these pills which were found and checked at customs. I came back to the office complaining about the hassles and Larry must have read some publicity into it. The next thing I knew, people were phoning me and saying, 'I hear you're leaving the Troggs'. It got out of control. We were meant to be flying out of the country a few days later and Larry came up to me and said, 'You're going to the airport separately from the others. Dave Wright is going to be there with his guitar and you're going to walk up at the last minute and say, "I'm not leaving after all!"' I said, 'Larry, I wasn't leaving in the first place! What's this all about?' But, what the hell, it made some very good publicity.

The media exposure appeared to spur Page on to even greater achievements. Suddenly, he was treating the Troggs as though they were songwriters of the stature of Lennon and McCartney. Reg Presley saw two of his compositions, 'Baby Come Closer' and '10 Downing Street', released in quick succession by the Loot and the Nerve, respectively. During the same month, the unlikely figure of bassist Pete Staples made his songwriting debut with 'Oh No', released on Page One by Bobby Solo. With Chris Britton and Ronnie Bond also preparing material, it was clear that all the Troggs had every opportunity to increase their earnings in the future. By the beginning of the summer, their gross intake for concert appearances had risen to £7600-a-month and additional royalties were coming in from record and songwriting sales. Page's elaborate plans for the late summer included an impressive series of Spanish one-nighters providing £800 per gig, almost double the Troggs' standard rate. Negotiations were also taking place for a much publicized 'behind the Iron Curtain' trip to Budapest. Without question, Larry Page's managerial potency had reached an all-time peak and the Troggs seemed to have the world at their feet. It was at this point that Page fell victim to an historical peripeteia which irrevocably altered and severely diminished his influence over the mid-sixties pop scene.

For all his ambition and adventure, Page never quite managed to convince the Troggs that extensive tours of Australia and America were unnecessary. Two years earlier, he had insisted that it was an absolute necessity to conquer America and verbally coerced Ray Davies into accepting the idea against his wishes.

With the Troggs, however, he completely reversed his policy and even the chart-topping success of 'Wild Thing' could not make him change his mind. Whenever the subject was brought up, Page had a ready-made list of objections:

> We'd had one big hit in America and that's not enough to tour with. American charts are based on airplay plus sales. Even at that time a number 1 record was no guarantee that you would pull in crowds. We'd had hits with the Kinks and they played in a classroom where they were putting desks together! I'd seen the big American tours, all the British groups going out there with 22 acts in Harlem. Everybody wanted to see America. 'We lost our balls, but we've seen America!' But that's no good. The idea was to *make* money. The people advising us, the publishers and the lawyers had all worked on the Beatles. None of them felt the time was right for the Troggs.

Page's protests were voiced with considerable conviction, but beneath the rational exterior there surely lurked strongly emotional feelings connected with his previous visit. The Kinks' tour of America had been the most important event in his managerial career up until that point and it had ended in disaster. Even while the Troggs were moaning about not being allowed to cross the Atlantic, barristers were exchanging arguments about the implications of Page's controversial departure during 1965. Clearly, Larry was in no hurry to tempt fate by returning to the States without a very good reason.

Although Page's position seemed more secure than that of most managers in pop history, the Fates were already conspiring against him. In mid-May, Drew Harvey and Derek Block were approached by the Troggs' former mentors, Barrett and Phillips, with a view to taking over the group's agency and management. On 5 June, Chris Britton extended the same invitation and informed the Troggs of his feelings. A meeting took place in Andover between Harvey, Block, Phillips and the Troggs, during which a suitable course of action was discussed. On 19 June, Page was still working feverishly on the Troggs' summer schedule when he received an undated letter from the group's solicitors terminating management, agency and recording contracts and demanding the return of all monies received from Page One. Later that day, Dick James received a similar letter purporting to terminate the three-year publishing agreement that he had signed with the group on 3 January 1967. Page sat down and shook his head in disbelief. After all he had done for the Troggs, they had rejected him in the same abrupt and unexpected manner as the Kinks two years before. Larry's first move was to drive to Andover in order to confront the boys, but they were already beyond his reach, having absconded to America.

The Troggs' visit to New York proved particularly illuminating. As soon as the American music business community learned that these chart-toppers were in town they converged on them from every angle. Suddenly, the country yokels from Andover were surrounded by the toughest lawyers and most controversial managers of the era. Britton recalls how they were almost swallowed whole by their new American friends:

> When we arrived we began to have various meetings with people but we weren't into their high pressure way of doing business. We were very nervous. They got us into a record company flat in Greenwich Village and were taking us out every evening and showing us a good time. It was great for a couple of weeks. Then things started getting a heavier end to them because we hadn't come up with anything and were still thinking and looking around.

Eventually, the Troggs were presented with a draft contract, but their problems with Page made them extremely wary of signing anything without expert advice. Unwilling to trust anyone in America, the boys placed a transatlantic call to Stan Phillips who advised them to do nothing until he arrived in New York.

Stanley Haydn Phillips may have been a small-time pop manager but he had clearly inherited that love of drama that characterized the actions of his great rival, Larry Page. Phillips took one look around him and convinced the group that they were completely out of their depth. While heavy-duty managers were still discussing what to do with the Troggs, Phillips plotted the Great Escape. In his mind, it became an intrigue of James Bond proportions and he refused to book a plane flight in case the airports were under surveillance by litigious assailants. Instead, the boys returned home on a Dutch liner in the happy company of a group of college kids. One adventure had ended and another was about to begin.

The indomitable Larry Page was already preparing himself for another court case and on 26 June 1967 he served a writ against Harvey/Block Associates and the Troggs claiming damages and seeking an injunction to restrain the group from looking for new managers. The case reached the High Court in July 1967, and in the preliminary hearing, the Troggs' counsel successfully argued against an injunction to restrain the group from engaging new managers. Such an injunction would amount to enforcing the performance of personal services by Page to the group and an injunction is never granted which would have the effect of preventing an employer from discharging an agent. Page, it was argued, was effectively in the position of an employer. His Lordship Stamp concluded that the obligations to Page involving personal services were obligations of trust and confidence and therefore could not be enforced. The 'personal services' ruling has been the bane of many a manager's life ever since.

The most distressing aspect of the Troggs' case for Larry Page was the broadsides levelled against his managerial integrity. Among the more serious allegations was one of cheating the Troggs. The findings of a chartered accountant sounded especially alarming: 'On investigation there was immediately revealed a complete state of chaos in the affairs of the group in the early months of their association with . . . Mr Page.' This provocative statement was later amended by the additional words 'in relation to US royalties'. Clearly, this was a reference to the unfortunate 'Atco business' that had so confused Britton and his fellows. Regrettably, however, the accountant was unable to particularize the 'chaos' that he had found and Justice Stamp concluded that Page's explanation of the position was *prima facie* convincing. Page must have felt relieved when the sagacious Justice Stamp upheld his managerial reputation by dismissing the allegations so forcefully:

> I can only say that having surveyed the evidence as a whole and having examined the particular allegations I am left with the impression that it is as likely as not that the Troggs' case is not only a made-up case, but a case made up for them — not, I hasten to add, by their legal advisers! It is almost entirely unsupported by documentary evidence.

Chris Britton still feels that Justice Stamp's words were rather harsh on the defendants:

> I wouldn't say it was a 'made-up case'. It was true that Larry was our agent, manager and record company. And part of the contract was that he would do his best endeavours, which he couldn't do if he was dealing with himself, so he shouldn't have signed us up for them all. He was turning around one day and saying, 'Hey, Larry, how about these boys getting a break from recording and going to America?' and with his record company hat on he'd say, 'No, no, we're going to make money out of them in England and you're going to get your share as manager!'

It seems from Britton's comments, and those made at the hearing, that Page's position as manager, agent and record company (with the additional involvement of his partner, Dick James, as publisher) was enough to create a severe case of entrepreneurial role conflict. However, Page still believes that his capacity to administer the affairs of the group in every sphere of the music business was not adversely affected by the various contractual inter-relationships:

> It meant I didn't have to go out and fight the world. I could control everything, and if you can control those things you're in a much stronger position. Otherwise, you're begging all the time. All I can say to Chris is since then he's been in a position where he can have separate managers and record companies and has it paid off for him?

The dispute between the parties was eventually settled on Appeal when the Troggs won back their management and agency rights. However, they had to fulfil the terms of their recording contract with Page One and, as Larry ruefully admits, the relationship between the parties was never the same. Only one more hit followed, the ironically titled 'Love Is All Around'. Looking back at that troublesome period, the Troggs betray predictably mixed feelings. Reg Presley's comments on Larry Page were terse and deliberately understated: 'He was a *very* lucky man'. Chris Britton, whose name was put forward as the first defendant in the court case, reveals that by the time the costs of litigation had been totalled up there were no winners. Although he still feels that the Troggs' suit was entirely justified, Britton admits that a High Court action may not have been the most sensible solution to their problems:

> We got a better deal but in doing so we lost the interest of our record company because they didn't know whether it was going to backfire in their faces again. I think the fact that there was ever a court case was more instigated by Stan and Lance than either Larry or us. I don't think we'd have thought of it ourselves. It was more an inter-management squabble than a group quarrel. We'd probably have sorted it out with Larry directly, but Stan's attitude was more along the lines of Queen's Counsel. Stan was working for our interests though. I don't think he resented his 5 per cent deal. He just thought Page wasn't doing it right.

One agreement that survived the Troggs' association with Page was the additional tie-up with Dick James Music Ltd. Due to the options clauses stipulated in their three-year contracts, both Britton and Presley still owe the company a number of songs. Presley in particular is still bitter about the standard contract whereby he assigned to James worldwide copyright of all his musical compositions. In Larry Page's estimation, however, Presley's problems were largely of his own making:

> They've had more bloody money out of there than you'd believe. Reg
> must be signed there for the next 200 years! . . . Reg used to go in there
> and say, 'Can I have an advance and I'll write X songs this year?' And
> Dick would say, 'OK', give him a big advance and he'd write next to
> nothing. He'd go in later and ask for another advance and Dick, like a
> prat, would give him another few grand. So there was a huge debt of
> songs and he kept doing this. Reg was always in there for money. I
> used to say to him, 'If you're not happy, write the songs and get out of
> it!' Dick gave him the opportunity time and time again.

Following his litigation with the Kinks and the Troggs, Larry
gradually became disillusioned with pop groups and increasingly
spent time selling minor talent and extending his production and
publishing concerns. It was clear that he had made several mistakes
as a manager, underestimating the troubled spirit of Ray Davies
during the Kinks' US tour and embroiling himself in disputes with
producers and agents. Had he been Epstein, a disaster like the
'Atco business' would have plagued him for far longer. But Page
was allowed to fade into the background and, unlike Epstein or
Oldham, retained his dominions, though there were several changes.
The once vibrant Page One fell into a state of limbo when the two
directors separated in order to pursue their own individual projects.
James founded DJM Records and Larry launched Penny Farthing.
Page's new record company retained few of the artistic ideals
associated with the great independent labels of the sixties. Whereas
he had once taken a healthy interest in such up-and-coming groups
as the Loot, the Nerve, Plastic Penny and Craig (featuring Carl
Palmer), Larry spent the seventies pulling in easier money with
horrendous one-off novelty discs such as Chelsea Football Club's
'Blue Is The Colour' and Danny LaRue's 'On Mother Kelly's
Doorstep'. He admits that his only hit discoveries were Daniel
Boone and Continental star Kincade. His forte for discovering
obscure garage groups and developing their image and musicianship sufficiently to produce million-selling records remained sadly
dormant and his once high media profile was replaced by a quiet
industry. As fellow 60s manager Simon Napier-Bell remarked:

> Larry is a careful, calculating person. He's still not a major record
> company but he's built up a catalogue that sells all over the world.
> There's no flamboyance there. I'd say 80 per cent of the people in the
> music business, including the top acts, have never heard the name
> Larry Page. But he's a very wealthy, extremely successful person.

The portrayal of Larry Page as an unflamboyant, behind-the-scenes worker seems strangely contradictory in view of his previous head-lining exploits. Yet, Napier-Bell's assessment seems largely correct. Larry may be a living legend in the annals of contract law and a seminal figure in the history of British pop management, but megastars, gossip columnists and trade paper scribes no longer beat on his door. However, there is some evidence to suggest that Page may revive his managerial activities sufficiently to re-establish his former media fame. For some time, he has been carefully developing the career of Jade, a teenage chantress who has already enjoyed television exposure and features in the daily national press. Page betrays a paternal protection for his young star and obviously spends considerable time warning her of the pitfalls of the music business. Although Larry hopes that the girl will take heed of his advice, he is cynical enough to know that the threat of usurpation is ever present:

> You read two court cases with Larry Page and you think, 'God help us!' But I've never screwed anybody. And that little girl, Jade, will go through her accounts and her contracts even more closely because of those past problems. She knows more about the business at her age than anybody. I've educated her. But if she wanted to leave us, what are you going to do? How are you going to stop her? All you can do is build up a relationship of trust and make sure the artiste gets every penny that's owed to them. I've always been honest with artistes, but they get greedy. Somebody once said to me, 'All artistes are animals, they're the enemy', and he's not far wrong! But I want to be friends with my artistes. I know Jade. I know Reg Presley and Chris Britton better than any psychiatrist could know them. You know *everybody* that you deal with. You've *got* to know them.

It might be assumed that Page's litigious history would at least ward off potential music business opponents. Incredibly, however, 20 years on, Larry is still fighting off rival pop managers in true sixties fashion:

> Jade has now been signed to me for years. Today, we get a call from somebody pointing out that he's got a signed contract with her. Isn't that lovely? He said to my secretary, 'Tell him I don't want any problem. I don't want lawyers. I just want money.' Bang! He can get the bloody lawyers! That's the game. *That* is our business.

Unexpected confrontations with the past are nothing new to Larry Page. Indeed, a close scrutiny of his music business career reveals an almost obsessive revisionism, as though some strange force was relentlessly driving him on to rewrite a happy ending to all his battle-scarred exploits. When his singing career foundered, Larry attempted to re-enact his fame vicariously by creating an artiste in his own name. The alter ego was a symbolic rejuvenation and a second chance for Larry Page (alias Lenny Davis) to become a national star. When Lenny failed to hit the big time, Page found another couple of Davies's and soon established the Kinks as a household name. When the group rejected their master, Page reacted with his customary trick of re-creation. The Troggs not only specialized in Kinks' covers but promised to provide a vicarious happy ending to their predecessor's unfortunate saga. Instead, they left Page in an almost carbon copy of the Kinks' court case.

Page was bitter and disillusioned about the Troggs' defection but he could never resist the temptation to turn back the clock and rewrite those bloody pages of pop history. By the early seventies he had won back the Troggs' management, thereby reversing any adverse public opinion associated with the controversial court case. The relaunched Troggs, which included Plastic Penny's Tony Murray in place of Pete Staples, achieved cult status in the United States, but in spite of some mischievous ploys, the old hit formula could not be rediscovered. Nevertheless, Page had achieved a reasonably happy ending, as Tony Murray confesses:

> The arrangement with Larry was satisfactory and the contract was quite good. He brought us over to the States and got us a half page in the *New York Times* which did us no harm. There was no animosity when we parted.

Although Page had righted the wrongs of history with the Troggs, a stinging thorn remained in his side that continued to fester. His old enemies, the Kinks, had not only survived their gruelling three-year court case, but went on to reap spectacular financial rewards in the lucrative US market. That irony was not lost on Page whose dream of conquering the Americas had been all-consuming during 1965. When I first interviewed him in 1982, the bitterness of those earlier years was still present. He portrayed the group as ungrateful animals who had bitten the hand that fed them. And how could he ever forgive Ray Davies who had testified in court that he *hated* his manager? These were Page's feelings as he catalogued the transgressions that probably cost him his rightful position in the pantheon of all-time great pop managers.

Fate has played many tricks on Larry Page over the years, but the strangest happening of all occurred in the spring of 1984 when he received a telephone call from Ray Davies. Nineteen years after their bust-up, the ever unpredictable Kink had decided to offer a truce. In one of the most remarkable turnabouts in rock history, Page agreed to place his hand back in the fire by taking over the Kinks' management for a second time. It says much about Page's psychology that he could place his negative feelings in a historical context. His former adversary, Grenville Collins, summed up the reconciliation with a humorous aside, 'He must be a glutton for punishment'. But Larry Page is no fool. With the influence he exerts on the Continent, he has the potential to restore the reputation of the Kinks in territories that they had probably forgotten existed.

The behaviour of Larry Page is habitual. He is again rewriting history. By winning back the Kinks, he has proved to himself and the world that his managerial charisma has not been eroded by the ravages of time. Whether the Kinks remain under his wing in the foreseeable future is now scarcely relevant. The victory is complete, for Page has already written himself into pop history as the manager who lost two of the most successful groups of the mid-sixties and then miraculously retrieved them during the successive two decades. Not content with that achievement, Larry has recently won back ownership of the name Page One. Is there no end to this retrospective re-assimilation?

Somewhere in Eire, that forgotten figure, Little Lenny Davis, plays on in a different persona, no longer dreaming of chart fame but vaguely aware of recent developments and no doubt wondering whether his former mentor will again defy the laws of time and complete a star-making process begun 25 years ago that should have transformed the diminutive Dick Hayes into a second Teenage Rage.

Gordon Mills was born in Madras in 1935, the son of a Welsh army sergeant stationed in India. Following the birth, the family returned to the home country and settled in Ton-y-Pandy. Like most working-class kids from his local community Gordon left school at 15 for an uncertain future. After three years' national service he became a bus conductor and seemed destined for a working life not dissimilar to many of his Ton-y-Pandy friends. What separated him from his fellows was a musical hobby which rapidly became more serious when Mills was dubbed the harmonica champion of Wales. That amateur award took him to the British finals at the Central Hall, Westminster, and on to Luxembourg where he represented the UK at international level. Along the way, he met another harmonica-playing prodigy, Ronnie Wells, and before long they joined the seven-piece Morton Fraser Gang and found themselves in panto at the London Palladium.

From 1957 to 1959, Mills gained considerable experience playing at some of the most famous theatres in the world. It was a tough life for the future millionaire who was barely surviving on £10 a week. As flatmate Ronnie Wells recalls: 'Gordon was so broke he used to borrow my shoes'. Along with singer Don Paul, Mills and Wells fell under the spell of fifties rock 'n' roll and were accused by Morton Fraser of allowing an *Oh Boy* attitude to creep into the act. When Fraser fired Don Paul for his James Dean moodiness, Ronnie and Gordon left in sympathy soon afterwards.

The rebellious trio teamed up again to become the Viscounts, a hard-working, close-harmony unit whose professionalism soon caught the eye of the ever-vigilant Larry Parnes. Under the Great Provider's aegis, they played all the major package shows providing backing vocals, comedy routines and parodic impressions of other acts.

Although the Viscounts were progressing, Gordon Mills still seemed a junior member in relation to the older and experienced Don Paul. Far from showing any strong managerial qualities such as leadership or efficiency, Gordon was all too likely to blunder through, appearing onstage in odd-coloured socks like an absent-minded schoolboy. On one occasion during Parnes' 'Rock 'n' Roll Trad Show' his lack of observation caused him to make a fool of himself before the entire cast, as Don remembers:

Every night, one of the artistes sang 'The Madison' and all the cast had to come on and dance across the stage. You'd done your act so you might be playing cards and this was the finale. As the tour went on, the amount of people turning up for the routine dropped until one day the words 'Madison Discontinued' appeared on the noticeboard, though they still sang it. Anyway, Gordon hadn't seen this notice and he ended up going out dancing on his own. He thought he'd be the hero and Jack Good would say, 'Good old Gordon'. I'll never forget that. We all fell about. Professional to the end was Gordon.

Although the Viscounts earned good money under Parnes, he was not in a position to push their recording career, so they switched agents, joining that pillar of Variety, Hymie Zahl. Much to Larry's tight-lipped astonishment, they charted soon afterwards with their umpteenth single, 'Short'nin' Bread'. More tours followed until Zahl secured them a residency at Paul Raymond's Celebrity Club. As part of the deal, the group had to play at the adjacent Revue Bar, famous for its striptease artistes. For Mills and his cohorts it was an experience to be relished:

> We were doing production numbers with all these nude women. We did about four or five shows from 6 p.m. onwards, then we went to the Celebrity restaurant. It was like a marathon. In order to relieve the boredom we got into smoking and drinking. One night we rolled this huge joint, took some puffs and went on. There were Japanese tourists sitting in the front rows with binoculars looking at the nudes; it struck us as hysterically funny and we just burst into laughter. They almost had to carry us off.

The Zahl era ended when the Viscounts moved to Michael Barclay and Philip Waddilove's ill-fated Audio Enterprises. When that company abruptly sank into liquidation, the boys took a backward step forwards by signing with another veteran Variety manager, Eve Taylor. The Queen Bee of Show Business was a redoubtable woman and although her managerial style was firmly grounded in the fifties, she had lately taken an interest in promoting gigs in true Parnes fashion. Thanks to Evie, the Viscounts toured with the Beatles and found time to register another hit, 'Who Put The Bomp?' By now they were known for their vocal pyrotechnics, quaint striped shirts and ubiquitous concert appearances. Mills meanwhile was emerging as a formidable arranger, painstakingly working on the Viscounts' distinctive harmonic blend. His colleagues began to notice that he seemed more interested in behind-the-scenes work than performing, but there was still little sign of any managerial astuteness. The elder Don Paul always remained the main man in the Viscounts, but he occasionally employed Mills' naïve cheek to good effect: 'If we needed something outrageous I'd always say, "Go on, Gordon, ask for it". Quite often, he was successful because he was never scared to ask for anything.'

By 1963, Mills was at last making an impact in the music industry, but it was neither as a performer nor a manager. Instead, Gordon unexpectedly achieved success as a hit songwriter. The Viscounts had all had a crack at songwriting, usually on the flip sides of their own discs. Mills had composed a song called 'I'll Never Get Over You' which was all but forgotten when relegated to the B-side of a flop 45. But thanks to Lionel Conway of Leeds Music, Mills' work was taken around Tin Pan Alley and eventually 'I'll Never Get Over You' became a big hit for Johnny Kidd and the Pirates. Mills also composed another of Kidd's biggest smashes, 'Hungry For Love', and hit lucky again when Cliff Richard recorded 'The Lonely One' which climbed into the Top 10.

Mills' songwriting success was a crucial development which effectively led to his departure from the Viscounts. In many respects, however, it was his love life that pushed him forward. Gordon was always a ladies' man. During the Revue Bar days, he dated a French stripper with the delightful name Melody Bubbles, but it was evident that the Welshman had his sights set on meeting a woman of greater sophistication. The lady who finally won his heart was Jo Waring, a talented and successful model. Following their marriage, Mills rapidly grew tired of life on the road, as Don Paul recalls:

> We travelled to Newcastle and Manchester to do television and Gordon kept saying, 'Do we *have* to go there?' I'd say, 'It's all right for you, Gordon'. He could more or less not go anywhere because Jo was earning a fortune. He'd already done well and she was against him touring because she couldn't bear him to be out of her sight. So she really influenced him to become a manager.

Mills' extra royalty payments ensured that he was even further ahead of his fellow Viscounts in terms of affluence and this economic imbalance ultimately split the group. Don Paul claims that there were no feelings of jealousy, but the Viscounts needed the income accruing from live appearances. With Mills gone, the group struggled on for another year, recruiting former teen idol Johnny Gentle as a replacement, but the spirit of the Viscounts was already dead.

In leaving the Viscounts, Mills had taken a big gamble on

developing a career in songwriting and management but, as Ronnie Wells reminds us, the man must have been born under a lucky star:

> When we used to do cabaret clubs up North there were these card schools, and Gordon could hold his own with good players. We didn't realize this until one morning he said he'd won £50, which was big money then. I wouldn't have thought of Gordon as a manager, but he was single-minded and ambitious and he had that all-important lucky streak. You've got to have a bit of that going for you and the signs were there in early 1964.

Mills was also fortunate in signing with the Colin Berlin Agency and learned much from the eponymous head of that organization. Although generally regarded as naïve in his Viscount days, Gordon was a quick learner, eager and willing to listen to the advice of music business veterans. However, it was chance rather than effort that brought him into contact with the artiste whose career he was to oversee for the next two decades. During a homecoming visit to Wales, Mills met up with Gordon Jones, an old friend from his days as a bus conductor. Jones took him to the Top Hat Club in Merthyr Tydfil to see a local group, Tommy Scott and the Senators. Scott had been billed as 'the twisting vocalist from Pontypridd', but it was not his choreography but impassioned vocal style that caught Mills' attention. After hearing a particularly dramatic version of 'Spanish Harlem', Mills went backstage and introduced himself. Although no big wheel in the music industry, Gordon certainly had clout as a hit songwriter and former Viscount. Backstage he sounded like a big time London agent and concluded matters by inviting Tommy and his Senators to look him up if they ever found themselves in the capital. Within weeks, Scott and the Senators arrived on the doorstep of his Notting Hill Gate residence begging for a chance to reap fame and fortune.

The ambitious Mr Scott may have had a booming voice but his *curriculum vitae* was unimpressive. Under his real name, Thomas Woodward, he had been a failed late-fifties Tommy Steele imitator. He later moved to London and recorded some demos for the legendary producer Joe Meek, but unfortunately they were never released. Returning to Wales with his tail between his legs, Tommy was next discovered by Decca A&R producer/scout Peter Sullivan and, following the recommendation of Dick Rowe, was handed over to Phil Solomon. Their association was short-lived, mainly due to the intervention of Bert Berns who dismissed Solomon's boy as a second-rate Elvis Presley. Mills, meanwhile, had decided to nurture Scott's career as a performer/vocalist. It was to be the perfect marriage of artiste/manager, not dissimilar to the relationship between Colonel Tom Parker and Elvis Presley, though based on friendship as much as profit. Mills was authoritative and forceful and immediately went beyond the terms of the standard management contract. It is said that they settled on a 50/50 split from the outset, a figure seldom seen in professional management contracts since the days of Larry Parnes. That Mills was worth every percentage point has since proved indisputable. Not only did he have a good business head, but the necessary creative input to ensure that his protégé developed along specific lines with the manager firmly in control.

Mills' first move was to rechristen his star Tom Jones after the Henry Fielding novel that had recently been transformed into an overly saucy feature film. With his backing group, renamed the Squires, Jones was installed in a Holland Park flat and placed on a small retainer. Mills, meanwhile, secured numerous gigs at American airbases and Irish ballrooms. Finally, the big moment came with Jones's debut Decca single 'Chills And Fever'. Contrary to Mills' expectations, it flopped. Jones was worried by the setback, believing perhaps that his chances of pop success were slipping away. The little money that he received during this period further dented his pride and in moments of re-appraisal he threatened to concede defeat and return to Wales. Unperturbed, Mills continued writing songs and a fruitful collaboration with Les Reed produced 'It's Not Unusual' which was submitted to Sandie Shaw as a potential follow up to her number 1 'Always Something There To Remind Me'. When Sandie elected to stick with her main songwriter, Chris Andrews, Mills reluctantly passed the song to his protégé.

Such was Tom's enthusiasm for 'It's Not Unusual' that his vocal completely drowned the accompanying choir and orchestration, and a second version had to be cut with an exceptionally loud brass backing. The new arrangement proved particularly effective and Dick Rowe credits Mills for ensuring that Jones was consistently kept on his toes: 'It wasn't until Gordon took over the management that things happened. Gordon is the best coach that I've ever heard. He could interpret a song and Jones would do it automatically.' By March 1965, 'It's Not Unusual' had soared to number 1.

Jones's early appearances on *Top Of The Pops* revealed him as a colourful pop star sex symbol with tight-fitting clothes, long curly hair embellished with a bow, and a rabbit's foot talisman dangling from his pants. The racy image, ostentatious hair ribbon and powerful sexy voice made him appear like a British version of P.J. Proby, who had first charted only months before. For a time, there was reputed rivalry between the two whose images were so close. However, unlike the self-destructive Proby, who allowed his onstage sexuality to extend to split trousers and cinema bans, Jones's performances were carefully held in check and his antics did not offend common decency. Nevertheless, Mills was unable to sustain Jones's recording career at a peak consistent with the success of 'It's Not Unusual'. The follow up 'Once Upon A Time', failed to reach the Top 30 and its successor 'With These Hands' was merely Top 20. In an attempt to reach a wider audience instantaneously Mills ensured that Jones recorded the theme song from the film *What's New Pussycat?* which fared exceptionally well in the States and maintained his profile in Britain. But even the film theme game could not forestall Jones's inevitable fall. The title track from the James Bond film *Thunderball* seemingly guaranteed another big hit, yet it fell outside the Top 30. As 1966 wore on, Jones became passé as a pop star and by the summer his chart run seemed over. No longer capable of pulling large audiences, Tom was back in workingmen's clubs whose boards he had trodden long before his rise to fame. Although his chart run was standard for the time, Mills rightly felt that something had gone terribly wrong. He wanted Jones to be a huge long-term international star, but the singer had fallen victim to the fickle adolescent pop audience who quickly realized that he was an old man in tight-fitting teenage trousers. It took Mills a little longer to reach the same conclusion.

Towards the end of 1966, Gordon noticed that Jones was attracting considerable attention from middle-aged women and from that point onwards a drastic image change was enforced. Out went the sexy clothes and rabbit's foot in favour of a mature tuxedoed image. Only the intense eroticism remained, with Jones stripping down to his shirt and sweating buckets as he bumped and ground to hits past and present.

By Christmas 1966, the unbelievable had happened. Jones's plaintive reworking of 'Green Green Grass Of Home' brought him back to number 1. He also achieved the distinction of being the first British Decca artiste to sell a million copies of a single in the UK alone. Overnight, Tom Jones was once more big business and from that moment forward his fortunes continued to improve. A consistent run of hit singles followed during the next few years including two more *New Musical Express* chart-toppers, 'Delilah' and 'Help Yourself'. More important than these UK chart achievements and record sales was Jones's gradual acceptance in the States as a Las Vegas performer. The second half of the sixties brought Mills closer and closer to his dream of establishing Jones on an international level with a pulling power that would rival Elvis

Presley. Having been dismissed as an Elvis clone only a few years before, Jones was at last challenging the weary king for his much-coveted crown.

Developing Jones's career was virtually a full-time job for any manager but Mills was determined to extend his interests, although he wisely resisted the temptation of diversifying too quickly. Unlike Oldham and the other charismatic mid-sixties managers, Mills was never likely to fall victim to his own ego. He studiously avoided signing temperamental pop groups, realizing that solo artistes were far easier to keep in check and develop in the long term. Even so, his next choice of artiste seemed a guaranteed loser and the signing suggested that Mills was placing sentiment before pragmatism.

The career of Gerry Dorsey, prior to Mills' intervention, was a history of successive failures. During the late fifties, he had appeared on *Oh Boy*, toured with Marty Wilde and recorded a flop single for Parlophone, 'I'll Never Fall In Love Again'. It was during this period that he first met Gordon Mills and they became close friends. Each was the best man at the other's wedding and when Gordon was searching for digs Gerry put him up at his Notting Hill Gate flat. They had both experienced hard times and often laughed at the days when Gordon was forced to do a moonlight flit to avoid paying overdue rent. But, whereas Mills was heading for millionaire success, Dorsey's career continued to spiral downwards. Dismissed as a poor man's Frankie Vaughan, he seemed an anachronism by 1963 and even less viable than the refugees from the Parnes stable, who at least had youth and boyish looks on their side. Dorsey's career hit rock bottom when he collapsed onstage in Manchester and was forced to retire for 18 months due to an extended bout of tuberculosis. Saddled with responsibilities, including a wife and two children, Dorsey found life on the dole extremely difficult. Often, Gerry and Pat Dorsey slept throughout the day to suppress their hunger pangs. By the time Jones's 'It's Not Unusual' had topped the charts they were living in an austere flat above a furniture shop in King Street, Hammersmith. Their room was lit by a bare bulb and decorated with a specially-framed cheque for 5s. 4d., which represented the total royalties accruing from Dorsey's last recording. Every morning, Gerry would see defeat staring him in the face and smile sardonically at the cheque which served as a testament to his failed artistic career. Unable to tolerate his pathetic existence, Dorsey decided to make another bid for recording success and in desperation turned to his old friend Gordon Mills. Although reluctant to take on another singer, Gordon could not easily forget Dorsey's kindness during the days when they were both struggling. By the end of 1966, Mills felt that the time was right to extend a helping hand: 'I had to break Tom before signing anyone else, but once I was a successful manager I knew I could help Gerry'.

Mills' first managerial decision was to kill off the old Gerry Dorsey and launch him as a completely new singer with a bizarre name. Just as Tom Jones was borrowed from Fielding, Mills once more delved into the world of literature to plunder the name of *Hansel and Gretel* creator, Engelbert Humperdinck. A deal was struck with Decca, who accepted Mills' terms in spite of some last-minute attempts to drop the Humperdinck mouthful.

Humperdinck's first break was as a surprise entrant for the Knokke Song Contest where he replaced Tom Jones at the eleventh hour. Clearly, Mills felt his new signing needed the exposure. Following the contest, Decca issued *'Dommage Dommage'*, which received considerable airplay but failed to chart. There were no such problems with the next release. Early in 1967, 'Release Me' dominated the number 1 position for five weeks, even holding off the Beatles' finest double A-side single, 'Strawberry Fields Forever'/'Penny Lane'. The follow up, 'There Goes My Everything', zoomed to number 2 and, by the summer, Humperdinck was back at number 1 for a further astonishing five weeks with 'The Last Waltz'. So, within eight months, Mills could boast the management of the two best-selling solo artistes in Britain with record sales unheard of since the height of Beatlemania. It is worth noting that Mills continued to write the flip sides of Jones and Humperdinck's singles, thereby securing half of the mechanical royalties from the biggest sellers of the era.

Mills' initial reservations about signing a second male singer had proved overcautious yet, in some ways, his concern was far-sighted. At first it was intended that Humperdinck would ingeniously complement Jones's sexuality by being sold as Mr Romance. His image was that of the Latin seducer in serenade rather than the overt bump and grind of sexy Tom. For a time, it worked, both in the sense of visual image and record material. But the dynamic between Jones and Humperdinck was always peculiar and grew more challenging as their popularity increased. It was inevitable that there would be some rivalry, for their careers followed an almost parallel course. They shared the same record label, broke similar sales records, starred in Talk Of The Town spectaculars, hosted hugely successful television shows and ended up selling themselves for millions on the Las Vegas circuit. In spite of their respective success stories, however, Humperdinck always seemed outdone by his stablemate. He was less secure than Tom about his standing with Mills and occasionally betrayed secret fears about his stage apparel and greying hair. Even this contrasted with Jones's more open displays of pop star vanity. When Tom had his nose job in 1967 it was common knowledge, and when, seven years later, he swelled to 15 stone, the embarrassment was transformed into a public display of macho pride. Tom announced that he was switching from beer to champagne, built a £250 000 leisure complex, trained every day and rapidly reduced his girth. No doubt his televised sweatbox performances burned off further calories thereby saving him from following Elvis into the heavyweight division. The macho image was further promoted by the overbearing presence of his hot-headed minder Dai Perry, who guaranteed that no trip was ever dull.

Although Humperdinck could not compete with Jones's high jinks without endangering his more conservative romantic image, he tried to match his partner's consumerism. Tales of Humperdinck and Jones embarking on spending sprees at jewellers and tailors are legion, but it was the Welshman whose spendthrift ways always created the most comment. Similarly, when Engelbert challenged Tom to a drinking contest, it was the latter who remained conscious till the bitter end. Their respective television shows also showed a contrast in quality and production with Jones attracting some of the biggest stars of the day and some of the most musically respected. Who can forget Jones singing lead vocal on 'Long Time Gone' with Crosby, Stills & Nash, or attempting to outdo David Clayton-Thomas at the height of Blood, Sweat & Tears' fame? Humperdinck could boast nothing as adventurous or arrogant in his run-of-the-mill shows, which, incidentally, were produced by Mills.

The rivalry between Jones and Humperdinck was ingeniously kept in check by Mills whose presence complicated matters. He was no ordinary business manager but functioned almost as a competitor, whose looks and dress sense matched that of his cabaret idols. Although he could compete with neither of them as a vocalist, he was more musically accomplished and his ability as a producer/musical director ensured that he had the clout to criticize their performances and influence their choice of material. Epstein has been called a mediocre businessman and he was also banned from Beatles recordings by the surly John Lennon; Mills, by contrast, was a tough negotiator and a greatly underestimated creative force. It was these dual talents that prevented Tom and Engelbert from challenging his authority. Even at the peak of their millionaire success in America they were always expected to show their manager the utmost respect.

While Mills could be authoritarian, his relationship with his artistes was based firmly on friendship. For a time, it seemed that

Gordon, Tom and Engelbert were like brothers, each boasting his own customized Rolls Royce and luxury home in Weybridge. They also jointly owned a custom-built plane and a 1000 acre farm in Sussex, both of which Mills regarded as practical investments, though they smacked of ostentation. That same jack-the-lad *nouveau riche* mentality was to be observed in Jones's spending sprees or in his short-lived frugal phase when he allowed one million pounds to accrue in his bank account, just for a laugh. The playboy image was reinforced by rumoured romances with models and singers. Jones was linked with a number of women, most notably former Supreme Mary Wilson, but, again, it was his stablemate Lothario who came off worst. In 1981, Humperdinck, by then 41, became embroiled in a paternity suit brought by 24-year-old Kathy Jenner, who claimed one million dollars on behalf of her daughter, allegedly an illegitimate offspring of the singer. Even while the Jenner action dragged on, another writ was served on the hapless Engelbert by a schoolteacher who allegedly suffered hearing damage at one of his concerts. Of all the singers who have broken the decibel limit, who would have thought Engelbert would be the one to suffer litigious threats for assaulting the ears? By this stage, however, Humperdinck was estranged from Mills whose intervention might have prevented such lawsuits from enveloping the beleaguered tenor.

Managing two millionaire superstars in the sixties and seventies did not prevent Mills from playing the field in search of new talent. Early in 1968 he launched US singer Solomon King in Britain with a Top 10 hit 'She Wears My Ring'. King was another powerhouse vocalist in the Jones/Humperdinck tradition, but lacked their sexual appeal. Although he scored again with the marginally successful 'When We Were Young', Mills found it difficult to sustain his career especially in the light of his stablemates' successes. That same year, Mills picked up the incorrigible Leapy Lee from an indignant Robert Wace who had dismissed the singer following an argument. Gordon struck lucky once more, for Leapy immediately notched up a fluke novelty hit with the Mills-produced 'Little Arrows'. Unfortunately, Leapy was far too erratic and self-destructive to consolidate his surprise success. He began drinking with East End villains and struck up a friendship with Diana Dors' husband, Alan Lake. One night at a pub in Sunnydale, Lake and Lee became involved in a fracas with a publican whose wrist was slashed with a flick knife. Leapy paid for this wideboy escapade with a jail sentence which did little to help his singing career. Following his release, Mills continued to use him occasionally as a freelance producer, but he eventually left England and was last heard of singing in bars in Majorca.

When Humperdinck and Jones's profits from recordings exceeded $20 million, Mills decided to move into the mogul game by establishing a management/recording company, MAM (Management Agency & Music). The acronym was deliberately chosen as an affectionate abbreviation for 'mother'. By the end of the sixties, MAM had expanded into an entertainment empire absorbing the Harold Davison Agency along the way and moving into other areas such as concert promotion, publishing, hotels and amusement machines. In 1969, MAM went public and the organization continued to grow during the early seventies.

The upsurge of MAM coincided with the discovery of Mills' third major artiste, Raymond O'Sullivan, humorously renamed Gilbert O'Sullivan after the two great composers. O'Sullivan was totally unlike Mills' previous artistes, boasting no sexual appeal or strong vocal talent. He had first written to Mills in 1969, enclosing a demo tape and photograph with a note explaining that he wished to succeed in showbiz and had therefore specifically chosen Gordon as his mentor. In truth, Gilbert was at the end of his tether having spent several barren years recording for CBS and Phil Solomon's Major Minor label. Mills was strangely intrigued by the boy and soon recognized a budding songwriting talent that could be transformed into greatness. According to legend, when O'Sullivan first arrived at Mills' office he was wearing a cloth cap and short trousers and had a pudding-basin haircut. His eccentric appearance did not put off the smartly-dressed millionaire entrepreneur who would shortly play upon that image to spectacular effect.

The launch of Gilbert O'Sullivan was greeted with quizzical looks and barely suppressed laughter by the music press. Even Mills' senior stars scorned Gilbert's singing ability and derided Gordon for wasting time on such a joke figure. Engelbert Humperdinck even had the audacity to suggest that Gilbert O'Sullivan was a ridiculous name! Such gibes merely encouraged the obstinate Mills to prove that he was right. O'Sullivan's debut disc 'Nothing Rhymed' was chosen as MAM's third single release and rapidly climbed into the Top 10. During the next two years O'Sullivan emerged as one of the most commercially successful songwriters/performers in the UK and secured a grudging respect from the rock music press while nonchalantly establishing himself as a mainstream MOR artiste.

O'During the early stages of his career, O'Sullivan retained the 'Bisto Kid' image which accurately reflected his prosaic lifestyle. While Engelbert and Tom drove around in Rolls Royces, drank champagne and partied in their mansions, Gilbert lived in a small Notting Hill bedsit and acted as though he was still a lowly-paid postal worker. He eventually moved into the grounds of Mills' Weybridge bungalow, but still survived on a meagre £10-a-week allowance. Although this fact would eventually be used against Mills as evidence of parsimony and exploitation, it seems clear that Gilbert's frugal lifestyle was largely of his own choosing. While residing at Mills' home, he preferred to stay in at night and was often employed as a babysitter. He even wrote one of his biggest hits, 'Clair', for the youngest of Gordon's four daughters. With a string of hits scattered throughout the early seventies, Gilbert was gradually coaxed into changing his image and under Mills' tuition began to appreciate a superstar lifestyle. He bought a Weybridge house, just like Tom and Engelbert before him, and was chauffeured around in a smart Mercedes by his brother Kevin. The pudding-basin haircut also disappeared, replaced by a perm, neatly complemented by trendy clothes. Meanwhile, his songwriting continued to improve, and he frequently acknowledged the creative input of his svengali manager/producer: 'He understands my songs. I even change some of my lines for him'.

Any suspicions that O'Sullivan's success was purely parochial were dashed when he broke through in the States. 'Alone Again (Naturally)', a million-selling US number 1, was followed by several other hits which established Gilbert as an international star. For several years it seemed that nothing could go wrong and O'Sullivan looked a sure bet to excel Elton John as the decade's most successful British singer/songwriter. Few realized that his peak period would soon be followed by a disastrous decline.

By the mid-seventies, Mills controlled the business affairs of three of the most lucrative performers in pop music history. The years of millionaire success, however, were slowly taking their toll on the great man. Although generally known as a no-nonsense workaholic, his lifestyle had gradually become more and more eccentric. Each year he disappeared on a safari holiday to Africa and returned with a number of exotic animals which were housed in the grounds of his Los Angeles home. Not content with allowing his party guests merely to visit his private zoo, Gordon decided to sneak a few privileged animals into the house and watch the hilarious results. His favourite animal companion was Ollie, a one-eyed gorilla whose antics always provided good fun, at least for Gordon. On one occasion, the unruly beast accosted a party guest and tore off her dress, much to the astonishment of the assembled company. This so amused Gordon that he later installed a couple of tiger cubs in the ladies' powder room in order to create an even bigger sensation. The results were predictably uproarious.

Before long, Mills boasted the largest private collection of orang-utans in the world, but his artistes began to wonder whether he was devoting enough time to their careers. Gordon immediately reassured Tom, whose Las Vegas earnings were immune to his mentor's extra-curricular zoological pursuits. The ever-uncertain Engelbert was not so easily appeased and by 1977 he had appointed a new manager, though he was still contracted to the MAM organization. As Gordon explained, 'I'm still his manager in name and law but that's all. He doesn't listen to me anymore'.

Although Mills was still one of the most powerful men in the pop game, some observers felt that he was losing interest in the day to day running of his company and indulging himself in an American Dream of his own imagination. Dick Rowe, by now also in the descendant as a force in the industry, noted a change in Gordon when he visited the States during the seventies:

> He believed in Tom Jones like Epstein believed in the Beatles. Then he went to LA and things started falling apart . . . He was living in cloud cuckoo land. The lifestyle is incredible if you're in the money and they believed their own publicity. I watched it from a distance and I thought, 'This is sad!'

Mills' apparent slackening of solicitude eventually caused concern to Gilbert O'Sullivan whose earnings had markedly decreased by the late seventies. What began as a minor disagreement over music publishing eventually blew up into one of the most spectacular court cases in pop history with O'Sullivan demanding the return of copyrights in his songs, plus millions of pounds in back royalties and damages. The case came before Mr Justice Mars-Jones in the spring of 1982 and the results were anathema to the shell-shocked Mills. The judge had been downright appalled by the admission that Gilbert was living on £10-a-week pocket-money at the time of his first few hits. After the accountants had opened their labyrinthine files and revealed the fate of millions of pounds, Mars-Jones concluded that the singer had been well and truly 'fleeced'. It was explained that between 1970 and 1978, O'Sullivan's recordings had grossed an estimated £14.5 million from which the singer received approximately £500 000 before tax. After hearing the evidence, the judge set aside the agreements between O'Sullivan and MAM as an unreasonable restraint of trade resulting from 'undue influence' which had led to an inequality of bargaining power. In short, the master tapes of all Gilbert's recordings were to be returned by Mills who was also ordered to repay every single penny he had made from the singer with the added penalty of compound interest. The judgement caused considerable panic in music business circles and prompted others, most notably Elton John, to follow O'Sullivan's lead with an even bigger action against the redoubtable Dick James. Elton failed to win the copyright of his songs, partly because the veteran James was a more experienced combatant than the unfortunate Mills who seemed at a low ebb during the early stages of the proceedings. Dick Rowe, sitting at the back of the High Court, was almost embarrassed by the mogul's wooliness under cross-examination:

> I was one of the witnesses in court. It was very sad for Gordon; I thought 'God, now we know the real strength of the man'. He didn't know what to say. The opposing Counsel just tied him up in knots and made him look like a fool. It must have been sad for Gilbert's people to see this man, the managing director of MAM, made to look like an ignorant office boy.

Although all seemed lost, Mills remained hopeful that the Appeal Court would overrule the decision of the caustic Justice Mars-Jones.

In the end, Mills lost the war to O'Sullivan and was forced to surrender the copyright of his songs. There were, however, some small victories. Mills' QC Michael Miller forcefully pointed out that, contrary to the original calculations, O'Sullivan had received £1.4 million and, after meeting his own expenses, was left with £964 000 — nearly double the sum quoted at the first hearing. After listening to the arguments, their Lordships remedied Justice Mars-Jones's ruling by allowing Mills and his companies a share of the profits for the work they had done in promoting and exploiting the star worldwide. They also concluded that Mills should receive credit for the tax that he had paid on behalf of the singer and that the original order to pay compound interest be amended to simple interest. The submissions of fraudulence and fleecing, though not overruled, were placed in a new perspective when it transpired that Mars-Jones's criticisms had been based partly on the assumption that publishing agreements dated February 1972 were made at that time, whereas in fact they had been made in 1970. Mills' culpability was therefore modified. His Counsel left the High Court with the opinion that the Appeal had been about one-third successful.

Following the O'Sullivan case Mills was left to take stock of his career. His great MAM empire had reached its expansionist limits and merged with Chris Wright's Chrysalis Group; Gilbert and Engelbert were history; his marriage was over. The one constant was Tom Jones, whose career he continued to supervise as vigilantly as he had done 20 years before. It was the last great manager/ megastar partnership to survive the sixties.

Epilogue

Gordon Mills' hard-working nature ensured that he was a difficult interviewee to pin down. Between 1983 and 1986 we corresponded and the ever-efficient Welshman faithfully promised to set up a long meeting on his 'next visit to England'. Later, we spoke briefly about the Viscounts, the early sixties and the fact that Gordon was anything but manager potential at the time. His frankness suggested that many revelations would follow. A third meeting during the summer of 1985 was postponed at the eleventh hour when Mills had to zoom across to France on business. He was always on the move, talking fast, providing snippets of interview material and promising a fuller confrontation next time around. We agreed there was much to discuss but the fundamental question for me was one that recurs throughout this chapter: what were the qualities that enabled Mills to transform such unlikely figures as Jones, Humperdinck and O'Sullivan into internationally successful artistes? That Mills should find one unknown star was unlikely, that he should fashion three was the stuff of miracles. Legendary svengalis like Parnes, Epstein and McLaren were greatly helped by cultural changes and found themselves at the forefront of massively publicized movements: anglicized rock 'n' roll, the beat boom and punk, respectively. But Mills had none of these. His discoveries were maverick solo artistes, out of time and out of step with fashion, and with no mass movement behind them. Yet under his guidance they became international stars with astonishing record sales. How did Mills do it? Perhaps it was his intuition, his persistence, his multi-faceted talents as A & R man, producer, writer, singer, musician and mogul or, more simply, that extraordinary streak of gambling luck that Ronnie Wells remembered from the Viscount days. Probably it was a combination of all these things. Whatever it was, I felt the mystery of Mills' superstar-making achievements could be captured during an intense, argumentative interview. It was a challenge to be relished and after three years' preparation I was fully charged. A date was finally set in July 1986.

Within weeks of confirming our interview, Mills had entered a recording studio with Tom Jones. During a session he complained of a stomach upset which was so painful that he decided to consult a doctor. Those close to Gordon would have found the news unalarming: he had been troubled with a stomach ulcer for several years, a legacy of the hard-working, heavy-drinking high life for which he was well known. Two years before, he had considered an operation to remove the ulcer, but eventually decided against it. It now seems probable that this 'businessman's ulcer' may have been far more serious than anyone imagined, for, in July 1986, doctors diagnosed that Mills had stomach cancer.

Confined to a bed in the Cedars Sinai Hospital, Gordon was visited by his perennial protégé Tom Jones. Within the space of a couple of visits Tom realized how serious his manager's condition had become: 'He was no longer there. There was no hope; he was dying in front of me'. Mills knew that he had cancer and asked Jones to tell him what his chances were of pulling through. Tom was frank enough with an understandably euphemistic reply of '50 : 50'. Ever the gambler, Gordon considered this comment for some moments and whispered, 'That's not bad odds'. The following day he was dead.

The sudden death of Mills, completely unexpected, and preceded by apparent good health, had an air of unreality about it. The news was broken to me on the day of our appointed interview. It left an illogical sensation of discomfort and sadness.

Mills' living epitaph is enshrined in the continuing international success of the singer he transformed into a superstar. Commentators such as myself are apt to bemoan the passing of Tom Jones from a rough-house rocker to a housewife heart-throb; as a personal manager, however, Gordon *had* to take Tom away from straight-forward pop or watch him fade away. In less skilful hands Tom might have followed the same disastrous path as his old sixties rival P.J. Proby. Their respective fates speak for themselves. Proby, the anti-hero, was banned, bankrupt and virtually forgotten for much of his performing life, while Jones became a millionaire. Without even bothering to record new material, he can still fill the Royal Albert Hall several times over whenever he returns to England. That is the level of fame and long-term security that Gordon Mills has given his protégé. And for both artiste and manager that achievement was far more important and desirable than transforming Tom Jones into a heroic failure with a small bank balance. As struggling working-class Welshmen they had already suffered enough of that in the fifties.

It takes an astute personal manager to understand the strengths and weaknesses of his artiste and perform his best endeavours in helping him to realize his potential and career aims. The Mills/Jones relationship remains a lasting model of manager and artiste in complementary unity.

Prior to the funeral of Gordon Mills at St Peter's Church, Hersham, Tom Jones provided the most memorable valediction that a pop manager is ever likely to receive from an artiste. His words leave little doubt about the man's pre-eminence as a personal manager and friend:

He was just part of my life. He taught me just about everything. He groomed me . . . he said he would guide me to become larger than life. There are parts of me which he totally created. We became much more than brothers . . . he took care of my life and now I will have to learn to deal with it.

The cult of the teenager which magically transformed gauche, insecure fifties youths into burning icons of pop star immortality had a less revolutionary effect on the paternalistic world of pop management. Starmakers were traditionally patriarchal figures, older and wiser than their innocent protégés. It was a stereotype that would only gradually be broken down. The novel image of the young entrepreneur was embodied in Larry Parnes who, rather astonishingly, was only a decade older than his boyish stars. Soon, Brian Epstein would reduce the age differential to single figures but it was not until late 1963 that British pop saw its first teenage tycoon.

Andrew Loog Oldham was born in 1944, but this did not prevent the short-trousered youth from developing an alarmingly precocious interest in mid-fifties London coffee bars. He even visited the celebrated Two Is at its peak and witnessed the first stirrings of British rock'n'roll. He was never the same again. After leaving public school with a handful of O levels and a sizeable ego, he launched himself on late-fifties London, determined to break into the pop business. Taking a circuitous route, he secured a job working for designer Mary Quant and supplemented his income by doubling as a waiter at Soho's Flamingo Club and Butler's Tea Rooms. The contacts he made in the fashion and music businesses enabled him to infiltrate several record companies, and he even released some singles under a number of amusing aliases, including Sandy Beach and Chancery Laine. Unfortunately, his singing ability did not match his ambition.

Andrew was sensible enough to realize that the chances of succeeding as a pop star were extremely remote. Following a period of self-questioning, he concluded that a far easier way to financial gain lay in publicity and management. A season on the road with teen idol Mark Wynter taught him much and after hearing the names of the most important impresarios in the business, Oldham presented himself at the door of the notorious Don Arden. Their relationship was short-lived since, for all his aggression, Arden was extremely conservative and resented the sensationalist press that Oldham consistently craved.

The redoubtable young blond upstart next approached Brian Epstein, who agreed to hire his services as publicist to Gerry and the Pacemakers and Billy J. Kramer and the Dakotas. The assignment was soon to end. Realizing that the Beatles were beyond his grasp, Oldham moved on once more. A chance encounter with Tony Calder, an ambitious agent who worked with Danny Betesh at Kennedy Street Enterprises, brought another change of scene. Within two years Andrew Loog Oldham had effectively charted the wayward course of British beat from London and Liverpool to Manchester.

Ever impressionable, Oldham tended to see himself as a second Mark Wynter, the new Epstein, or Don Arden Mark II, but perhaps the most important role model of all was Phil Spector. The enigmatic American producer, with his shades and flash limousines, looked more like a thirties gangster than a music business mogul. Andrew followed him around London, listening intently to all his words and aping his mannerisms. Eventually, he returned to daylight office hours carrying a pair of dark glasses and a new philosophy.

By early 1963, Oldham vowed to follow Spector into production but quickly realized that in Britain a less strenuous route to success could be achieved through management. All he had to do was find a group, just like Brian Epstein. Following a tip from *Record Mirror*'s Peter Jones, Andrew drove to the Station Hotel in Richmond and experienced the sound of the Rolling Stones.

Oldham talked his way into the Stones' camp and quickly persuaded them to abandon their founding father, Giorgio Gomelsky, in favour of his charismatic leadership. Still an unknown, in spite of his peripatetic experience, Oldham sought a backer. His first choice, Brian Epstein, declined, thereby losing the opportunity to control two of the biggest groups of all time. Fortunately, show business agent Eric Easton elected to take a chance. On 3 May, the Rolling Stones were signed to Impact Sound, the company that Oldham and Easton had formed to supervise recording sessions. Easton was initially intent on ousting the grimacing lead singer, but Oldham insisted that Michael Jagger could be transformed into a sex symbol.

The next plan was deciding upon a record label. Fortunately for Oldham and the Rolling Stones, Dick Rowe was still smarting from the loss of the Beatles and, following a tip from George Harrison, he also found himself in the hallowed Station House. Dick recalls the day with amusement:

> George Harrison told me that I ought to sign the Rolling Stones and I'd never even heard of them. I picked up my wife and we went straight to see them. I went in there wearing dark glasses and it was like the Black Hole of Calcutta. They were thumping away and my wife thought they were very interesting. I then looked around and saw that there were no girls. It was all boys in twos and threes jumping up

and down to the rhythm on the balls of their feet. I'd never seen anything like that. It was incredible. It caught my imagination.

Although Rowe had been alienated by the suave Brian Epstein, he maintained a certain affection for the wide boy enthusiasm of Eric Easton's young partner:

> Eric had the agency and put up the money to start with. But he couldn't quite cope with Andrew. . . When you're older you don't know how much rope to give a young man. Andrew always knew what he was doing; it was written all over him. Unlike Epstein, it was all he had, therefore he had to be more aggressive. In retrospect, he wasn't very clever to sign with us for three years. But the deal was good for them and good for the company. Oldham was the driving force. He drove me. He was exciting and had tremendous flair.

From the outset, Oldham attempted to gain as much control as possible. He insisted on independently producing the Stones' debut 'Come On', even though his previous experience in the studio was non-existent. Although the single eventually had to be re-recorded at Decca, Oldham made his point by stressing that the raw, uncluttered production he so favoured was precisely what the kids wanted.

On the day of the single's release, the Stones were granted a prestigious appearance on *Thank Your Lucky Stars*. Against his better judgement, Oldham reluctantly acceded to the demands of television producers by forcing the group to don matching houndstooth jackets with velvet collars. While this was occurring, Andrew announced another bombshell by ousting Ian Stewart from the group on the grounds that he was 'too ordinary to be a pop star'. Stewart accepted the decision stoically and stayed on as roadie and occasional pianist.

While 'Come On' was creeping into the lower regions of the Top 20, Oldham had retired to France suffering from psycholithic poisoning. He returned in time to see them through the trauma of a follow up, the Lennon/McCartney number 'I Wanna Be Your Man'. At that point, the Stones were still recording cover versions and Oldham was desperate for original material. Eventually, he locked Mick and Keith in a room and refused to release them until they emerged with a song. Their early efforts, 'It Should Have Been You' and 'Will You Be My Lover Tonight?' (both recorded by the late George Bean), were insufferably bland, but Oldham would not be denied. In his scheme of pop, Jagger/Richard *had* to be the next Lennon/McCartney.

The early months of 1964 saw the Stones catapulted to fame amid a torrent of controversy. Their long hair outraged elder members of the community, even those who had lately accustomed themselves to the sight of Beatles' mop tops. While the momentum gathered, Oldham took a sidestep and finalized a promotional Stateside visit which proved premature and anti-climactic. Without a hit, the Stones were dismissed as a cheap hype, and it was only as the tour reached its final days that they salvaged their reputation with sell-out concerts, heavily promoted by the influential disc jockey Murray The K.

Shortly after returning to Britain, the Stones finally hit number 1 with 'It's All Over Now' and pandemonium followed. The Beatles had already produced teenage hysteria on an unprecedented level in pop, but the Stones generated a new, uglier reaction that frequently spilled over into violence. On 24 July at the Winter Gardens, Blackpool, the group hosted the largest ever rock riot on British soil. As Mick Jagger wiggled his backside and turned up his protruding lips, the lunatic element in the Stones' audience vented their feelings by smashing chandeliers and demolishing a Steinway grand piano. The show ended with 50 fans being taken to hospital for treatment. One week later, a concert appearance in Belfast was terminated after 12 minutes while hysterical girls were dragged away from the venue. The next month there was further trouble in Manchester. And so it went on.

Far from showing concern about the Stones' bad boy image, Andrew Oldham appeared to revel in the chaos. He spoonfed the press with pre-planned headlines such as the famous 'Would You Let Your Daughter Go Out With A Rolling Stone?' and showed every willingness to exaggerate their supposed rivalry with the Beatles. At early concerts, where the Stones received a tepid welcome, Oldham was an indefatigable cheerleader. One apocryphal story portrays him crouching in the back row seats of an auditorium screaming at the top of his lungs in an attempt to stir up some genuine fan hysteria. He was also the scourge of other people's press conferences. A Pye reception for Petula Clark was virtually disrupted by the dramatic entry of Oldham and his long-haired colleagues who seemed intent on stealing everyone else's limelight. Wherever he went, Oldham drew extreme reactions. Loved by many up-and-coming would-be whizz kids, he was simultaneously reviled by important elder members of the record business who longed to see this upstart receive his comeuppance.

For one moment, in the eventful summer of 1964, it seemed that Oldham had burned himself out. With hindsight, it appears that he had decided the time was ripe to mythologize his own entrepreneurial career. The pop press recoiled in astonishment as the news filtered through that the Stones' svengali was quitting the business. In a self-effacing statement to *Melody Maker*, the noble Oldham turned his back on millionaire success, apparently destroyed by his own ambition:

> The truth is I didn't come into the pop business just to make money. If that had been my only intention I would have concentrated on making a lot more. As it stands, I've done okay. But money can't buy you happiness, although you can't have happiness without money. I've made a lot and spent it. Right now, I plan to get away from the scene for quite awhile. I'm going to mess about doing what I want to do — I'll buy a joint in Portugal and spend some time there. It's cheap. I'm in a bit of a state, really. Don't know what I want, frankly. The doctor says I've got an ulcer. That's from no sleep, and worrying about perfection. Failure in anything is terrible. Success — that's everything. When I do something it has to be 100 per cent properly done, or nothing . . .

Oldham was not to know that some of those publicity-grabbing words would later prove prophetic.

Oldham and the Stones quickly demonstrated that they were not the product of some short-lived trend, and as the months passed their importance in the pop world increased. 1965 was the year of the breakthrough, when both America and Britain conceded that there was substance beneath the Oldham hype. The Stones' three number 1 hits that year ('The Last Time', 'Satisfaction' and 'Get Off Of My Cloud') put their musical and songwriting supremacy beyond doubt and their emphatic victory in the *New Musical Express* chart points table emphasized their overall consistency. It was also a great year for publicity. On 18 March, three of the Stones were arrested for urinating against a petrol station wall and fined £5 for 'trespassing'. The press loved the story almost as much as Andrew Oldham did.

In spite of all his escapades, Oldham had yet to achieve his ambition of emulating the wealth and power of Brian Epstein. While the Liverpudlian had quickly branched out with a stable of groups, Oldham got little further than supervising the exotic named Mighty Avengers, who were fed several Jagger/Ri songs, but failed to break big. The Stones, meanwhile, wer ing little money from their American tour and at home O arguing with his latest co-promoter, the perpetually tr Stigwood. Oldham's response to these niggling mo to accept an audience from that aggressive Ameri

Allen Klein. The small, overweight New Yorker had recently boasted that he would replace Brian Epstein as the Beatles' manager and, having failed in his bid, decided to woo the Stones instead. Klein's irrepressible confidence rapidly won over the impressionable Oldham, and the other Stones agreed to accept his services as business manager. In effect, this meant Oldham now had even more time to concentrate on their publicity and recordings, but the deal was not achieved without a hitch. The much abused Eric Easton refused to take all this lying down and began legal proceedings which dragged on interminably. Klein responded immediately by demonstrating his own managerial prowess at boardroom level. He walked into Decca's offices, confronted the magisterial Sir Edward Lewis and renegotiated the Stones' contract for an unprecedented $1.25 million in advance royalties. As so often with Klein's business activities, there was a sting in the tail. The money was paid into a US subsidiary, Nanker Phelge Music, over which Klein was to exercise complete control. In later years, this would be used as ammunition for lawyers representing the Rolling Stones in their lengthy action against the 'Robin Hood of Pop'.

Freed from the tedium of workaday business management, Andrew's imagination took full flight. In the first of a series of charismatic overreaching gestures, Oldham decreed that the Rolling Stones would soon be celluloid heroes. With the Beatles having already achieved worldwide success in two feature films, Andrew was determined that his group must outdo them. Instead of pursuing the traditional pop star production with a comic scenario and some well-chosen songs thrown in, Oldham insisted that his boys must be treated as serious actors. The film, therefore, would have to be intelligent, thought-provoking and controversial, closer to Paul Jones's *Privilege* than the Beatles' *Help!* For a brief period, Oldham boasted that he would win the rights to Anthony Burgess's *A Clockwork Orange*, seemingly unaware that Stanley Kubrick had already pre-empted him with a timely offer. Instead, Andrew persuaded Decca to invest a sizeable sum into a film based on Dave Wallis's book *Only Lovers Left Alive*, a tale of mass suicide in which teenagers inherit an anarchic Britain. Months passed, and eventually the capricious Andrew abandoned the idea, preferring an even bigger movie boasting the directorship of the prestigious Nicholas Roeg. The rigours of pursuing a long-term movie deal seemingly proved beyond Oldham's patience and further changes of mood followed. Eventually, he decided to fulfil an old ambition by penning his own *meisterwerk*, *Back Behind And Front*. Unfortunately, that too was uncompleted and as the months turned into years, the ones' cinematographic aspirations remained unfulfilled. Oldham, the great overreacher, had begun his spectacular downward spiral, but nobody in the pop business had yet detected the already evident signs of hubris.

For a time, Andrew seemed to see himself as some grand pop patron of the arts. When the charts offended his royal tastes he would invest considerable sums in advertising revenue in order to push some favoured song of the moment. The Righteous Brothers' Spector-produced 'You've Lost That Lovin' Feelin'' was championed in favour of Cilla Black's opportunist UK cover and swiftly went to number 1. Pleased with the results, Oldham again played god, interceding on behalf of the then unknown Mamas and the Papas who were amazed to read a portentous half-page testimonial in *New Musical Express* extolling the virtues of their debut single, 'California Dreamin''. Oldham's lengthy promotional poem ended with a postscript allaying any suspicions of self-interested hyping: 'I didn't write it; I didn't publish it; I didn't produce it and I didn't release it — I just like it.' Such was the man's delightful eccentricity at its peak.

Andrew's willingness to promote new talent, when time permitted, had been evident as early as 1964 when he surprised the pop world with a new discovery, Marianne Faithfull. The 17-year-old former convent girl, with her innocent face and elegant demeanour, was as far removed from the image of the Rolling Stones as the human mind could imagine. Yet, this same paragon of virtue would later be deeply wounded by the monster that Oldham was nurturing for public consumption. Before falling fully under the influence of Mick Jagger, Marianne achieved considerable success in her own right. Under Oldham's tutelage, Jagger and Richard even managed to write their first undeniably important song for her, 'As Tears Go By'. Marianne enjoyed other hits, including 'Summer Nights' and 'This Little Bird', but in spite of such successes she never felt comfortable as a singer. Like Oldham, she was perpetually restless and eager to break into different fields, most notably, serious acting. As her fame increased, she became notoriously difficult and tempestuous in the recording studio. By 1965, Oldham could no longer spare the time to oversee her career as vigilantly as he had once done. Other producers and caretaker managers were frequently frustrated by this wily girl who would constantly moan, 'Andrew is the only person who understands me'.

Andrew, of course, was no longer purely concerned with artiste management, even though his clients were Britain's second most popular group. What he now desired was the power of a Phil Spector, and, in the British music business, the most logical route towards achieving that aim lay in record production and record company ownership. Andrew effectively combined both roles with the formation of Immediate, Britain's first major independent record company. The label even boasted a reassuring, if pompous, motto: 'Happy To Be Part Of The Industry Of Human Happiness'. Unlike most earlier independents, Immediate was not marketed under a corporate logo, but paraded its existence in grey and black. For those already seduced by Andrew's high-powered publicity and whizz kid mythologizing, Immediate was tantamount to a revolution in the British music industry.

When Immediate's first release, the McCoy's 'Hang On Sloopy', climbed into the Top 10, Oldham's Midas touch seemed beyond doubt. By the summer of 1966, the much respected though commercially unsuccessful Chris Farlowe, also benefited from his association with Oldham and was rewarded with a number 1, 'Out Of Time'. Even relative chart failures, such as Twice As Much, best remembered for their Peter and Gordon public school enunciation, were served well by Jagger/Richard songwriting and Oldham publicity, receiving extensive radio airplay as a result. While the press extolled the brilliance of Oldham and the innovative policies of Immediate, a few cynical voices in the record industry began to wonder where this young upstart was getting his money. It was only in later years that other aspiring moguls, such as Simon Napier-Bell, realized precisely why they could not compete with the great Oldham:

> Immediate was a business joke because Andrew said, 'Right, I'm going to form a record company and have a hit'. So he went to other record companies and bought, at exhorbitant prices, records that were US hits and were obviously going to be hits in England. He came back and released them on Immediate but he was losing money. He was paying more for the English rights than the records could possibly make, even if they went to number 1. But it was a very good ploy. If I started a record company I would do that — but you do it for window dressing and you know bloody well you can only do it once or twice. You've got to get the thing on a sound commercial base afterwards. But Andrew was more interested in keeping up a high profile . . . There just wasn't enough money coming in to cover it . . .

In spite of Napier-Bell's criticisms, the remarkable fact was that Immediate maintained its high profile and gradually attracted more and more influential artistes to its ever-growing roster. Whatever mysteries lay hidden in the ledgers, Oldham never once betrayed the possibility that he was anything other than pop's latest precocious millionaire. Visitors to his flat in Ivor Court duly noted the stuffed humming-birds encased in a glass dome, the chair carved to resemble a peacock and the leather rhinoceros which graced the hearth. In the street outside his office one might find any number of vehicles that Andrew had purchased like a child collecting dinky toys. The Sunbeam, MGB and Lincoln stood alongside his most prized possession, a gleaming silver Rolls Royce equipped with a record player, telephone and cocktail cabinet. As he paraded his shiny possessions, the 22-year-old infant tycoon spoke like a record business veteran:

> I was an angry young man years ago simply because I hadn't got any money. Now, I suppose, I'm very nearly one of the people I hated so much. The success story was as much luck as anything else. I had to learn the hard way and pass through a lot of phases — like aping Phil Spector. You get bitten, but you must experience it to know where you're going. You also have to have a fantastic ego and you go through a stage of thinking you're more important than the artistes. I went through this with the Stones, but I'm sorted out now.

In spite of his assurances, Oldham was not quite the leopard who had changed his spots. It was true that he was now married with a young son, but domesticity had not blighted the hard-man image that he had carefully nurtured since entering the business. He still enjoyed employing minders, like the menacingly named Reg the Butcher, and even at the height of his fame, he could be riled by a relatively innocuous gesture of defiance. When the Yardbirds indulged in a spot of pop star rivalry with the Stones, the traditional 10-minute feud extended to include their respective managers. Simon Napier-Bell made an unintentionally sarcastic remark to Andrew over the telephone, which caused the young mogul to react with an indignation more suited to the hot-tempered Don Arden. In a grand theatrical gesture, he instructed several of his boys to pay a surprise visit to the office of the cheeky entrepreneur, but Napier-Bell was nowhere to be found. Not wishing to play Andrew's games, he had immediately sought legal protection, the results of which were predictably amusing:

> My lawyer sent a letter to Andrew saying 'We understand you sent a couple of gentlemen around to see Mr Napier-Bell . . .' and pointed out that if anything happened to me in the next few weeks, including a complete accident, he'd very likely end up in jail. My lawyer could have gone on record and any accident I had, even if it was unrelated to what he was doing, might have looked very much as though it had been instigated . . . Anyway, my letter came back torn in pieces which

is madness because not only have I sent a letter but he's sent back a receipt! He actually sent it back — 'Yes, thank you — received and read!' He put himself in a crazy position . . . It was a typical Andrew Oldham childish thing to do. Andrew's not childish now, but he was then. He's changed a lot.

For Oldham, of course, the gesture was all. He was not a violent person and his ripping up of the letter demonstrates how disinterested he was in the entire matter. The pop business was his playground and Napier-Bell had seemed like a pushy pupil spoiling for a scrap. When the pair next met there was no mention of the letter nor any indication of animosity on Oldham's part. Evidently, he had forgotten that the incident had ever taken place. It was just another Andrew Oldham fantasy.

During 1966, the Rolling Stones consolidated their position as Britain's number two group, but Oldham seemed to be growing apart from them. His once noticeable svengali-like influence over Jagger had clearly waned, and as the relationship cooled, Andrew's involvement with the Stones' everyday lives became largely negligible. With Klein running their business affairs in his own inimitable style and the efficient Les Perrin conducting press relations, Oldham was drawn more and more away from pop group management. But it was to be the decisive events of early 1967 that resulted in his departure from the court of the Rolling Stones.

It was already well known in pop-music circles, and widely suspected by the general public, that the Rolling Stones took drugs. The extrovert behaviour of Brian Jones had already attracted the attention of the scandal-seeking *News Of The World*, but, betrayed by their own enthusiasm, the paper's rapacious reporters had made the unfortunate error of confusing the blond star with the far more newsworthy figure of Mick Jagger. When the singer read of his inaccurately reported drug escapades, he promptly issued a libel action against the newspaper. It was to prove a disastrous error which merely invited further speculation into his narcotic habits. Like most of the major pop figures of the day, Jagger dabbled in soft drugs and, with his coterie of hip friends, it was unlikely that he could survive public and official scrutiny for the length of time that a libel case demanded. In February 1967, Jagger's discretion was finally undermined when the police raided Keith Richard's home in West Wittering and promptly arrested the inhabitants on a number of drug-related offences. Although Jagger's only transgression was the possession of several pep pills, the arrest caused a considerable stir. The controversial drugs trial which followed momentarily transformed the Stones into sympathetic figures, hounded by an insensitive and vindictive Establishment. The clement mood of the nation and the quality press was ripe for the type of exploitation that Oldham had once so loved, yet he remained mysteriously silent throughout the entire affair.

Oldham's absence during the Stones' greatest crisis was, no doubt, an expression of his growing impatience with their lifestyle. He disapproved of their fraternization with drugs dealers and hangers on, though not particularly from any moral standpoint. It was, quite simply, bad business and non-productive. Frustrated by their bohemian cool, Andrew made a last, desperate attempt to re-assert his authority during the recording of *Their Satanic Majesties Request*, but the Stones ignored his advice and adopted a defiantly obtuse attitude throughout the proceedings. Oldham left the sessions in disillusionment and surrendered his management of the group to Allen Klein shortly afterwards.

By the end of 1967, Oldham was still resplendent in his role as record company mogul. In spite of his estrangement from the Stones, there was no shortage of established groups willing to place their future in his hands. The most successful of his inherited hit-makers were the Small Faces, fresh from a tempestuous relationship with Don Arden and a brief association with Robert Wace. Demoralized and confused, the Small Faces needed the commitment and enthusiasm of an inspirational svengali. For a time, Oldham played the role well and Ronnie Lane still regards him as the best manager that the group encountered during their stormy career. Under his guidance, they achieved a second run of expertly-crafted pop singles, including 'Here Comes The Nice', 'Tin Soldier' and 'The Universal'. Amid this spree, they recorded the chart-topping album *Ogden's Nut Gone Flake* which won a string of awards for artwork and design. Yet behind the outward success, the Small Faces were still in a financial mess. Oldham had allowed them to indulge their creative whims in the studio for over a year and the recording costs proved astronomical. As ever with Oldham, sound economics were surrendered to grandiose schemes and although his gamble with the Small Faces paid some dividends, the group's relationship with Immediate gradually deteriorated. Complications concerning their settlement with Don Arden sapped their confidence and soon other creditors were snapping at their heels. It was no great surprise when the group finally split amid confusion and acrimony on New Year's Eve, 1968.

Oldham's other involvements with artistes were less than memorable. He inherited the peripatetic Herd, following their defection from managers Howard and Blaikley, but was unable to repeat their commercial success. In truth, Oldham was far too busy attending to the administration of his record company to stabilize an evidently difficult group. Following the Herd, there were other successes, most notably, P.P. Arnold, who recorded several minor hits for Immediate including Cat Stevens' 'The First Cut Is The Deepest' and Chip Taylor's 'Angel Of The Morning'. P.P. Arnold had backed the Small Faces on 'Tin Soldier' and was herself accompanied by another promising outfit, the Nice, whose controversial revamping of Bernstein's 'America' was an underground hit. Steve Marriot, formerly of the Small Faces, also returned to the label with the supergroup Humble Pie, which later went on to achieve considerable success in the States.

Although Oldham could have made substantial sums developing the careers of artistes such as Humble Pie and the Nice, the financial plight of Immediate required his full attention. Humble Pie passed into the hands of the high-powered American entrepreneur Dee Anthony, while the Nice appointed Tony Stratton-Smith as their new manager. Tony soon found himself waging a fruitless war against Oldham in order to further the group's career in America:

> My last meeting with Andrew Oldham was at the Speakeasy when we threatened to have a punch up as a result of the way he was failing to give any support when the Nice badly needed it in America. We were stuck with Andrew at a time when he was distributed by CBS but at Clive Davis's personal instruction he was not allowed to enter the CBS building. So it was very amusing to be with a record company that was itself on an answering machine in a Central Park apartment. Nor could we go to CBS because officially we weren't their artistes, we were Andrew Oldham's artistes. We couldn't get any action on the records. It was one of the most frustrating years of my life.

By late 1967, the pop business was rife with rumours that Oldham and Immediate were in serious financial difficulties. By April of the following year, the company was in liquidation, thereby confirming the long-held suspicion that the great Oldham had overreached himself once too often. In spite of his grand fall, the influence of Oldham's brainchild cannot be overestimated. He inspired a generation of entrepreneurs to establish new, thriving independent record companies that challenged the majors at their own game and provided new outlets for important artistes whose work was previously considered uncommercial or esoteric. Ironically, one of the people who benefited from Oldham's example was his former combatant Tony Stratton-Smith, whose experiences with Immediate taught him many lessons when he later founded the independent

Charisma Records:

> Oldham's Immediate was brilliant. They had a marvellous A&R policy, they developed some great artistes. But, unfortunately, there was no genuine commitment with what they were trying to do. It was all on top — not the music, but the organization. We had this absurd situation at the end where Andrew appointed his personal barber as a general manager. This poor chap was really paid to sit there and listen to managers' gripes and say he'd look into it. It really was a joke. I had a love/hate thing for Immediate; I learned a lot of good things from it, creatively, but, as the way they went down at the end tended to prove, there wasn't a lot of integrity there.

Oldham's managerial career effectively ended with the liquidation of Immediate, but he remained in the music business, achieving varying success in the States as a record producer. In terms of the history of pop management, Oldham is a crucial figure, the first of the great creative young managers of the mid-sixties. His influence on the music business during that period was incalculable and his achievement as a publicist and mastermind behind the Stones' rise to fame assures him a place alongside the all-time greats of pop management. While his importance is beyond question, however, his contemporaries still question the depth of his vision. Tony Stratton-Smith concludes with an intriguing perspective:

> I always used to think that he was of the ilk of [Who manager] Kit Lambert. But whereas Kit had the charm and the intellect which gave another dimension to the razzmatazz and brilliant promotional ideas, Oldham was just the brilliant promotional ideas. He didn't have the intellect or clout that Lambert later showed with the Who. I also felt that Oldham placed himself, for a period, so close to Mick Jagger almost to suggest to the world that he had created Jagger, as if he were the svengali. But when you saw them working together, this was transparently not true. Jagger was always his own man. Oldham had lots of nerve, which you needed then to be successful in the business. In many ways I liked and admired him but, at the end of the day, I didn't respect him.

In spite of Stratton-Smith's reservations, there remains a body of managers who still maintain that Oldham was *the* great svengali of mid-sixties pop. Simon Napier-Bell believes that Oldham virtually created the Rolling Stones and even the normally sober Ken Pitt waxes enthusiastic on that same myth:

> Oldham was unique in that he was one of the Rolling Stones. It was

almost as if there were six schoolboys and one of them wasn't any good so they pointed at him and said, 'You be the manager.' It worked because everything about his personality fitted in so beautifully with the boys. I don't think he was a good manager in the administrative sense — but he was the man to promote them and dream up those wonderful stunts . . . He couldn't be in one place long enough to manage. He was a rolling stone.

In 1963, Harvey Lisberg was a graduate articled clerk working for pitiful wages, made bearable only by the sure knowledge that such deferred gratification would be amply rewarded upon qualifying as a chartered accountant. The tedium of work encouraged him to search for a compensatory hobby that might somehow combine his flair for business with a lifelong love of music. Like many of his contemporaries, Harvey was fascinated by the Beatles and their suave, mercurial manager, Brian Epstein. As a confident 23-year-old with a head for figures, an eye for image and an ear for good straightforward pop, Lisberg decided to emulate the lepidopterous Liverpudlian by embarking on some part-time talent spotting. In the unlikely setting of a church hall in Davyhulme, Manchester, he discovered a teenage group, the Heartbeats, led by a baby-faced singer with an irresistible charm, ideally suited to the teen market. The kid was Peter Noone, a former actor who had achieved a flicker of national fame playing Len Fairclough's son in the popular television series, *Coronation Street*. His professional experience and cherubic looks convinced Lisberg to sign the group, which later emerged as Herman's Hermits.

Lisberg's first move was to find a sympathetic producer and his choice proved crucial in establishing the group as a hit act. The man of the moment was Mickie Most, a former pop singer who had recently scored hits with the Animals and the Nashville Teens. Mickie liked the cute-looking Noone who reminded him of an adolescent John F. Kennedy, a resemblance that augured well for the American market. In mid-1964, a record deal was finalized with Columbia, and Most took the group into the studio to cut a cover of Goffin and King's 'I'm Into Something Good', a number then enjoying US Top 40 success for Earl Jean. The song rapidly climbed to number 1 in Britain, and even hit the US Top 20, outselling Earl Jean in the process. Lisberg was now a qualified pop manager, a role that inevitably cost him his accountancy finals.

By early 1965, Herman's Hermits had switched to covers of late-fifties high school songs, including the Rays' 'Silhouettes' and Sam Cooke's 'Wonderful World'. Their success in introducing relatively obscure American oldies to British listeners was reversed in the States, where they concentrated more on numbers with an English slant. A throwaway album track titled 'Mrs Brown You've Got A Lovely Daughter' shot them to the top of the US charts in the midst of a much publicized Manchester invasion. For six consecutive weeks, Freddie and the Dreamers, Wayne Fontana and the Mindbenders and Herman's Hermits occupied the coveted number 1 spot and during an incredible week at the end of April were one, two and three in the *Billboard* Hot 100. This was a feat previously matched only by the Beatles so, not surprisingly, radio and television producers were falling over themselves in their attempts to discover whether this latest invasion constituted the eclipse of Merseybeat.

The man who held the fate of all these artistes in his hands was the celebrated Danny Betesh, whose Manchester-based agency, Kennedy Street Enterprises, was responsible for their bookings worldwide. Lisberg placed great faith in Betesh whose career development was uncannily similar to his own. They had both entered the pop business while working as articled clerks though, unlike Lisberg, Betesh was searching for additional income rather than pursuing a hobby. At the end of the fifties he ran a small ballroom, and after qualifying as a chartered accountant in 1961 moved into agency work, booking local acts such as Freddie and the Dreamers and Dave Berry. In 1963, he struck lucky, for his first big tour was the famous Roy Orbison/Beatles package. The 21-date tour was an astonishing success and established Betesh as one of the most important new promoters in the country. Now he had America at his feet begging to see acts who, several years before, were struggling to fill church halls. Freddie and the Dreamers were despatched first and the response could not have been better. After appearing on the television programme, *Hullabaloo* their old 1963 hit, 'I'm Telling You Now', zoomed to number 1. Amazingly, other former successes followed suit within days, including 'You Were Made For Me' and 'I Understand'. The Americans seemed spellbound by the zany antics of Freddie Garrity, whose high-wire aided leaps and crazy dance routine added an element of slapstick comedy to the standard beat group formula. Earnest American journalists noted Garrity's choreography with interest and, ever aware of the ephemeral power of such crazes as the Twist and the Hully Gully, demanded to know the name of the new dance. Garrity paused for a second and then announced, 'It's called the Freddie'. When this 'revelation' was heavily publicized, the group rushed out a novelty single, 'Do The Freddie', which gave them another Top 20 hit. If Freddie Garrity could become a mini-superstar in four weeks, what would the Americans do when they saw the fresh-faced Peter Noone? Betesh and Lisberg learned the answer to that question towards the end of 1965 when sales figures confirmed that Herman's Hermits had sold over 10 million records in less than a year.

Within weeks of landing in America, Herman replaced Freddie Garrity as flavour of the month, but due to clever promotion and an ever-increasing teenage following, he maintained his standing for a considerable period. Lisberg, meanwhile, was enjoying the role of pop mogul and soon found himself besieged by hustlers and hangers-on. He was offered film scripts and various dubious deals, all of which were politely declined. One morning, he arrived at his recently acquired New York office only to be confronted by a man smoking a giant cigar. It was the renowned producer Sam Katzman, who had flown in from Hollywood and refused to leave until a deal was agreed. Harvey threw up his hands and exclaimed for the umpteenth time, 'I don't want to do a bloody film!' The wily producer would not be denied, however, and after much pleading convinced the exasperated manager to allow his boys to perform two numbers in a cameo short. The conversation was beginning to sound like dialogue from a forties B-movie and, as if realizing this, Harvey half-jokingly announced: 'I'm not doing it unless I get a Cadillac'. Katzman merely snapped his fingers and drawled, 'You got it'. The following morning Lisberg was amazed to see a huge, white Cadillac parked in the street outside his office. Overnight, all his Hollywood fantasies had come true. In addition to the car, he received a cheque for £50 000 — a sizeable sum for two days work in Hollywood. The movie, *When The Boys Meet The Girls*, featured Connie Francis in the lead role and was described by Lisberg as 'the worst film ever made'. Katzman seemed pleased enough, however, and lined up Herman's Hermits for another celluloid embarrassment called *Hold On!*

The films negotiated by Lisberg spawned several hits including 'Listen People' and 'A Must To Avoid'. Meanwhile, the group traded mercilessly on their image as quaint English boys, singing such maudlin cockney music hall songs as 'My Old Dutch' and 'I'm Henry The VIII, I Am'. Incredibly, the latter reached number 1 in the States, even in the face of competition from the Byrds' 'Mr Tambourine Man', the Rolling Stones' 'Satisfaction' and the Beatles' 'Help!' Fortunately, British listeners were spared this archaic material, for neither of Herman's US number 1s were released as singles in the home country. Most of the credit for Herman's hit run has been given to producer Mickie Most, though Lisberg rightly maintains that this reputation needs qualifying:

Mickie felt uncomfortable when he didn't select the records, and our biggest three were the ones he didn't select — 'Mrs Brown You've Got A Lovely Daughter', 'I'm Henry The VIII, I Am' and 'Listen People'. Against that, he did choose the number 1 'I'm Into Something Good'

> . . . I'm not trying to put Mickie down, incidentally. He's very talented at picking stuff. He's equally talented for taking credit. I was also a good picker, so it didn't really matter. But he wanted the glory . . . That was his lifeblood.

By the end of the sixties, Lisberg's first discoveries could look back on 18 US and 20 UK hits.

In many respects, the longevity of Herman's Hermits was extraordinary. While most of their better contemporaries floundered or underwent long periods of struggle, Noone and the group breezed through the sixties, seemingly immune to the many mini-musical revolutions that threatened to extinguish them. Their worldwide record sales taught Lisberg an important lesson that he was never to forget:

> If they had been any good, it would have been so much the better. But I wasn't satisfied; I didn't have a band that could develop. I saw other bands that were miles better than Herman's Hermits musically, or any way you like, and they couldn't get arrested. I just live with that. It happens to be a fact of life. It proved to me that in those days it didn't have that much to do with musical talent.

Many managers might have fallen victim to delusions of grandeur with such a pulsating hit machine under their thumb, but Lisberg was never allowed this luxury. For, early in 1965, he signed another Manchester group whose career proved an unmitigated disaster. The Mockingbirds were a quartet that included in their ranks two major artistes of the future, Graham Gouldman and Kevin Godley. On paper, they looked chart certainties and Lisberg initially made all the right moves in forwarding their career. Like Herman's Hermits they were signed to Columbia and, for their first single, Graham came up with the classic 'For Your Love'. The song was demoed and presented to Columbia for release, but, incredibly, they turned it down. Lisberg was stunned by the decision and immediately passed the song over to Mickie Most explaining that it would be ideal for Herman's Hermits. Most was unimpressed, however, and his rejection left Harvey with a classic song that neither of his artistes were allowed to record. Eventually, 'For Your Love' ended up in Giorgio Gomelsky's hands and his group, the Yardbirds, took the song to number 1 in the *New Musical Express* charts. For Lisberg, this success was a mixed blessing, for he could not rid his mind of the knowledge that a great song had been given away needlessly.

The Mockingbirds released five singles during the next two

years and all of them failed to chart. It was a remarkable run of bad luck that still provokes some puzzling questions. Neither Lisberg nor the group can explain why their songs bore the kiss of death while the extra-curricular compositions of their singer-songwriter, Graham Gouldman, seemed blessed by the hand of Midas. Every time a Gouldman-written Mockingbirds single flopped, the group would shake their heads in disbelief while cataloguing his other chart successes: 'For Your Love', 'Heart Full Of Soul' (Yardbirds); 'Look Through Any Window', 'Bus Stop' (Hollies); 'Listen People', 'No Milk Today', 'East West' (Herman's Hermits); 'Tallyman' (Jeff Beck).

As the months passed, new ideas were discussed and there were several attempts to break the Mockingbirds by changing record companies and producers. Giorgio Gomelsky and Paul Samwell-Smith tried their luck and failed. The group even switched to Andrew Oldham's fashionable Immediate label for a one-off single, but fared no better. Eventually, they ended their days on Decca surrounded by other sixties relics. Although Lisberg should not be held entirely responsible for their failure, it is difficult to escape the conclusion that a more concerted promotional push was needed to boost their chances. Other managers would have invested hard cash in radio plays, engineered a bizarre publicity stunt or even paid a chart-fixer, but Harvey preferred to allow the records to fail on their own merits.

Lisberg eventually despaired of the Mockingbirds, but took comfort in the knowledge that Gouldman was one of the best pop songwriters in Britain. Not surprisingly, Graham quickly struck out for a solo career, but the curse of the Mockingbirds appeared to blight his progress. Several flop singles culminated in the American release of an album, *The Graham Gouldman Story*, which swiftly found its way into the bargain bins. Throughout this period, Gouldman continued songwriting and production work for other artistes and even found time to form a couple of short-lived studio groups, High Society and the Manchester Mob. One of the sessioners involved in both these projects was singer-songwriter, Peter Cowap, who so impressed Lisberg that he signed him up. Like Gouldman, however, Cowap failed to secure chart glory in spite of a near hit with 'Crickets' in 1970.

Graham Gouldman's songwriting skill drew Lisberg towards a number of acts over the years including Wayne Fontana who, since splitting from the Mindbenders, had achieved minimal chart success. 'Pamela Pamela', Gouldman's eighth hit composition, provided the necessary breakthrough, but further success was not forthcoming. In retrospect, Lisberg admits that he could neither control nor develop Wayne Fontana's career:

> I never really 'managed' him because he was impossible. He was wild! If he'd been correctly handled or took direction he would have been huge. But it was all down to songs — the wrong songs, the wrong production . . . Mickie Most just did what he wanted, but with Wayne, he never did the right songs.

Resurrecting the career of a fallen artiste is never easy as Lisberg discovered later in the decade when he briefly managed the Herd. The group had left Billy Gaff, Howard and Blaikley and Andrew Oldham and were searching for a new mentor to restore them to the charts. After only three months, however, Harvey found himself so bogged down in their personnel problems that he politely withdrew his services.

Unlike many managers, Lisberg did not place his faith in temperamental pop artistes alone, but spent much time developing songwriting talent. The short lifespan of many sixties groups convinced Harvey that the public were fickle in taste, unpredictable and easily led. For a manager to survive in the business, diversification seemed the best course of action and the recent phenomenal success of Lennon and McCartney suggested that young songwriters were a sound investment. Lisberg was astute enough to spot commercial potential in two up-and-coming composers, Andrew Lloyd Webber and Tim Rice, and agreed to represent them. It was a frustrating period spent fruitlessly attempting to convince record companies and theatrical impresarios that *Joseph and the Technicolour Dreamcoat* was a viable proposition. Decca eventually agreed to release the album but, even then, Lisberg met further brick walls while trying to stage the musical in London. His confidence was not helped by teasing jibes from Graham Gouldman and others, who felt that his championing of Rice and Lloyd Webber was a colossal blunder. When the songwriting duo announced that their next project was to be a musical entitled *Jesus Christ Superstar*, Lisberg lost heart and turned his back on a fortune:

> I thought, 'Well, I can't see that being right for a Jewish boy somehow!' It felt uneasy. I'd played *Joseph* to people and they thought it was a load of crap. I felt they could happen, but I never had the tenacity, mainly due to the subject matter of *Jesus Christ Superstar*. If I'd stayed with them I would have been in a different league as far as theatrical work is concerned, which has always been my first love anyhow.

As the end of the sixties approached, Lisberg seemed a likely candidate for retirement from the management field. Most of the celebrated pop managers of the decade including Andrew Oldham, Larry Page, Simon Napier-Bell, Howard and Blaikley, Peter Walsh and Ken Pitt all bowed out in favour of less taxing ventures. The influx of accountants, solicitors and anonymous agencies had weakened the power of the typical sixties charismatic manager and left many feeling disillusioned amid the facelessness of seventies rock. Lisberg survived this managerial purge for a number of reasons. Unlike certain of his fellows, he had not been dragged through litigation, bankruptcy or tempestuous relationships with his stars. Herman's Hermits had proved a smooth-running operation, allowing Lisberg to relax and enjoy life in Manchester free from the pressure of the London entrepreneur. While other managers hogged the limelight and encouraged media interest in their activities, Lisberg remained a veritable unknown outside the industry. Looking back, Harvey contrasts himself with the great personality managers of the sixties:

> I was more interested in money than ego. I wasn't interested in self-aggrandisement or building up an empire like Shell Oil. I was just interested in meeting nice girls and enjoying healthy pastimes. I was 23 — I had a lot of energy! People like Kit Lambert felt they were part of their groups, which was nonsense. Fortunately, I never wanted to be one of Herman's Hermits. I was a manager. I wanted to be Epstein or Colonel Tom Parker.

If Lisberg really wanted to be an Epstein he was certainly contradicting his comments about ego and empires. Epstein was the fantasy model for many sixties managers, but Lisberg was a totally different species. Less neurotic and grandiloquent in his schemes, he was content to proceed at a cautious pace. The accountancy training he had undergone years before remained a useful tool, particularly when new seventies artistes began searching for business-orientated managers. Sensing the dawn of a new era, Lisberg increased his power in the industry by forming a partnership with his old friend Danny Betesh. As a director of Kennedy Street Enterprises, he could now combine his managerial skills with one of the most reputable agents in the business.

Although Lisberg had successfully extended his sphere of influence, there remained the problem of deciding where to channel his energies. The record business was in a state of flux and it was difficult to predict whether pop, progressive or washing-up music would prove the best investments for a secure and lucrative future. Predictably, Harvey covered his options by aiming at a number of different markets. When Herman's Hermits ended their chart run he stayed with Peter Noone in the hope that a solo career might prove fruitful. Harvey credits Mickie Most for setting that career alight by selecting David Bowie's 'Oh You Pretty Things' as a hit single. Unfortunately, Noone failed to capitalize on its success and gradually wound down his recording career.

Lisberg, meanwhile, was now taking Gordon Mills as his career model and seemed intent on discovering a middle of the road performer in the Tom Jones bracket. While plotting Noone's solo career, he had simultaneously launched Tony Christie, a singer whose vocal mannerisms were remarkably similar to the Welshman of his dreams. Christie charted immediately with 'Las Vegas', a place where his manager would clearly have loved him to perform. Unfortunately, Tony lacked the charisma of Jones and failed to crack the American charts let alone successfully infiltrate the gambling capital of the world. Nevertheless, his success in Britain was consistent over the years with a short string of hits including 'I Did What I Did For Maria', 'Is This The Way To Amarillo', 'Avenues And Alleyways' and 'Drive Safely Darling'. Lisberg enjoyed the hit run, but admits that they had problems with songwriters, insistent on pushing their own material when it had evidently lost its commercial appeal. With Christie's career in the balance, Lisberg pulled out following a serious disagreement over career development:

> I managed him for seven to eight years. I packed it in eventually because he refused to do the part I got him in *Evita*. He was on the original soundtrack and they wanted him to do the stage version and he just didn't want to know. I thought, this is ridiculous, inflexible, stupid. I couldn't believe it. It's horrible when an act gets to that level and you feel that they're over the top.

In spite of his involvement with balladeers and boyish teen idols, Lisberg was irresistibly drawn back to the bane of his managerial life — Graham Gouldman. The former Mockingbird was as inventive as ever and continued to plot a musical course as diverse as Lisberg's zig-zag managerial road. In the summer of 1968, he even joined the struggling Mindbenders, but his cursed luck struck again and they folded within three months of his arrival. Gouldman shrugged his shoulders and returned to session work, taking up an offer from Giorgio Gomelsky to produce some material for the manager's recently launched Marmalade label. Seeking assistance, Gouldman reunited with ex-Mockingbird Kevin Godley and an old schoolfriend, Lol Creme, and together they began work on the album. Unbelievably, Gouldman's perennial bad luck struck again when the unpredictable Gomelsky announced that he could no longer afford to finance the project.

Ever-resourceful, Gouldman soon found himself back in work when Lisberg negotiated an intriguing deal with the prodigious Kasenatz-Katz Organization. The New York-based company were the leading purveyors of bubblegum music and had already astounded the world with such legendary acts as the Kasenatz-Katz Singing Orchestral Circus, the 1910 Fruitgum Company, the Ohio Express and Crazy Elephant. Most of their groups were non-existent and the often infantile songs were the bastard creations of faceless writers, session musicians and singers. Since they had so many group names in their catalogue, Kasenatz-Katz were always looking out for writers and could not resist a composer of Gouldman's experience. The former boy wonder was despatched to New York and went through a gruelling work schedule that offered minimal aesthetic satisfaction but considerable financial rewards. As Lisberg noted, 'It was a total disaster but great fun'. Anxious to return home, Gouldman persuaded the Kasenatz-Katz Organization to extend their operation to England, and dragged in Godley and Creme as musical drones. Together, they hacked out up to 20 tracks a week, even using their own double-tracked falsetto voices in place of unaffordable female backing vocalists. They rightly regarded these absurdly low budget productions as hit factory fodder, but the discipline and ingenuity involved in maximizing limited studio resources was to prove extremely valuable experience.

The Kasenatz-Katz sessions were completed at Strawberry Studios, a workshop recently opened by ex-Mindbender Eric Stewart and former Dakotas' roadie Peter Tattershall. It was there that Godley, Creme and Stewart began tinkering with various instruments and studio equipment and accidently created an extremely unusual and commercial pop song. Released under the group name Hotlegs, 'Neanderthal Man' rocketed to number 2 in the British charts establishing the studio trio as unlikely hit artistes. Once again, the luckless Gouldman had been left out in the cold, while the musicians he brought together prospered. The irony was compounded when the song also cracked the US Top 30 and went on to sell over two million records worldwide as well as spawning a moderately successful album, *Thinks School Stinks*. Gouldman was allowed the consolation of joining the group on a highly successful British tour, following which Hotlegs became inoperative. It soon became clear, however, that the quartet could go on to fulfil Lisberg's latest dream:

Ultimately, I wanted a group that could just carry on writing, performing and not have to put up with all the crap that I had had with Mickie Most, like *not* doing good songs such as 'For Your Love' and 'Bus Stop' and having to give them to the Yardbirds and the Hollies.

Lisberg's studio wonders were eventually signed by former pop singer, novelty exponent and UK label boss Jonathan King, who also gave them a new name — 10cc. After charting with the falsetto high-school pop pastiche 'Donna', they began a chart run which continued almost uninterrupted for the rest of the decade. 10cc virtually re-invented pop at a time when the British charts lay in the hands of the glitter and techno flash brigade. As a result of their years of studio work, they were not only more musically competent and imaginative than their contemporaries but also blessed with a historical perspective that recognized the Great Tradition of pop and demanded its continuation. This they achieved by borrowing from and assimilating the finest teen music of the fifties and sixties and adding their own magical sprinkle of seventies technology. Their wit and word play appealed to the same intellectual critics who weekly scorned the tinsel superficiality of Slade, T. Rex, Gary Glitter, the Sweet and all their ilk. A string of UK hits including 'Rubber Bullets', 'The Dean And I', 'Wall Street Shuffle' and 'Silly Love' culminated in the tragi-comic chart-topper 'I'm Not In Love', which also provided a belated US breakthrough. By this time, however, their once unshakeable camaraderie was waning.

Throughout 1976 the group struggled to stay together, but in spite of some odd flashes of wit, such as 'I'm Mandy Fly Me', it was generally accepted that their work lacked the sparkle of earlier days. When they split into two factions towards the end of the year, it came as little surprise to their critics or their harried manager:

> The group kept splitting up. One was leaving one minute and another the next. Godley and Creme just decided that they wanted to be film producers. If ever they are, good luck to them, but, by God, they're going to sweat in the meantime. They turned their back on huge success because they couldn't stand it. They were great, brilliant, innovative — and what did they do? A triple album that goes on forever and became a disaster.

The work Lisberg refers to is the grandiloquent *Consequences*, subtitled 'The Story of Man's Last Defence Against an Irate Nature'. Consisting of seven songs over six sides, the work was intended to launch the gizmo gadget, a guitar attachment that seemingly created new sounds previously unheard in the history of music. The press turned on the once-unpretentious 10cc duo and dismissed the entire proceedings as a ridiculous display of pompous ego gratification. *Consequences* went down in pop history as the ultimate coffee-table album.

Following the split, Stewart and Gouldman retained the 10cc tag and attempted to carry on as if nothing had happened. They charted on a couple of occasions and even pulled off a surprise number 1 with the mock-reggae 'Dreadlock Holiday', but their recordings demonstrably lacked the charm, wit and imagination of previous days. The 10cc hit machine effectively ground to a halt when Eric Stewart was involved in a car crash in January 1979 and suffered deafness in his left ear. Micro-surgical operations were carried out in an attempt to correct the condition, but by the time he returned to resurrect 10cc, the group seemed passé. In spite of all their vinyl successes, Lisberg was left with a feeling of anti-climax:

> I think they should have been bigger. The only reason why they weren't, aren't or ever will be is because of their snobbery. It was absolutely impossible to convey one ounce of artistic feedback to 10cc. All you could do was say you didn't like something. They believed they knew it all. And they had a lot of success. You don't argue with people who are turning out number 1s. But, in my heart, I felt if only they'd put on sequined jackets or got something additional that the kids could have got off on — then they could have been as big as Pink Floyd.

For a time, Lisberg continued to manage both 10cc and Godley and Creme, but when the latter also began to write hits, the political situation became extremely delicate. After long consideration, Harvey decided to leave Kevin and Lol to their own devices and stick with the less problematical Gouldman and Stewart. A decade on, it seems unlikely that either faction will regain the power or wit that characterized their early-seventies recordings, though they still have much to offer in other spheres of the music business. In spite of Lisberg's frustration, the unfashionable image of 10cc has proved a strength as well as a weakness for unlike most of their glam rock contemporaries, old age and changing fashions have not irrevocably destroyed their pop careers.

The success of 10cc during the early seventies convinced Harvey that he had his finger on the pulse, so, eager to embrace the new era, he launched into the progressive music market. The first of his 'underground' signings was Julie Driscoll, a talented singer previously managed and recorded by Giorgio Gomelsky. Driscoll had been involved in a couple of Graham Gouldman's multitudinous studio escapades and Harvey made no secret of his respect and admiration for her talent. Although he managed her for nearly three years she apparently never worked during that period. However, Lisberg takes no responsibility for her strange reluctance to perform: 'It wasn't my fault, she just didn't feel up to it!' The most amusing result of Driscoll's low profile was her increased popularity among university entertainment officers who consistently pestered Harvey for bookings. Although he retaliated by gradually increasing her fee from £400 to £2000, their eagerness to secure the girl who brought life to Dylan's 'This Wheel's On Fire' never waned. Eventually, this most unusual and hilarious manager/artiste relationship ended when Julie married former King Crimson pianist Keith Tippett.

Lisberg's next idea was to break into the seventies albums market with a prestigious art rock band, but rather than choosing a new act, he signed Barclay James Harvest. Formed in early 1967, the band were major exponents of techno flash rock and one of the first of their era to include a mellotron in their live performances. After several hard years on the road, however, their career was at a crossroads. Their albums were selling poorly and financial problems threatened to push them into bankruptcy. Lisberg took over in the midst of the crisis and soon found himself out of his depth:

> I was interested in getting into that area and away from Herman's Hermits. In fact, a mile away from Herman's Hermits. . . But I didn't know what I was taking on. It was an absolute quagmire of personality problems. It made Herman's Hermits look like a Sunday school outing.

Harvey had to use all his accounting knowledge to stabilize the group financially, and, for a time, all went well. The band even performed on *Top Of The Pops* and scored a shock Top 50 hit with a live EP. More importantly, Lisberg found them a hot-shot American producer, Elliot Mazer, who worked on their much-publicized album *Time Honoured Ghosts*. Expectations were high following its release, but the sales proved disappointing. Amid their disillusionment, the group split with Lisberg on the grounds that he had failed to break them in the States. Ironically, they have made little headway there since, though they remain a major attraction on the Continent. The only consolation for Lisberg and Kennedy Street Enterprises was retaining the publishing from the period of their four-year management.

One morning in early 1977, a tape arrived at Kennedy Street Enterprises, and after listening to several tracks, Harvey declared the group chart certainties. Sad Cafe were a strangely eclectic unit whose repertoire offered a selection of white soul, tinged with jazz and dramatic ballads. Their staunch, workmanlike performances proved enormously popular in Manchester and several years earlier they would have received highly-acclaimed reviews as a 'fine band'. In the year of the punk explosion, however, their chances were virtually non-existent. With three-chord minimalism, spiked hair-cuts and nihilistic politics offering the quick route to fame, Sad Cafe were obviously in for a long slog. After two albums, *Fanx Ta Ra* and *Misplaced Ideals,* Lisberg decided to bring in Eric Stewart as producer in the hope that a hit single might result from the sessions. The experiment worked and Sad Cafe finally broke through with *Facades*, which included three hits: 'Every Day Hurts', 'Strange Little Girl' and 'My Oh My'. Although their following slowly increased, they failed to capture the headlines from lesser outfits and remained a relatively minor league attraction, much to their manager's frustration:

> They were unfashionable, provincial hicks. Some of the songs should have been hits but they weren't very good at songwriting. They needed to be stronger to break through. They gave a good show — they gave their all. But it wasn't good enough.

By the end of the seventies, Lisberg was sick of the music business and refused to sign any new acts. He continued to manage 10cc but admits that this amounted merely to servicing an already established unit. Instead of temperamental rock stars, Harvey began managing successful snooker players and still has a vested interest in the game. From 1980 to 1982 he stopped seeing new groups or listening to the radio. His disillusionment stemmed partly from an aversion to post-punk movements combined with a growing belief that the media and record industry were consistently churning out rubbish:

> I don't think you can ever underestimate the gullibility of the public. Don't talk to me about art! The public will take what they're given. People can turn around to me and say exactly the same thing about Herman's Hermits: 'They didn't have quality and you shoved it down our throats'. And it's true. Even today, and possibly more so with video, things are packaged. They're made to look fashionable, anarchistic, grotesque, scandalously sexy, bisexual or anything else that goes. It's background noise which DJs will tell you is wonderful. What's quality? There's no quality in it.

Lisberg's words betray the cynicism of a McLaren, yet he remains a victim of the business that he derides. Kennedy Street Enterprises represents the establishment end of the Manchester music scene and in spite of his catholic tastes, Lisberg is extremely conservative. Significantly, while Slaughter and the Dogs, the Buzzcocks, Magazine, the Drones, Spherical Objects, the Passage, Joy Division and the Fall raged around his ears, Harvey doggedly persisted with Sad Cafe. He has always been associated with eminently unfashionable artistes whose anonymity reflects his own managerial persona. Certainly, Harvey has consistently maintained a low profile, though as a business manager and accountant, this is hardly surprising. Yet, his self-image is not that of the provincial businessman. Remarkably, he castigates the accountants and solicitors that have infiltrated the music business since the end of the sixties, even referring to them as a 'cancer'. In his own mind, he remains the frustrated creative manager, trapped in a role not of his own choosing:

> I've got a lot of good ideas on the musical side. I've created a lot of things. I got hold of Peter Noone who was a little yob in a club and I made him into a world superstar. I did the same with Tony Christie, and the same with 10cc and Sad Cafe. You can't keep doing that unless there's something there . . . You can have a tremendous influence on a band artistically, which can be done in the foreground, like Mickie Most shouting how great he is, or in the background, like myself. I preferred being in the background, but now I'm not so sure whether that was right . . . I'm much more artistic than my image suggests and that suits me. I know what I want.

Precisely what creative input Lisberg was directly responsible for remains a mystery and one cannot help feeling that there is an element of self-delusion in his svengali notions. The starmaking fantasies are probably fuelled by his formidable successes as a business manager over the years. When pushed he concedes that few, if any, artistes listened to his creative ideas and this has clearly proven enormously frustrating. Underlying past glories is the knowledge that some dreams remain unfulfilled:

> I've never had an act that can deliver on stage. It must be a wonderful thing. With all the success I've had I can never look back to a great performance. With 10cc I could say it was a fantastic sound or of Sad Cafe I could say it was good, but a little passé. And Tony Christie was always in the shadow of Tom Jones.

The catalogue of failed dreams sounds depressing and, as if realizing this, Lisberg changes tack and like a latter day Muhammed Ali, announces that he is making a comeback. For the past few years,

Kennedy Street Enterprises has concentrated on promoting, publishing and agency work, but Lisberg is now eager to discover new pop talent. At the time of our meeting, he had recently signed a young group who were willing to accept his creative ideas and career directives. As Lisberg bluntly stressed: 'I've got a new act now and I'll do just what the hell I like with it'. Like all managers with a new act, Harvey believed Bürlitz might prove his biggest find to date, but it was not to be. Now in his mid-forties, and with a history of unfashionable acts behind him, it seems doubtful whether Lisberg will ever *create* a visually exciting and musically dynamic pop group. He can, however, claim a significant contribution in placing Manchester on the world musical map. Although he retains an engagingly bombastic tone, there are already signs that the hunger of discovery may have been sated once too often. His ambivalent feelings about the power and glory that top flight management offers are finally betrayed in a revealing aside: 'These big acts want blood. They're not going to get mine'.

The rise of Ken Howard and Alan Blaikley to positions of power in pop management is an unlikely tale. During the early sixties the duo were happily employed at the BBC, working in television drama and current affairs. While assigned to the police series *Z Cars*, Ken decided to compose a cash-in record featuring Joe Brady (alias PC Jock Weir). On the strength of the television audience ratings, Pye agreed to release 'The Great Train Robbery', but due to its controversial subject matter, the single caused a minor furore, resulting in a nationwide ban. Undeterred, Alan and Ken continued to write songs while searching for suitable vocalists for recording purposes.

A friend recommended a visit to the Mildmay Tavern in Islington, where the Sherabons had a residency. Upon arrival, Howard and Blaikley discovered a middling pop group whose saving grace was a female drummer, the presence of whom guaranteed publicity in the mid-sixties pop world. The Sherabons were pleased to accept some Howard and Blaikley songs and when their producer elect, Joe Meek, selected 'Have I The Right' as a single, a management deal was quickly completed. Ken Howard admits to being rather taken aback by it all:

> We never dreamed of being managers. We hated the image. Nothing that we'd ever done before — school, university, the BBC — was in any way connected with that sort of world. People were amazed when we went into it, but it was a time of great mobility.

One advantage the management team had over some of their rivals was a knowledge of the law. Ken Howard's father was a reputable West End solicitor and provided excellent advice on drawing up contracts. Basing many of the terms on the standard Equity agreement, he produced a document that was unusually geared in the artiste's favour.

Although the Sherabons had won an excellent management contract, they failed to attract much record company interest. HMV wrote a particularly dismissive letter suggesting that the Joe Meek-produced 'Have I The Right' had 'no commercial potential whatsoever'. Several nail-biting months passed before Pye finally intervened with an acceptable offer, dependent upon the group changing their name. One afternoon, Pye MD Louis Benjamin heard Ken Howard humming Jimmy Rodgers' 'Honeycomb' and, recalling that the Sherabons' drummer was nicknamed 'Honey' Lantree, he rechristened them the Honeycombs.

Following a couple of prestigious television plugs, 'Have I The Right' began selling in large quantities and by late August 1964, it was number 1. Amid the celebrations, the press leaked the fact that songwriter 'Howard Blaikley' was, in fact, a thinly-disguised pseudonym for two BBC employees. The broadcasting authority responded with an ultimatum — either Ken and Alan cease this extra-curricular employment immediately or surrender their posts forthwith. Much to the amazement of their friends and supervisors they gambled on a career in pop, as Ken explains:

> Everybody counselled us against it. They said, 'You're mad — you can't leave the BBC. It's your career. How can you throw it up, after six years, for this ridiculous pop business?' But it wasn't difficult at all. At that time pop music was the thing that England could excel in.

Ken and Alan were obviously overwhelmed by their champagne start in the pop business and when 'Have I The Right' effortlessly sailed into the US Top 10, their future as major pop moguls seemed assured. Meanwhile, Louis Benjamin, their saviour at Pye, confidently predicted that the follow up single, 'Is It Because' would climb to number 1. Everybody believed that the Honeycombs could do no wrong. But pop fans can be fickle creatures and following a dramatic reversal of fortune, the group found themselves with a follow up that failed to register a Top 30 entry. They were the only chart-topping act of the year that could not exploit their number 1 success and this was a matter of grave concern.

Reviving the chart fortunes of the Honeycombs proved immensely difficult, particularly as the group seemed relatively unconcerned about their status in the pop world. According to Howard, they preferred singing in pubs to appearing on television and reacted to their chart-topping achievement with humble satisfaction rather than awe-inspiring egomania. Their lack of ambition was also reflected in lacklustre live performances which often ended in jeers from over-expectant members of the audience. In desperation, their managers temporarily sent them abroad where pop-starved fans were less discriminating.

While Howard and Blaikley urgently sought another potential hit, the Honeycombs slowly disintegrated before their eyes. Bespectacled guitarist Martin Murray developed a crush on Honey which was not reciprocated. To make matters worse he broke his leg, and by October 1964 was gone. A promising cover of Ray Davies's 'Something Better Beginning' and a comeback hit with

Howard/ Blaikley's 'That's The Way' kept the group's name alive
for another year, but further line-up changes and poor morale
blighted their progress. It was a measure of Howard and Blaikley's
desperation that they encouraged the group to record Shakespeare's
sonnet 'Who Is Sylvia?' as a novelty single. The gamble failed, no
further successes followed and the Honeycombs completed their
inexorable slide into cabaret.

In spite of the Honeycombs' ultimate failure, Howard and
Blaikley felt indebted to the group, not only for dragging them into
the pop business with a number 1 hit, but also for introducing them
to their next discovery. It was during a Honeycombs gig that
Martin Murray rushed backstage to inform Alan Blaikley of an
amazing support act whose flamboyant antics were causing a sensation. Blaikley needed only a few minutes to realize the enormous
potential of this crazy quintet:

> They would throw guitars around, throw each other around; it was a
> tremendous extrovert act. They were immensely experienced. They'd
> been in the Star Club, the Reeperbahn and Butlins. The act was
> extremely risqué for the time. Their comedy routines were really very
> blue — but funny. The singer had a great patter and could get away
> with murder.

Upon returning to London, Alan Blaikley told his partner about
this unusual group — Dave Dee and the Boston. At this point, the
Salisbury quintet were managed by Southampton promoters Bob
James and Les Canon, who were happy enough to surrender the
management reins in return for future agency rights. On the
strength of their live performance, Jack Baverstock signed the
group to Fontana and assigned them to a young American producer,
Steve Rowland. Meanwhile, Howard and Blaikley saddled them
with one of the longest group titles in pop history — Dave Dee,
Dozy, Beaky, Mick and Tich. The nicknames were actually genuine
and fully conveyed the zany nature of this comic outfit.

The main problem that Howard and Blaikley faced in 1966 was
getting the boys extensive airplay on radio. After two flop singles,
'No Time' and 'All I Want', a devious plan was hatched to cajole
producers and disc jockeys into airing the group's discs. The
management threw an elaborate party at Ken Howard's home in
Swiss Cottage, attended by virtually every influential media figure
in the music business. Mid-way through the evening, Ken and
Alan ushered the bemused guests into a bus and transported them
to the Burton's Ballroom in Uxbridge where they watched the
climax of a Dave Dee, Dozy, Beaky, Mick and Tich concert. They

were then shuttled back to the party and plied with more drink. At one stage, a semi-inebriated Radio London executive was heard to exclaim: 'If they sound as good on record tomorrow as they did tonight, I'll make them my pick of the week'. The following morning he dutifully played their latest record, 'You Make It Move', and before long it crept into the Top 30, much to the relief of the songwriting duo.

Under Howard and Blaikley's tutelage, Dave Dee and Company had an incredible run of 13 consecutive chart hits in under four years. It was strictly formula pop, but executed with a camp flair and theatricalism that proved alarmingly irresistible. Ken Howard recalls how the formula was expertly rehashed on each successive release:

> Every record with them was a challenge to top the one before. We connived to think of crazy ideas and scenarios. They were really actors; if you gave them a plot they would act up on it, whether it was a whip in 'The Legend Of Xanadu' or a motorbike in 'Last Night In Soho'. They would suggest ideas too. There was no stopping it. We could do anything.

Time and changing musical fashion finally caught up with the group in the late sixties and Dave Dee left for an unsuccessful solo career before moving into A&R.

On the strength of their chart successes, Howard and Blaikley contracted a number of artistes to short-term management deals. This allowed the prolific duo to release an ever-increasing number of songs from one-shot artistes in the hope of scoring further hits. Jack Baverstock of Fontana was more than pleased to offer two-single recording deals in the hope of finding another Dave Dee, Dozy, Beaky, Mick and Tich. Countless faceless artistes were caught up in this hit factory process including the Wolves (from Wolverhampton!), Alan Dean and his Problems, Peter Anathan and Gary Wright. Of all these brief flirtations, only Gary Wright later emerged as a major success, achieving three US Top 20 singles during the late seventies.

The next breakthrough for Howard and Blaikley came not from scouring pubs in search of talent but following the advice of their producer friend, Steve Rowland. In partnership with Ronnie Oppenheim, Rowland had formed RR Records and the premier act on the label, the Herd, were growing restless with their lack of hit success. Ken and Alan checked out the group at the Marquee, but were unimpressed by their stage act. The vocalist, Andy Bown, was stuck behind an organ, thereby robbing the Herd of a strong vocal point. The only time their performance came to life visually was during a solo spot by the guitarist, who sang lead on a Dylan cover. In spite of their shortcomings, Howard and Blaikley felt the group could be developed and agreed to take them on, backed by Rowland and Fontana. Not surprisingly, the Herd's manager, Billy Gaff, was less than pleased with this decision. He had, after all, bought them equipment and put considerable work into breaking the act. Following a loud argument in the living room of Ken Howard's house, he was finally appeased and fully reimbursed for his financial outlay. Gaff, like so many other managers in this book, learnt the hard way that artistes are capricious creatures. Strengthened by experience, he went on to become a very powerful manager in the seventies, brilliantly guiding the career of Rod Stewart.

Howard and Blaikley's first task as managers of the Herd was to restructure the unit, elevating Peter Frampton to lead vocalist. A psychedelic single, 'I Can Fly', revealed the group in unhappy transition, with both Bown and Frampton trading lead vocals. In order to bury the old image, Howard and Blaikley urgently required a quick, quality follow up. Luckily, such a song was already available: 'From The Underworld'.

In common with the Honeycombs' 'Who Is Sylvia?', 'From The Underworld' was an attempt by Howard and Blaikley to translate their favourite literature into pop. Such academic pretensions from one of the most blatantly commercial songwriters of the sixties left even their record company perplexed:

> They didn't think it was commercial. But Alan and I really believed in that song mainly because we'd been to the same school and had done Virgil's *Orpheus In The Underworld* as a set text in Latin. We'd gone to some trouble to transform it into a pop song keeping many of the original allusions. It was totally lost on the record-buying public, but we liked it!

Thanks to extensive plugging by disc jockey Alan Freeman, the record fulfilled its promise, peaking at number 6. Flushed by success, the songwriting duo pulled a similar trick with the follow up, this time citing Milton's *Paradise Lost*. Suddenly, the Herd found themselves in a peculiar position. They were a jazz-influenced trio with certain artistic aspirations and in a different situation might have developed into a 'progressive' band. With Howard and Blaikley however, they were inevitably regarded as a commercial pop group and the spurious profundity of their song titles fooled nobody, except perhaps themselves. Although the recently promoted lead singer, Peter Frampton, seemed content to remain in the shadows, his publicity-conscious managers had other ideas. During the desperate moments prior to an important television appearance, Howard was appalled to see Frampton swanning around in an old sweater and jeans. With no stage clothes available, he grabbed a pair of scissors and spontaneously transformed the singer's sweater into a geometric nightmare, complete with a sexy bare shoulder. Ken recalls how the Frampton look created a mini-sensation: 'Everybody talked about it. We got letters. Kids were seen shortly afterwards wearing similar garments. Talk about image!'

Unfortunately, Frampton was never allowed to recover from Ken Howard's publicity-grabbing exercise. Suddenly, the reluctant pop hero became front cover material for every teenzine in the land. His boyish good looks prompted *Rave* magazine to dub Peter 'the face of '68', a tag that dogged him for over a decade. Frampton's overnight success brought film offers, prying photographers, worshipping fans and undreamed of publicity for the Herd. Unfortunately, the pressures of stardom were not welcomed by the angst-ridden singer, as Howard reveals:

> We realized he had a fantastic face for photographs. He was a very good-looking kid. As soon as he assumed the lead we started selling records. He got this great fan following which was terrifying for him. He used to weep and sob. I felt terribly sorry for him; he wasn't ready for it, didn't want it, couldn't cope.

With the Herd established as fully-fledged pop stars, Howard and Blaikley abandoned the literary allusions of yore and wrote a straightforward ditty entitled 'I Don't Want Our Loving To Die'. The group were now at the peak of their career, but fame brought ego problems and petty jealousies. They began to resent Howard and Blaikley's commercial songwriting and, intoxicated by success, seemed intent on composing their own hit material. Moreover, as they had demonstrated in their affairs with Billy Gaff, the Herd were quite capable of cold expediency if a favourable opportunity arose elsewhere. Perhaps it was not too surprising that they were drawn towards the charismatic Andrew Oldham, whose wealth, style and managerial credibility proved irresistible. Ken Howard remembers his disappointment upon learning of their abrupt defection:

> We suddenly found the van in the street outside the house: its tyres had been let down. They said, 'We're going to go to Andrew Oldham'. What could one do? One couldn't sue them. It was particularly hurtful because we had a number 2 record and had notched up three

hits. They were poised for very big things. We just thought, 'Why?'

The Herd's Faustian lust for glory ultimately caused their down-fall. In Andrew Oldham they discovered a manager whose own expediency made them appear like novices. He gave them all they wanted, namely 'Sunshine Cottage', a Peter Frampton composition intended to follow 'I Don't Want Our Loving To Die' into the Top 10. The single flopped spectacularly and the Herd never even came close to retrieving their chart fortunes. Oldham no doubt fulfilled his obligations, but he was a man who always had more important schemes on his mind. The Herd had been exposed as three-hit-wonders and Oldham had neither the energy nor commitment to save their floundering career. In any case, it was probably too late to forestall their seemingly inevitable self-destruction. Of course, Frampton went on to US superstardom years later, but it was a long road back from the wilderness and Howard hints that the scars remain: 'He's had an extraordinary career, that boy. But, in a way, I feel sorry for what's happened to him. I don't feel he's very happy.'

By the end of the sixties, Howard and Blaikley were beginning to tire of their reputation as purveyors of puerile pop songs. Apart from their own stable they had also written bland Eurovision material for Lulu and a string of singalong hits for other artistes. What they needed was a new challenge and an opportunity to prove that they could write something more substantial than lowest common denominator pop. So it was that Howard and Blaikley launched themselves into the progressive music scene, picking up artistes whom they would once have run a mile from. Like many of their contemporaries, they ultimately failed to achieve the transition from sixties to seventies management, but this had little to do with their lack of entrepreneurial skill or even an inability to pen suitable material. In truth, by the end of the decade management was no longer a fun business for anybody. Zany, fun-loving groups like Dave Dee, Dozy, Beaky, Mick and Tich seemed a dead breed, replaced by tougher career-orientated individuals. Even teenage pop stars were taking themselves and the music business so seriously that full-time management had lost much of its former sparkle. During their twilight years, Howard and Blaikley suffered a run of bad luck, including an unpublicized tragedy that blighted their management career.

The first of their new-style discoveries was the promising Flaming Youth, featuring Phil Collins. The group recorded a concept album, *Arc 2*, but in spite of some excellent publicity the record failed to take off. Disillusioned, Howard and Blaikley soldiered on until their attention was drawn to another emerging talent. The

publisher Roy Berry, from Campbell Connolly, introduced them
to a former member of Fairport Convention who was apparently
intending to record some commercial material. Ian Matthews
initially seemed a godsend and Howard and Blaikley buried themselves in work intent on breaking the artiste internationally. They
wrote several songs on the *Matthews' Southern Comfort* album,
using the pseudonym Steve Barlby. In part, this was a joke on the
music establishment which had always dismissed Howard and
Blaikley as superficial composers. Suddenly, some uninformed
critics were applauding their writing ability and there must have
been several red faces when Steve Barlby's true identity was revealed.

Ian Matthews can have few complaints with Howard and
Blaikley's early efforts. They wrote songs, provided good publicity
and even created the famous Matthews' Southern Comfort T-shirt.
Against the odds they issued a belated cover of 'Woodstock' which
had already failed as a single in the UK by the then illustrious
Crosby, Stills, Nash & Young. Amazingly, the single climbed to
number 1 in the autumn of 1970 and also reached the Top 30 in the
States. Sadly, however, Matthews' Southern Comfort were doomed
to remain one-hit-wonders and Ian left to pursue a solo career.
According to Ken Howard there were frequent ego clashes in the
group and even at the peak of their success, with 'Woodstock'
topping the charts, they were far from content. Ian felt unhappy
about appearing with them on *Top Of The Pops* and, in desperation,
Ken Howard was reduced to pushing notes under the door of his
Highgate flat to try and persuade him to reconsider. Like many of
the early-seventies singer-songwriters, Matthews had a wilfulness
which frustrated a traditional manager such as Howard:

> Ian was a great talent but a very difficult personality inasmuch as he
> was a perfectionist who knew exactly what he wanted whether it was
> commercial or not. In many ways, I do respect him for his single-
> mindedness. On the other hand, he was a pain in the neck to manage
> . . . He could have been huge.

Career differences between Matthews and his management reached
a head prior to a performance at Manchester Town Hall. Ian left
the gig abruptly, boarded a train and returned home, leaving
Howard to sort out the mess. At the end of the evening Ken turned
to his partner and said, 'I don't ever want to manage anybody
again'. Although the duo retained their management interests for a
further couple of years, it was not a happy period. Southern
Comfort remained a second division unit along with Dando Shaft,
another club favourite that Ken and Alan had signed in a moment

of wayward enthusiasm. The ever-unpredictable Ian Matthews went his own way, but failed to achieve the worldwide commercial success that many writers had predicted.

The problems that Howard and Blaikley experienced with Ian Matthews merely confirmed their growing antipathy towards management as a profession:

> We never wanted to manage anybody. We never enjoyed managing people . . . I think there's something intrinsic in the management/artiste situation that makes it almost impossible for you to be friends with your artiste. They will place you in the role of being a schoolmaster or a crook. When you're on the road travelling around and you're dead tired, there's got to be someone you can blame. An artiste will say, 'It's alright for those lazy bastards, we're the ones doing the work'. In the end, it's got to come down to that. That's why, on the whole, the relationship between managers and artistes is dreadful.

In retrospect, Ken Howard claims that it was the successive failure of Flaming Youth and Ian Matthews that finally ended the long-term management agreement between himself and Alan Blaikley. However, there is another obscure combo whose brief career also played an important part in that decision. Windmill were an aspiring pop group whose work and appeal was not that far removed from Dave Dee, Dozy, Beaky, Mick and Tich. Perhaps they were an anachronism, but their existence seemed to suggest that there could still be fun in the over-serious seventies rock business. Howard and Blaikley held great hopes for them, but, just as their career prospects were beginning to improve, tragedy struck. While travelling from East to West Germany, the group were involved in a fatal accident. Lead singer Dick Scott and his wife were killed instantaneously when their car careered from the road and hit a tree. The subsequent dissolution of the group seemed to symbolize the death of Howard and Blaikley's pop sensibility. The innocence and fun-loving nature of their compositions seemed decidedly inappropriate during the austere seventies. Although they continued writing and achieved a modicum of success, their impact was severely lessened, and the loss of management ensured that they were no longer actively involved in any artiste's long term career. The talented duo still write musical soundtracks for West End shows, Howard works in film production, while Blaikley earns his living as a psychotherapist. No other figure in this book has used his managerial apprenticeship to such appropriate effect.

The pre-managerial exploits of Tony Stratton-Smith are exotic enough to warrant several chapters of a fully-fledged biography. While many of his contemporaries spent the fifties scouring Tin Pan Alley in search of potential British pop stars, Stratton-Smith was happily watching county cricket and football matches. For eleven years he served as a sports journalist, moving confidently from the *Birmingham Gazette* to the *London News Chronicle, Daily Sketch, Sunday Despatch* and *Daily Express*. If fate had taken a different course he might have lived and died in that profession. For, in February 1958, he had been ticketed for a flight from Belgrade to Munich to cover Manchester United's European Cup progress. Remarkably, he was assigned elsewhere at the eleventh hour and missed the tragic air disaster that all but destroyed one of the greatest soccer teams of that era.

By the early sixties, Stratton-Smith was slowly establishing himself as a freelance journalist and writer, contributing towards a number of football annuals. Soon, he had visions of ghosting full-scale biographies of the great footballing stars of the fifties and sixties, including Pele, Denis Law and Alfredo di Stefano. The books never appeared, but he was happy enough to sell their stories in the form of serialized newspaper articles. Apart from the odd stint at writing, Stratton-Smith appears to have spent most of his time lounging around at the Copacabana beach where he had retired following the Chile World Cup. There he met composer Antonio Carlos Jobin who casually suggested he should pursue a career in music publishing. Upon returning to England, Tony still had doubts about this advice and his initial reservations were to prove correct. His naïveté and earnestness as an aspiring publisher made him an easy target for street-wise musicians and songsmiths in search of a quick buck. Down at the Giaconda coffee bar in Denmark Street, Strat was regarded as a joke figure, easily cajoled into buying worthless songs for sizeable advances. Sadly, he squandered a considerable amount of money and finally closed his office in disillusionment. Most of the copyrights he had bought with such faith and enthusiasm were consigned to the rubbish bin.

Chastened by his failure, Stratton-Smith returned to his former occupation as a writer and completed work on *The Rebel Nun*, a biography of the martyr Mother Maria Skobtzova. It was during this period that he first met Beatles' manager, Brian Epstein, who was searching for a writer to ghost his autobiography. Tony spent several days with Epstein in Holland discussing the project, but eventually declined the offer which was later taken up by publicist Derek Taylor. Although Stratton-Smith narrowly missed establishing himself as the first celebrated rock biographer, his meeting with Epstein had proven inspirational:

> I learned a great deal from Brian, especially that a manager's role is a creative one. He has to create a situation in which his artistes can happen. That requires a lot of skills and disciplines that are quite outside the law and accountancy . . . I'd like to think that I was one of the managers who felt that way. Unfortunately, very few of them exist now.

Stratton-Smith embarked upon his managerial career in 1965, and, rather fittingly, his first discovery was a Liverpool combo. Paddy, Klaus and Gibson were a talented trio of musicians recommended to Strat when he was searching for sessioners to demo one of the worthless copyrights that remained in his files. At that point, the group was managed by ex-Viscount Don Paul, who urgently needed financial backing to purchase equipment and gain media attention. In return for £250, Paul agreed to give Stratton-Smith 10 per cent of his 25 per cent management commission. Before long, Stratton-Smith secured the group a residency at London's trendy Pickwick Club, where his chequebook was in frequent use. Unfortunately, after spending a fortune entertaining disc jockeys, journalists and celebrity musicians, he unexpectedly lost the group to Brian Epstein. The Beatles' manager had been pestered by John Lennon and George Harrison into offering the group a home at NEMS and, predictably, they accepted. Although Stratton-Smith and Paul received some financial compensation, Tony later felt that the transfer deal was a mistake:

> I had regrets because I think they should have made it. They weren't a Top 20 band but they had a marvellous live feel. I think the way I was handling them, building them through the clubs and delaying a record debut was, with hindsight, the best way. With NEMS, record after record came out and they were put on tours and I don't think they really had time to develop.

During early 1966, Stratton-Smith discovered another potential talent in the form of Liverpool singer Beryl Marsden. The Woolworths shop assistant had already gained enormous experience singing with various Merseybeat groups, as well as appearing at Hamburg's celebrated Star Club. Sensing her potential abroad,

Tony shipped her off to France where she achieved a modicum of success. Unfortunately, financing the act incurred losses of £50-£100 per week and lucrative bookings at home were rare. In an attempt to secure Marsden a higher media profile, Stratton-Smith approached a chart-fixer and paid £150 to hype her single 'Who You Gonna Hurt' into the *New Musical Express* chart. According to Tony, the fixer even had the foresight to send Beryl a bouquet several days before the chart was published. That same week the singer was interviewed by *NME* in their 'Newcomers To The Chart' feature. Ever unpredictable and obtuse, the diminutive 18-year-old virtually unhyped her own record with an incredibly frank and insouciant aside: 'I don't actually like the record. I've never cared much for it and I didn't think it had a chance of getting into your Top 30'. Poor Strat could have been forgiven for retiring from pop management on that frosty November day. The following week 'Who You Gonna Hurt' disappeared from the *NME* Top 30 listings and did not even register an entry in the *Record Retailer* Top 50. Stratton-Smith was amused by this embarrassing anomaly and began to take an ominous interest in the methods used by these clandestine hypers. The results of his research would be used to controversial effect later in the year.

In spite of her brief chart success, Beryl seemed unwilling to knuckle down to Stratton-Smith's conscientious career plans and proved one of the most undisciplined artistes he ever had the misfortune to deal with:

> Beryl was a marvellous girl flawed by a kind of Liverpudlian bloody-mindedness. There is a Liverpool thing and if you're not part of it, it's very difficult to cope with. . . I had to hire a Liverpool minder for her and he was the only guy who could actually get some sense out of her. Often, if a gig didn't suit her, she would actually lock herself in her flat so that nobody could get in and she couldn't get out. Many a time, this minder had to go through a window to get her.

Although Stratton-Smith was unable to break this temperamental singer in England, the Continentals evidently took her to their hearts. Unfortunately, Beryl's success overseas was severely arrested by a sudden attack of flight phobia, which Tony related with resignation:

> Once she was due to go to Germany for an important television show. She knew exactly what it involved. But when she got to the airport she refused to fly. I knew she'd flown before. God knows what was going through her mind. It caused a terrible commotion: police were involved,

British Airways said they'd virtually ban her from coming near the airport. After a few months of that I had to have an emergency operation brought on by nervous exhaustion, overwork and anxiety. I then backed off to rethink what I should do.

With two extremely talented, but unsuccessful, acts under his belt, Stratton-Smith's finances were already dwindling, yet he retained enough faith to back a couple of other hopefuls, the Creation and the Koobas. The former were one of the most inventive groups of the period, and certainly the best of the post-Who mod bands. Pete Townshend duly informed the press of their talent and in a fit of generosity reputedly invited lead guitarist Eddie Phillips to join the Who. Their success seemed assured and this time Stratton-Smith was taking no chances. He promoted their single 'Makin' Time' with expertise, and eventually it crept into the chart on 7 July 1966 at number 49. Amazingly, though perhaps not when one remembers Beryl Marsden, Stratton-Smith was suspected of arranging a fix, and the disc failed to appear the following week. It was unbelievable. Here was Strat with a *bona fide* hit and the ruling powers didn't believe it! The irony was completed the following week when, in a fit of indignation, he paid £270 (in advance) for the record to be reinstated. The fixer promised instant action but the record failed to recover its placing.

Stratton-Smith's cursed luck with hypers and chart compilers eventually prompted him to take the law into his own hands. Dissatisfied with the techniques of profiteering fixers, he devised his own system of hyping and effectively cut out the middle men. Without consulting the group, Tony spent £600 'pushing' their next single 'Painter Man', and this, combined with more legitimate promotion, secured a placing at number 36. Although he considered a further investment, Stratton-Smith concluded that if the disc failed to progress naturally at this point it was probably a loser anyway. Sadly, this was the extent of Creation's chart progress. Their prospects as a creative unit took a savage blow when key writer/lead vocalist Kenny Pickett was ousted from the group following a struggle over leadership. Although Creation traded on their reputation in Germany until as late as June 1968, they never recovered from the loss of Pickett. Once again, Stratton-Smith was forced back to the drawing board but at least there was still the Koobas.

Stratton-Smith had stumbled across the Koobas in late 1965 and immediately fell victim to their charm. Initially, their prospects seemed promising, particularly after appearing as support on the Beatles' last tour of England. Such an accolade might have proven enough to break an ambitious combo, hungry for fame, but sadly the Koobas were not of this breed. Their greatest flaw was an inability or unwillingness to write all their own material, which by the late sixties was almost a prerequisite for long term success. Before long, the Liverpudlian group hit a downward spiral, drinking frequently and languishing in a false sense of luxury provided by their over-fastidious manager. In retrospect, Stratton-Smith admits that he was largely responsible for pampering them to death instead of forcing them to face the inevitability of failure:

> I think that was the only band I ever spoiled and I regret it. Their career became more important to me than was healthy. I was putting far too much time into this one band in an attempt to crack them and I think you lose your objectivity if you do that. It just becomes a question of 'Oh, we'll carry on, Strat will always be there to pay the hotel bill and buy a drink'. I was virtually supporting them out of my own pocket which is a terrible mistake, particularly if you can't afford it.

By 1968, the Koobas were still dangling from Strat's purse strings unaware that their foolishly philanthropic mentor was several steps on the road to the bankruptcy court. A temporary reprieve from financial worries was secured via a prestigious support on a Jimi Hendrix Experience tour of Switzerland which enabled the group to rekindle some of their lost morale. Sadly, this fragile lifeline came too late for a group whose innate lack of motivation would inevitably negate what little opportunities were bestowed upon them. The continued failure to produce a competent writing team within the ranks precipitated their dissolution, leaving Stratton-Smith a wiser but poorer man.

The failure of the Koobas forced a nail into Stratton-Smith's managerial coffin, and for a time he seemed more than willing to accept a premature death. Abandoning the music business, he stoically returned to the world of book contracts and film scripts, much to the hungry anticipation of his once-spurned agent. All went well, and Tony seemed assured of the prosperous future that he had inexplicably rejected three years before. Within months, however, his security was totally undermined by the intervention of the Nice.

Of all the groups he had so far handled, the Nice clearly had the greatest potential and were already a well-respected club act whose recorded work on Immediate had received favourable reviews. Unfortunately, their association with manager/label owner Andrew Oldham was not without its problems, as Stratton-Smith recalled:

> With respect to Andrew Oldham, I don't think he ever really had any

faith in them. He didn't try hard to help the band, or even hang on to them. I think he totally underestimated what the Nice were about. That's why they brought me in. They wanted somebody who would pick up their career by the scruff of the neck and slam them into concert halls. Happily, I was able to do that for them, with their help.

Although Tony remembers this period with some affection, he admits that the group caused him a few minor headaches. When Keith Emerson unceremoniously burned a canvas effigy of the United States flag during a dramatic rendition of 'America' at the Royal Albert Hall, a lucrative Stateside tour was placed in jeopardy. It later took all of Stratton-Smith's diplomacy to persuade the US consul that the Nice would not repeat the incident. Agent Lenny Poncher was equally concerned and advised the group to postpone their tour until after the Presidential elections, adding ominously that he could not guarantee their personal safety. When the boys finally arrived at New York's Fillmore East, Emerson duly repeated his fiery stage act, shocking both his manager and a large proportion of the audience who catcalled, 'Go home limey'. Even the Fillmore's owner, Bill Graham, disapproved of the action and fell out with the Nice for some considerable period.

The problems that beset the Nice in the States did not prevent Stratton-Smith from extending his empire at home. Viv Stanshall was so impressed by Strat's handling of the Nice that he presented him with the Bonzo Dog Doo-Dah Band. The group had a management contract with the publishers Gerry and Lillian Bron, but the couple were more than willing to release this zany bunch of eccentrics. Managing the Bonzos was probably too great a strain for any manager though Stratton-Smith held the post for a year. During that period he struck lucky, for the Bonzos scored a surprise hit with 'Urban Spaceman', a track produced by Paul McCartney (under the pseudonym Apollo C. Vermouth) prior to his arrival. The Bonzos proved a happy diversion from Stratton-Smith's more serious ventures and his one regret was that, like the Nice, they failed to win strong support from their American record company.

In many respects, Tony's frustration with certain record companies provided the circumstances that finally transformed him from a failed sixties manager into one of the most celebrated entrepreneurs of the early seventies. After serving four years' apprenticeship in management, he realized that his financial woes had stemmed not merely from temperamental and extravagant artistes, but a record industry that cleverly exploited creative talent through severely one-sided contracts. In the mid-sixties, EMI and Decca Records controlled the show and their only serious challengers,

Philips and Pye, merely reflected the policies that the duopoly had established years before. Stratton-Smith vividly recalls negotiating at length with Pye in order to raise the Koobas' royalty rate from two to two-and-a-half per cent. And this was far from the worst deal on offer to an unknown group during that period. It was not until the late sixties that the winds of change swept through record company offices, altering the outmoded conventions that had kept artistes, and many managers, under the corporate thumb since the Tin Pan Alley days. This mini-revolution was caused by a number of complex factors. The elevation of pop music to the status of a minor art form encouraged many groups and singers to take their work more seriously and this was reflected in their attitudes towards the business. More importantly, several long-sighted entrepreneurs including Robert Stigwood, Larry Page, Andrew Oldham and Kit Lambert were intent on branching out from management in order to secure control of preserves previously held by the corporators. This desire for entrepreneurial autonomy, coupled with the artistes' growing awareness of the importance of their product, spelt danger for many record companies. In retrospect, Stratton-Smith credits Roland Rennie as one of the major figures responsible for breaking the EMI/Decca duopoly. Rennie had defected from EMI in the mid-sixties in order to help set up Polydor Records in the UK. As a matter of policy, Rennie spent extravagantly, buying up talent on an unprecedented level and offering large advances that forced the majors to compete in a more open market. Inevitably, the balance of power shifted and artistes and managers achieved a bargaining strength they had previously lacked. Stratton-Smith found himself in an unusually strong position for two important reasons. Firstly, his tastes in music had always veered towards the progressive rather than the popular so he was always likely to attract the fashionable artistically-conscious 'underground' bands, many of whom rejected the old style Tin Pan Alley merchants and the mid-sixties whizz kid 'bread heads'. Secondly, by 1969 Tony had broadened his interests by founding his own record company with a select roster of artistes reflecting his own personal tastes. Obviously, Stratton-Smith was heavily influenced by predecessors such as Stigwood, Blackwell, Oldham, Lambert and Page, but his small-scale operation promised a closer-knit family unit in keeping with the post-hippie ethos of the period.

The dangers implicit in managing an artiste and owning his record company have already been noted in the career studies of Page and Oldham. The role conflict that inevitably seems to result from a label/management tie-up would ultimately force Stratton-Smith to choose between two careers but, for a time, he worked effectively in both spheres and established himself as one of the most popular managers of the new decade.

Within the first two years of the formation of Charisma Records, Stratton-Smith signed a number of artistes to label/management deals and the majority of these proved relatively successful. Rare Bird (co-managed by agent Terry King) charted in February 1970 with the haunting 'Sympathy', and went on to reach number 1 in several European countries. The management deal lasted eighteen months but Rare Bird never capitalized upon their early promise, a fact that Stratton-Smith puts down to lack of motivation:

> I don't think they were ever a first division band, though they were top of the second division. I remember getting extremely annoyed with them at Stockholm University where they patronized the audience. It was almost as if they were doing them a favour by being there, and I hate to see a band do that. If an opportunity has been created you should seize it.

The tragedy of lost opportunities was a fate that bedevilled several Charisma acts over the years. One month after Rare Bird charted, the Nice officially disbanded, much to Stratton-Smith's regret:

> The Nice were genuinely exciting, innovative and moving. There were nights when they were so good, they could bring you to tears. In fact, one of the few times I broke down in tears in this game was when I realized it was all over. I knew it was a mistake — they should have given it a couple of more years.

It is worth noting that the Nice would have split four months earlier had Stratton-Smith not persuaded them to embark on a farewell British tour. At least they went out in a blaze of glory and helped to establish Charisma as a potential force in the record industry by endowing the label with their final two albums, *Five Bridges Suite* and *Elegy*.

Following the success of the Nice and Rare Bird, Stratton-Smith continued to search for new talent, often picking up unusual acts that did not conform to the standards set by unadventurous A & R men from the major labels. One such artiste was Peter Hammill, whose band Van Der Graaf Generator entered into a long-term association with Charisma. Stratton-Smith had great faith in the band but a major breakthrough proved elusive:

> Peter Hammill was the most talented lyric writer I ever worked with. In those early days I thought 'This is it!' I persevered with the

Hammill family albums making something like 19 in 11 years. It was the biggest output of any of our bands — and I failed. We reached a solid cult audience and couldn't cross over. Eventually, it was economic suicide to carry on. It's a great loss to the collective taste that he didn't make it internationally. He was an important and unique figure.

Although Stratton-Smith seemed instinctively drawn towards the progressive art school acts of the early seventies, there was also a lighter side to his musical taste that surprised a few people. When publisher Barbara Hayes played Strat a rough tape of a song titled 'We Can Swing Together', the last thing she expected was an enthusiastic response. When he excitedly exclaimed that the harmonica player could achieve the same impact with the instrument as Ian Anderson had done with his flute, Barbara must have felt that the head of Charisma had lost his marbles. One year later, Lindisfarne were Charisma's most successful act yet. Their second album, *Fog On The Tyne* topped the charts and hit singles followed with 'Meet Me On The Corner' and 'Lady Elenor'. For Stratton-Smith they fulfilled an old ambition:'Lindisfarne achieved what I had hoped the Koobas would achieve — a success based on empathy with their audience. Lindisfarne were a far heavier writing team. They didn't play particularly brilliantly — but that didn't matter.' Throughout 1972, Lindisfarne played numerous festivals and their unpretentious and infectious music established them as crowd favourites. While Stratton-Smith and Terry King retained managerial control it seemed they could do no wrong.

The success of Lindisfarne enabled Stratton-Smith to develop the careers of some of the less commercially-minded artistes on his label. Both Audience and Bell & Arc benefited from his patronage, but neither achieved anything more than middling status in the early-seventies rock world. Lost opportunities, incompatible personalities, insufficient talent or plain bad luck may explain the relative failure of Charisma's second division acts. Tony remembers the ill-fated Bell & Arc as examples of the kind of group that, due to circumstances beyond a manager's control, fail to realize their full potential:

> I think Arc would have been better not to have been involved with Graham Bell, who was brilliant, but unmanageable. He was an artiste whom we spent a lot of money encouraging, but it never really worked. Graham could be bloody-minded and not helpful to himself. I was very excited by their first album, but some things just don't happen.

By the early seventies, Charisma had established itself as the independent home of British underground music. Much of the record label's distinctive charm came from Stratton-Smith's proud, paternal interest in all the artistes under his charge. As a socialite supreme, he could often be found after normal office or pub hours at the Speakeasy or other London clubs. There he would hold court, often listening to the problems of various musicians and advising on everything from tax to drug busts and personal relationships. Although he may occasionally have overestimated the maturity of certain Charisma musicians, his respect for their intelligence produced excellent artiste/management relations. Such was the case with the next major act to join Charisma. In spite of their youth, Genesis conducted themselves like seasoned businessmen, fully aware of their strengths and limitations. Stratton-Smith provides a perceptive overview:

> Beneath that rather nice, middle-class demeanour, they are truly dedicated to what they're doing and they are 100 per cent professionals. They maintained a semi-formal relationship with me. They always rang for an appointment, never just dropped in from the street. They were polite and liked all their affairs handled in a business-like manner. They were never one of the lads. Genesis had dignity.

Stratton-Smith later learned that Genesis had almost broken up prior to his arrival. They had already been given a shot at fame and glory, recording an unsuccessful album for Decca, *From Genesis To Revelation*, under the auspices of Jonathan King. King had christened the group, produced them, and evidently perceived their potential, but his initial interest rapidly waned. As an unrepentant pop merchant, Jonathan had little patience for the unnecessarily complex material that the group clearly preferred to record. Without the patronage of King and Decca, Genesis' chances looked bleak, but, fully realizing the odds stacked against them, the individual members quit school and college and adopted the mantle of professional musicians.

By early 1970, Genesis had found themselves on the books of agent Terry King, who allowed them to support Rare Bird. The magnanimous headliners immediately spotted their potential and Graham Field advised King to entice Stratton-Smith along to check them out. Tony was first introduced to Genesis at Eastbourne and following several calls from Peter Gabriel, instructed producer John Anthony to arrange a London gig in order to present the group to Charisma Records. This live 'audition' took place during a short residency at Ronnie Scott's and proved enormously successful. Having received the blessing of his staff, Stratton-Smith signed Genesis that very night, killing competition from Island and Threshold Records.

The progress of Genesis proved slower than anybody could have anticipated and a series of setbacks tested Stratton-Smith's nerve and commitment. After investing heavily in their Charisma debut, *Trespass*, he was confronted by the shock news that Anthony Phillips and John Mayhew had quit the group. Although Tony had half-expected Mayhew's departure, the loss of Phillips was extremely worrying: 'Anthony was in relatively frail health and couldn't stand up to touring, so he and the band had to make the decision. He was a man of high intelligence and an important influence. His leaving was a major setback.'

After endless auditions, Genesis finally emerged with a settled line-up, adding Phil Collins (drums) and Steve Hackett (guitar).

Genesis were effectively relaunched at London's Lyceum, then shuttled off on an ingenious package tour with Lindisfarne and Van Der Graaf Generator. Although their live reputation improved, they were still subject to self-inflicted disasters. In June 1971, at Friars Aylesbury, Peter Gabriel became so engrossed in his performance of 'The Knife' that he leapt recklessly from the stage and landed in a heap amid the assembled throng. This spontaneous display of acrobatic suicide resulted in a broken ankle, and while the crowd cheered, the singer was carried off by St John's Ambulance men. Another long lay-off ensued during which the group completed the poor-selling but well-received *Nursery Cryme*. The balance sheets made ominous reading and Stratton-Smith was forced to employ all his rhetoric to save the group's recording future:

> I said to a certain lawyer: 'If Genesis leave Charisma, then so do I'. I'd built the label for that kind of artiste. I had a kind of clairvoyance about them. I knew this was a band of incredible quality. You had to give them time to grow. I never had a moment's doubt.

Stratton-Smith's commitment was partly vindicated by the third album, *Foxtrot*, though the sales still left much to be desired.

In order to distract attention from Genesis' financial short-comings, Stratton-Smith chose to busy giddy minds with foreign quarrels and laid plans for a Continental invasion. Before long, Genesis emerged as mini-superstars in France, Belgium and Italy, much to their manager's relief:

> The Latins took them to their hearts. Genesis had melody and a wistfulness in the music and an element of fantasy that transcends

language. The Latin market broadened our economic base at a time when we were still trying to build in England.

1973 brought major successes for Genesis and Charisma. A cut-price live LP proved a clever marketing exercise, the studio album *Selling England By The Pound* was a steady seller and 'I Know What I Like' became a surprise hit single. Most managers would have chosen to reap the rewards of their investment at this stage, but, incredibly, Stratton-Smith backed down. Having managed virtually every group on the Charisma label since its inception in 1969, he surprised many of his contemporaries by announcing his retirement from management in late 1973. Like several of his predecessors, Stratton-Smith found the dual role of manager/label owner an intolerable burden. The crux had come during the summer when Genesis' three-year contract with Charisma had ended. Suddenly, Tony was in the bizarre position of negotiating with himself over the future of his charges. Obviously, this was not in the best interests of the group so he advised them to bring in their lawyers. At the same time, he recommended Tony Smith as his replacement. Smith was a well-known concert promoter who had worked extensively with Strat over the years and seemed the perfect choice for the second phase of Genesis' career. Mr Charisma evidently had no regrets about these far-reaching decisions:

> I had to make that choice and for me I made the right choice for my peace of mind. Whether I made the right choice economically is a totally different question. But, extraordinary as it may sound, I've never been highly motivated by money. I enjoy making things work much more. I knew Genesis were going to be enormous in America. What they needed was the hard-nosed, super tour manager, setting up these tours and logistics and sitting on the record company's neck. That's a particularly time-consuming skill in itself and I really didn't want to do it.

In many respects Stratton-Smith timed his exit well. The break-up of Audience and the rapid decline of Lindisfarne, who had split in half during 1973, obviously played an important part in persuading him that the game was up. Sacrificing Genesis, however, must have been a difficult decision. In retrospect, their international success during the mid-seventies should be seen as a tribute to Stratton-Smith's faith, perseverance and determination at a crucial stage in their development.[1]

From 1973 to 1985 Stratton-Smith steered Charisma through the ups and downs of the record industry, and during that period the label signed a diverse number of artistes including Monty Python's Flying Circus, Patrick Moraz, Bo Hansson, Brand X, Hawkwind, Sir John Betjeman, John Arlott, Rick Wakeman and, more recently, Malcolm McLaren, Julian Lennon and the Opposition. In most respects the original ideals of the company remained intact, which was no small achievement.

Looking back over Stratton-Smith's remarkable career one cannot help being struck by the number of dramatic upheavals he forced upon himself. Journalist, writer, music publisher, manager, record company mogul — the list betrays a diversity that inevitably leads to accusations of dilettantism. When I last spoke to Strat he laughed at this suggestion but said that it might contain a grain of truth:

> There were times when that might have been a fair charge against me. We all get the seven-year itch and back off. I don't think that's an uncommon thing with entrepreneurial souls in the music industry. Of course, it's not an option that's open if you're an employee. Some of them should have a few sabbaticals; they'd be better for it. I think the periods when I have loosened my grip on things have been damaging to this company. And I say that without arrogance. I don't intend to let it happen again.

Tony Stratton-Smith wound down his interests during the mid-eighties, selling Charisma to Virgin in 1986. During the same period his contemporary Gordon Mills had lost MAM to Chrysalis and I was struck by the parallel fates of these once-thriving independents. Having surrendered their companies, Mills and Stratton-Smith had at least bought time to enjoy their middle age. Sadly, Mills died of stomach cancer in July 1986, aged 51. Eight months later, Tony Stratton-Smith, aged 53, also died suddenly of stomach cancer. A service in his memory was held at St Martin-in-the-Fields attended by a telephone directory of musicians, journalists and Charisma personnel. It was a fitting tribute to one of the most important and likeable rock entrepreneurs of the seventies.

---

[1]It has unfavourably been stated elsewhere that Genesis were £200 000 in debt when they left Stratton-Smith, but this figure was, in fact, a reference to unrecouped advances paid by Charisma. The sum actually gives a favourable indication of the record company's commitment to the group. In the event of Genesis' dissolution or failure to record, such monies would have been written off automatically as per contract. As Stratton-Smith concluded: 'In the 15 years since Charisma began we have made our contribution to creating nine individual millionaires. I don't think that's a bad record.'

Simon Napier-Bell maintains that he was born under a lucky star. He has a point. Although his birth coincided with the start of World War II, it was the perfect year for a future rock 'n' roll manager to enter the world. Four years younger than Elvis Presley, Napier-Bell would catch the tail end of the fifties as a teenager, and begin the swinging sixties at the magical age of 21. By that time, he could look back on a childhood and adolescence which had provided both security and adventure.

Like Brian Epstein, Napier-Bell attended several well-known public schools, none of which gave him any lasting satisfaction. As a disgruntled 17-year-old he had already decided to forgo a conventional career in favour of the rebellious world of jazz. His private income enabled him to indulge that dream and, armed with a trumpet and a suitcase of clothes, he set forth for Canada. A year on the road was enough to quash his musical ambitions. Although he met several of his jazz heroes, most of them turned out to be unrelenting bores, reduced to playing popular dance music at weddings. Still, the trip was not without its adventurous moments. In Montreal, a homosexual horn player slipped him a Mickey Finn and while Simon the sleeping beauty dreamt of international fame, his trousers were surreptitiously removed. He escaped molestation by a matter of seconds.

Leaving Canada for a hitch-hiking tour across America, Napier-Bell returned to Europe as restless as ever. A sojourn in Spain followed, involving various sordid exploits along the route. By the end of his adolescent years, Napier-Bell had decided to pursue the pleasure principle in adult life. His sexual experiences and hedonistic lifestyles ensured that he would easily adapt to the permissiveness of swinging sixties London. Indeed, he already looked poised to take his place as one of the most epicurean pop managers of the era.

In spite of his apparent immaturity, Napier-Bell managed to curb his excesses for the first few years of the sixties. He settled into the 'family business', making documentaries and television commercials for his father's film company. Eventually, he formed an additional firm, Nomis (Simon spelt backwards) which specialized in the buying and selling of second-hand film. A settled career in the enterprising realm of film production seemed likely, but Napier-Bell had two problems. His threshold of boredom was abnormally low and he was easily distracted by ephemeral excitement.

By 1965, the inexorable slide into decadence could no longer be forestalled. Simon was a frequent visitor to Soho and the wilder haunts of London and it wasn't long before he was sucked into the nerve centre of the pop élite. Clubs such as the Scotch of St James's, the Ad Lib, the Scene and the Cromwellian became regular resorts for the bleary-eyed film-maker, who was gradually transformed into a creature of the night. In the subterranean semi-darkness of celebrity-filled dives, he became used to the sight of drunken, pill-popping pop stars, desperately drinking away their 15 minutes of fame. It was there also that he heard tales of the new managerial aristocracy: Epstein was the undisputed king, but beneath him there was a battalion of flashier, more aggressive sharpshooters, men like Andrew Oldham, Larry Page, Gordon Mills and Tony Secunda. It had not escaped Napier-Bell's notice that they were all roughly his own age. And in that golden year of 1965 who could deny that any one of them might sneak up on Epstein and claim the throne for himself.

Although he was at least two years behind the pack, Napier-Bell entered the hunt for managerial glory at the fag end of 1965. His first 'discovery' was Diane Ferraz, a West Indian teenager who had auditioned for one of his television commercials. Rather haphazardly, he teamed her up with another young hopeful, Nicky Scott. At least the racial mix was original and Simon used that fact to considerable effect by accusing several apathetic television and radio producers of exercising racist policies. Apparently, they were sufficiently intimidated by the fear of adverse publicity to play the duo's discs on a regular basis. What began as a potentially successful venture, however, ended in disillusionment as the twosome suffered a series of chart misses. Simon faithfully stuck with them until their demise in late 1967. The news was broken to him after the group returned from an elongated stay in Paris: 'Diane fell for the bass player. It was the classic end to a group that hadn't quite happened'.

The failure of Scott and Ferraz had no discernible adverse effect on Napier-Bell's managerial reputation. He quickly learned that the music business and record-buying public have a delightful habit of brushing past failures under the carpet. As long as you can create a high proportion of successful artistes your starmaking infallibility remains unquestioned. Armed with this knowledge, Napier-Bell decided to shorten the odds by progressing in three directions simultaneously.

Early in 1966, he was approached by *Ready Steady Go* producer, Vicki Wickham, with the novel idea of co-writing some English lyrics for an Italian song that Dusty Springfield had found during her unsuccessful bid to win the San Remo Music Festival. Simon had already written a song for Diane Ferraz and Nicky Scott so felt experienced enough to take advantage of the offer. According to legend, 'You Don't Have To Say You Love Me' was knocked off by Simon and Vicki in the space of an evening. The speed of its execution is belied by the quality of the song with its surprisingly sophisticated lyric. It provided Dusty with her only UK number 1 and was later covered by a variety of artistes, most notably Elvis Presley. The amount of songwriting royalties received by Napier-Bell more than compensated for a short evening's work.

The international success of 'You Don't Have To Say You Love Me' thrust the young songwriter into the limelight and enabled him to pursue the third stage of his entrepreneurial education: record production. His break came when he was approached by one of the most famous and respected groups of the era: The Yardbirds. Under the guidance of Giorgio Gomelsky, they had already achieved four consecutive Top 10 hits, each more inventive and adventurous than its predecessor. The unfortunate Gomelsky was a tempestuous character renowned for his erratic brilliance as a producer, but somewhat less concerned with the complications of management. He had already lost the Stones to Andrew Oldham and now the Yardbirds were seeking a younger, more charismatic manager in the Brian Epstein mould. Napier-Bell could not believe his luck and immediately took them on for his then customary 20 per cent remuneration. Rather naïvely, however, he neglected to take any management commission on their songwriting and publishing.

The departure from Gomelsky had placed the validity of the Yardbirds' EMI contract in some doubt and Napier-Bell took advantage of the confusion to negotiate new terms. It was a classic piece of opportunism. His bargaining power was substantially strengthened by the presence of Philips, who were waiting in the wings with a counter offer of £33 000. Realizing that Napier-Bell had no fear of litigation, EMI agreed to fork out £25 000 which was more than enough to secure a truce. With money in hand, Napier-Bell took the group into the recording studio and set about writing and co-producing their next hit. 'Over Under Sideways Down' was conceived as a single compendium of the eclectic work that they had produced under Gomelsky's guidance. By mid-sixties standards, it was an intriguing composition, though Napier-Bell maintains that his primary aim was to play safe:

I felt it was extremely important to come up with a cohesive style because Giorgio Gomelsky had jumped from one style to another. To take another step into the unknown without Giorgio's musical background was too dangerous. So I said the single should be a bit of blues and chanting. They put it together on that basis. It worked and I was pleased.

Having established his credentials with a Yardbirds Top 10 hit, Napier-Bell assumed that the group would expand their chart catalogue. Unfortunately, such prospects were hampered by internal disputes, rivalry and endless bickering. Simon had little patience with their petty squabbling and openly derided their artistic pretensions as naïve. As far as he was concerned they were just another pop group, capable of generating sizeable sums of money. Sadly, the Yardbirds failed to enjoy the fruits of their wealth and Paul Samwell-Smith in particular found himself increasingly alienated by the rock 'n' roll excesses of his fellow members. His conservative image, already evident in the press photos of the period, accurately reflected a maturity that seemed decidedly out of place in such a rebellious ensemble. It came as little surprise to Napier-Bell when this malcontent quit the Yardbirds in July 1966. Paul's parting words were refreshingly frank and pinpointed the frustrations of a talented record producer trapped in an uncomfortable pop star role:

> I'm too old at 23 for all these screaming kids leaping about. I don't think I'll be missed in the group— no one really noticed me on stage. I might just as well have been a dummy. A robot could have done what was required of me.

Although Samwell-Smith had been an important creative force in the Yardbirds, they were perfectly capable of surviving his departure. After all, the previous year had seen Jeff Beck replace Eric Clapton, whom guitar fans regarded as a near deity. It was Beck who now stepped in to take greater control of the group's direction but he made a crucial error in insisting that Jimmy Page be recruited as a replacement bass guitarist. Coincidentally, Page had been offered Beck's job back in 1965 but turned the post down in favour of more steady work as a session musician. Now, he saw the chance of establishing his reputation outside the recording studio. Napier-Bell was convinced that the arrival of Page spelt trouble. The new boy had a strong personality, oozed ambition and, worst of all, was an excellent lead guitarist. Once he grew tired of fingering a bass, there would likely be a clash of egos and in a group as combustible as the Yardbirds that could prove disastrous.

By the time Napier-Bell assembled the boys in the studio for their next single recording, they were no longer talking to one another. Seizing artistic control, Simon decided to risk his arm with an ambitious aural experiment in true Gomelsky fashion. In order to speed things up and avoid unnecessary conflict, each member of the group contributed his vocal or instrumental piece separately. The final product was a delightfully chaotic song appropriately titled 'Happenings Ten Years Time Ago'. Record reviewers of the period couldn't decide whether it was a classic or a piece of pretentious rubbish. Derek Johnson of *New Musical Express* summed up the ambiguous feelings of his fellow critics with a cautious headline: 'Great — But What's It All About?' That question also seemed to bother radio programmers who regarded the song as rather too esoteric for day-time listening on the Light Programme. The pirates were somewhat more receptive but the overall lack of plugging meant that the song barely scraped into the chart. Napier-Bell blamed this major setback on a number of factors largely stemming from his inexperience:

> I didn't have any background of managing so I was learning it as I went along. I was possibly missing out in areas I should have known about. Maybe I should have been at the record company every day fighting for promotion. I'm sure Giorgio was. But I had enough to cope with being a producer and a manager. It was a miracle I'd ever got that far.

Amid the turmoil, Napier-Bell managed to persuade the group to follow up their 1964 live album with a belated studio work bearing the imaginative title *The Yardbirds*. During the same period, he pre-empted his rival, Kit Lambert, by securing the group a cameo part in Michelangelo Antonioni's mildly controversial celluloid paean to swinging London, *Blow Up*. Antonioni had originally considered the Who for the part, but seemed happy enough when Beck demonstrated a similar penchant for demolishing guitars onstage. After the filming was completed, Beck continued his extravagant acts of auto-destruction, which neither endeared him to the group nor Napier-Bell, who was forever replacing their equipment.

By the autumn of 1966, the rivalry that Napier-Bell had predicted between Page and Beck was beginning to ignite. The Yardbirds now boasted two excellent lead guitarists, united in an uneasy alliance. In the battle of nerves that followed, it was Beck who proved the most fragile. During an American winter tour, he fell victim to tonsillitis, temporarily withdrew, and finally found that he had been ousted. It proved the symbolic, if not concrete, finale to the Yardbirds' troubled career.

Meanwhile, Simon Napier-Bell was still trying to put his life in order. The Yardbirds had seemed so obtuse and obstreperous that the idea of finding another group was almost unthinkable:

> I thought I'd never touch management again. Personal groups are objectionable and I don't just mean pop groups. Groups are generally imposing. With the Yardbirds, I was either in charge *or* the scapegoat. There was a lot of pressure on me and no background knowledge to deal with it. They communally fought like mad; they were a dour group. Plus I was about the same age, which didn't help.

Retreating from the pressures of the pop scene, Napier-Bell took an extended holiday in sunny St Tropez. However, even at such a safe geographical distance, he was still vulnerable to the solicitations of starry-eyed young hopefuls. While he sat drinking his champagne cocktails and soaking up the French sun, strange occurrences were taking place at a nearby *gendarmerie*. Two English musicians, John Hewlett and Chris Townson, had been arrested on a vagrancy charge after being found wandering penniless around the resort. Hewlett had convinced his captors that he could raise bail and was temporarily released in order to collect the money. When his predatory eyes feasted on a famous young manager idly indulging himself on champagne and caviar, Hewlett knew that his prayers had been answered. Turning on the charm, he mesmerized Simon with tales of a stupendous group whose looks and musicianship could tear the British charts apart. Simon was so taken with the young lad's cocky charm that he immediately produced the requisite bail money and flew back to England, eager to resume his managerial career. Puzzled journalists were highly amused by the haughty manner in which he described his latest protégés: 'I bailed them out and discovered that they were a group, and one of the conditions of my bailing anyone out is that they work for me for three years'. It wasn't long, however, before Napier-Bell realized that he had been rather hasty in taking these musicians to his bosom. He first saw them perform, billed as the Silence, in the queer setting of a swimming pool situated in a remote town called Burford Bridge. His abiding impression was that they were the worst group he had ever seen.

Although Napier-Bell had been sold fool's gold, the Silence did have some redeeming qualities. They were, in almost every respect, the complete antithesis of the Yardbirds: good-looking, fun-loving, enthusiastic and positive. For this, Simon thanked his gods and forgave the group for their inept musicianship. Since Hewlett had been responsible for securing Napier-Bell's patronage, the Silence was rechristened John's Children. The paternalistic title also ensured that the young bassist would remain immune to any unforeseen internal shake-ups.

Having stabilized the group, Napier-Bell next used his influence to win them a valuable recording contract with EMI. When their first single, 'The Love I Thought I'd Found', failed to sell, Simon decided to take an unusual gamble by switching his efforts towards the US market. With financial backing from White Whale Records, he recorded a fake 'live' album, *Orgasm*, but the title caused such a stir that it was deleted before reaching the record shops and remained on permanent hold for a further three years. Napier-Bell was shattered by the news and flew back to England with the air of a man who had just seen a fortune slip through his fingers.

In the meantime, John's Children had found an unexpected following in the form of London's emerging hippie contingent. Initially, Simon was taken aback when the group tore up their smart, white suits but he soon grew accustomed to the sight of kaftans, silky shirts and beads. More importantly, he realized that their lack of musical craftsmanship could be disguised under the free-form banner of 'psychedelia'. What they desperately needed was a fluke hit single in order to grab the coat-tails of the Move and the Pink Floyd. Napier-Bell decided to improve their chances by employing the services of a chart-hyper. One of the most proficient fixers of the day was Harvey Freed, whose services were used by a number of managers, including Don Arden. In return for a few hundred pounds, Freed lifted the single, 'Just What You Want', to number 28 in the *New Musical Express* chart. It was hoped that this push would generate sales, but the single dropped out of the *NME* listing the following week and, perhaps not surprisingly, did not even enter the *Record Retailer* Top 50.[1] Nevertheless, Napier-Bell was content with the minimal chart exposure provided by Freed: 'It certainly needed it. It was an appalling record. I'm astounded that even hyping could get it into the charts.'

The heavy-handed promotion of 'Just What You Want' ensured that John's Children increased their small following and improved their reputation as a live draw. However, they needed a big hit in order to recoup Napier-Bell's investment, so the next plan was a change of record company. Simon concluded that their 'psychedelic'

---

[1]Harvey Freed changed his name and later emerged as a leading figure in seventies British management. I will be conducting a more rigorous investigation of his later career in 'The Strange Case Of The Pop Group That Never Existed', a chapter from the forthcoming book, *Rock Around The Queen's Bench: Famous Court Cases In Pop History.*

image would be better promoted on a hip, independent label, such as Track Records, which was about to be launched by his great friend, Kit Lambert. Although Lambert's entrepreneurial expertise had yet to be severely tested, Napier-Bell was overwhelmed by his energy and commitment and envious of the chart success he had achieved for the Who. The fact that Lambert frequently tottered on the brink of disaster like a drunken tightrope walker, and yet always staggered home in triumph, made him seem larger than life. Simon accompanied Kit on many boozing sessions around the élite establishments of Mayfair and the sordid clubs of Soho and never ceased to be amazed by the man's upper-class disdain, exaggerated homosexuality, and irresistibly anarchic spirit.[1] Even if Track failed to break John's Children, the group's association with such a fashionable label would surely benefit their short-term career.

Kit Lambert also took a great interest in another of Napier-Bell's recent discoveries. At that time, Marc Bolan was something of a problem child. He had achieved some success as a model before launching himself as a folk singer under the name Toby Tyler. After a couple of unsuccessful singles with Decca, he turned up one evening at Napier-Bell's door and announced that he was going to be a star. Simon was impressed by his self-assurance and charm, even though his ego was insufferable. Even then, Bolan was filled with delusions of grandeur about his talent, songwriting skill and singing ability, yet there was no doubting his originality. Napier-Bell's problem was deciding how to translate Bolan's eccentric elfin image into a form that would prove acceptable to the mid-sixties record-buying public. Rather unwisely, he had gambled on a Christmas release, 'Hippy Gumbo', which predictably flopped. Since then, Bolan had been a thorn in his side. It was Kit Lambert who came up with a plausible solution to the problem. He suggested that Bolan be drafted into John's Children, replacing guitarist Geoff McClelland. Surprisingly, the change was achieved with considerable ease, as Napier-Bell testifies:

Marc definitely wanted to be a solo star. He never saw himself as

---

[1]Kit Lambert was, of course, one of the more flamboyant and charismatic managers of the mid-sixties. He attempted to create the Who in his own image, encouraging their self-destructive tendencies and later pushing them towards extravagant projects, most notably the 'pop opera' *Tommy*. As a manager, Lambert had a number of faults and it is generally accepted that he lacked business acumen. The incredible publicity that he has received over the years has tended to glamorize and occasionally overstate the importance of his contribution to managerial history. After a decade-and-a-half of unparalleled self-abuse, Lambert was declared unfit to oversee his business affairs and ended his days as a Ward of Court. In 1981 he died following a fall at his mother's home.

anything else. But I persuaded him that John's Children would be a good stepping stone. I felt that if he was singing with John's Children people would get used to his voice and he'd begin to find a market.

Napier-Bell was convinced that Bolan's induction would propel John's Children to the top. He had already written their first single for Track, a catchy and imaginative song, 'Desdemona'. Unfortunately, the BBC detected sexual connotations in the line 'lift up your skirt and fly' and promptly ignored the single thereafter. Although some compensatory play was received on pirate radio, the disc was effectively buried. Bolan was particularly disappointed by the fate of 'Desdemona' and although a follow up, 'Midsummer's Night Scene', was quickly prepared, the release was cancelled at the eleventh hour. It was clear from Bolan's attitude that he would not be a member of the group for much longer.

The morale of the group was temporarily boosted when they embarked on a tour of Germany supporting the Who. It was to prove one of the most eventful episodes in their career. From the outset, Napier-Bell decided to take full advantage of the situation by ensuring that his group upstaged the Who at every opportunity. He instructed lead singer Andy Ellison to leap into the audience and create as much pandemonium as possible. He openly encouraged onstage violence on a scale seldom seen since the Kinks' 1965 tour. And in case all else failed, he equipped Marc Bolan with a heavy silver chain and instructed him to lash the bare backs of his fellow Children towards the climax of the set. Not surprisingly, these gigs caused a veritable riot and frequently left the Who uneasily contending with a near demented audience. The reverberations were even felt back in England where the letters column of *Melody Maker* described John's Children as '. . . the most atrocious excuse for entertainment I have ever seen. They issued forth a barrage of sound bearing no resemblance to anything on earth . . . It was sickening'. By the time the entourage reached Ludwigshafen, the authorities were all too aware of the reputation of John's Children. In spite of the presence of riot police, however, Napier-Bell succeeded in provoking further violence and placed himself and the group in danger of losing their lives. Eventually, they departed like war casualties, leaving behind a boiling cauldron of chaos and destruction.

During the drive back home Simon decided that the boys deserved a holiday, so he took them on a detour across Europe. Eventually, they landed in Luxembourg, where they spent an evening watching Ravi Shankar in concert. Bolan was particularly taken with the idea of a musician sitting on a rug surrounded by admirers in an incense-filled auditorium. At the time, Napier-Bell considered this an understandable reaction to the recent mayhem caused by John's Children and thought no more about it. A month later, Bolan left the group.

Marc's leaving speech to his manager left little doubt about the depth of his self-confidence: 'He told me he was going to form a group called Tyrannosaurus Rex because that was the biggest animal there'd ever been in the world and he was going to be *that* big'. Originally, Tyrannosaurus Rex was conceived as a quintet and Bolan placed an advertisement in *Melody Maker* for suitable musicians. Almost immediately, an impromptu gig was booked at the Electric Garden which was to have a marked effect on Bolan's career development, as Napier-Bell recalls:

> He was so high-flying at the time and so full of himself. He really thought that the best gig would come from bringing people together and he'd just get up and it would all happen. So he turned up with five people, got some equipment and went onstage. He'd never played a note with them before! It was one of the worst things that ever happened to anybody. About thirty people shuffled in and out again. That was the moment when he knew he'd have to play an acoustic guitar sitting on a rug where nothing ever could go wrong.

While Marc Bolan was sorting out his future, Napier-Bell found himself in Los Angeles witnessing the 1967 Summer of Love. With the words 'flower power' indelibly imprinted on his consciousness he came scurrying back to London, grabbed the remnants of John's Children, pushed them into the studio and recorded the evocatively titled 'Come And Play With Me In The Garden'. In order to publicize the record, he had the group photographed completely nude with a few well-placed flowers covering their private parts. Posters of this Edenic scene were plastered around the country, but even that was not enough to get John's Children a hit record. They made one final attempt, fully clothed in winter, but again nothing happened. Shortly afterwards, Hewlett and Townson had a silly argument and the group fell apart. Although their demise had seemed on the cards for some time, Napier-Bell was saddened by his failure to bring them success:

> It disappointed me because I cared about John's Children. They were a heavy investment for the sixties, £40–£50 000. They'd actually learned to play and 'Desdemona' should have been Top 5. I wanted to break a group from scratch. All the other contemporary managers had done that.

The demise of John's Children seemed ill-timed but allowed Napier-Bell to concentrate on the flighty career of Marc Bolan.

Tyrannosaurus Rex rapidly found their niche, playing to a small, devoted band of hippie followers and selling liberal quantities of vinyl on the fashionable Regal Zonophone label. Although Simon enjoyed the status of titular manager, his understanding of Bolan's career intentions seemed hopelessly outdated. Marc had now entered a completely anti-commercial phase and regarded 'bread heads' with hippie disdain. In order to prove his point, he was playing small-time gigs at schools and colleges for a relative pittance. After attending one such performance, Napier-Bell roughly calculated the audience figures and rubbed his hands in glee. When Marc next appeared at his office, he confidently confided: 'I'll get on the phone and up your fee to £50 a gig. It's easy'. Bolan was mortified by such a flagrant admission of avarice and chided his manager with a few well-chosen words: 'No, man. I don't want to do that. It wouldn't be nice. It wouldn't be cool.' Napier-Bell could hardly believe his ears. Here, for the first time in his career, was an artiste who was turning down legitimately earned money. Such a notion was almost beyond the comprehension of Napier-Bell, but he soon became attuned to the Bolan philosophy. After several months, however, it was obvious that the once-influential pop mogul had become a liability to his idealistic charge:

> I finally realized that being connected with me wasn't helping him in the slightest. He wouldn't let me manage him. Nothing seemed to be going forward. I really didn't see how I could get him a better deal. We felt he'd have better credibility as a wandering minstrel.

By the close of the sixties, Simon Napier-Bell had followed the lead of many of his contemporaries by retiring from management. In 1969, he founded a production company called Rocking Horse with Ray Singer, who had recently worked on Peter Sarstedt's number 1 hit 'Where Do You Go To, My Lovely'. Simon later made light of this period, but he now admits: 'We were very serious about producing. We wanted to be good producers and it was the most serious time'. For the first few weeks they struggled, but eventually Simon cajoled an American record company mogul into paying an advance for an imaginary group. Soon, more advances were forthcoming from rival companies and the duo attempted to produce some worthwhile product. They recorded a couple of albums with Forever More (who later emerged as the Average White Band) and a minor league outfit called Fresh. The remainder of their projects consisted of conveyor-belt pap recorded by anonymous groups picked up on the London pub circuit. Soon, they grew weary of rehearsing second-rate groups and reverted almost entirely to session musicians: 'We didn't even have to do an album at a time. We just booked the studio for a month, cut a hundred tracks and got the lead vocalist from each group and made the album'. These cut-price productions ensured that Napier-Bell ended the sixties on a financial high, but he was also extremely bored. Seizing the moment, he invested his money, said his farewells and retired to Spain.

By the early seventies, the name Simon Napier-Bell had been consigned to the history books. He would be remembered as one of the many charismatic managers of the mid-sixties, a late starter whose achievements were overshadowed by others such as Andrew Oldham, Larry Page and Tony Secunda. He had written a number 1 hit, of course, but as a manager he had failed to break a major act. One Yardbirds Top 10 hit was the sum total of his managerial achievements.

The statistics of managerial fame were of little consequence to Simon Napier-Bell during the early seventies, for he was leading a life of unrepentant self-indulgence, touring the world on an extended holiday that looked like never ending. Occasionally, he would produce the odd record in Australia and Indonesia, but his hedonistic lifestyle left little time for serious pursuits. After five years, however, the spending spree came to an end. Rather optimistically, Simon had assumed that he could survive on interest alone, but the growing rate of inflation was eating into his assets. Eventually, he decided to return to work.

It was a new Simon Napier-Bell that landed in England in 1976. No longer the reckless playboy, he vowed to put his music business experience to good use and avoid the excesses of the sixties. However, one characteristic that had not been altered by time and travel was his unshakeable self-confidence. Even before he descended from his aeroplane, Simon had worked out a breezy schedule and could be heard boasting: 'I'll pop across to a record company tomorrow, find a group by Tuesday evening, sign them on Thursday and get the record deal worked out by the next Monday'. In fact, it took the best part of a week for Napier-Bell to schedule a one-hour lunch date for the following month. The prodigal son of sixties pop was dejected to learn that his name had been virtually forgotten.

It took several days on the telephone before Simon managed to contact the few influential business people capable of putting something his way. At this stage, he was totally uninterested in management and merely wanted to re-establish his name in publishing and production. Word slowly spread of his 'comeback', and a series of hopeful young groups knocked on his door proclaiming themselves 'the future of rock'. They were uniformly awful.

While ruminating on the appalling state of the music industry, Napier-Bell was approached by another of those insufferably persistent young singers in search of stardom. However, this latest whelp had a novel request — he wanted Simon to transform him into a manager. At the time, it seemed a good idea. Danny Morgan was a young hustler, seemingly capable of ferreting out exciting young groups, and his management tie-up would leave Napier-Bell free to concentrate on producing records without interference. However, the only marginally successful outfit that Morgan discovered for his mentor was Urchin, which later evolved into Iron Maiden.

The lack of instantaneous hit acts bothered Napier-Bell, and he soon became disillusioned with his apprentice manager. Morgan remained incredibly persistent, however, even in the face of blank disinterest. He begged Simon to see another of his 'marvellous groups' and finally won a brief audition for their lead singer, David Sylvian. Napier-Bell's reaction upon seeing the heavily made-up, stylish blond singer of Japan was a combination of excitement and unerring conviction:

> From the second I saw Dave Sylvian, I knew he was a superstar. It was the same old thing. Knowing somebody's a superstar doesn't mean they're going to be a superstar this week. It could be next week, or never. But I jumped in. I was out of touch with the scene so I wasn't aware of any problems with Sylvian's image, music or style. I just thought it was all fantastic.

Napier-Bell was so taken with Japan that he immediately signed a deal without bothering to check the musical undercurrents of the day. He splashed out several hundred pounds on equipment and transport, but the group seemed financially insatiable. Before long, his investment was running so high that he relieved Danny Morgan of administrative responsibility and went all out to break the group himself. After an eight-year absence, Simon Napier-Bell was once again an aspiring pop manager.

From 1976-7, Simon invested virtually all his energies into breaking Japan, but, incredibly, he could not even win a record deal. Suddenly, the majors were less interested in signing long-term acts than snapping up the current hit favourites from local clubs. Cursing his luck, Napier-Bell vowed that if he again reached the top he would do his utmost to ensure that his power was greater than that of all his contemporaries. Such a conception would have been beyond his imagination 10 years earlier when he flitted around like a butterfly, propelled by wealth, caprice and luck. Now, for the first time in his career, he was losing a small fortune on a group that the entire music business regarded as unfashionable and ephemeral. After a year, the spiralling debt became increasingly worrying, but somehow Simon held on to his belief:

> I never lost faith in their ability to happen, but I kept looking back and remembering Marc and John's Children. I could see exactly the same thing happening to Japan if I didn't get it right. But I couldn't. All I could do was bring it to an end.

In order to take his mind off the Japan crisis, Napier-Bell decided to invest some money elsewhere. One day, the irrepressible Danny Morgan burst into his office and exclaimed, 'You've never seen anything like it'. The object of his latest ecstatic effusion was London, a punk group he had seen one night at a local club. Simon agreed to check them out and was astonished to discover a cavern filled with ghastly-looking creatures sporting safety-pins, bin-liners and spiked haircuts. The rapport between the group and the audience was one of mutual disrespect and the most fervent followers indicated their feelings by spitting at the musicians, who replied in kind. As Napier-Bell remembers: 'It was the most incredible thing I'd ever seen'. He signed London without a moment's thought, guaranteeing them £150 000 in the process. It was several weeks later before he realized that the group was not unique but commonplace:

> I was out of touch. I didn't go to clubs where 16–18 year old kids went. I tended to go to places where the music business had always gone. There were about 15–20 other places with groups doing exactly the same thing and the record companies had already stumbled on them.

So, for the second time in a year, Napier-Bell had made a rash decision that made him feel extremely foolish. On this occasion, however, he moved quickly and was fortunate to discover a record company that was equally out of touch. MCA immediately made an offer for the demo tape he had recorded, thereby repaying his hasty investment.

In retrospect, Napier-Bell claims that London were unlucky to miss out on the punk rock boom of 1977. Their chance came and went with the single 'Everyone's A Winner'. Unfortunately, MCA found themselves in a disadvantageous position, lacking both the promotional clout of the corporators and the hip credibility of the new independent labels. When London foundered, Napier-Bell was in no mood to pick up the pieces. He disliked them intensely as personalities and from the way they acted, the feeling was evidently mutual. Whenever they visited his luxury flat, he would be subjected to a torrent of abuse, laced with frequent expletives. Initially, Simon put this down to inverted snobbery, but he later learned that much of their street urtication was mere affectation. One Sunday afternoon, he phoned London's drummer, Jon Moss, expecting to be greeted by the rough tongue of a bedsit landlady. Instead, a posh middle-class voice could be heard calling to her son, 'Jon, dear, it's for you'. Moss was not pleased to discover that his punk credibility lay in ruins.

As the memory of London faded, the Japan problem became more acute. 'Simon's folly' now boasted a £100 000 deficit, with no sign of a record deal. It was at this point that an extraordinary series of auditions took place in London. With punk still at its peak, the German record company Ariola/Hansa had boldly marched into the capital, determined to seek out new talent. Completely ignoring the austerity dictated by punk, they erected posters of an alluring, buxom blonde astride a motorcycle, brazenly extending her tightly-clad white wrapped buttocks. Beneath this image were the words, 'Would you like to be a pop star?' Simon immediately concluded that any record company still using such obvious sexploitation coupled with that apparently archaic term 'pop' might well find a home for the eminently unfashionable Japan. Fortunately, Hansa liked the group, so Napier-Bell wasted no time in finalizing a deal. By his usual standards, the terms were extremely poor, but at this stage he would have signed them for anything. After a year in the doldrums, Japan were at last ready to record the album that their manager believed would rocket them to international fame.

The 1978 debut, *Adolescent Sex*, was, in Napier-Bell's words, 'a disaster' which set them back even further. The critics were so abusive and unmerciful that Simon was left wondering whether his managerial involvement had contributed to the purge:

> They saw it as music business manipulation — the old Simon Napier-Bell svengali touch taking the group and dressing them up. But I imposed nothing on them. That was part of my new approach in coming back to the business. I realized that a manager with experience had to find artistes that were totally self-contained, artistically and creatively. What I offered was tremendous experience and ultimately power.

By 1978, most critics had dismissed Japan as second-rate Roxy Music copyists and that impression was reinforced by the release of

their third album *Quiet Life*. Sylvian's Bryan Ferry-tinged vocal
was more evident than ever and the aural comparisons were compounded by the involvement of Roxy's former producer, John
Punter. By this time, even Napier-Bell was forced to concede that
he had failed:

> I decided I just had to stop. It was a practical business decision. You
> cut your losses and start again. It was no use. I hadn't broken them.
> Perhaps I was the wrong manager. I couldn't go on bleeding my
> money. It probably wouldn't have been any use to them anyway.

The proposed split with Japan was probably the most torturous
decision of Napier-Bell's managerial career. He had always had a
reputation as a cynical, self-interested dilettante, with little regard
for the aesthetic importance of pop music and even less for the
music business. Now, for possibly the first time in his career,
Napier-Bell was forced to consider the moral implications of his
expedient philosophy:

> It wasn't easy. I didn't know how the hell I was going to tell them.
> They had really devoted their lives to this thing. You couldn't just say,
> 'Go and get a job'. They'd lost their chance and cut themselves off.

After scheduling a meeting at his house, the troubled entrepreneur
prepared a leaving speech and attempted to act as sombrely as
possible. However, when the group breezed in, full of humour and
enthusiasm, Simon's sentimentality overcame his customary
cynicism. After a few minutes he blurted out a rather different
speech from the one he had rehearsed: 'Well, I thought we'd have a
meeting to decide how we're going to crack this thing'. From that
moment, he knew that he was stuck with Japan indefinitely. What
may have seemed a financially ludicrous decision ultimately placed
his managerial career in a far more favourable light. It enabled him
to take his rightful place alongside those immortal charismatic
managers of the mid-sixties, such as Oldham, Page, Secunda and
Lambert. Eventually, Napier-Bell would also break a group from
scratch. Equally importantly, his flighty image could now be
qualified by evidence of genuine commitment. The spirit of
Epstein, Calvert, Pitt and Stratton-Smith, men who had based
their principles on faith and perseverance rather than easy money,
had finally entered Napier-Bell's managerial consciousness.

Simon's grand gesture of loyalty was not rewarded by the gods
of pop for some considerable time. In a desperate attempt to
diversify, he invested heavily in NOMIS rehearsal studios, a

splendid complex situated in Hammersmith. However, the running costs of the operation proved prohibitive in a period when record companies were spending significantly less money on elaborate albums projects. Clearly, Napier-Bell had again blundered, though, paradoxically, his public image was improving:

> I had Japan on one side and NOMIS on the other. Everyone was saying, 'Napier-Bell's really come back! Magnificent studios; wealthy man'. I was thinking, 'Bloody hell, I've just lost about a million pounds in four years and my name's beginning to get known. But soon I'll be known as a bloody idiot'.

As the decade ended, Napier-Bell spent even more heavily on promotion in an almost obsessive effort to break Japan at any cost: 'We thought up this terrible publicity stunt — "The most beautiful man in the world" — which David hated, but something had to be done'. It was still not enough. After reviewing past record sales, Hansa declared that they would not finance another Japan album.

Ironically, when Japan switched to the Virgin label, Hansa changed tack and attempted to restrain the group through the courts. Fearing that Japan would miss out on the New Romantic boom, Napier-Bell reluctantly conceded that a compromise was the only logical solution: 'Our costs were £50 000 and the group were costing me £2000 a week. An injunction process can be kept going for a year and they were prepared to go on. Therefore, we had to make a settlement'. By the time the dispute was settled Japan's debt to their manager was so great that even a million-selling number 1 single would have brought negligible rewards. Fearing that the historical debt would overwhelm them, Napier-Bell magnanimously wrote the sum off. It was a risky, though clever, decision which restored confidence and enabled Japan to forge ahead and earn their manager some long-overdue commission.

Throughout 1981, the increasingly fashionable Japan enjoyed minor hits and finally broke big the following year with a gold album, *Tin Drum*, and a Top 5 single, 'Ghosts'. After six years' hard work it was a treat to be savoured:

> They were so well known it was extraordinary. They'd singlehandedly created the New Romantics who were having hits all around them. Duran Duran dressed like Japan and even begged the group to produce them, then they went off and made a sensible commercial hit record. Japan would not do that. They played their own esoteric music. But it gelled on *Tin Drum*. And when it gels, it sells!

What seemed like a happy ending was to prove frustratingly transient, for on the brink of major worldwide success, Japan informed their manager that they were splitting. Playing cautious, Napier-Bell ordered them not to announce their decision until after the *Tin Drum* promotional tour. However, it was obvious from the number of solo projects they were undertaking that something was amiss. The animosity and political skirmishes within the group soon worsened when bassist Mick Karn's girlfriend ended up in Sylvian's arms. Although it seemed certain that Napier-Bell would be defeated by the cumulative mini-dramas he somehow persuaded them to undertake a second tour, even though the warring factions had not spoken to each other for over a year. His hope that another few months together might cool them down sufficiently to reconsider their break up proved over-optimistic, however, and from the first date onwards the tension backstage was unbearable. Accepting the inevitable, Simon appeared at the fourth date and informed the assembled company, 'OK, you can finish the tour and break up'.

Following the Japan débâcle, there were some serious questions that the middle-aged entrepreneur needed to ask himself. After six years back in the music business, he had barely broken even, so was it worth going on? Fortunately, his soul-searching proved reassuring:

> In the end, I decided that I'd become a good manager. I'd got an enormous knowledge and was obviously very good at dealing with people and being the effective balance between the record company and the artiste. So I decided to move swiftly to the most commercial and potentially the biggest outfit I could find.

In order to strengthen his position, Napier-Bell teamed up with fellow manager Jazz Summers (Danse Society, Blue Zoo, Late Show) and founded Nomis Management. Meanwhile, the inchoate superstars that he had dreamed of unearthing appeared abruptly one Thursday evening while he was watching *Top Of The Pops*. There before his eyes was the transfixing sight of a leather-clad duo performing their latest hit 'Young Guns'. Never in his life had Napier-Bell seen such a visually powerful symbiotic relationship between two male performers.

The pursuit and capture of Wham! took many months and was followed by a stupendous legal battle with their record company, Innervision. That particular drama ended with the duo signing to Epic Records. With Napier-Bell generating the publicity machine into overdrive, the group emerged as world-beating chart stars in 1984 with a string of million-selling singles, including 'Wake Me

Up Before You Go-Go', 'Careless Whisper', 'Freedom' and 'Last Christmas'. The following year brought even more accolades including a historic trip to China and a stadium tour of the States. By February 1986, however, the manager/artiste relationship had ended in acrimony and misunderstanding when it was learned that Nomis intended to sell their interests in Wham! to Kunick Leisure, one of whose clients was Sol Kerzner, owner of the notorious Sun City. The 'Kunick Incident' precipitated Wham!'s dissolution and effectively brought down Nomis Management. The reversal of fortune was so sudden that Jazz Summers found it difficult to take in: 'One minute we were managing the biggest act since the Beatles, then within 10 days we'd lost them . . . and a £5 million deal'.[1]

Napier-Bell was surprisingly stoical about the loss of Wham!, realizing perhaps that George Michael would one day want to run his affairs alone. As it was, the years spent managing Wham! enabled the middle-aged entrepreneur to enjoy a deserved managerial fame far greater than he ever could have imagined in the sixties. His tireless self-publicity engineered column inches that rivalled those of Parnes and Epstein at their peaks. Napier-Bell is a seasoned media manipulator and knows how to provide ready-made self-analytical assessments which neatly mingle pride and humility in precisely the correct amounts. While boasting of the millions he has made, he likes to linger over financial *faux pas*, a technique that inevitably makes his triumphs even more impressive. That same boastful humility was at work in his scanty sixties memoir *You Don't Have To Say You Love Me* in which he reduced his managerial career to one long party of self-indulgent excess. He made it all sound easy and, by implication, contrived to place his meagre managerial achievements alongside those of the sixties greats. Most rock critics lazily accepted the hyperbole, mistakenly assuming that he must have been a sixties managerial god. Others fell into the trap of accepting his self-mythologizing, cynical, con-man persona as fact rather than caricature. Jazz Summers laments the loss of the well-rounded Napier-Bell to the pasteboard figure of media fame:

---

[1] The Napier-Bell/Wham! saga grew to such overwhelming proportions that I was left with no choice but to farm the entire story off into a separate book: *Wham! Death Of A Supergroup*. There, free from word restriction, I was able to deal at luxurious length with the complex relationship between Nomis, Wham!, CBS, Innervision and music publishers Morrison/Leahy. The Wham! book is intended to complement this chapter, while also providing fuller details of the managerial career of Napier-Bell's partner, Jazz Summers.

Simon's actually very loyal to people but he's his own worst enemy because he loves that word hype. He's almost addicted to it . . . The reason why he has never been taken seriously is because he's always practised that hype. People obviously think he's lucky or doesn't know what he's doing so they don't take him seriously. But when you go to Japan or China, they take him *very* seriously.

The old hype shows no signs of abating as Napier-Bell launches into an ever-increasing number of unlikely schemes. These include an aristocratic soap opera, *The Legacy,* a musical based on the trial of deposed Liberal leader Jeremy Thorpe, a new hit boy duo, Blue Mercedes and the setting up of a new label, Music UK. The latter consists of an amorphous bunch of artistes (Cher Perrier, Matt Belgrano, Paul Aaron and Roy Gayle) who corporately represent 'the Voice of Young Britain'. Whether the experiment will prove successful remains to be seen, but its existence confirms that Napier-Bell has long since abandoned the idea of returning to his early-seventies tax havens: 'I won't retire again. I'd drop dead. I can't stand not working. It was a silly thing to think I could do it. Now I just want to be active and work'. In spite of his assurances, however, there are occasional asides which suggest that he recognizes the absurdity of his situation in the pop world: 'I'm 48. I'm successful. I'm quite well off. I've spent my life running around doing silly things for 19-year-olds who, in five years' time, will know just how stupid they are'.

Tam Paton's long apprenticeship in the music business began during the early sixties. He had previously spent several years in the army and then returned to a secure, uncomplicated life working in his parents' potato merchant business in Prestonpans, Scotland. Still craving excitement and glamour, he decided to make full use of his leisure hours. For a brief period, he joined a traditional Scottish dance band, but this proved far from exciting. Eventually, he discovered an alternative in what seemed a new musical fad — rock 'n' roll. Fired by enthusiasm and bad piano playing, he persuaded several friends to form a seven-piece showband, The Crusaders. Paton acted as their agent and publicist, always demanding three months' notice for bookings, even if their date sheet was blank. Soon they were performing all over Scotland and England, supporting such acts as Eden Kane and Billy Fury.

The Crusaders continued playing for several years, but never looked like breaking free from the standard showband circuit. Their hopes of a possible major breakthrough were rekindled when they entered a beat group contest, sponsored by Oxfam. After winning a series of heats in Scotland, the band were invited to the grand final at the Prince of Wales Theatre in London. With debts mounting, the contest represented their last chance of glory, but morale was shattered when they finished a lowly tenth. The blow effectively ended the Crusaders' six-year career. In retrospect, the real significance of the contest was not the dissolution of the Crusaders, but a never-to-be-forgotten meeting between Tam Paton and Brian Epstein. The Beatles' manager was one of the judges at the event and, towards the end of the evening, Tam managed to accost him for a brief chat:

> I was very depressed. I asked him where he felt we'd gone wrong. He said the music was good, but we lacked image. I thought to myself, 'What's this image the guy's talking about? It's got to be the music'. You'd always had the Glenn Miller *sound* or the Benny Goodman *sound* — people wanted to hear not see the group.

Although Paton initially dismissed Epstein's advice, he was haunted by his criticisms for the rest of his career.

The death of the Crusaders forced Tam to return to the family business. There he remained for six months, until one day the manager of Edinburgh's Palais de Dance phoned offering a job. He persuaded Tam to form a new 10-piece showband from the ashes of the Crusaders and accept a full-time residency at the Palais. It was a period of stability that lasted two years. By 1967, however, the staid, evergreen Tam Paton Orchestra was finding it difficult to cater for the teenage audiences that invaded the hall every Thursday night. As a result, the Palais decided to employ local pop groups for one gig a week. Paton was asked to choose them and because the fees were so small, he was advised to concentrate exclusively on semi-professional units. Not surprisingly, Tam was frequently approached by young, inexperienced kids in search of a gig. The most persistent of the bunch were two schoolboys, Alan and Derek Longmuir, who had recently formed a group called the Saxons. By the time Paton auditioned them, however, they had changed their name to the Bay City Rollers. They played relatively uninspired covers of old Beatles songs, but their dedicated teenage following seemed unconcerned about such trivialities. Suddenly, Paton recalled the prophetic words of Epstein and realized the importance of image. When the group requested his services as manager, Tam was ready to take his next big chance.

Initially, Tam sought advice from another local manager who, upon seeing the Bay City Rollers, dismissed them as a complete waste of time. The snub merely served to strengthen Paton's characteristic stubbornness. Using half-remembered contacts from his Crusaders days, he secured the group a residency at the Top Storey Club and set up an endless series of one-nighters throughout Scotland. At this stage, the Rollers were a sextet, but the line-up was seldom settled, as Paton remembers: 'There was a lot of dead weight in the group. Members were getting engaged to be married and bailing out left, right and centre. You'd get somebody in, they'd settle for six months and then leave'. In the meantime, Paton lost his own residency at the Palais when the club was closed following a series of knifings. Turning down a similar residency in Belfast, he returned to the family business as a lorry driver while attempting to administer the Rollers' affairs in his spare time. It was an exhausting couple of years spent working all day and driving half way across the country for nightly gigs.

Apart from lack of sleep and poor financial remuneration, the Rollers frequently found themselves in danger of physical assault. At one gig a dispute ensued between the group's roadies and some local thugs which ended in a near riot. On other occasions half-drunken members of the audience, jealous of the Rollers' pretty-boy looks, would attempt to pick fights. Paton was always amid the throng and sometimes went to desperate lengths to protect his charges. Several times he was knocked to the floor by gangs of

youths and barely rescued in time by club bouncers. The black
eyes and broken nose that Paton sported so often during these early
days merely convinced his friends of the magnitude of his folly.

Such indignities might have proved easier to bear had the
Rollers' career prospects seemed promising. Unfortunately, competition on the Scottish circuit was intense and they were forced to
travel frequently in order to publicize their existence. Tam was
literally living from hand to mouth as the outstanding bills increased
from month to month. In order to improve the quality of the
group's stage act, Paton and the boys invested in some expensive
equipment. Disaster struck several weeks later when their van was
broken into resulting in the loss of several uninsured amplifiers and
guitars. Their financial prospects were now so poor that it was only
the charitable intervention of music-shop owner Peter Seaton that
saved them from extinction. Seaton loaned them equipment for a
considerable period and sought no payment in return. It was one of
the few lucky breaks that Paton received during his early days in
management.

The major shortcoming of Paton as a manager was his lack of
connections in London. He had achieved considerable success
with booking agents by blitzing them with hundreds of photos of
the group, but these publicity tactics had little effect on record
companies. In early 1971, however, Paton's luck changed. While
the Rollers were playing at the Cave's Club in Edinburgh, a posse
of record company talent-spotters, including Bell Records' president, Dick Leahy, producer Tony Calder and agent David Apps,
were auditioning groups in Glasgow. That night the city was
fogbound, so they drove to Edinburgh where similarly turbulent
weather prevented them from taking their flight back to London.
Forced to remain in the city overnight, they booked into an hotel
and, following the recommendation of one of Tam's friends, visited
the Cave's Club. The fan hysteria they witnessed there was so
frenzied that two of the parties decided to sign the group. Paton
was already dangerously out of his depth:

> I was as green as grass . . . The straw was coming out of my ears. I
> knew how to get work, I knew how to get photographs and I knew if a
> gig was £40 there'd be £5 needed for petrol and £15 for HP. But I
> didn't know anything about getting advances. It was a completely new
> ballgame for me.

Eventually, Tam signed with Calder's production company. Tony
sent up a film crew to capture the Rollers on celluloid and signed
the group to Leahy's Bell Records. They next received the pro-

duction talents of Jonathan King and gained a surprise Top 10 hit, 'Keep On Dancing'. In spite of this success there were more troubling line-up changes and, to make matters worse, Calder's production company went into liquidation. It would be several years before Paton retrieved the lost advance.

The success of the single seemed a prelude to disaster. When the follow up flopped, most people wrote off the group as forgotten one-hit-wonders. The Rollers were now eating up so many different line-ups that Paton had been forced to retain another group, Kip, who remained in Edinburgh as a pool of potential replacements. The lure of marriage proved irresistible to these love-lorn boys, but Paton continued to convince himself that each new line-up was an improvement on its predecessor. By this time, past experience had made Tam a hard taskmaster. In order to stabilize the group, he insisted that they follow special rules designed to govern their conduct and prevent the mass exodus that had plagued previous line-ups. It was this decision that later led to Paton being characterized as the svengali of pop.

Learning from past mistakes, Paton was reluctant to sign to any one particular agency, but played them off against each other in order to get work. Eventually, however, he signed the group to Barry Perkins, which led to a brief tie-up with manager Peter Walsh. Many groups might have abandoned Paton at this stage but the Rollers were too confused for such Machiavellian tactics. Tam recalls this period with some amusement:

The group and I were marched into Peter Walsh's office and it was beautiful . . . I was wandering around in jeans and in the group's eyes Peter was probably what they imagined as a manager. Somebody sitting there with a big moustache and big names in his past. Luckily, that didn't wash with the group because by this time they were hanging on to me like grim death! They really believed that everything I was doing was right for them.

Paton's influence over the group appeared to be growing in strength with each passing month. Ken Howard and Alan Blaikley were brought in by Bell to write the third record, 'Mañana', which won the Luxembourg Song Contest but failed as a single. Howard was astonished by the behaviour of this group, who never swore or drank in his presence. One night, he recalls, they were frolicking in a swimming pool when Tam appeared and instructed them to go to bed *instantly*:

They immediately stopped and went off to bed as meek as lambs. I have seen many groups over the years but never anything like that. Tam was a svengali, a Scottish patriarchal figure. The Rollers were 'zombie-like'. It was almost as if they had a switch in their brain. Whenever you'd ask them to do something they'd come to a halt and direct you to Tam.

Howard's recollections indicate that Paton was no longer taking any chances with the group and they knew he meant business. Although the svengali image would later be used to great effect as a publicity-grabbing device, past and present Rollers testify to its reality at certain stages of their career.

Having failed with Howard and Blaikley, the Rollers took on the services of famed Eurovision songwriters Bill Martin and Phil Coulter. This led to further friction within the group, particularly from Nobby Clark who was determined to record his own material on the flip sides. After failing to chart with 'Saturday Night', the Rollers seemed poised to call it a day. As Paton remembers, 'Their social lives were being obliterated and so was mine'. Even the oldest member, Derek Longmuir, fell into a depression and threatened to quit. For Paton it might well have seemed a blessing in disguise. He was already heavily in debt and had borrowed additional money from his parents to support the group. The only sensible solution to his problems was to dissolve the Rollers and cut his losses but Paton could not bring himself to destroy his dream so he persuaded the boys to struggle on 'for a few months more'.

In a desperate final fling, Paton borrowed a few hundred pounds and organized his own publicity campaign, sending 10 000 photos of the group to addresses culled from fan club magazines. Meanwhile, the Martin/Coulter team finally came up with that long-awaited hit. 'Remember (Sha La La)' climbed into the Top 10 and effectively relaunched the group's career. Amid the excitement, the inventive Paton worked overtime on presenting the group's image. Previously, he had dressed them in pink suits, black bow ties and see-through trousers and now he added tartan shirts to identify the boys with Scotland. Another of his short-lived groups, Bilbo Baggins, were the first to sport the fashion, but after Eric Faulkner took to sewing tartan on his trouser legs, the Rollers made the uniform their own.

A new image and chart comeback proved insufficient to prevent Nobby Clark or John Devine from quitting the group and the ever-resourceful Paton was forced to bring in singer Les McKeown and rhythm guitarist Stuart 'Woody' Wood to bolster the collapsing unit. Fortunately, Paton had promoted the Rollers' collective image so effectively that radical personnel changes had little effect on their popularity. During the next year they scored a string of hits culminating in two successive number 1s, 'Bye Bye Baby' and 'Give A Little Love'. Rollermania had arrived.

The summer of 1975 was a season of fainting fans, worried ambulancemen, overworked security officers and full-scale riots. Meanwhile, the Paton publicity machine ensured that the image remained unspoiled. Press biographies frequently stressed that the boys were clean-living, eligible bachelors so dedicated to their work that they had no time for girls. Far removed from the wacky world of rock 'n' roll, they drank milk not beer and, like the Beatles before them, played before royalty. The promotional tactics were a throwback to the fifties, when anodyne wholesomeness was seen as a necessary accoutrement to pop star success. Paton admits he played up the image to its logical extreme:

> We pushed the celibacy and non-drinking a lot in the early days. I made a big point out of it. I tried to turn them out as a nice group, different from the others around at the time who were getting pissed and dragging females up to their rooms.

The press inevitably caricatured Paton as a ruthless hirer/firer and puppetmaster. They loved to catch him out at every opportunity and his acquiescence ensured that he was easy prey. Once he was asked to pose for a photo outside the gates of his house, Little Kellerstain. The following week's newspaper headline said it all: 'Locked Behind The Gates of Colditz'. Paton initially shrugged off these tabloid tales:

> I was prepared to accept the svengali image. They said I was this terrible guy who stopped the Rollers having girlfriends and locked them in behind barbed wire. I still have barbed wire around the house now and I don't have any groups.

As with everything else in Paton's life, the puritanical image was pushed too far and although he wisely played along with the press for a brief period, they would ultimately have the last word.

The phenomenal success of the Rollers brought Paton further problems in the form of pirates and poachers. Although Tam had attempted to secure control of the group's lucrative merchandising rights, his efforts were rendered impotent in the face of worldwide exploitation. Meanwhile, opportunist sharks and reputable businessmen were eagerly vying to buy him out. One consortium offered £60 000 for his management contract, but the offer was declined. Even Bell Records supported a change of management, preferring to deal with an office in London rather than an unpredictable Scot who always insisted on travelling with his group. On many occasions, it was suggested to Tam that he would be better off accepting a job as a glorified road manager and transferring the administration to more experienced entrepreneurs. Always, he refused, and it is easy to understand why. For Paton, the Rollers were not merely a business asset, but the embodiment of all his frustrated dreams and ambitions. It was an emotional commitment, the value of which transcended commercial considerations, no matter how tempting. Like Epstein, Paton allowed his group to fill an important gap in his life. For a time, Tam and the Rollers had a mutual dependence which sustained their relationship, even in the midst of apparent chaos.

Although the Rollers were universally derided as a British weenybop phenomenon, they broke through internationally in 1975, topping the US charts with 'Saturday Night' and completing a lucrative American tour. However, as with every previous Rollers breakthrough, triumph was quickly followed by near disaster. The first sign of a newspaper backlash came in November 1975 when a 75-year-old widow died after being hit by Les McKeown's car. The following night, during a performance at Southampton, the distraught singer ran from the stage in front of 2000 shocked fans. Although there was sympathy from some quarters, certain members of the press were already sharpening their knives. In the ensuing case, McKeown was charged with reckless driving and banned for a year. It was hardly ideal publicity for the clean-living, fun-loving boys.

Although the hits kept on coming throughout 1975-6, both Paton and the Rollers gradually collapsed under the intolerable pressures brought by international success. McKeown again found himself in trouble, this time for supposedly firing an air gun at fans camped outside his house. Paton recalls the incident:

> There was a girl shot in the head and he was acquitted. Even though the road manager said he'd done it, a lot of people thought he was covering up. Whether he was or not, I don't know. I wasn't there . . . Les certainly never said to me he fired the rifle. He wasn't a bad kid. None of them were. The pressure just built up and we were all on cloud nine.

What had started out as innocent, zany fun, based on a cross between the Beatles and the Osmonds, was rapidly developing into a nightmare of death and destruction. A Manchester police sergeant died trying to control fan hysteria and although this could hardly be blamed on the group, it seemed to focus press attention on the darker aspects of the Rollers phenomenon. As it turned out, investigative journalism was not needed to discredit the group. The self-destructive tendencies of Paton and the Rollers would provide enough sordid revelations to keep the Sunday papers in business for the rest of the decade.

1976 proved the year of disaster, and the prelude to Paton's ultimate downfall. At this point, the myth of the milk-drinking, celibate Rollers ruled by an iron-fisted svengali could still sell papers, but it was no longer helping the group's career prospects. Rumour and innuendo increasingly hinted that the group were merely the private sexual playthings of another gay pop manager. This, however, was completely untrue, as became evident in later years when the boys confessed their bedroom secrets. Paton also maintains that the puritanical purge, so often associated with his management, was severely relaxed at the peak of their success:

> Guys were coming up and saying '. . . they're poofs!' The fact was the Rollers did have their casual sex . . . not with my approval, but I turned a blind eye. The only thing I ever said was 'Be careful — don't get any paternity suits'. That was good management. It was my job. In the early days I was strict, but not after they'd taken off. It didn't really bother me what they did or who they had in their bedroom.

Unfortunately, not everybody saw it that way. During the succeeding years, Paton's reputation as a sexual svengali proved a difficult cross to bear. Often people would abuse and pick fights with him for no apparent reason and it became increasingly unwise to appear locally in public. Tam remembers the resentment of his fellow Scots with some bitterness:

> If you go to the States and somebody drives to work in a Cadillac people will say, 'Hey, isn't he lucky? What a beautiful car!' But over here if you drive into a place with a Rolls people will say, 'Look at that dirty bastard. How did he manage to get that? What about the workers?' And they'll spit on you. They hate success. Eventually, I had to get rid of my Rolls because it was scratched, scraped and filthy things were written on it. And that is a strain.

By mid-1976 Paton was in a desperate state. The pressures of trying to fend off predatory managers, negotiate with record companies, sooth the Rollers' internal disputes and come to terms with an increasingly antagonistic public eventually proved too much for the self-styled svengali. At the height of the Rollers' fame, with every day presenting new crises, Paton suffered a nervous breakdown. Tam recalls driving to the infirmary with shooting pains in his neck, while the top of his head went completely numb. The doctor informed him that it was not a brain haemorrhage, but the first symptoms of an impending breakdown brought on by nervous tension. Even eight years later, Paton has yet to recover from the experience:

> It's still with me today. I'm the worst hypochondriac in the world. The other day I was working and the side of my face became warm and I thought I was having a brain haemorrhage. One night I was sitting here and I could hear my heart beating; I panicked, and thought it was the last burst before it stops. I phoned my nephew who's a surgeon and he said, 'I think you should be more concerned when you can't hear it beating'. Even Raymond, who's lived with me for years, says the same thing. It's got to the stage where they just ignore me. But that period of my life did affect me.

Today, it sounds a little comical, but, back in 1976, Paton's mental health left a lot to be desired. A specialist prescribed regular tranquilizers and advised Tam to give up managing the group. Although he briefly considered that possibility, he found it impossible to release the reins. Instead, he struggled on, gradually coming to terms with the pressures that had almost destroyed him. In later years, Paton admitted he found it difficult to kick the valium habit, but he seldom indulged in hard drugs. Indeed, Tam remembers only one instance of such experimentation during these troubled times:

> I only ever once took an LSD trip — and I cried for three days. But I'll tell you, I felt great afterwards. I think I bottled up a lot inside and during those three days I was able to cry and get everything out.

Although the trip proved therapeutic, he was still plagued by fears and depression. In his worst moments, Paton even considered taking his own life:

> I was definitely on the verge of suicide. There's no doubt about it. I was frightened of death, being a hypochondriac, but at the same time I wanted to go before anything took me. It sounds crazy. You may think I was going off my head and, in many ways, I was.

Paton's breakdown had predictably disastrous effects upon his charges, whose vulnerability was fully exposed in the spring of 1976. Impressionable and insecure, they merely reflected their mentor's own neuroses in an extraordinary series of traumas and near suicides. Having only recently recovered from the McKeown crisis, the Rollers found their image again in danger due to problems with Eric Faulkner. For some time, Tam and Eric had been at each other's throats over the thorny subject of employing outside writers to compose their hits. It was clear that Paton had little confidence in the Rollers' songwriting ability. Still obsessed by the importance of image and exasperated by the constant bickering, he found it increasingly difficult to play the diplomat:

> I remember telling Eric Faulkner: 'Go away and write your hit songs'. I was constantly on about his weight and that made him hate me. He felt it didn't matter if he was 20 stone, that people would still pile in to see him. But it doesn't work like that. I don't care who it is, even Led Zeppelin — there's an image there . . . I wanted them to become middle of the road but Eric wanted to go into a Meatloaf or Zeppelin scene. He couldn't get the 'we're going heavy' phrase out of his head.

At this stage Tam was probably correct to stick to his guns. A radical shift of musical policy by the Rollers would have been as laughable as the Tremeloes' ludicrous attempts to transform into a 'heavy' group at the end of the sixties. Of course, Faulkner's vision of 'heaviness' was no doubt considerably more lightweight than Paton suggests, and later in their career his arguments would prove convincing. For the present, however, formula singles and pretty-boy looks were deemed necessary so Faulkner continued to battle with his rapidly expanding girth. During a tour of Australia a doctor had prescribed amphetamines to suppress his appetite, but this brought unforeseen problems. By the time he returned to London, Eric was taking four or five pills a day and his sleep patterns were totally disrupted. By his own admission, he had become a walking zombie. Like Tam, he experimented with LSD, though the only ill effects of the trip came from attempting to devour a giant packet of cornflakes at one sitting. It was the use of barbiturates that proved most dangerous to his welfare and quickly led to an attempted overdose.

Paton somehow managed to get himself and Faulkner back on the rails, but there were additional problems with Alan Longmuir. Incredibly, he also admits to attempting suicide during this period of flux. Understandably, Paton was concerned about his protégés' psychological welfare and it is not too surprising to learn that, in the event of a total collapse, there were several substitutes waiting in the wings. The main contender was 17-year-old Ian Mitchell, who had previously achieved some success on the Northern Ireland showband circuit. By early 1976, he was living in Tam's house while awaiting the possibility of forming a new group in Scotland. Mitchell later confessed to the tabloids that he unintentionally ousted Longmuir from the group by informing Tam of some pictures showing the guitarist kissing a girl. Although the incident occurred, it was clearly a minor infringement taken completely out of context. In reality, Alan had tired of the group and seemed more interested in spending time on his farm or with his girlfriend from Dollar. Towards the end of his stay, he began to let the image slip, occasionally appearing unshaven and reminding the world that his teenage days were almost a decade away. Although he was destined to return to the group in 1978, there was no doubt that his enforced exit was a blessing in disguise. Longmuir later suggested that life as a Roller was intolerable, and added that he had always been much happier as a plumber.

The new line-up with Ian Mitchell saw Paton finally back in control, and seemingly recovered from his nervous breakdown. Certainly, in Mitchell's eyes, Paton still retained his legendary authoritarianism:

> Everybody was frightened of him. He was a very frightening man. I was scared shit of him as well. If he said 'jump' you jumped. He never threatened — it was absolutely voluntary. . . We were afraid of him. But don't ask me why. I haven't got a clue. He just projected this control.

There were even signs of Paton branching out as a manager with new talent, and his latest discovery, 16-year-old Gert, was revealed to the world in a blaze of publicity. Tam was confident that the bairn could crack the Japanese market and become an international star. It turned out to be little more than a combination of false hopes and hype. Gert had looked lovely fronting a group in Denmark, but when Tam put him in a studio, he found to his dismay that the boy was a terrible singer. Poor old Gert scuttled back to Denmark shortly afterwards, and all Tam was left with was a slightly reduced bank balance and sly rumours that he had kidnapped the youngster!

As the months passed, the Rollers' old gripes returned. There were further showdowns about songwriting as the hit records gradually dried up. Mitchell remembers Tam as the perfect manager for the Rollers but believes that he was losing direction during their later days:

> They were living on image. But where could they go from there? He created the Rollers and made them successful throughout the world, but, by this time, it was obvious that the kids had stopped wearing the

tartan and were listening to the records. And that was the problem. Once it started dying off he didn't know what to do, he panicked. That brought on the nerves and the internal arguments within the band. They wanted to mature musically rather than on hype. They wanted to be credible on vinyl.

Mitchell's theory is that Paton resisted allowing them total artistic control because he feared that if they were successful his influence over them would wane. Alternatively, if they failed, the band would probably break up. Either way Paton would lose. Tam maintains that as songwriters the group left a lot to be desired, while Mitchell suggests that he underestimated their talents, ignoring Faulkner's obvious potential as a hit composer of such songs as 'Money Honey'. The retrospective arguments solve nothing, but ably demonstrate how intense the conflict must have been at its peak.

Tam's twilight years as manager of the Rollers makes disheartening reading. Although he rightly maintains that the group were allowed their casual sex, even Paton was unprepared for the debauchery that he witnessed on the next American tour. Mitchell feels that the episode filled his mentor with disillusionment:

> I can remember him arriving three days late and we were all in the rooms with birds and rumping buttery queens . . . When it all started he booked himself out of the hotel. He had the hump. The Rollers was Tam's baby and it hurt him to see his creation being abused. I think it really did him a lot of damage to walk in and see everybody destroying the image of being good boys.

The Rollers' outrageousness was clearly becoming more alarming. Mitchell recalls a typical example of such behaviour:

> I'd had about ten bottles of Budweiser . . . and a couple of Quaaludes. They really make you randy, especially if you've been drinking. I ordered some room service and when the maid arrived I put my hand up her dress . . .

The startled maid rushed from the room and later accused Tam of rearing a bunch of animals. Other members of the Rollers were equally indiscreet, but because much of this over-indulgence occurred during foreign tours, the salacious details remained a well-kept secret.

It was inevitable that the celibate image of the Rollers would be destroyed eventually, but Paton maintained the facade upon his return to the UK. He even spoke wistfully about his own missed chances of settling down at 21 with a wife, a council house and six kids. These particular sentiments appear to have been totally genuine. Indeed, Tam even became engaged to a London art student, Marcella Knaislova, though the affair did not last.

In spite of the occasional short-lived hopes, the Rollers continued on their rapid downward spiral. Ian Mitchell gradually lost interest and frequently clashed with Paton over musical policy and image. Although the money was reasonable and the sex freely available, Mitchell felt weighed down by the need to maintain a false image. Prior to the return of Alan Longmuir, Pat McGlynn joined the group, though by this time it hardly seemed to matter which Roller came or went. Realizing that their appeal was waning in the UK, Paton looked to America and Japan for a resurgence of interest. He successfully negotiated a 13-week US television series which he hoped might transform the group into a seventies-style Monkees. Of course, the Rollers were far from convincing as individual personalities and the entire deal was placed in jeopardy due to delays and arguments. When Paton returned to Britain, he was confronted by five lawyers each demanding better deals for their respective clients in the group:

> It was an impossible situation. NBC were ready to throw it in. When we eventually got out to Los Angeles to do the filming, there were arguments about cars and private swimming pools. We had problems with Eric and Woody who felt they were Lennon and McCartney. I thought I was going crazy; I thought this is mental — this is the end.

In April 1978, the Rollers sacked McKeown, reputedly because he insisted on recording a solo album and mocked Faulkner's songwriting pretensions. He returned briefly for an important Japanese tour but was estranged from the others throughout the visit. According to Paton, four security guards were employed in order to prevent trouble. Understandably, McKeown declined a similar offer to tour Germany, leaving the Rollers to find a replacement.

By this point, Paton's influence over the group had all but vanished. The man they had once feared was now treated like a lowly employee. The Rollers insisted that they would choose McKeown's replacement and Tam heard nothing more until one day there was a phone call from Dublin requesting his presence. When he arrived at the airport there was no car waiting to pick him up, so he took a taxi to their hotel. Upon arrival, he was embarrassed to discover that they were interviewing possible candidates to replace him as personal manager. Eventually, he was introduced to the new Roller, South African Duncan Faure. Paton advised against signing the lad, fearing that his South African passport might cause the group problems obtaining work in certain countries. The other Rollers refused to listen to his arguments and insisted that he continue with plans for the German tour. Realizing that there would be problems, Tam refused to accompany them, but sent an employee in his place. Predictably, the Rollers played to half-empty halls on certain dates which led to further bickering and disenchantment. Paton recalls how his long-term association with the group finally ended in anger and bitterness:

> They told me I was sacked unless I got my arse out there. I told them they'd hear from my lawyer. There was a lot of abuse on the telephone. Alan and Woody were obviously pissed out of their heads and didn't know what they were saying. Derek came on the next morning and tried to talk things over but I'd really had enough. There was nothing left there to manage. The monster had got out of control and was destroying itself. Ten managers couldn't have held that group together. The only thing that could save them was a period of realization that they were finished.

The Rollers didn't have long to wait. Without Paton at the helm there was little chance of them saving their faltering career. Record companies rapidly lost interest and dismissed the group as a passing fad. Soon they became mid-seventies curios hopelessly adrift in a new age.

For a time, Paton remained confident that he could create another Bay City Rollers. Waiting in the wings were Rosetta Stone, a group that had already made some headway in Japan and seemed a perfect vehicle for his managerial skills. Although Paton gained them some useful television exposure and threatened to add new boy Limahl to their ranks, it all came to nothing. They lost confidence in his starmaking, sought new backers and found obscurity.

In June 1980, Tam Paton returned to his home, Little Kellerstain. Weary, disillusioned and still stinging from a £12 000 overdraft, he turned his back on management. During the next six months, he found himself caught in a tangled web of false friends, sycophants and hangers on. The circumstances that created Paton's downfall were not entirely of his own design. In 1979, his reputation had been considerably damaged following a burglary at Little Kellerstain. The culprits were revealed as 'rent boys' (male prostitutes), a fact that immediately placed Paton's moral conduct under suspicion. According to Tam, rumours were spread around clubs that he enticed teenagers to Little Kellerstain, doped and then seduced them. The effects of such gossip proved particularly detrimental, as Paton recalls:

> I was very lonely because people were afraid to come near me. People
> came up here and were frightened to take a drink in case I dropped
> something into it. Once my house went on fire and the firemen
> wouldn't go in there. I really created my own loneliness.

Toward the end of the year, Paton was visited by a former
provincial journalist who suggested the possibility of writing a
biography. However, it soon became apparent that his real interest
was in Paton's supposed sexual relations with the Bay City Rollers.
Although Paton rightly assured him that no such relationship
existed, he was told that £65 000 could be gained from such
revelations. Eventually, the journalist settled in as a permanent
guest and became increasingly involved in life at Little Kellerstain
until Paton began to resent his presence. Finally, he was asked to
leave and immediately went to the police and told of strange
goings-on, allegedly involving drugs and illegal sexual activities.
Strangely enough, Ian Mitchell claims to have been painfully aware
of the danger that Paton was courting. According to Ian, Tam was
'going a bit haywire' and needlessly fuelling the rumours concerning
Paton Place. Prior to police intervention, Mitchell phoned Paton
and warned him that a raid was imminent, but his former manager
laughed at the suggestion and denied that anything untoward was
happening. Shortly afterwards, the police arrived at Paton's gates
and he was taken into custody for a week before being released on
18 December. There were no drugs discovered at the house, but
the police felt they had sufficient evidence to press charges and
Paton was subsequently brought to trial. It was an extraordinary
case, which still leaves many puzzling questions unanswered.

In May 1982, Paton was sentenced to three years' imprisonment
at Edinburgh High Court for committing indecent acts with a
number of youngsters aged between 15 and 20 years. In addition,
he was charged with supplying them stupifying alcohol and allowing
blue movies to be shown at Little Kellerstain. Today, Paton does
not claim to be innocent of any of the charges, but maintains that he
admitted certain things which were untrue, particularly regarding
the reputed number of sexual offences.

In the aftermath of Paton's sentence, newspapers speculated
upon the existence of a secret file, allegedly implicating other guilty
parties. Paton was apparently 'torn between letting the whole thing
blow over or seeking justice and exposing the real beasts'. The
mention of this mysterious file caused consternation in certain
quarters. Ian Mitchell remembers receiving phone calls from several

music business people who were in a state of near panic after reading this statement. According to Paton, however, this was all a gross exaggeration and no such incriminating file is in his possession.

Looking back at the trial, it seems hard to believe that Paton received such a stiff sentence. Many figures in the music business were shocked by the custodial sentence, not least Ian Mitchell who clearly has strong feelings about the matter:

> That whole trial was absurd. If he'd been down here (in London) he'd have got off. The evidence was absolute rubbish. What did he do? Give a couple of kids a drink and a smoke and show them a copy of *Emmanuelle*. Who's really interested?

The answer to Mitchell's last question is 'virtually everybody'. The sentencing of Paton produced the expected sensation in the Sunday newspapers, but was he really the perverted svengali that everyone assumed? Certain aspects of his case suggest not.

The sexual assaults were, of course, the most serious charges, but even the judge suggested that these so-called 'kids' were actually young men and willing partners. Paton recalls seeing a youth on the stand whom he had never previously met, and others he barely knew. Yet another was a young gay who had deliberately sought out Paton's company. In retrospect, it is easy to see how Tam's notorious reputation as a 'svengali' was used against him during the trial:

> One guy had come around and hung about. It was stated that he wanted to be a pop star. I never promised to make him a pop star. He couldn't sing — I believe I did tell him that. Don't get me wrong, I feel more sorry for the kids, or young men, who were dragged through this because it was a horrific experience for them. The whole thing should never have happened.

During the course of the trial a whip was produced, as well as photos allegedly revealing the former manager in a compromising position with young boys. One of the photos featured Ian Mitchell perched upon Paton's knee and squeezing his cheek. Tam explains how this came about:

> We were doing a tour of Germany with Rosetta Stone. The bar was closed and Ian wanted this pint so he sat on my knee put his arm around me and said: 'Come on, give me that pint of beer'. Somebody took a photograph and that was me 'being fondled by boys'.

Mitchell did not attend the trial, but when I enquired about this incident he supported Paton's testimony with a carbon copy statement. He also added that, in his experience, Paton had never made any improper suggestions, let alone actions, to any member of the Bay City Rollers.

The second of Paton's convictions was for showing pornographic films at Little Kellerstain. Here again, there is confusion and controversy over the nature of these films. Paton admits to screening a number of blue movies, most notably *Tina With The Big Tits,* a soft porn item that he regarded as comical:

> The jury laughed at *Tina With The Big Tits* and the judge wasn't amused . . . I mean anyone who got a sexual kick from these movies had to be crazy or really hard-up. There was plenty of exposure, but it was really more comedy. It was the kind of thing you could put on at a party and even women could sit and watch . . . Most of the guys here were past the stage of being perverted and corrupted.

Unfortunately, certain films alluded to in the trial went far beyond the scope of *Tina With The Big Tits.* Paton maintains that several hard-core homosexual movies, later shown in court, had been planted in his house by a certain individual. Although Paton was cleared of this particular charge, the shocking nature of the films and attendant innuendoes left him in a very weak position. The additional pressure of knowing that his 80-year-old parents were under constant strain during the trial convinced him that he should conclude matters quickly. Paton recalls the events that led up to his admission of guilt:

> Two homosexual movies were shown in court. After they'd been shown what was the point of going on with the court case? They showed a heterosexual jury a film they didn't even understand. It was very hard core. I was in more of a position to understand it than the heterosexual jury and I had to sit and watch this revolting thing and realize it had been planted on me . . . They tried to make out they were home-made movies. They weren't. I'm not interested in making home-made movies with kids having sex. It doesn't bother me. That didn't even turn me on.

Worse was to follow when the news broke that Paton had pleaded guilty on these charges. As expected, journalists had a field day, leaving Tam in a state of weary disillusionment. He still maintains that the reporting of the case was sensationalized and grossly exaggerated:

> I came out that day and read: 'Depraved manager's hideaway' and 'What happened in the sauna' . . . I thought, 'God, what's happening? What's going on? Little Kellerstain?' If I'd been outside the court, read that paper and thought it had all been true I'd probably have shot the guy they were talking about. But here they were talking about *me*. And it was nothing like that. It was completely twisted and distorted.

Paton also dismisses fanciful reports that he was dragged from the court screaming: 'I'll take them all with me'. In fact, Tam simply smiled at the press when judgement was given and walked out stoically to begin his long sentence. It was an extraordinary end for one of the most famous managers in pop history.

Prison life can often be a trying and painful experience for those convicted of sexual offences. There is always the danger of being beaten up or ostracized from other prisoners. Fortunately, Paton was able to establish his credibility among fellow inmates at a very early stage. A couple of days after arriving in prison, Tam was walking in the square when suddenly a young kid began calling him obscene names. When the boy spat at him, Paton retaliated by cracking his jaw, an action that resulted in a cooling-down spell in solitary confinement. Word quickly spread about the incident and soon the Rollers' manager found himself accepted and respected by both inmates and prison officers. He was given a job of trust, working in reception for a year, until the parole board reviewed his sentence. Paton explains how institutionalized life strengthened his character:

> It gave me a little more faith in humanity because I discovered that there were a lot of nice people in jail that understood everything that happened to me going right back to the Rollers. We were all equal. For years before that anyone who spoke to me or came near me always wanted something. Here I was and I couldn't give anyone a thing. I couldn't even give them tobacco because I needed every ounce myself. That made me regain my confidence which I think I'd started to lose.

During the year that he spent behind bars, Paton was able to place his life and crimes in a clearer perspective. But even following his release in May 1983, Tam found it difficult to rationalize his dramatic fall:

> In years to come, people will laugh at my court case. The day I was released I drove out and I thought, what was it all about? Society got

their pound of flesh and that's what they wanted. They were able to drag me through the gutter and rip me apart. They were really able to get at this 'monster'.

For a brief period, it was rumoured that Paton might return to management, pick up the remnants of the Bay City Rollers and try again, but instead he lay low, concentrating on areas of business far removed from the pop scene. When the subject of a comeback is broached he still seems defensive but speaks frankly about his new view of life:

> I'm happy to be out of management. By being in that scene I had the press chasing me and dragging every skeleton out of my cupboard. I only want to be allowed to live. I don't go around dragging kids into cars because, believe me, that's not me. Sex isn't very important to me at all. I think I'm slightly past the stage of sex. All I want to do is have a successful property company and let people forget me.

Paton's views are not entirely consistent here. Although he claims to crave anonymity, it is evident that he has strong feelings about his court case which he wishes to make public. Whether such speculations will ultimately prove beneficial is debatable. In a revealing aside, Tam hinted that certain parties had cautioned him to steer clear of writers and journalists:

> Even the people I spoke to in jail said that it's better for me to lie low until the press has loosened its teeth. What interest am I? There are thousands of guys like myself. I know what it's all about — that I managed the Rollers to get them into bed. But it's garbage; that wasn't even in my mind. It didn't have to be the Rollers. I could have gone and picked other people up. They thought I was a svengali and had them locked up out here — that's rubbish. It's not my mind that's sick, but the people who write that kind of thing or believe it. Anyone who wants to make a quick buck goes and writes about me. And they've got an open door because I was convicted.

A perusal of certain newspapers suggests that Paton's criticisms are not far wrong.

Paton ultimately emerges as a figure of pathos, almost destroyed by an absurd dream that he pursued for much of his life. He is likely to be remembered as a hard-hearted svengali though such an image is difficult to reconcile with the physical reality of Tam Paton today. By his own admission, he is a neurotic, smoking incessantly and betraying a slight nervousness that seems totally out of character in a 'puppetmaster'. Clearly, the portrait that has been painted of Paton in the popular press is a spurious likeness of the man. Of course, myth has always been preferable to reality in the pop business so perhaps it is not too surprising that Paton's name has become synonymous with the phrase 'svengali'.

My brief glimpse of life at Little Kellerstain proved particularly rewarding. Prior to my arrival, Tam had been entertaining the maiden aunts of the community with tea and cakes. As he wryly noted, 'It makes a change for me'. Although Paton has obviously won back the trust and respect of many locals, not everyone has forgotten the old stories. While I was there the phone rang incessantly and, according to Tam, the caller was a persistent youth looking for a break in the music business. Although the ex-Rollers manager declined to accept the call, he could not bring himself to be rude to the boy. Such courtesy does not seem advisable in present circumstances. Obviously, for some star-struck kids the legend of Paton Place lives on.

The attitude of the local police seems less easy to gauge. Coincidentally, while I was interviewing Paton, a police officer arrived to discuss some minor driving offences. Laughing, Tam admitted that the transgressions had occurred while he was in the company of Her Majesty's prison. The rapport between Paton and the local constabulary was extremely cordial but not everyone shares my optimistic appraisal. Ian Mitchell provides a much-needed reminder that Paton must question the motives of everybody with whom he associates. Old myths die hard, and any relaxation on Paton's part could prove catastrophic. Thomas Paton may walk a free man, but his every action seems likely to elicit some form of public scrutiny and as Mitchell ominously confides:

> I'll tell you something else — they're watching him right now. I know that for a fact. They're watching his every move and all they want is one instance and they'll bang him up again so fast his feet won't touch the ground.

The turbulence and mayhem that Malcolm Robert Andrew McLaren was to wreak on the British Isles during the mid-seventies has been exhaustively analysed over the years. Insatiable greed, monomaniacal ego gratification and situationist subversiveness have each been considered as the aetiology of punk, but for the real root cause we need to travel back even further. Much of the confusion, conflicting imagery and insurrection that characterized the movement was portentously present in the eccentric childhood of the man credited with its invention.

Malcolm was born into a Jewish North London middle-class family one year after the A-bomb fell on Hiroshima. Behind the doors of the large Victorian house in which he spent his formative years, a Dickensian scenario unfolded. Malcolm found it difficult to accept his step-father, businessman Martin Levi, and became increasingly estranged from his mother. Although the presence of an elder brother, Stuart, restored a semblance of intimacy, even that relationship would not survive beyond adolescence. Whatever chance Malcolm had of living a normal childhood effectively ended when he was placed in the custody of his eccentric maternal grandmother.

Malcolm Edwards, the family name he adopted and retained until the end of the sixties, adored the Victorian grandparent whose unconventional behaviour and copious *esprit* he had both inherited and imitated. He learned to laugh at her outrageous stories of a scarcely believable past spent selling fake paintings to a gullible bourgeoisie. That this great swindle was perpetrated by a responsible elocution teacher, herself reared by strict Victorian parents, made the tale even more irreverent and exciting. Between apocryphal anecdotes, Malcolm was inculcated with a selective education, quickly learning to appreciate art and music in a self-consciously precocious fashion. The most important lessons that his grandmother imparted, however, were attitudinal rather than factual. The youngster was encouraged to question his elders, to accept nothing at face value and to disregard the myopic rules of the Establishment. Not surprisingly, such ill-advised licence soon brought young Malcolm into conflict with the educational authorities. He spent much of his primary school days hiding underneath his desk, a position which offered a particularly impressive view of pre-pubescent female underwear. More than once, Malcolm's mischievous grandmother trudged along to the head's study to learn of the outrageous exploits of her recalcitrant charge. At the end of every meeting her anticipated disapprobation would be undercut by a motto which Malcolm learned to prize above all others: 'Boys will be boys'.

In spite of his rebellious behaviour at primary school, Malcolm sailed through the Eleven Plus, thereby gaining admittance to the prestigious Whitechapel Foundation. During his first year, he briefly fell under the influence of his elder brother who was already promulgating the mesmeric glamour and primal stimulation of rock 'n' roll music. Interestingly, it was those two doomed stars of the era, Eddie Cochran and Buddy Holly, that most excited young Malcolm's imagination. The inarticulate Cochran, whose demigod dreams were enshrined by tragic death, was regarded by Malcolm as the quintessence of rock 'n' roll. Malcolm carried his fascination for fifties feretories and fashions into the new decade and seemed discomfited by the sudden emergence of the Beatles during his final year at school. It was to another doomed rocker that Malcolm clung for purity and inspiration: Johnny Kidd. In later years, he would claim that Kidd had a greater sociological impact on British youth than Bob Dylan, a perspective that betrayed how blinkered his outlook had already become.

By the time Malcolm Edwards embarked on his record-breaking eight-year sojourn at art school, he had dismissed the world of pop music as irrelevant and obsolete. It was to the artistic community that he now turned for inspiration, revelling in the bohemian lifestyle of a disgruntled and playfully cynical young student. He avoided both the wrath of the authorities and the beckoning of full-time employment by systematically moving from one educational establishment to another. During the sixties, Edwards attended Chiswick Polytechnic, Harrow Art School and Croydon College of Art, before completing his formal education at the University of London's Goldsmith College.

The Harrow period (1964-7) brought him into contact with Vivienne Westwood, an energetic young woman who was to have a profound effect on his future career. A primary school teacher with an art school background, Westwood later became interested in design and the use of fashion as a political tool. She regarded Malcolm as the most exciting person she'd ever met and maintains that he was even more dynamic then than he is today. Their relationship was intense and extremely volatile, but they always remained close and in 1969 Malcolm fathered a son, Joseph.

During the same period, the migratory Malcolm had enrolled at Croydon College of Art where he met another important ally, Jamie Reid. The pair became involved in various student demonstrations, made a film on the history of Oxford Street and, most significantly, fell victim to an avant-garde political movement whose theories would later be translated into McLaren's distinctive style of pop management.

The *Internationale Situationiste* was founded in Italy in the summer of 1957. Combining Marxist and Dadaist thought, the fellowship sought to enlighten the proletariat by attacking the passivity of consumerism, deriding the mindlessness of work and exploiting the creative possibilities of enforced unemployment and increased leisure time. The movement espoused its doctrines through sharp provocative slogans such as 'culture is the inversion of life', 'the more you consume, the less you live', 'be reasonable — demand the impossible' and 'it is forbidden to forbid'. The sloganizing was reinforced by perpetrating 'situations' conceived to pervert established codes and values and make the individual aware of the repressive politics of the modern technological world. What most appealed to Malcolm, however, was the spiteful fun with which the situationists executed their absurd stunts. Ten years later, he would distil that spiteful potency to spectacular effect in the seventies pop world.

By 1971, the art school years had come to a close and the eternal student finally found himself adrift in the hostile commercial world. It was time for a change of plan and a fresh identity. Borrowing money from friends, he leased premises at 430 King's Road under his new name, Malcolm McLaren. His dream was a boutique catering for the heroes of his youth, those menacing Teddy Boys who scoured the streets of fifties London, wearing gaudy Edwardian-style draped jackets and drainpipe trousers. Let It Rock soon attracted a select clientele impressed by Vivienne Westwood's ability to design fifties-style garments which looked authentic and original.

Among the scattered celebrities that frequented this anachronistic Chelsea emporium was that doyen of pop sensationalism, Screaming Lord Sutch. McLaren was fascinated by the diminutive rock screamer who had risen to national fame without ever appearing in the charts. He even offered extremely generous discounts on clothes just to hear precisely how Sutch had engineered his absurd political campaigns. It was already apparent to McLaren that Sutch's electoral battles with Harold Wilson and other prominent politicians represented the supreme example of situationism in sixties pop. What proved doubly interesting was the way Sutch had employed strikingly visual images to colour his impish personality. The African tribesman of the Two Is coffee bar and the cutlass-wielding buccaneer of pirate radio were just two of the roles that the plumber's mate from Harrow had acted out in the pursuit of national notoriety. What McLaren did not realize was that in listening to Sutch he was receiving the wisdom of that great posthumous professor of pop sensationalism, Reg Calvert.

When Sutch appeared at the 1972 rock 'n' roll revival show at Wembley Stadium, he was mildly amused to discover McLaren selling tacky souvenirs of the event. The sprightly entrepreneur was still full of questions, but his air seemed more confident, as though he had stumbled on a secret formula that could make him a fortune. As he packed away his collection of unsold T-shirts, Malcolm announced that the next major movement in pop music would not merely be linked with a fashion, but created by that fashion. He cited Epstein's manipulation of the Beatles' dress style as an example but indicated that a more radical approach would be necessary for the decadent seventies. In all his conversations, however, it was clear that McLaren regarded the under-15 market as his target group. If events had taken a different course, he would probably have launched a teenage group not dissimilar to the Bay City Rollers. Malcolm always had a strange attraction to tartan. Fortunately, he was beaten to the draw by that Scottish patriarch, Tam Paton, who realized many of McLaren's dreams several years later. The success of Paton's Rollers eventually forced McLaren to re-adjust his sights and plunge headlong into a search for a negative copy of this latest phenomenon. His revised plan betrayed an attitude reminiscent of Oldham and the mid-sixties charismatic managers: flashy, controversial and devil-take-the-hindmost.

The Bay City Rollers were already reaching their peak when McLaren finally entered the management field. In the meantime, he had moved away from fifties rock 'n' roll with a new boutique, Sex. Out went the Teds and in came the raincoat brigade in search of rubber underwear to liven up their weekends. The group that best exemplified Sex were a bunch of high-heeled, leather-clad, outrageously made-up Americans whom McLaren had befriended two years before.

It was late 1973 when the New York Dolls wandered into Let It Rock, braving the aggressive stares of indignant Teds in order to try on drape jackets and hear Eddie Cochran on the jukebox. McLaren was impressed by their nerve and enchanted by their sleazy tales of life in the Bowery, surrounded by drunks, junkies and prostitutes. The previous year, the Dolls' drummer, Billy Murcia, had overdosed on drugs, a testament to their hard-living image, but now they were back promoting a much-neglected debut album. McLaren immediately jumped on the bandwagon and began following the group around the country. He popped up at their Christmas gig at Biba's and two weeks later he was on the road to the Paris Olympia. There, he chatted garrulously to celebrated *NME* scribe Nick Kent who remembers him as 'the proverbial kite lost in spring', enthusing about the Dolls as if they were the most exciting rock act of all time.

Although McLaren knew embarrassingly little about the development of pop music since the mid-sixties heyday of the Stones, he desperately sought to fill in those missing years with endless questions followed by arm-waving dismissals of hippies, singer/songwriters and seventies supergroups. The music press, which he suddenly began reading voraciously, confirmed his impression that teenage rock 'n' roll had become uniformly tame. The only article that excited his imagination was a brief piece on Larry Parnes, which suggested that the Great Provider had added an 'e' to the surnames of his young demi-gods for numerological reasons. For some reason, Malcolm thought this the most amusing and ingenious conceit he had heard in years.

By the end of 1974, McLaren had begun his apprenticeship as a manager overseeing the rapidly disintegrating New York Dolls. When he arrived in New York, he was faced with five bickering musicians who had upset promoters, alienated their record company and all but lost their original impetus. Against the odds, he bullied them into rehearsing a new repertoire and set about restructuring their image and regulating their creative output. He discouraged David Johansen from writing with Johnny Thunders, arguing convincingly that the Dolls' best songs were Sylvain/Johansen collaborations. The relegation of Thunders to a solo spot in the act reflected McLaren's personal preferences at the time. He respected Johansen's intelligence and was frequently seen in his company, and although he also betrayed a sneaking admiration for the recalcitrant Thunders, the boy's flirtation with heroin proved disconcerting. Both Thunders and Jerry Nolan were known to frequent some of the seediest areas in New York, basking in a twilight world that was beyond McLaren's experience.

A far bigger problem facing the Dolls was Arthur Kane's fall into alcoholism. The Dolls' bassist was frequently incapacitated and on more than one occasion roadie Peter Jordan had been forced to perform in his place. McLaren urged the group to replace Kane with Richard Hell from Television, but Johansen's intercession and Hell's reluctance combined to save the bassist from dismissal. In despair, Malcolm briefly took a part-time job as a window cleaner in order to pay for a 'cure'. It was clear that he was determined to 'manage' the New York Dolls in spite of themselves.

What McLaren needed was some old-fashioned sensationalism in order to thrust the jaded Dolls back into the public eye. When the group introduced a new composition, 'Red Patent Leather', his scheming brain conjured up a wild idea. Overnight, the Dolls were transformed into communist propagandists and plans were hatched for the infamous 'Better Red Than Dead' tour. With his usual theatrical flair, McLaren designed a stage set featuring the group in red uniforms, backed by a giant poster of Chairman Mao and several hammer and sickle flags. A copy of Mao's *Little Red Book* was placed in Johansen's hands before every concert with the intention of infuriating any right-wing Americans in the audience.

Although the communist imagery attracted media attention, the Dolls failed to receive the expected sympathetic response from several prominent New York rock scribes. In order to save the group from further critical castigation, David Johansen played the diplomat, explaining that the Maoist trappings were part affectation. The press received a different response from the surly Thunders. Upon being asked, 'Are you a communist now?', Johnny turned to his interrogators and retorted, 'What's it to ya?' McLaren was overjoyed. In his mind, Thunders had summed up the perfect rock 'n' roll attitude in four barely articulated words. For weeks afterwards, Malcolm kept repeating Thunders' phrase at every opportunity, as though acting out the part of Marlon Brando's Johnny in *The Wild One*.

The sudden rise of Thunders to heroic status coincided with Johansen's fall from grace. Increasingly, McLaren found it difficult to compromise in the decision making and Johansen was far too intelligent and single-minded to knuckle down. With Arthur Kane grimly hanging on, Thunders mouthing dissent and Malcolm expressing frustration, the Dolls were clearly heading for a split. Events reached a head when Thunders rebelled and accused Johansen of wimpishness. As they exchanged insults, Thunders found new ammunition by reminding the vocalist that he had previously played in a 'hippie' band. Malcolm was momentarily stunned, then horrified. All his life he had hated hippies and to discover that he had been nurturing a former flower-child was anathema. Poor Johansen had no opportunity to refute the exaggerated allegation because McLaren's disillusionment was beyond repair.

By the spring of 1975, the New York Dolls were on the brink of extinction, but Malcolm still felt in control. The gossip around the Bowery area was that he knew no fear. He had booked the Dolls into several shady dives where hoodlums were known to cream off the house's profits as a matter of course. Yet there would be McLaren dutifully counting receipts and actually demanding the group's money in full. Remarkably, his antagonists were so impressed by his nerve and barrow-boy humour that they laughingly acceded to his whims. His showmanship and braggadocio duly impressed several other promising outfits, including Television and Blondie.

The possibility of managing a group as musically adventurous as Television was superficially attractive, but McLaren felt little empathy with vocalist Tom Verlaine. He was denounced as a poet and a hippie in the same scathing tone that Malcolm reserved for all wordsmiths from Donovan to Bob Dylan. However, Television still boasted the presence of the one figure whose management McLaren desired above all others. The fact that Richard (Myers) Hell had once edited a poetry magazine and dropped acid like any self-respecting hippie was conveniently ignored by the star-spotting English entrepreneur. For Hell had a charisma and aggressive dress style that proved irresistible to McLaren's confrontational boutique mentality. With his spiked hair, deadpan New York drawl and ripped clothes festooned with safety pins, Hell seemed the perfect vehicle for McLaren's full-blooded assault on the rock establishment. Unfortunately, Malcolm was neither persuasive nor astute enough to win Hell's confidence and by April 1975, his plans were dashed. The Dolls disintegrated in Florida and while their erstwhile manager was prevaricating, Johnny Thunders and Jerry Nolan flew back to New York and persuaded Hell to form a new group, the Heartbreakers.[1]

Although the New York Dolls always seemed doomed to self-destruction, McLaren felt a profound sense of failure following their demise. Disillusioned, he returned to England, intent on building a new group in the tradition of the Bowery. Shortly before his Stateside sojourn, he had expressed interest in an inchoate unit which included his Saturday shop assistant, Glen Matlock. Matlock had formed an unlikely alliance with two unemployed youths, Steve Jones and Paul Cook, who introduced him to their leader — musician, songwriter and former classmate Wally Nightingale. The cataclysmic Wally managed to gain nocturnal access to the BBC's Riverside Studios and there the quartet rehearsed a repertoire of Small Faces covers and Nightingale originals. Wally even provided them with a cheekily suggestive group name — the Swankers.

McLaren agreed to take the Swankers under his proprietorial wing and soon found himself attracted towards the delinquent duo Cook and Jones. He loved to hear how they bunked into seemingly impregnable rock venues and gatecrashed prestigious private

---

[1] In order to earn a reasonable living, David Johansen and Sylvain Sylvain retained the name New York Dolls for a further eighteen months. The sickly Kane went through a series of groups, and eventually overcame his drinking problems.

parties. They could even wax ecstatic on the late lamented New York Dolls, whom they had once seen supporting their heroes, the Faces, at Wembley Stadium in 1972. What most impressed McLaren, however, was Steve Jones's credentials as a petty thief. Malcolm always had an inexplicable fascination for criminals and loved to hear the stories that circulated about Jones and Cook breaking into the houses of rich pop stars in order to furnish themselves with musical hardware. These Robin Hood exploits betrayed an anarchic playfulness which no doubt reminded McLaren of vintage sixties situationism.

McLaren's first managerial decision was to sack the bespectacled Wally Nightingale, thereby gaining complete control over the group's creative direction and image. The favoured Steve Jones was temporarily thrust into the lead vocal spot and the Swankers were renamed Q.T. Jones and the Sex Pistols (Q.T. was a title borrowed from a sex magazine and a pun on 'cutie'). After several abortive low-key gigs, it was evident that Jones was a poor front man, so he reverted to guitar, leaving his mentor to search for a new singer.

McLaren's vain attempts to recruit the perfect vocalist were both desperate and farcical. Initially, he wasted valuable time attempting to persuade the ever-reluctant Richard Hell to leave the Heartbreakers. Abandoning that dream, he turned to Sylvain Sylvain, Johnny Thunders, and even Nick Kent's singing girlfriend, Chrissie Hynde. All of them strenuously resisted his plans and as the weeks passed, Malcolm grew more restless and eccentric. At one point, he even threw up his hands and decided to take the job himself. It was a well-kept secret, but Malcolm had once fronted the New York Dolls performing an off-key but enthusiastic cover of Marv Johnson's 'You Got What It Takes'. Embarrassed about his vocal shortcomings, McLaren eventually sought professional advice. For several weeks, his pop star delusions were sustained by infrequent vocal exercises. Suddenly, everybody noticed that whenever Malcolm walked down the street he was always singing a song. Fortunately, he quickly came to his senses, realizing that at 29 he was rather old to be challenging the Bay City Rollers. The single remnant from his brief 'pop star' phase was an unrecorded self-penned composition humorously titled 'If I'm Not Gonna Be A Rock 'n' Roller I Might As Well Be A Thief'.

Recovering his managerial poise, McLaren relentlessly drove the embryonic Sex Pistols into a semblance of mild competence. Steve Jones was taken in hand by Nick Kent and given some rudimentary guitar lessons, which proved surprisingly successful. For several months, Kent rehearsed with the group but his status always seemed tenuous. With his formidable knowledge of the rock business, he was clearly far too worldly-wise for a permanent post. As later events showed, McLaren could never tolerate an equal for any length of time.

In retrospect, it seems remarkable that Cook and Jones, rebellious, incondite and unreliable by nature, knuckled down so meekly to McLaren's ever-increasing demands. For all their naïveté, however, they were sharp enough to realize that the strawberry blond shopkeeper wasn't in this game for the good of his health. Blithely ignoring the political digressions that occasionally spewed from his mouth, they stoically soldiered on. Their motives were clear: they wanted to be pop stars, just like the Faces. And like all aspiring working-class pop idols, they were willing to work themselves silly to please their middle-class manager.

McLaren's hilarious quest for the perfect Pistol was getting beyond a joke. The search was even extended to gay clubs and before long an array of bright young things passed through the doors of his boutique in search of fame and finance. Most of them couldn't sing a note to save their lives and visibly seized up when presented with a microphone. On more than one occasion, Kent angrily demanded to know what McLaren was playing at. The embarrassed entrepreneur shrugged his shoulders, feebly adding, 'I don't know precisely what I want, but I'll know it when I see it'. In truth, McLaren was finding it difficult to match the face to the singer and the singer to the group. From his predominantly visual perspective, the look was all important. He therefore went to extraordinary lengths to incorporate strikingly inept individuals into the lead singer role. When the results proved predictably disastrous, Malcolm would utter a vaguely reassuring 'Er, maybe you'd be more comfortable holding a guitar. You won't have to play it, just hold it'. For a man with the reputation of a ruthless hirer/firer, McLaren could be blindly sentimental at times.

After all the aborted 'auditions', the supreme Sex Pistol was finally discovered swanning around McLaren's boutique one afternoon. The green-haired John Lydon with his manic stare and sullen demeanour had all the visual ingredients of an anti-star. According to legend, he secured the post after a self-mocking rendition of Alice Cooper's 'School's Out', accompanied by the boutique jukebox. For McLaren, he represented everything that the Pistols needed, and more besides. Genuinely menacing onstage, his pent-up malevolence would be released in a devastating diatribe that could not fail to provoke. Offstage, he betrayed all the characteristics of a precocious misanthrope: suspicious, sarcastic, cynical, condescending, cantankerous, purblind and obtuse. With his stage name, Johnny Rotten, the kid was instant caricature and hardly seemed human at all. Even more than Parnes' creations, Rotten's persona represented the playing out of a moral allegory in the pop universe. Rotten was a veritable Pyrocles — the fiery temper that burns itself and others while seeking fame.

Following Rotten's recruitment in the summer of 1975, McLaren finally felt that the group was a complete entity. There was a brief moment of doubt when a second guitarist, Steve New, began rehearsing in Kent's place, but the lad was quickly dismissed for the unforgivable crime of acting like a hippie. For the remainder of the year, the Sex Pistols appeared sporadically, playing support to more musically accomplished acts. They seemed just another no-hoper teenage group whose deafening repertoire lacked even the sophistication of a second-division heavy metal act.

What separated the Sex Pistols from the young acts of the period was their unwillingness to respect their elders on the rock circuit. Even during the early stages of their career, McLaren made no attempt to tone down their obnoxious and aggressive behaviour. The first reported act of Sex Pistols violence occurred during a St Valentine's Day dance at High Wycombe, supporting McLaren's old friend, Screaming Lord Sutch. The group had turned up without a PA system and, as a favour to McLaren, Sutch allowed them to borrow his equipment. After playing three numbers excruciatingly loud they were dismayed to find that the audience had not even noticed their presence. Rotten prowled the apron of the stage with a leering grin, admonishing the students to clap. His ruse worked, and before long a pocket of hecklers began chanting 'Off, Off, Off'. Their chorus gradually grew louder and louder until they could be heard above the deafening sound of the Sex Pistols' instrumentation. Rotten responded by throwing a bottle into the crowd which inevitably provoked further unrest. The indignant students replied in kind and the set ended amid a hail of debris. During the ensuing scuffle, Sutch's equipment was badly damaged and he was forced to go on later with a faulty microphone. The rival musicians almost came to blows backstage until McLaren intervened and promised to reimburse Sutch for his losses. Long after the Sex Pistols had gone home, the garrulous old Lord of Horror Rock was still debating their significance:

> The effect it had was to make you think about it all the time. My band said, 'What an amateur lot of useless bastards they are'. I said, 'But look at all the bands who've supported us. How many of them do you remember?' They created something that night. All the crowd reacted against them.

Another person who observed the pandemonium at that Valentine's Day rout was promoter Ron Watts, who wasted no time in offering the Pistols a gig at the 100 Club. With further performances at the Nashville and Marquee, the group finally broke into the standard gigging circuit. However, it was not long before the music community realized that the Sex Pistols were no ordinary group. Their public appearances had become minor events attracting a new breed of teenager, radically different from the tartan hordes that followed the Bay City Rollers. The outlandishly spiked hair, torn clothes and safety pins were the legacy of Richard Hell and a fashion that McLaren was now turning into a commodity. It was only a matter of weeks before the music press found a term to describe this burgeoning underground movement: punk.

By the spring of 1976, the Sex Pistols' supporters had invented their own set of inverted values, symbolized in such creations as an anti-dance (pogoing) and a perverse form of adulation (gobbing). The virulent power of this new movement came as no surprise to McLaren, who claims to have orchestrated the entire idea. Clearly, he had learned the lessons of pop history well. Whatever else, it is doubtful whether punk would have happened quite so spectacularly had it not been for McLaren's all-consuming fascination with the career of Larry Parnes.

What most impressed McLaren about his fifties predecessor was the influence that he exercised over his artistes, the media and the record industry. Frequently, McLaren asserted a truth which no rock critic has ever dared suggest: 'Parnes *was* British rock 'n' roll'. One of McLaren's favourite theories was that the power which Parnes wielded during that epoch-making era could somehow be revitalized in the barren, decadent seventies. For a time, Malcolm genuinely wished to emancipate British youth in the same way that Larry had brought the dreams of stardom to multitudinous teenagers of the fifties. Like Parnes, he would unleash a battalion of exotically named pop stars, plucking them from dead-end jobs and dole queues like some avenging socialist angel. These were noble aims indeed and McLaren was not without his supporters. By the late summer of 1976, however, this idealistic vision of a teenage community was to be undermined by McLaren's fatal attraction for the monster he had created.

In the wake of the Pistols, other notable punk groups rapidly emerged, including the Damned and the Clash. The latter boasted the managerial guidance of Bernard Rhodes, a McLaren acolyte who had supervised the Swankers during Malcolm's absence in America. The faithful 'Bernie boy', as McLaren demeaningly referred to him, was now in the forefront of punk politics, promoting the Clash as teenage urban guerrillas in striking contrast to the non-doctrinal jack-the-lad Pistols. Although the Rhodes/McLaren friendship continued throughout this crucial period, the community spirit that Malcolm had propagated only months before was sacrificed before a rapacious self-interest. With the music press and record companies sniffing a sensation, McLaren knew that he could create an impact beyond his wildest ambitions. He even adopted a new slogan which left little doubt about his designs: 'Beatles, Rolling Stones, Rollers, Sex Pistols'. With unabashed elitism, McLaren ordered his group not to associate with their punk rivals and severely reprimanded Matlock after seeing him fraternizing with a member of the Damned. The golden dream of a Parnes-inspired community had been jettisoned in favour of a full-frontal assault by the Pistols as an institution in themselves. Such reasoning was to make any subsequent moral considerations largely irrelevant.

The violence that erupted in London clubland during the summer of '76 represented the evil face of punk, and it was this visage that would later encourage moral condemnation of the entire movement. McLaren was sufficiently in control of the Sex Pistols at this stage to gauge the climate but, inflamed with a recently acquired lust for power, he set out to wreak havoc. Suddenly, every Sex Pistols show had to be an event. If Johnny Rotten could not create uproar onstage, then the pandemonium would have to be provided by hard-core supporters in the audience. Malcolm found the perfect disciple for his rabble-rousing in the appropriately nicknamed Sid Vicious.

Vicious was dangerously unstable and subject to psychopathic outbursts which would finally prove beyond McLaren's control. Goaded on by friend Rotten, Vicious ensured that Sex Pistols gigs were not for the fainthearted. Although much of the violence associated with those summer performances was undoubtedly spontaneous, and perhaps inevitable in view of the intensity of the music and the ferocity of the pogoing, it was Vicious's presence that led to the spilling of blood.

The most celebrated victim of violent assault was former Pistol associate Nick Kent. During a Pistols performance at the 100 Club, he was accosted by Vicious, who proceeded to dance maniacally in front of him. When Kent attempted to move away, his aggressor whipped out a bicycle chain and swung the weapon menacingly towards his head. Meanwhile, Sid's sidekick moved in for the kill: 'It wasn't Vicious I was worried about, but Jah Wobble who was holding a knife to my face. He really wanted to cut me. It was a chilling moment'. Distracted by Wobble's flashing knife, Kent momentarily wavered, allowing Vicious to execute a perfect hit. As blood gushed from Nick's scalp, Ron Watts entered the fray, restraining Vicious from inflicting further injury. Fortunately, the wound was superficial, but the publicized flailing caused a dangerous precedent. Kent still believes that McLaren was cogniscent of the bloody scheme, for he was conspicuous by his absence when the blow was struck.

By September, further fights had been reported during punk gigs at Dingwalls and the Nashville. As each pub and club announced the banning of punk nights, the Sex Pistols and their ilk were forced underground. It took Sid Vicious to force the nail in the coffin. During the 100 Club's much-touted Punk Rock Festival, he became involved in a glass-smashing incident which ended in near tragedy when an innocent girl was blinded by a flying splinter. McLaren has always been characteristically blasé about the negative aspects of the Pistols phenomenon, but his cavalier comments on personal injury and intimidation still sound crass and insensitive:

> The violence was magnificent; it was something that gave all those kids a terrific identity, made them proud of their future. So someone got blinded? Well, there are far worse things happening in places with far worse causes. One person blinded, a couple of people badly hurt — the achievement outweighed it completely.

Such perverse logic not only assuaged Malcolm's conscience but convincingly sustained his delusion about the social importance of the Sex Pistols.

With record company interest looming, McLaren strengthened his position by forming Glitterbest Management. Jamie Reid was offered the post of art director and his girlfriend, Sophie Richmond, took on secretarial duties. It was this back-up team, aided by the ever present Vivienne Westwood, that kept McLaren sane during the stressful months ahead when the Sex Pistols hit the nation's headlines like no other group had done since the heyday of the Beatles.

Attracted by the idea of pitting his wits against a corporation, Malcolm signed the Pistols to EMI for £40 000. The release of their debut single, 'Anarchy In The UK', caused mild controversy with its simplistic politicizing and oblique references to 'Anti-Christ'. However, it was their obscene language on Thames Television's *Today* programme which rocketed them to national infamy. The tabloids had a field day sensationalizing this event under such banner headlines as 'Off . . . Off' and 'The Filth And The Fury'. The publicity excelled even McLaren's situationist expectations, but notoriety brought its own anonymous admonitions. As Christmas

'76 approached, the Pistols' nationwide 'Anarchy Tour' was crippled by a series of abrupt cancellations. In desperation, EMI attempted to persuade McLaren to tone down the Pistols' obnoxious behaviour and curry favour with influential tabloid journalists. It was a classic misreading of McLaren's personality, for he was already transforming the Pistols' odious conduct into a *cause célèbre* among the more self-consciously radical elements of the music press. His love of provocation and incendiarism outweighed the need for short-term record sales and concert receipts, though reconciling political theory with profit was proving increasingly difficult.

Towards the end of 1976, Malcolm had threatened to disengage the Pistols from EMI if the label did not improve its promotion of the group's product. However, the corporation was already questioning the sagacity of the signing and, unknown to McLaren, the executives were prepared to call his bluff. Early in the New Year, events reached a head when the group was once more reprimanded in the press for allegedly vomiting in the departure area of Heathrow airport. Within days of this incident, EMI announced that they were terminating the Sex Pistols' contract, albeit having lost £40 000. Malcolm was left with the demulcent words of the managing director ringing in his ears: 'Why not try Virgin?'

McLaren quickly won over Virgin, but at the last minute decided that he would rather infiltrate another corporate structure. In the meantime, he oversaw the sacking of Glen Matlock, whose desire for a more professionally-minded Pistols ran counter to Malcolm's anarchic whims. The new boy, Sid Vicious, confirmed McLaren's dictum that attitude was more important than ability. Nevertheless, it would be Matlock's contributions which provided the qualitative bulk of the Sex Pistols' musical legacy.

By early 1977, McLaren's ambiguous intentions were becoming nakedly revealing. The recruitment of Vicious appeared to demonstrate that the old situationist was still searching for fresh excesses to shock the nation. Yet, in his heated negotiations with various record companies, McLaren was betraying the avaricious self-interest of a traditional Tin Pan Alley manager. There remained the lurking suspicion that all this talk about politics was a cheap con, cleverly conceived to disguise a capitalist in Robin Hood's clothing. Maybe he was only in it for the money after all. Whatever else, his dealings with A&M were sharp enough to elicit a swift £50 000 cheque. On the day of the signing, deliberately staged outside Buckingham Palace to prepare the world for the next single, a number of rumbustious incidents occurred. The group invaded the offices of A&M and in a drunken free-for-all defaced walls and damaged a toilet. That same night, the recently appointed

Vicious lived up to his name by hospitalizing a friend of Bob Harris, the diffident presenter of BBC's *Old Grey Whistle Test*. One week later, Malcolm skipped down the stairs of A&M's offices clutching another cheque for £40 000. The Pistols were once again without a record label. McLaren's ego was rampant.

A&M's *volte face* was sufficiently melodramatic to frighten off other potential investors and after suffering rejection from five more labels, McLaren felt obliged to place economic necessity before politics and art by once again entertaining the attentions of Virgin. In many respects, Virgin was the complete antithesis of everything Malcolm stood for. Founded by a young, bearded, middle-class, former public schoolboy with a flair for entrepreneurial expansionism, the label literally oozed the suburban hippie mentality that McLaren despised. Yet Richard Branson was to prove Malcolm's nemesis. Unlike the older executives of EMI and A&M, he was unfazed by bad publicity, sharing McLaren's love of sensationalism and outrage. From the outset, Branson was potentially dangerous because he had the personality to tolerate and contain McLaren while siphoning off the Pistols' energy for the lasting benefit of Virgin Records. Understandably, Malcolm's initial reservations became largely irrelevant when Virgin placed £90 000 on the negotiating table for world rights, excluding the US, France and Japan.

The pact between Virgin and Glitterbest proved particularly beneficial to the Pistols during their reckless assault on the British media's most sacred cow. The release of 'God Save The Queen', which climbed to number 1 in the *NME* charts during Jubilee Week, caused even greater commotion than the widely censored 'Anarchy In The UK' and persuaded Virgin to mount a publicity campaign pleading for liberality. McLaren still regards the macabre single and attendant outrage as the most significant event in the Pistols' career, for it literally tore into the heart of British Nationalism in a frighteningly comic fashion that came closest to an act of genuine situationism.

Ever inventive, McLaren next organized a boat party on the Thames which allowed the Pistols to wax anarchic outside the Houses of Parliament. After disembarking from the appropriately named *Queen Elizabeth*, several of the anti-royal revellers found themselves under arrest. The assault upon Her Majesty presaged the ominous appearance of menacing mobs masquerading as the general public. Jamie Reid's foolhardy wearing of a 'God Save The Queen' T-shirt, provocatively displaying Her Majesty's safety-pinned nose, encouraged McLaren's once-revered Teddy Boys to break the art director's nose and leg. Johnny Rotten was the next victim, slashed with a razor along with his colleague, producer Chris Thomas. Within two days of this attack, drummer Paul Cook received a good thrashing topped off with the crunch of an iron bar across the head. When the Pistols subsequently went into hiding, the violence spilled visibly on to the streets. The most prominent trouble spot was the King's Road, which still housed McLaren's latest boutique, Seditionaries. Significantly, the warring factions consisted of Teds and Punks, the two youth sub-cultures which the red-haired boutique-owner had so lovingly nurtured. Having ignited the passions of youth, McLaren was now in danger of being consumed by the conflagration.

Many acolytes claim that the Pistols died a slow death following the Jubilee caper and there is much truth in the argument. Publicly pilloried, unable to perform and unwilling to write, they fed upon their own egos while the momentum slowly faded. It was at this crucial stage that McLaren chose to distance himself from the group, plunging headlong into his next venture — the Sex Pistols film. What began as a distraction grew steadily into an obsession and finally a grand folly which was to drag McLaren through the High Courts.

McLaren's fatal attraction for a full-blown Pistols movie was partly a nostalgic hangover from his art school days. He had once made a film about the history of Oxford Street and even attempted a biopic of Billy Fury which foundered under the weight of an impossible budget. Old habits were to die hard. With the Pistols, Malcolm was determined to step outside the traditional rock celluloid cash-in by creating something outrageously new and ambitious. His first choice as director was Russ Meyer, the soft porn merchant responsible for such cult sexploitation movies as *Beneath The Valley Of The Dolls*, *Supervixens* and *Ultravixens*. Meyer began the project in earnest and after rejecting several writers commissioned his old friend Roger Ebert, who completed a racy, comic script titled *Who Killed Bambi?*[1] Unfortunately, the film was dogged by ill luck and questionable judgements. Meyer insisted on various rewrites, while McLaren frequently intervened with wild ideas that proved impossible to implement. As the budget steadily rose, Meyer found himself in conflict with Rotten whose antipathy towards the project was frequently voiced. Even

---

[1] The title, a parody of Walt Disney's sentimental box office smash *Bambi*, refers to a scene in which a degenerate rock star callously shoots a deer. Coincidentally, McLaren's sixties sensationalist counterpart, Reg Calvert, had once done precisely that in a characteristic moment of madness. In spite of his conversations with Screaming Lord Sutch, the seventies svengali was unaware of this uncanny happening.

more alarmingly, the solid investments which McLaren anticipated from various backers proved naïvely over-optimistic. With Glitterbest's resources stretched to the limit, Malcolm was forced to concede defeat and cancel the film. The unfortunate Meyer was left to seek financial redress through the courts.

In tackling the movie business, McLaren was clearly out of his depth but he gamely struggled on as imagination once more overran practicality. In the succeeding months, scriptwriters Jonathan Caplan and Peter Walker came and went, while costs spiralled beyond recognition. A second film script, *A Star Is Dead* (another parodic title) was completed, then jettisoned amid confusion and financial uncertainty. Finally, much to McLaren's disappointment, the grand design fell into the hands of the then inexperienced Julien Temple, who had been waiting in the wings since filming the abortive Anarchy Tour and Jubilee boat trip fiasco. Within the space of a year, McLaren's celluloid dream had been transformed from a lavish Hollywood extravaganza into a low-budget feature.

McLaren's pursuit of cinematographic glory not only cost him his reputation as a shrewd operator, but severely weakened his influence over the Sex Pistols. The perpetually disaffected Rotten was now displaying undisguised contempt for the manipulative games of his playful manager. McLaren responded by concealing vital information from his charge, fully realizing that such a course would only exacerbate existing tensions. As always, the svengali could not resist the petty drama of manager/artiste rivalry.

Rotten proved a worthy opponent, gaining in strength and intelligence as the Sex Pistols' fame spread. Many new wave writers were already apotheosizing the spiky-haired youth as the spokesman of his generation, a view which McLaren regarded as laughable. Nevertheless, the assimilation of the Pistols into the hard rock mainstream now seemed an inevitable process. Their next single, the melodic 'Pretty Vacant', was even featured on *Top Of The Pops*, a decision which McLaren bitterly resented. Predictably, the long-awaited debut album, *Never Mind The Bollocks, Here's The Sex Pistols*, rocketed to number 1 amid partisan claims extolling its all-time classic status. In truth, it was a patchy affair, dominated by previously released songs which merely underlined that the Pistols were running short of ideas. For McLaren, the album crystallized his dilemma in reconciling economics with attitude. He welcomed the revenue that the product generated, but regretted falling into such a predictable rut.

The Pistols had begun with an attitude that combined fifties rock 'n' roll sullenness with a vaguely anarchic desire to introduce chaos into the lives of their doleful supporters. Malcolm had always explained the phenomenon as an attack upon the record industry and Establishment. Thus, the Sex Pistols turned outrage and prohibition to proselytizing effect by scorning rock venues in favour of strip clubs, and using the singles format to bombard kids with simple but effective slogans. The naïve lyrics of 'Anarchy In The UK' expressed an attitude rather than an argument. What did we expect? Poetry? McLaren and Rotten regarded poetry as the secret language of middle-class hippies. Yet, here were the Sex Pistols pandering to genteel record buyers by producing that most desirous of commodities: the LP record. The mild furore over the album's title made the project seem like another situationist wheeze, but it was actually McLaren cashing in the 'attitude' for an irresistible profit.

The concept of 'The Great Rock 'n' Roll Swindle' was now uppermost in McLaren's mind. He had already conned the record industry and 'emancipated' the kids, but now they were to be swindled too. The bestselling album was to be followed by, of all things, a US tour. Clearly, the Pistols were cleaning up, with Rotten playing a prima donna rock star and Malcolm slumping into the traditional money-grabbing managerial role. Yet McLaren could not fully contain his mischievously anarchic nature within the confines of a simple profit-making venture.

The American tour was the battleground on which McLaren's dual nature confronted itself. Unable to resist the money, he had secretly hoped that the US visit would be vetoed by immigration control. In reply, he intended to mount an anti-American tour of Russia or China, re-employing the old New York Dolls' trick. His dream was scuppered when the Pistols were granted visas. Confused about his motives, McLaren vowed to outwit his avaricious nature by plotting a course fraught with danger. He wanted to make an easy profit in the hardest possible way.

McLaren's awkwardness was evident from his first discussions with the Pistols' American record company. Warner Brothers envisaged a large-scale tour, culminating at Madison Square Garden, but McLaren insisted on playing obscure towns and cities, including redneck areas of the South. The provocative itinerary guaranteed that the tour would not pass without incident. Indeed, the Pistols would be fortunate to escape with their limbs intact.

Warners' consternation, fuelled by McLaren's stubbornly uncooperative attitude, increased tenfold upon witnessing the eccentric behaviour of Sid Vicious. In the preceding months, Sid had inexorably fallen into heroin addiction, egged on by the shrill-voiced, corpse-like companion on whose arm he uneasily rested.

Nancy Spungen, a former Heartbreakers' groupie, had insinuated herself into the Sex Pistols' circle, and established a mutually dependent relationship with its most unstable and psychotic member. The periodic beatings that Vicious dished out to his paramour were par for the course in the twilight junkie environment which they increasingly inhabited. More than once, McLaren had attempted to separate the ill-starred duo, but Spungen clung fast with the desperate tenacity of a hardened addict. While Virgin sought to cure Vicious's habit, McLaren gradually grew accustomed to his excesses and even encouraged his wild animalistic behaviour. Sid needed little prompting for he regarded America as the perfect platform on which to indulge his rock star fantasies.

As the tour progressed, the once incendiary Johnny Rotten was eclipsed by his colleague's lust for infamy. During rehearsals Sid stabbed himself with a knife and later, onstage, proudly displayed the wound to his ghoulish followers. This was no act of purgation but self-infliction designed solely to draw attention and outrage. With his senses heightened and tolerance of pain increased, Sid amused himself by grinding broken bottles into his arms and chest. Photographers and fans paid scant respect to Rotten, whose whinging theatrics paled alongside the genuine menace emanating from the malcontented guitarist whose bare chest displayed the bloodily engraved plea: 'GIMME A FIX'.

Although Vicious baited homosexuals in Texas and bled regularly onstage, the performances were anti-climactic by Pistols standards. McLaren became increasingly disillusioned with Rotten's haughtiness and branded him a rock star quisling. Rather than watch Warner Brothers transform his monster into a stadium showpiece, McLaren racked his brains for another situationist stroke.

The notion of transporting the Sex Pistols to Brazil in order to be filmed playing with train robber Ronnie Biggs was McLaren's most bizarre conceit to date. The anachronistic coupling was certain to transform the Pistols story into a black Ealing comedy, but McLaren's grotesque fascination with the exiled criminal was unquenchable. Although Jones and Cook laughingly agreed to the ruse, Rotten accused McLaren of pulling a cheap publicity stunt and refused to be cajoled. Seizing the moment, the self-styled svengali turned on his protégé, and after winning support from the others informed Rotten that he was fired. Within weeks, the Sex Pistols were scattered across the globe like agents of pandemic destruction.

The headline-grabbing Vicious had been unable to make the Rio trip due to temporary incapacitation following several heroin binges. It was no matter: McLaren had already decided to extend the joke by promoting Ronald Biggs as the Pistols' new lead singer.

With remarkable swiftness, the dispossessed penurious convict found himself signing a Glitterbest contract and clutching a cheque for £1000.

The Rio escapade produced another controversial single, 'God Save The Sex Pistols', later retitled 'No One Is Innocent (A Punk Prayer)'. Jamie Reid's graphics, with the message, 'Cosh The Driver', provided a chilling reminder that it was not all fun and games. But if McLaren hoped that his followers would applaud the Rio carry on, he was to be disappointed. The pro-Rotten lobby of the music press derided the Diaghilev of punk as a desperate man, wringing blood from a corpse. His tactics were deemed self-aggrandizing, whimsical or irrelevant, rather like a Sutch political campaign. Many of their objections were well-founded but they failed to appreciate McLaren's love of irony, his economic and artistic dilemma and, most crucially, his message that the Pistols were not a precious pop group but a mouthpiece for an absurdist rationale. Rock star hagiography had no place in the Pistols saga, which was why Biggs was such a suitable replacement for the foolishly apotheosized Johnny Rotten.

The firing of Rotten forced Julien Temple to complete the Pistols movie without its most celebrated anti-star. Instead, McLaren was pushed to the foreground as a scheming manipulator, rewriting history in order to glorify his Machiavellianism. Significantly, it was arch-delinquent Steve Jones who emerged as the leading support, with Rotten relegated to old footage and Matlock written out of the script.

The backdrop to *The Great Rock 'n' Roll Swindle* was the real life deterioration of its sole surviving myth. By early 1978, Sid Vicious had surrendered himself to a lethal mixture of Spungen and heroin and as the year progressed his behaviour became increasingly erratic. He genuinely wanted to complete the film and at times betrayed a desperate need for the ego gratification provided by cinematographic immortality. Yet his drug habit made him impossibly inefficient and unpredictable. Camera crews were frequently frustrated by his non-arrival, whether due to incapacitation or junkie arrogance. He also grew to hate McLaren, whose waspish sarcasm and festering cynicism seemed increasingly unbearable.

The frequent and frenzied clashes between the addicted artiste and overbearing manager culminated in a hilarious encounter in Paris. The forlorn Julien Temple had been attempting to persuade Vicious to record 'My Way', but when they entered the recording studio the petulant junkie refused to sing a note. When McLaren was informed of the wasted studio costs the following morning, he became incensed. From his hotel bedroom he phoned the still drowsy Vicious and launched into a vitriolic monologue, cataloguing the performer's infinite shortcomings and adding brusquely that the boy was finished. Unbeknown to Malcolm, however, Sid had passed the receiver to Nancy Spungen, and while the invective oratory continued, the defamed one was scurrying towards his master's suite. McLaren was still hurling abuse when his bedroom door was abruptly smashed by an interloper dressed in jackboots and swastika underpants. As Sid lunged forward, the wily Malcolm made a break for the door and was chased down the corridor while astonished chambermaids screamed havoc. Eventually, Malcolm dived into a lift but as the door slowly closed the irrepressible Sid burst through. By the time the elevator reached its destination McLaren had been pummelled. Furious with embarrassment and indignation, he immediately packed his bags and returned to England, leaving Temple to finish the film alone.

After recording Eddie Cochran's 'C'mon Everybody', Vicious returned to New York intent on living out his rock star junkie role. Before his departure, he played a farewell London gig, 'Sid Sods Off!' in a parachronistic ensemble featuring Glen Matlock and Steve New. He already appeared to be half-blind and some said he smelt of death. Meanwhile, Cook and Jones were playing in pick-up groups across England. Devoid of McLaren's influence, they resembled nothing more than a poor man's Faces. The Sex Pistols' tawdry tale had apparently ended in anti-climax.

Punk's autumnal ennui was dramatically shattered on 12 October 1978 with the shock news of Nancy Spungen's death. Rumours rapidly spread that the lovers had arranged a suicide pact from which Sid reneged at the last moment, however those who had witnessed his wilful mortification with blades and broken bottles found this explanation highly implausible. The speculation surrounding Spungen's death was never officially resolved, though Sid reputedly confessed to both the police and a trusted associate. The latter's testimony, supported by taped evidence at the time but embellished by retelling over the years, arguably provides the most faithful reconstruction:

On the eve of the killing, Vicious and Spungen were staying at the Chelsea Hotel. By some grotesque twist of irony their room number was 101, the place where inhabitants of Orwell's 1984 confronted their worst imaginable fears. The nightmare that was to destroy Vicious began pleasantly enough when Nancy received some urgently needed cash from an old friend, eager to book Sid for some club dates. This unexpected windfall temporarily alleviated concern about raising money for their narcotic needs, but Sid was nevertheless impatient. The barbiturates he had consumed to stave off the worst effects of opiate withdrawal had made him hyperactive and aggressive. In his frenzy, he stormed down the corridors of the Chelsea Hotel, banging on doors and screaming 'I wanna score'. Eventually, he was confronted by a burly negro whom he provoked into a pointless fight. Debilitated by drugs and alcohol, Sid offered only token resistance and received a sound thrashing. By the time he crawled back to room 101, Vicious was a bloody mess with a nose that had been punched out of joint. Nancy's reaction was characteristically scathing; she slapped her lover across the face. In the circumstances, it was no more than he deserved for messing up another evening. Unfortunately, her blow made contact with his damaged nose and, almost instinctively, Sid grabbed the nearest object to fend off his attacker. That object was an open-bladed knife.

The sudden shock was quickly followed by resignation, and even acceptance of the deed. Both Sid and Nancy had long been used to the sight of blood and the wound seemed superficial. Foolishly, they withdrew the weapon without thought and failed to bandage the small gash. Minutes later, they were hugging and kissing and shortly afterwards Sid volunteered to try and score once more. On this occasion, he was more cautious, stalking the backstreets in silence, intent on finding his quarry. In his narcotically-distorted time scheme, Vicious was unaware of the hours that passed while Spungen expired in a pool of blood. By the time he returned to room 101, police were already surveying the scene.

When Malcolm received news of Sid's arrest he could barely contain his excitement. The Pistols had been moribund since the Rio incident and their image had degenerated to that of any other washed-up rock group. Now, suddenly, there was a scheme to end all schemes. If McLaren could free Vicious the world might yet see the first pop group led by a psychopathic killer. This made Biggs look farcical, Rotten tame and irrelevant, previous outrage incidental; Vicious was now the man, and with Spungen out of the way, the svengali could re-assert control. McLaren's callousness was even betrayed publicly when he swiftly marketed a Sid Vicious T-shirt bearing the message: 'I'M ALIVE. SHE'S DEAD. I'M YOURS'.

It was not until McLaren arrived in the States that he realized the extent of Vicious's mental instability. Released on $50 000 bail supplied by Virgin, the punk star was in dreadful physical shape and seemed determined to blot out the memory of Spungen by any means available. On 22 October, while suffering withdrawal pangs, he locked himself in his bathroom and lacerated his right arm with a razor blade and broken light bulb. McLaren was summoned to his room and witnessed a pathetic, nauseating spectacle. Vicious lay half-naked, surrounded by a pool of blood, with urine running down his leg. Staring at his old master through a myopic, semi-conscious haze, he implored: 'Get me some downers. I want to die'. Here lay the saviour and future of the Sex Pistols: an emaciated, incontinent, morbific degenerate. McLaren recoiled with repulsion, his perennial complacency rudely shattered. For one of the few times in his life he was confronted with a genuinely torturous moral dilemma. He could either grant Vicious the dog's death that he desired or take measures to save his life. McLaren made his humanitarian decision and summoned an ambulance.

Within weeks of his near suicide, Vicious was back in prison. A night at New York's Hurrah had ended in a scuffle when Sid assaulted and cut Patti Smith's brother, Todd. The following day he was sentenced to a detoxification course at the hardy Riker's prison. Since saving Vicious's life, McLaren had lost the mono-maniacal zeal for violent outrage. He spoke optimistically about Sid's chances of recovery, betraying an almost paternal concern for the self-destructive youth. His latest plan was to remove the boy from the drug-infested New York environment and record an album of 'family favourites' in Miami. But before that could occur, McLaren had other battles to fight.

The old enemy, Johnny Rotten, had made surprising progress in his statements of claim against Glitterbest and was confidently preparing for a High Court war of attrition. With Russ Meyer also threatening legal retribution, McLaren's business organization was under serious threat. As the weeks passed, Malcolm's confi-dence visibly eroded and that old familiar laugh was replaced by a falsely authoritative voice, grown shrill with pyrogenous argument. His most severe verbal assaults were reserved for the hapless Julien Temple who was puzzlingly denounced as a 'public school fascist' and a worthless slave. Temple remembers McLaren at the end of his emotional tether, permanently red-faced as though his rage was beyond appeasement. The lines of his face had also extended, forming a perfect letter 'M' just above the nose.

Temple's friendship with McLaren did not survive *The Great Rock 'n' Roll Swindle*, but he was not the only victim of the svengali's purge. With his empire crumbling, McLaren turned on other old friends, convinced that they were contributing to his fall. In his worst moments he suspected that some unidentifiable assailant might make an attempt on his life. His feelings of victimization, imaginary or otherwise, suggested that he was ill-equipped to manage, let alone manipulate, the psychological drama of a High Court action.

A fortnight before the hearing, McLaren's downward thrust on Fortune's Wheel was almost complete. On 3 February 1979, a news-paper headline left the pugnacious entrepreneur feeling demoralized and dejected. It read: 'Sid Vicious Dies In Drugs Drama'.

The final act of Vicious's life created almost as much mystery as the death of Nancy Spungen. On 1 February he had again been freed on bail and spent the evening celebrating privately with his mother and new girl friend, Michelle Robinson. Before retiring to Michelle's bed, he injected himself with a lethal dose of heroin. He died peacefully in his sleep. Although romantic suicide was suspected, it seems more likely that Vicious had simply over-estimated his tolerance level following detoxification.

The tabloids' attempts to transform Vicious's death into a punk *Romeo And Juliet* could not disguise the sordidness of the entire affair. McLaren was filled with self-reproach following the news, still believing that his presence might have saved Sid from self-destruction. His guilt was only partly alleviated by the comforting words of friends who confirmed that he had done everything possible to protect his doomed protégé.

The two-week High Court hearing concluded with a receiver being appointed to disentangle the labyrinthine financial affairs of the ravaged Pistols dominion. Mid-way through the proceedings, McLaren's co-defendants, the capricious Cook and Jones, had pulled a surprise *volte face* by belatedly siding with the disaffected Rotten. In the circumstances, the sagacious Justice Browne-Wilkinson advised the parties to forestall further legal action concerning the ownership of the Sex Pistols' name and related interests, by settling matters out of court. It was revealed that Glitterbest had received £880 000 up until the end of December 1978, but apart from £30 000 in the company bank account neither the Pistols nor their management had any assets beyond the income invested in publishing agreements and the yet-to-be released film, *The Great Rock 'n' Roll Swindle*. It was therefore paramount that a receiver be appointed immediately to exploit funds resulting from the movie.[1]

McLaren interpreted the judgement as tantamount to a victory for Virgin Records. He has always maintained that Richard Branson dethroned him by financing Rotten throughout the proceedings; the Virgin supremo has consistently refuted the allegation, arguing that there was no competition between himself and McLaren over who should control the group.

Branson's defensive argument was lost on McLaren as he flew to Paris, dejected and broke. In his bitterness, he believed that his adversary intended to rub salt in the wounds by reuniting the Matlock-era Pistols. The fact that Rotten had recently formed Public Image Limited and was barely on speaking terms with the

---

[1] The destination of the monies locked in receivership was eventually decided in the Sex Pistols' favour following a High Court decision in January 1986.

remaining Pistols was not sufficient to suppress such unreasonable fears. Branson, meanwhile, insisted that his primary aim was to promote peace between the two camps in order that Virgin could work effectively with both PIL and the remnants of the Pistols. With striking diplomacy, he despatched a telegram reassuring the fallen svengali of his good intentions and willingness to collaborate on future projects. McLaren's reply was a hearty laugh. In private, he suggested that Virgin were attempting to purchase his soul, a metaphysical conceit guaranteed to further alienate his opponent. Branson was left to release the remaining substandard Pistols recordings which were rightly dismissed as deplorable.

McLaren's self-imposed exile in Paris coincided with a number of fanciful schemes: he intended to work with Serge Gainsbourg; to record a cover of Edith Piaf's 'Je Ne Regrette Rien' as an amusing comment on the Sex Pistols fiasco; to direct a pornographic film. All of these grandiloquent ideas came to nothing. Instead, he accepted employment collating public domain soundtrack material for a blue movie company. One afternoon, while sifting through classical scores at the Beaubourg Music Library, his concentration was distracted by a selection of ethnic recordings. Amazed by the sheer wealth of non-European music, McLaren convinced himself that the next major trend in pop music was at his fingertips. By the time he returned to London his magpie mind was full of theories about pre-pubescent fashion, ethnic music and the importance of theatrical costume.

One person who took an exceptional interest in McLaren's outpourings was Adam Ant. The minor league bad boy of punk already looked a shade passé and was anxious to promote a radically different image in the hope of attracting a new audience. McLaren suggested a look based on his old sixties heroes Johnny Kidd and the Pirates, with a dash of Red Indian warpaint for additional visual effect. He also played Adam a few ethnic records, including the African Burundi drummers. Armed with these ideas, the ex-punk created a new persona which later transformed him into one of Britain's most commercially successful pop stars.

While Adam Ant slipped through his fingers, McLaren found new inspiration in the unlikely setting of a McDonald's hamburger joint. There, his eyes feasted upon a coloured youth carrying an enormous portable cassette recorder. The ghetto-blaster was making such a racket that the kid was eventually ordered to switch it off or get out. Disdainfully, he hoisted the machine over his right shoulder and, without uttering a word, left the establishment, still dancing and finger-popping to the music. McLaren was so impressed by this display of arrogant cool that he rushed home and wrote a song extolling the virtues of home taping and portable recorders. The song, 'C30, C60, C90, Go' was incorporated into a television programme that he was scripting, portentously titled *An Insider's Guide To The World Of The Music Industry*. Inevitably, McLaren's contribution was deemed too controversial for the broadcasting authorities, but he retained the copyright of the songs and decided that they must be recorded by an unknown artiste.

Rather than hunting down the kid from McDonald's, McLaren set out to find a female equivalent of Frankie Lymon, the American teenage singing star of the fifties. The search ended at a Kilburn dry cleaners where he first met Annabella Lu Win, a 14-year-old Burmese girl with no previous musical experience. She had a good voice and exceptionally clear intonation which proved particularly useful in enunciating the svengali's rhetorical lyrics. Borrowing three of Adam's Ants, Malcolm formed a makeshift backing group which shortly became Bow Wow Wow. Poor Adam Ant was dismayed to discover that his hymenopterous helpmates would not be returning.

Like the Sex Pistols before them, Bow Wow Wow had a brief but unfruitful liaison with EMI. 'C30, C60, C90, Go' was a spectacular debut, but failed to scale the higher chart echelons. Malcolm maintains that it was 'hyped out of the charts' for political reasons, but his explanation sounds unconvincing. When the next offering, 'Your Cassette Pet', also barely scraped into the charts, McLaren realized that paeans to home taping were not enough.

In order to enliven Bow Wow Wow's image, a second lead vocalist was recruited. Lieutenant Lush was an outrageous glam-rock androgyne who could not resist stealing the limelight from the svengali's *ingenue*. When his presence became too distracting and overbearing, McLaren informed the egocentric lieutenant that he was fired. Like Adam Ant, Lush went on to reap far greater rewards fronting the million-selling Culture Club.

McLaren's association with Bow Wow Wow petered out with a series of dubious publicity stunts. The jailbait Annabella had her head shaved into a Mohican style and began appearing in tribal clothes designed to reveal a sizeable proportion of her still developing breasts. There was further controversy when she was photographed semi-nude on an album cover pastiche of Manet's *Déjeuner Sur L'Herbe*. Her mother was not amused.

By the summer of 1982, McLaren had become bored injecting new ideas into Bow Wow Wow, whose record sales remained unspectacular. They were also showing strong signs of independence and rebellion, which augered badly for any future publicity campaigns. Rather than facing further flak from Annabella's mother,

McLaren allowed the group their freedom. Unfortunately, Bow Wow Wow rapidly foundered and Annabella went into the wilderness from which she has only recently returned as an older, and hopefully wiser, woman. Perhaps the greatest irony in the Bow Wow Wow saga was that McLaren's two rejects, Adam Ant and Boy George, were the artistes who went on to make the big financial killing.

The managerial career of Malcolm McLaren effectively ended with the demise of Bow Wow Wow. By the mid-eighties, he was investing time and energy pushing himself as an artiste. His obsession with ethnic music reached fruition on a surprisingly well-received debut album, *Duck Rock*. That was followed by *Fans*, a crazy fusion of pop and high opera which brought 'Madame Butterfly' into the Top 20. Whatever reservations one may have about McLaren's methods and the shortcomings of his music, his imagination deserves respect. What seems most remarkable about his topsy-turvy managerial career is that it should end with the svengali playing the role of the artiste. Although there is a great tradition of 'singer managers' in British pop (Gordon Mills, Don Arden, Larry Page, Andrew Oldham, Adam Faith, Marty Wilde *et al*) McLaren may be unique. For he is not the star who became a svengali, but the svengali who became a star.

Surveying McLaren's managerial career, it is possible to pinpoint certain turning points and important crossroads that strongly contributed to his success and infamy. Long ago, he set out to establish a community of young groups, but abandoned that dream in the pursuit of notoriety with the Sex Pistols. In retrospect, however, McLaren partly achieved his idealistic aims. The negativism that the Pistols represented was countered by a number of positive achievements. In their wake, hundreds of groups appeared from nowhere in what was the most spontaneous rush of youthful adrenalin since the mid-sixties beat boom. Other kids produced their own fanzines, drew cartoons or presented their bodies as works of art. Many of the new musicians proved inept and politically fraudulent — but who could deny that they made an impact? And as Malcolm rightly notes: 'They made a few bob too!'

As for McLaren, the image of the benevolent svengali is delightfully double-edged. For every left-wing critic who glorifies the working-class victories of punk, there remains the knowledge that behind it all was a middle-class opportunist in search of money. Or was he? The image of McLaren presented in *The Great Rock 'n' Roll Swindle* has a false ring, but his avarice should not be underestimated. The most forceful and pertinent phrase he used during our conversation was the wonderful refrain: 'Show us your money pal'.

If McLaren really perpetrated a great rock 'n' roll swindle, who were the victims? The record industry? The public? The Sex Pistols? If the answers are yes, then it should be added that McLaren also conned himself. Following the Pistols' demise, he was virtually flat broke. In the end, he sacrificed the profit for the event and, by the immoral standards of *The Great Rock 'n' Roll Swindle*, revealed himself as gullible and self-deluded as the punters who fell for his scheme. But it would be unfair to judge McLaren by those perverse standards alone. We now know that as a business-man he left much to be desired, but the same has been elsewhere said of Epstein. What McLaren should be remembered for is the dynamic effects of his management, not merely on the fortunes of a few groups, but on an entire generation of young kids. In this respect alone, he equalled the achievements of Brian Epstein and Larry Parnes.

McLaren's victory was momentarily won in the heat of aesthetic confusion. With their own standards and DIY record labels, the kids could effectively deride such concepts as art and technique and even dismiss history in an ageist glorification of the present. The complacent British record industry, for all its market research, could not prevent a spanner from entering the works. The offending tool was soon removed, but considerable damage was done, mainly to the careers of self-important elder rock statesmen, many of whom suddenly found themselves obsolete.

It is easy to romanticize punk as the great leveller and the means by which the kids won back rock 'n' roll and found a voice to express their social woes. Yet, paradoxically, the more you rhapsodize about the redeeming values of punk, the further you move away from the message of the Sex Pistols. For their role was never to instruct or proselytize; there never was a direct message from them beyond a fatalistic jack-the-lad acceptance of booze, birds and quick money. Steve Jones, Sid Vicious and Johnny Rotten were selfish, insular and often reactionary. Like the proles of *1984*, they merely sought animal gratification. And that may well be the final irony of McLaren's message.

Rob Gretton's introduction to the music business was similar to that of many unassuming young managers of the late seventies. He was, quite simply, a fan who suddenly found himself caught up in the zeal of punk and went on to manage his favourite group. Self-styled svengalis and street-wise tycoons proliferated in the wake of McLaren, but the majority were swallowed whole by the rapacious music business. Few achieved any real entrepreneurial power and were merely pasteboard figures in comparison to the great creative masters of the sixties. Artistes were more cynical, demanding and independent than ever before and the old-style autocratic manager was deemed an anachronism. Once the punk ethic had been eroded by the lure of the capitalist record industry, pampered pop groups found themselves 'managed' by embarrassingly dependent and ultimately redundant yes-men. Beyond this legion of failed svengalis, however, there were some hard-working and imaginative managers capable of growing in stature alongside their newly successful discoveries. They diversified their interests, bought or founded record labels and strengthened their artistes' reputations. One such manager was Rob Gretton.

Gretton's pre-managerial career was decidedly inauspicious. A bored insurance clerk, he abruptly decided to leave his job and seek travel and excitement abroad. Accompanied by his girlfriend, he worked in a kibbutz for seven months before returning to Manchester and signing on the dole. Early in 1976, the first rumblings of punk were heard in the city and although Gretton had previously never bothered to listen to white rock music, the energy and aggression of this movement proved irresistible. Rob struck up a friendship with Slaughter and the Dogs and began travelling with them, contributing fivers towards the petrol costs, just to be part of the show. He even provided them with a £200 loan to record their first single. Although Slaughter and the Dogs received a considerable amount of press in the heyday of punk, they never quite managed to hit the big time. However, Gretton still looks back at those early days with some affection:

> They were quite a strange group. They used punk fashion to a certain degree, but they were more like glam rock. Their heroes were the New York Dolls, Bowie and Roxy. They ended up more like the Damned than the serious side of punk . . . The music they played was great, but no one seemed to like them, except the Sex Pistols.

Gretton stuck with the group for the occasional gig, mainly because he enjoyed visiting London. By his own admission, he was always regarded as a hanger-on, a starry-eyed supporter who even ran the Slaughter and the Dogs fan club. In most respects, he was the complete antithesis of a professional music business manager.

Working on the road enabled Rob to meet other young groups and managers whose tales proved particularly educational. Enthusiasm and commitment were more important than experience in the early punk days and, following his stint with Slaughter and the Dogs, Gretton continued promoting punk groups in Manchester. Acts such as Siouxie and the Banshees, Johnny Thunders and the Heartbreakers and the Buzzcocks were among the bookings, but the financial remuneration was poor. On a couple of occasions, Gretton got badly stung when groups failed to appear and these setbacks effectively ended his short career as a punk promoter. Instead, he continued working part time as a disc jockey at clubs such as the Electric Circus and Rafters.

Rafters was a punk cellar incongruously situated beneath a cabaret club named Fagins. It was there that Gretton first saw the group that would establish his name as a manager. Warsaw had only played a handful of gigs prior to that evening and most of those were badly received. In order to compensate for their lack of musical experience, lead singer Ian Curtis was playing the role of a Mancunian Iggy Pop. Towards the end of the set, he smashed a pint glass on the dance floor, jumped from the stage and rolled around in the debris. Gretton was mildly amused by the spectacle, but nobody regarded the group highly or even expected them to survive in the face of competition from dozens of more accomplished units.

Rob Gretton soon became bored with playing records at Rafters and sought a more consuming interest. He briefly managed a local punk group, the Panik, and produced their prophetically titled single, 'It Won't Sell'. Within four months, however, they disintegrated, the victims of disorganization, non-rehearsal and a lack of transport.

Coincidentally, the Panik's drummer, Steve Brotherdale, had also played in Warsaw, whose progress was still decidedly uneven. The emergence of a London group, Warsaw Pakt, had forced them to change their name to Joy Division and they were desperately searching for a chance of fame at the Stiff/Chiswick Records Challenge, a talent competition featuring the best of Manchester's many undiscovered new wave groups. Unfortunately, Joy Division were not scheduled to appear until the early hours of the morning, a decision that filled them with rancour. They spent most of the night running round complaining to the organizers, almost as though there were some conspiracy afoot. Their irrational indignation amused Gretton, but he was unprepared for what followed. At 2.30 a.m. they took the stage and played a blistering handful of songs to a select but tired clientele. Gretton was one of the few people who appreciated the emotional intensity of their performance:

> I thought they were the best group I'd ever seen. There was something really weird about them. I'd met them before because they used to come to Rafters and ask me to play records by Kraftwerk; they always asked for pretty weird stuff. It was around then that people first said 'Fascists' because they dressed so differently. They were smart, punky, but not scruffy; it was unusual. And the music was absolutely wonderful.

That night Gretton lay in bed and for some reason couldn't get this group off his mind.

Rob Gretton was not the only person stunned by Joy Division's performance. Tony Wilson, a presenter of Granada Television's music programme *So It Goes*, was well known as a champion of new wave. He had already given the Sex Pistols and the Buzzcocks their first television airing, so it was hardly surprising that his presence at the Stiff/Chiswick Challenge raised a few hopeful eyebrows. One person less than enamoured with Wilson was Joy Division's singer Ian Curtis, who had attempted, without success, to secure a guest spot on Wilson's programme. Although this was hardly surprising given the intense competition among Manchester groups, Curtis almost regarded the rejection as a personal affront. Accosting Wilson at the bar, Curtis harangued him at great length, though such treatment had little effect on the television presenter. In his time, he had met many obnoxious young kids from do-it-yourself groups and was well used to gratuitous insults. Like Gretton, Wilson was there at the end of the evening and saw Joy Division's bile translated into an emotive live performance. He was transfixed. The two most important catalysts in the group's history had been converted on the same evening by a performance that virtually everybody was too tired even to notice.

Several days after the Stiff/Chiswick Challenge, an unusual incident occurred. Gretton was in a public phone box in Manchester when he noticed a familiar figure in the adjoining booth. It was Bernard Dicken, Joy Division's lead guitarist. Gretton immediately stopped his telephone conversation, accosted the youth, and reiterated his favourable impressions of the group and their music. To his great delight, the musician explained that Joy Division urgently needed a competent manager. Rob recommended himself and within a week he was part of the team.

Gretton was kept busy during his first few months with Joy Division sorting out their complicated recording history. Shortly before his arrival, the group had completed recordings for an album signed to Richard Searling, an employee of RCA Records. Searling soon found another partner, John Anderson of Grapevine Records, who agreed to split the studio and production costs. Their investment soon prompted an offer of a one-album deal from RCA but the record was destined never to appear. Ever fastidious, Joy Division took exception to the mixes and quibbled about the terms of the contract. Gretton was equally concerned about a record deal to which he had not been a party, and took the contract to a Manchester solicitor. After reading the document, the lawyer concluded that the terms were extremely good. Crestfallen, Rob approached Rabid Records' legal advisers who were not so impressed and advised him to contest the rights. His combatants were unwilling to fight over such an ungrateful group and eventually agreed to dissolve the agreement and surrender the mixes for £1000. Even then, there was a long delay before Joy Division could raise the necessary sum to buy back their freedom.

After almost signing to producer Martin Hannett's Genetic label, Gretton turned his attention to the omnipresent Tony Wilson, whose entrepreneurial endeavours were proving particularly interesting. Apart from his television work, the industrious Wilson was managing A Certain Ratio and had recently established the Factory Club as a showcase for up-and-coming Northern groups. Wilson further extended his interests by founding an independent label, Factory Records. His partners in the venture were Alan Erasmus, an ex-actor with whom he co-managed Duretti Column, and Peter Saville, an art student who specialized in designing record covers and posters. The aforementioned producer, Martin Hannett, was recruited several months later, ensuring that Factory was one of the most professionally-run independent labels in the country. Joy Division appeared on the company's first vinyl offering, *A Factory Sample* and several months later Gretton agreed to sign a recording contract. Rob explains why he chose an independent in preference to such major labels as RCA and WEA:

> I was in my do-it-yourself frame of mind. The punk ideals appealed to me, but nobody else believed in them! To McLaren, signing with the majors fitted in with his situationist philosophy — getting in there and creating havoc. We were the opposite. We'd broken big in Manchester and realized that if we signed to Factory, a Manchester label, it wouldn't harm us. We were convinced it would work, if not on a sales level then on a cult level. The music was so good, it had to work.

Between 1977 and 1980, Joy Division's musical development was nothing short of staggering. The cacophony of Warsaw had been replaced by a distinctive and later much copied use of bass and drums as lead instruments. The greater precision and fluidity in their playing had also allowed Ian Curtis to mature as a vocalist/performer. The former Iggy Pop imitator was now renowned for his own distinctive style of neurotic choreography, like a demented marionette on invisible wires. By the autumn of 1979, however, Curtis's performances were drawing attention for a much more serious reason. At the Factory Club the lead singer suffered an epileptic seizure prior to going on stage and was advised to sit out the performance. Embarrassed by the mild fuss, Ian insisted on appearing and suffered no further ill effects. The following month he had to be led offstage towards the end of a concert and at another gig shortly afterwards felt too ill to play an encore. Over the next few months, Curtis continued to perform with Joy Division, never missing a show and completing an arduous but successful Continental tour in January 1980. By the following spring, however, it was evident that he was seriously ill. A performance at the Rainbow ended with the singer falling into the drum kit as he was taken by another seizure. The following week he suffered several brief blackouts while onstage yet somehow pulled through without cancelling. The state of Curtis's health must have been particularly worrying for Gretton since the group were scheduled to embark on their first American tour the following month. Rob recalls his feelings during this troubled time:

> I wasn't worried as a manager, I was worried as a friend. We didn't have to cancel any gigs, except three performances in Scotland. Looking back on it, the whole thing was getting more and more stressful, and the stress was bringing on the fits. Sometimes he was bad, but normally he was OK for weeks or months. The fits were usually brought on by tiredness. It was getting worse and worse towards the end . . . On some gigs he'd come offstage, have a fit and insist on going back on. The fit would last for a minute and then he'd be very embarrassed and would insist on acting more energetically than usual.

On 18 May 1980, the eve of Joy Division's trip to America, Ian Curtis was found hanged. The verdict was suicide. According to press reports a note was allegedly found bearing the words: 'At this very moment I wish I were dead. I just can't cope anymore'. With the group in a state of shock, the projected US tour was cancelled. It was only in the next couple of months that the public fully realized the import of this tragedy, for it quickly became evident that Curtis had taken his life at the peak of his creativity as a recording and performing artiste. It was inevitable that posthumous Joy Division releases would be afforded a sympathetic reception, but nobody could have anticipated the quality of the work which was issued that summer. The single, 'Love Will Tear Us Apart', was probably the finest of 1980, a haunting account of a broken relationship sung by Curtis in a voice that few realized he possessed. The succeeding album, *Closer*, was even better, a journey into the abyss that ended in exorcism. Seldom has an album articulated such a sense of despair, yet simultaneously offered such a therapeutic release. Instrumentally, the work showed maturity in every area, leaving little doubt that Joy Division were not merely on the brink of greatness — it had already been achieved. The Joy Division story ended with *Still*, a double compilation of their remaining material, most of it in primitive form.

As with many suicides involving creative figures, a degree of speculation inevitably followed the Curtis tragedy, though little information emerged. It was later stated that he had made two previous attempts to take his life following a period of depression, but neither Joy Division nor their manager confirmed such speculation. The posthumous tributes to the singer, the circumstances leading up to his death and the extremely introspective nature of *Closer* each contributed to the public image of Curtis as a melancholic character destroyed by his own demons. This representation effectively placed him in the tradition of the doomed Romantic poet, bravely exploring the darker areas of life and ultimately sacrificing himself to his art. For many fans, tragic death was thus translated into heroic sacrifice. Myth and reality often become confused by elegy and it is interesting to learn that Gretton's characterization of Curtis contrasts strikingly with that of rock hagiographers:

> The way they described Ian dying was so far from the way I perceived it that it's not worth getting annoyed about. There was no great depression, no hint at all. The week before, we went and bought all these new clothes; he was really happy. A lot of his problems were personal, with his wife and not so much to do with the group. It obviously affected us and we knew all about it. We could advise him, but we couldn't do anything about it.

The contention that Curtis's death was primarily a personal tragedy unconnected to his work or lifestyle may have validity. Yet even Gretton cannot measure the extent to which Curtis's creativity may have contributed towards the personal problems which caused his death. Is it possible that the self-absorption and introspection produced by his artistic endeavours may have aggravated neuroses and created the potential for suicide? Anyone familiar with Joy Division's work cannot have failed to observe the workings of a writer whose speculations on the self seemed at times extremely close to despair. Although Curtis's introspective art probably provided a purgative function enabling him to defeat despair, it is equally plausible that his entry into the abyss created a downward spiral which became irreversible. Gretton acknowledges the illogicality of the act: 'The whole thing was a bolt out of the blue. It was something that none of us understands to this day. Ian wasn't that sort of person. He was a happy-go-lucky type, not a depressive'.

The fact that so many of Curtis's compositions documented a confrontation with despair will inevitably encourage listeners to equate the suicide with the art. Gretton's eminently reasonable attempt to divorce the two and interpret the artiste's death as a tragedy of personal circumstances, unconnected with his work, would be entirely convincing were it not for the enduringly disturbing power of those lyrics and music and the abiding memory of an onstage persona that embodied manic confusion.

There was never any question of Joy Division surviving the death of Ian Curtis. Long before, they had unanimously agreed that in the event of any line-up changes, a new group name would be coined. This staunch refusal to trade on their past reputation resulted in a completely new repertoire which excluded even their hit single, 'Love Will Tear Us Apart'. Meanwhile, Factory splashed out on a US advertising campaign to promote *Closer*. It was delightfully incongruous to witness a full page ad for the album in *Rolling Stone*. Even more surprisingly, a billboard on Sunset Strip bore the stark message: '*Closer*— Joy Division— FACTUS 36'. According to Gretton, this was partly whimsical for Factory knew that few Hollywood inhabitants had ever heard of Joy Division. The rescheduled Stateside tour during the summer was a testing ground for life without Curtis. Understandably, the main problem lay in selecting a singer from the group to fill Curtis's role. Steve Morris soon found himself under great pressure as vocalist and occasional synth player, and eventually returned to his drum kit. With Bernard emerging as the new singer, the group decided to incorporate the synth more fully into the act, which meant recruiting a new player upon their return to England. Rather than auditioning an established musician, they chose a relative unknown in the form of Steve's girlfriend Gillian Gilbert.

The restructured group barely had time to draw breath before they found themselves involved in a minor controversy. Gasps of disgust were heard when it was revealed that the remnants of Joy Division would henceforth be known as New Order. The title was variously dismissed as 'stupid', 'ugly, dangerous and highly irresponsible'. The liberal music press vainly attempted to persuade the group to drop the name and avoid being dubbed closet fascists, but it was already too late. New Order pleaded innocence and soldiered on.

Although the subject of the group's name may seem relatively innocuous today, the contemporaneous music press had good reason to be censorious. The punk movement had been accompanied by an unhealthy interest in Nazi paraphernalia and many kids were decorating themselves with swastikas as a symbol of rebellion against their conservative elders. For a time, such shock tactics were dismissed as mere fashion but before long the fascist imagery was causing considerable concern. It was widely suspected that organizations such as the National Front were infiltrating pop music in order to seek out young recruits. Moreover, some of the less savoury characters in the skinhead Oi movement had been voicing racist slogans and encouraging violent behaviour. A twin assault from Rock Against Racism and the Anti-Nazi League was successfully combating the National Front and before long the music press also entered the fray. Suddenly 'fashionable fascism' was deemed extremely tasteless and socially irresponsible. That Joy Division/New Order should be included in such a purge was in some ways surprising; neither their song lyrics nor public statements hinted at any right-wing sentiments and not one swastika was ever seen on their person. No doubt their contention that the name 'New Order' merely meant 'another beginning' was sincere. Nevertheless, the unfortunate ambiguity of the term could scarcely be denied, particularly in the political climate of 1980. In effect, the group were simply asking for trouble. The outcry would have been less vocal if the controversial name was perceived as an isolated incident but, as everyone knew, the group had long been suspected of tacitly supporting fascism. Gretton claims that such rumours began as early as the Warsaw days and were based solely on the forties-style dress and hairstyles favoured by the group. Since then, there had been an unfortunate catalogue of coincidences that left them extremely vulnerable to such attacks. Their vinyl debut on the compilation *Live At The Electric Circus* was prefaced by the announcement: 'You all forgot Rudolf Hess'; the EP *An Ideal For Living* depicted a member of the Hitler Youth and a photograph of a Jewish boy guarded by a Nazi stormtrooper; the name Joy Division itself was reputedly taken from a book detailing the sexual exploitation of Jewish girls in a Nazi concentration camp. And so it went on. Even the agency chosen to promote their gigs bore the unfortunate name Final Solution. The rumours might have subsided if the group had played well-publicized political benefits or conducted a sustained series of pro-left-wing interviews. Instead, they maintained their customary silence, no doubt concurring with Gretten's nonchalant dismissal of the entire controversy: 'If you know it wasn't like that, why bother? They've already said it so there's no point'.

In spite of the critical ballyhoo over New Order, Gretton seemed unwilling to take advantage of the publicity, preferring to allow the group to develop at their own pace. The eagerly awaited debut album, *Movement*, did not arrive until November 1981 and for many it failed to live up to the promise of the two pilot singles, 'Ceremony' and 'Procession'. Live appearances brought equally conflicting responses from audiences too steeped in the legend of Joy Division, as Gretton explains:

> We're quite an unusual group in that we do what we want to do and that doesn't always fit people's expectations. Sometimes people are disappointed because we don't put on a show. New Order play encores if they feel like playing them. They don't feel they have to just because the crowd want it.

It took a further year before New Order finally established themselves as a commercial entity independent of their illustrious history. The turning point was probably March 1983 when the long-awaited second album, *Power Corruption And Lies*, and an additional 12-inch single, 'Blue Monday', hit the shops simultaneously. The latter was a spectacular success, charting on two separate occasions and finally emerging as the biggest-selling 12-inch single of all time. In the wake of the phenomenal chart comeback of 'Blue Monday', there was renewed interest in Joy Division's back catalogue and before long a repromoted 'Love Will Tear Us Apart' was climbing the Top 20. According to Gretton, the single was out of stock for some time because the stamper had been worn down and the original tapes mislaid. By the time these tapes had been retrieved from abroad, back orders had accumulated in excess of 12 000, which persuaded Factory to repromote the disc. Gretton was far from surprised by the topsy-turvy chart achievements of Joy Division and New Order and maintains that he could manipulate the national Top 40 with consummate ease:

> The Joy Division and New Order catalogue sells all the time. If we

wanted to, we could make every Joy Division and New Order record a hit again by not pressing them for six months and then reissuing them. We sell about 2000 copies of *Closer* a month — that's 25 000 a year. If you deleted that for 12 months there'd be 25-30 000 people trying to get it. It'd probably have a knock-on effect too because the distributors would order 3000 copies instead of 1000.

The idea of Gretton creating Top 40 anarchy by mischievously deleting and repromoting Factory's back catalogue is an amusing, if unlikely, proposition. Nevertheless, by resisting the lure of major labels and acquiring a financial interest in Factory, New Order have achieved a greater control of their product than virtually any other hit group of the era. Most of the money they have accrued from the sales of their discs has been poured into the Hacienda Club in Manchester, an asset that has enabled Gretton to develop his entrepreneurial interests in fresh and challenging directions. The Gretton/New Order/Factory set up closely resembles a family business that prefers independence to easy profit and although the temptation to surrender to the majors must be ever present, Rob sees no reason for a change of policy:

> We're not as rich as if we'd gone to a major, but we're a lot less compromised. If Joy Division and New Order had been signed to a major we'd sell a lot more records but we'd lose a great deal of control and wouldn't be able to do many of the unusual things we do with sleeves and choice of singles. I think New Order look upon Factory as their own label, even though the deal is 50:50. The only reason to leave Factory would be to do it ourselves so we could take 100 per cent, which we could do, but they're our friends.

One consequence of Gretton's parochial thinking has been a lack of international success. An unwillingness to release singles from albums has hardly endeared New Order to Continental distributors and their standing in America leaves much to be desired. Although they remain a respected, independent cult group, it has proven extremely difficult to compete with major record companies in the rock marketplace. Gretton concedes that it has not been easy to communicate his ideas to the inhabitants of the New World: 'They're very business-orientated, and Factory and us aren't really like that. For us, it's more like a full-time hobby'.

When speaking about New Order, Gretton frequently uses the word 'we' rather than 'they', seemingly confirming the generally held belief that he is less a manager than a fifth member of the group. This is a dangerous delusion that has preoccupied and spoiled many aspiring young managers over the years. Fortunately, Gretton is not a starry-eyed gofer, riding on the coat-tails of a commercially successful group, but a cynical realist who knows his limitations better than most. He once described himself as one of life's great losers and provided the following assessment of Joy Division's future: 'I can't see them making any success . . . if they do become big they will have sacked me'. Although history has apparently proven Gretton wrong, he remains modest about the group's accomplishments:

> I don't think Joy Division really did become big — I meant mega global success like Duran Duran. Maybe they could have done it; they'd probably have been as big as New Order. But we never did achieve mainstream success. Even New Order's albums haven't sold that well. A hundred-odd thousand isn't big league. We're successful in a peripheral way and we've shown people that there is a different way of doing it. We aren't striving for commercial success, so it's a bonus if we get it. I think we've been quite lucky; I could easily have seen us being recognized after we'd broken up.

The uncompromising nature of Gretton fits well with the artistic temperament of New Order and such shared characteristics will no doubt ensure their continued relationship on both a personal and business level. When discussing New Order, Gretton betrays all the hallmarks of a one-act manager and expresses no interest in overseeing other groups, even though he chooses many of the acts signed to Factory. It is difficult, therefore, to predict whether he would remain in management if his prize group dissolved or fell from grace into obscurity. Consciously or otherwise, Gretton has already anticipated that question by diversifying into record company and promotional work. His related interests in Factory and the Hacienda virtually constitute full-time jobs in themselves, so even if there are no further managerial activities, Gretton will not be a forgotten man. All things considered, he has come a long way from those Manchester dole queues of the mid-seventies.

The transformation of Stephen Pearce from illiterate school-leaver to independently-minded music business entrepreneur is an intriguing case study of self-belief overcoming adversity. A misfit and under-achiever, he could barely read and write when he left Dagenham's Eastbury Comprehensive School in 1979. During his final year, the 16-year-old had been put on a work experience scheme at a warehouse, and like many of his fellow pupils ended up labouring. At least his earnings were sufficient to secure a mobile disco unit on hire purchase. Armed with a small collection of records, he worked Monday nights as a disc jockey at the gaudy Chelsea Drugstore playing 'electronic music/disco'. This was followed by a residency at the Clarendon in Hammersmith, only minutes away from his new home.

The fringe interest in electronic music soon attracted the attention of young pop journalists who duly noted the antics of the eccentric disc jockey now known universally as Stevo. Before long, a Stevo-compiled 'electronic music' chart was featured in the pages of *Record Mirror* and this was succeeded by a 'futurist chart' in the rival music paper *Sounds*. The publicity ensured that Stevo was engulfed by packages containing obscure privately-funded singles and roughly-recorded demo tapes. Eventually, the futurist chart featured more demos than records and such was the saturation that Stevo announced the possibility of recording a compilation. Choosing the artistes was no problem, for several groups were interested in securing Stevo's services as a manager, realizing that an appearance on his album was the gateway to a wider audience. Initially, the idea was to record the best of the current fringe groups such as Throbbing Gristle, Classix Noveaux, Clock DVA and Cabaret Voltaire. Perversely, but heroically, however, Stevo elected to feature complete unknowns, using his more obscure demo tapes as a guideline. The inaccurately-spelt but appositely titled *Some Bizzare Album* included songs by four acts who went on to achieve greater fame — Soft Cell, Depeche Mode, The The and Blancmange. Stevo made no attempt to tart up the performances, preferring the rawness of the original home-recorded demos. He now claims that the entire package cost a mere £250.

By late 1980, Stevo was undergoing a self-improvement course in which he was both master and pupil. Since leaving school, he had taught himself to read and write and adopted a healthy aversion to priggishness that was manifested in an endearingly forthright manner:

> Whenever I hear a new word I ask what it means. I always stick my
> neck out. It's self education. How many people do you know who,
> when they're in a conversation and hear a phrase they don't understand,
> keep their mouths shut? They're the idiots.

Some would argue that Stevo's well-documented brusqueness was
a method of over-compensating for his lack of education. Whatever
its psychological origins, this pent-up aggression was to prove
intimidating enough to be extremely useful in negotiating with
record companies. From the outset, the teenager was unpredictable,
tempestuous and idealistic in his aims and demands. You either
accepted his eccentricities and altered standard business procedure
or refused to have anything to do with him. No middle ground was
ever offered.

The first group to be signed to a Some Bizzare management
contract and subsequently licensed to a major label was the Leeds
duo Soft Cell. Stevo had received a copy of their debut EP *Mutant
Moments* and was impressed enough to hitchhike to Leeds in order
to see them perform at the Warehouse. Their sleaziness was so
appealing that he immediately offered a management tie-in and
returned to London in search of a corporate outlet. Fortunately,
Soft Cell's contribution to the *Some Bizzare Album*, 'Girl With The
Patent Leather Face', was deemed one of the better tracks on the
compilation and encouraged Phonogram to consider a licensing deal.

Eventually, Stevo won a small advance for the group and taxed
the patience of Phonogram by insisting upon a clause allowing him
a weekly supply of sweets for the duration of their contract. It was a
characteristic eccentricity from a youth who would later show his
disdain for record company executives by sending a teddy bear to
business meetings in his place. The furry delegate would be armed
with a cassette which included an exhaustive soundtrack of Stevo's
demands. The unusual negotiating tactics were frequently reflected
in Stevo's irreverent expostulations on standard management and
recording contracts:

> I haven't looked at the management contract with Soft Cell since I
> signed it. The last Some Bizzare contract consisted of three pages —
> straight to the point; no bullshit. My attitude towards contracts is that
> they're signed because it's a necessity. You try telling a lawyer or a
> record company that you've got a verbal agreement . . . But if Marc
> Almond wanted to leave Some Bizzare, that contract would be torn
> up. It would never go to court. There's no ties with anyone's destiny
> on the label.

The Phonogram connection enabled Stevo to win the ear of producer Daniel Miller, whose Mute Records was one of the major outlets for electronic music during this period. Miller agreed to work with Soft Cell and produced the next 45, 'Memorabilia'. Although Stevo was never actively involved in the creation of Soft Cell's music or image, his influence during the recording session of 'Memorabilia' should not be underestimated:

> I remember walking into this little East End studio at 10.30 a.m. I was drunk. It was Daniel Miller's birthday and he'd been up all night, so I said, 'Happy Birthday, Daniel' and spewed all over the floor. It stank. I still reckon that's what gave the record its raw edge. Have you ever tried mixing a record in those conditions? You just want to get out of there.

Daniel Miller did not survive another session as Soft Cell producer.

For their next vinyl offering, Soft Cell chose Wire producer Mike Thorne for a spirited cover of Gloria Jones's northern club favourite 'Tainted Love'. Stevo predicted a hit, but even his optimism could not have encompassed the breadth of Soft Cell's commercial success. 'Tainted Love' not only topped the UK charts, but played an elongated game of snakes and ladders in the US, eventually notching up a record 43 consecutive weeks. A string of Top 5 hits followed, including 'Bedsitter', 'Say Hello, Wave Goodbye', 'Torch' and 'What'. Yet in spite of the consistent chart hits, Soft Cell were never happy with their pop star role. Although their romanticized sleaze and glamorizing of squalor separated them from more traditional teen idols, there seemed no escaping the pop machinery of which they were a part. Implicit in Soft Cell's rise to fame was a playful self-destructive streak that they shared with Stevo. Rather than pursuing success to its logical extreme, the Some Bizzare way was to pervert its course in the hope that something more daring and original might emerge from the debris. Almond found his self-destructive secret weapon in an alter ego — Marc and the Mambas.

The Mambas project was initially conceived as a one-off but, paradoxically, the international success of Soft Cell ensured its longevity. For Stevo, the dual existence of Soft Cell and Marc and the Mambas was akin to a statement of policy from Some Bizzare:

> Once something becomes a commodity in the sense that it's selling on the strength of the name, rather than the merits of the music, that is the time when it will please a capitalist, but, at the same time, it's a disgrace for art.

Many managers would have suppressed the Mambas offshoot and concentrated on the prize-winning group, but Stevo always revelled in the knife edge uncertainty of Almond's extra-curricular pursuits.

The sabotaging of Soft Cell's pop star image continued with the recording of *The Non-Stop Exotic Video Show*, a visual accompaniment to their previous albums, *Non-Stop Erotic Cabaret* and the mini-dance mix *Non-Stop Ecstatic Dancing*. The most controversial part of the original video was a sketch accompanying the song 'Sex Dwarf'. The ever-inventive Almond had hired a dwarf to take part in a scene that was conceived as a parody of both *The Texas Chainsaw Massacre* and sado-masochism films in general. The setting was a meat factory where a masked girl is chained to a table and has to endure the sight of a jock-strapped Almond busily rubbing raw meat into her body, while semi-nude cohorts cavort in the background to the sound of a revved-up chainsaw. Unfortunately, an unexpurgated pirate version of the video rapidly found its way on to the market and what was intended as a parody became misinterpreted as genuine pornography. Even the *News of the World* picked up on the story, a fact that Almond and Stevo regarded as absurdly ironic.

While the controversy reigned, Stevo and Marc were undertaking some selected club appearances to promote the recent *Non-Stop Ecstatic Dancing*. Rather unwisely, Stevo had decided to take in some smaller venues and it was at one such appearance that the Some Bizzare supremo and his pop star sidekick almost lost their lives. Patrons were bemused when Stevo entered the disc-jockey booth and repeated the words 'Yes, yes. Hello, It's highly psychological' for 15 minutes, while the sounds of Cabaret Voltaire and the *Sooty Show* were mixed in the background. The tension increased when the controversial sex dwarf video was screened. By now, the resident disc jockey was up in arms, haranguing Stevo for ruining the evening. Amid the drama, a punch was thrown at Almond, and a skirmish swiftly ensued which culminated in the club bouncers besieging the Some Bizzare duo in a barricaded dressing room. Eventually, the pop star and his manager escaped only to discover that their enemies had taken revenge by demolishing their car. On the way home, Stevo vowed never again to DJ in the provinces.

The determinedly erratic career of Marc Almond had provided enough instant success to ensure that Stevo was a name to be reckoned with. Even the most conservative record company A & R man could not ignore the chart achievements and enormous sales of Soft Cell, and this curiosity inevitably drew them to other Some Bizzare artistes. It was obvious that Stevo could have made a financial killing by milking Soft Cell until the hits ran dry, but instead he invested all his efforts and ready cash into launching Some Bizzare as a haven for an élite group of esoteric acts. Under his management some of the most uncommercial acts in rock history were able to infiltrate the heart of the corporate record industry and reach a mass audience for the first time.

By Some Bizzare standards, The The were both extremely accessible and capable of achieving international success, yet their career development was decidedly uneven. Formed in 1979 by Matt Johnson and Keith Laws, the group went through some 13 different members before eventually emerging as a one-man unit. Unlike virtually all their contemporaries on Some Bizzare, The The actually boasted some managerial involvement prior to the arrival of Stevo. Tom Johnston, the cartoonist on the *Standard*, had promoted their first gig at the Africa Centre on 11 May 1979 and paid the studio costs for their debut single 'Controversial Subject' on 4AD Records. This act of faith prompted The The to take their career more seriously and early the following year they played some gigs for Stevo, contributed a track to his compilation album, and finally signed with Some Bizzare on Friday 13 February 1981.

The The subsequently recorded a single 'Cold Spell Ahead', but 4AD still had a one-record option, so Matt Johnson was temporarily released from his Some Bizzare commitments to work on a solo album, *Burning Blue Soul*. The term 'solo' was something of a misnomer since by this time Matt Johnson and The The were one and the same. Nevertheless, the 4AD album did not appear under the The The moniker, a decision that Johnson regrets to this day.

The critical response to *Burning Blue Soul* was generally enthusiastic but the album was not promoted sufficiently to achieve strong sales, though by independent standards Johnson could hardly complain. It was clear that Stevo had another potentially commercial artiste on his hands, but the selling of The The was not proving easy. Matt had been rejected by virtually every major record company and even the larger independents expressed only mild interest. The final indignity, a rejection letter from Rough Trade, convinced Stevo that it was time to earn his management commission.

By the spring of 1982, Stevo was sufficiently established with Soft Cell to convince the doubting A & R men that Matt Johnson was worthy of record company patronage. Accordingly, Phonogram/Decca agreed to invest £8000 in a one-off single 'Uncertain Smile' to be produced in New York by Mike Thorne. Stevo maintains that their attitude was along the lines of 'All right, let's give the weirdo Matt Johnson a chance'. Annoyed that they had not trusted his instincts two years before, Stevo pulled a stroke at the eleventh hour and refused to sign the contracts binding Johnson to Decca. On the eve of their departure to New York, he threatened to pull out of the deal unless a waiver was signed enabling Johnson to shop elsewhere. After completing the single 'Uncertain Smile' (a new recording of 'Cold Spell Ahead') Stevo ditched Decca and allowed CBS to secure the rights to the single for a figure variously estimated between £40 000 and £75 000. Although this manœuvre gained Stevo a reputation as a McLaren-like wheeler-dealer, Johnson maintains that they owed no loyalty to Phonogram, whose interest in developing his career was insignificant in relation to CBS.

The protracted negotiations with CBS were conducted with typical Stevo eccentricity. While the majors wrangled with each other, CBS head, Maurice Oberstein, decided to confront Stevo over dinner in a West End restaurant. When his secretary phoned Some Bizzare, however, she was told that Stevo would only be available under his own conditions. Oberstein was instructed to turn up at a Tottenham Court Road bus stop at midnight and await the arrival of the young upstart. Remarkably, he agreed to this demand and that very same night found himself hanging around the West End in the pouring rain. Stevo and Oberstein walked past each other three times before eventually driving to Trafalgar Square where they signed a deal while sitting on one of the lions. Even today, Stevo admits that the Matt Johnson signing was one of the strangest and most confusing episodes of his managerial career.

Initially, The The looked likely candidates for chart fame and both 'Uncertain Smile' and the follow up, 'Perfect', proved moderately successful. Early in 1983, Johnson entered a 24-track recording studio in New York to work on his second album, *The Pornography Of Despair*. Although the sessions seemed fruitful, the album took longer to complete than expected and Johnson eventually decided that it was out of date. Several of the tracks later appeared elsewhere, but it was destined to remain the missing link in his recording career, which reached new heights with the release of *Soul Mining* in November 1983.

Soul Mining proved a cult classic, and even readers of *The Times* were informed of Johnson's enormous potential. The founder of The The maintains that the zeal of his manager was a crucial factor in bridging that long gap between single and album:

> It was Stevo's faith in me that was one of the reasons I stuck with him. I'd been rejected by everybody, but he was a very motivating influence. Most of Some Bizzare is filled with insecure paranoids, including Stevo . . . He is so erratic. There's things he's done that you wouldn't

believe. He's totally eccentric and mad, but he had the faith and it paid off in the end.

Johnson went through a period of frustration with CBS and following *Soul Mining* retreated to work on a number of projects including short stories, soundtracks and a pseudonymous album of cover versions. He eventually re-emerged in 1986 with *Infected*, a devastating and arresting comment on the spiritual, economic, sexual and moral malaise of contemporary Britain.

Stevo's success in securing major record deals for both Soft Cell and The The encouraged him to branch out further in search of the unusual. A self-confessed Throbbing Gristle fan, Stevo invited Genesis P. Orridge's current group, Psychic TV, to join his thriving stable. As one of the most subversive ensembles working on the fringes of rock music, Psychic TV seemed well suited to Stevo's label and management. Their work, frequently bordering on the obscene, had always incited a strong critical response, yet they seemed doomed to live a twilight existence, like some Victorian freak show that elicits momentary curiosity only to be followed by revulsion and rejection. Always a champion of the apparently unacceptable, Stevo was determined to channel their work through a major corporation and privately boasted that he would let loose Genesis P. Orridge and company in a 24-track studio with a full-blown string section. Virtually everybody told him that the idea was ridiculous and he must be insane. Yet this was just the type of challenge that appealed to Stevo's mischievous nature and he made good his boast by securing Psychic TV a licensing deal with Warner Brothers. As usual, the negotiations concluded with a non-recuperable treat for the artiste, this time in the form of a year's supply of baby food for Orridge's offspring. For a time, the unlikely coupling of Psychic TV and Warner Brothers worked reasonably well, but Stevo eventually found himself enmeshed in contractual arguments with the corporation. There was also a political clash between Stevo and Genesis P. Orridge which eventually resulted in Psychic TV leaving Some Bizzare in order to pursue their increasingly eccentric ideas and arcane recordings.

Although Stevo initially established himself as a discoverer of new talent, he now sees his role as providing a gateway for artistes at various stages of their career. Such was the case with the signing of Cabaret Voltaire, whose work he had admired for several years:

They'd done everything in their own studio on 8-track but they needed more clarity in separation to make something harder in a 24-track studio. It's like rolling a ball down a corridor: unless you can take a side door and change radically it's difficult. I'd always been a Cabaret Voltaire fan, and something needed to happen so I went up to Sheffield and said, 'I want to sign you'. What I love about Cabaret Voltaire is that they don't believe in remixes. They believe in going for it and things actually come together spiritually. The whole label is orientated on that psychic level.

The selling of Cabaret Voltaire proved less difficult than most of the other Some Bizzare acts. They had already established a cult following and boasted an extensive back catalogue including seven albums, two cassettes and five EPs. Throughout this period they had remained remorselessly independent, re-investing their royalties into new projects until their experimental 'sound collages' demanded bigger financial backing. The desire to extend their operation meant a leap into the Some Bizzare followed by infiltration of the majors. Stevo wasted no time in securing a £50 000 advance from Virgin, a label that had previously struck gold with two other Sheffield groups, the Human League and Heaven 17. As usual, Stevo demanded an array of free gifts including a compact disc machine on signature, a set of matching luggage for the first European television show, a waterbed and a bubble car. Not surprisingly, the patient folk at Virgin found it virtually impossible to locate a bubble car and suggested a toy replica as an alternative. A compromise was eventually reached and Cabaret Voltaire went on to record several albums for Virgin/Some Bizzare, maintaining steady sales along the way. As Stephen Mallinder explained to me at the time: 'It's quite good to be old-fashioned capitalists, but we also make sure that we get what we want. Nobody pushes us. People give us ideas and if we're happy we go along with them'. Cabaret Voltaire maintained their independence by continuing to run their own small independent label, Doublevision, but Mallinder was positive about Some Bizzare's important contribution:

> The liaison helped. Some Bizzare got us involved with a major company and we had our interests looked after very well. The previous labels that we'd been on were independent by their nature and tended to leave you to your own devices, which is OK, but quite negative to an extent. At least at Some Bizzare if something goes wrong or they don't like it, you get insulted. And that can work as positive encouragement.

Stevo's willingness to push Some Bizzare into ever more adventurous and seemingly uncommercial directions was further evinced by the signing of Berlin's Einsturzende Neubauten, the first foreign act connected with the label. At this point, Stevo was bored with conventional 'rock' instruments, scorning the traditional lead guitar, bass, rhythm guitar and drums in favour of avant-garde experimentation. As he evangelically pontificated: 'Rock 'n' roll is more than those instruments, it's in people's adrenalin, which must be smashed out'. Stevo could not have chosen a more appropriate group to smash out the listener's adrenalin than Einsturzende Neubauten. Renowned for their use of 'industrial instrumentation', they gave Britain an unforgettable introduction to the bleakness of 1984 with *The Concerto For Machinery And Voice* in the ornate setting of London's ICA. Among the 'instruments' featured at that notorious concert were a concrete-mixer, cement-breakers, concrete-pounders and pneumatic drills. The show climaxed with Neubauten attempting to hack their way through the stage with a chain saw. Eventually, the audience went wild and destroyed the PA system in an orgy of destruction.

Like all of Stevo's artistes, Neubauten have gained considerable publicity and a hard-core following that has not waned. Although they spend much time abroad, Neubauten have established a strong rapport with several of the other Some Bizzare artistes, thereby confirming Stevo's conception of the label as some form of eccentric extended family:

It's like West Indians feel safe moving into an area where there are other West Indians. Some Bizzare is like either a mental hospital or a community. It's for artistes who've got integrity but are paranoid or insecure or who feel that no one can relate to them. They know if they come to Some Bizzare they'll be appreciated and understood.

The sound of clanging metal was also heard on the UK's equivalent of Neubauten— Test Department. Of course, the comparison virtually ends there, for Test Department are more than urban metal-bangers. Their work may involve spending considerable time in scrap-metal yards, but apart from hammering a variety of industrial wastage into mesmerizing rhythm, they are adept in the field of video, photography and soundtrack recordings. Stevo was quick to spot their potential and signed them to Phonogram through Some Bizzare. Like most of their fellow artistes, Test Department have been allowed to develop their ideas without obstruction from their corporate benefactors. Even their debut album, *Beating The Retreat*, was released in the unusual form of two 12-inch singles in order that the sound quality would be exemplary. Their live dates also reveal a determination to avoid traditional 'rock' venues. What other group would combine such an odd variety of venues as the Arch 69 Waterloo, the ICA, Heaven, Annadale Bus Station and the

Sir Henry Wood Hall? Yet Test Department are anything but wilfully parochial and have shown considerable willingness to tour the States and the Eastern Bloc. They have also been eager to confront contemporary issues, playing alongside the South Wales Miners' Choir in a display of solidarity. Like Cabaret Voltaire, they seem assured of a long life on the periphery of what is liberally called avant-garde rock music.

While Some Bizzare expanded to incorporate the likes of Psychic TV, Einsturzende Neubauten and Test Department, it was still Marc Almond whose record sales kept the company afloat. By early 1983, however, the money-spinning Soft Cell was spiralling towards self-destruction and threatening to take Some Bizzare out of the black and into the red. The old conflicts with Phonogram intensified following the release of Soft Cell's 'Numbers'. The record company had little faith in the single and in order to bolster its hit potential they employed the standard marketing trick of including an additional freebie — Soft Cell's massive-selling 'Tainted Love'. What they had not reckoned on was the extreme reaction of Stevo who does not take kindly to record companies overstepping the mark:

> When I found out, I was fuming. I phoned up Marc, he came over and we thrashed their office, smashed all the gold discs and stuck a pair of scissors in their speakers. At the end of the day, you're not going to be pushed around and they'll never do it again. If they think they can do things like that maybe they're not used to people who want a say in their own destiny.

The 'Numbers' fiasco ably demonstrated Stevo's determination to secure artistic control, but it also proved one of several nails in Soft Cell's coffin.

By 1983, Almond was plunging deeper into the Marc and the Mambas project which culminated in the release of a double album, *Torment and Torereos*. This was Almond's most extreme and personal document to date, an absurdly melodramatic revelation of the darker side of his personality. The unrelenting intensity of the work alienated many reviewers and when *Record Mirror* flippantly dismissed the entire album, Almond literally blew his top. Armed with a bull whip, he ran round to their offices and berated the reviewer at some length. The following week Almond announced to the world that he was retiring from the pop business. Although the statement was soon retracted, it was true in essence. Marc and the Mambas split up and Soft Cell struggled on long enough to release a farewell album at the end of 1984. Since then, Almond has toured with a new unit,

Marc and the Willing Sinners, and signed to Virgin via Some Bizzare. He still charts infrequently and throughout the long process of falling apart has somehow managed to combine cult credibility with pop stardom. His continued success is a testament to Stevo's faith and one reason why the motley crew of Some Bizzare still attract the attention of world-weary corporate A & R representatives.

What is especially interesting about Some Bizzare is the way artiste and manager seem so strongly linked in their interests and outlook on life. At times, it seems almost as though Stevo were carefully selecting artistes to reflect various aspects of his personality. The wayward Marc Almond, for example, displays the mischievously commercial face of his mentor, beguiling teenagers with a mixture of overt sentimentality and mildly subversive sleaze. Matt Johnson is the hard voice of reason, the warning bell in Stevo's head that can occasionally be heard in such asides as 'but you've got to be sensible'. Then there is the anarchic side of Stevo's personality, the completely unreasonable, unrelenting, uncompromising spokesman of hard core. The art terrorist in Stevo, which is still the scourge of record companies everywhere, has been embodied most forcibly in the myriad identities of that enigmatic figure Jim Foetus.

The Australian-born Jim Thirlwell arrived in England during 1979 and in a brilliant display of fantasy and self-obsession created his own microcosm of the record industry. By 1980, he had saved enough money to found Self Immolation, a small independent label which promised 'recorded works of aggression, insight and inspiration in reaction to the general malaise and poison rife in the music scene'. Rather than waiting for rock critics to categorize his label's music, Thirlwell provided them with ready-made slogans such as 'hard art', 'aesthetic terrorism', 'bleed now pay later', and the often quoted 'positive negativism'. Assuming the role of managing director, Thirlwell launched his artistic enterprise with a series of releases by a school of musicians known collectively as the Foetus family. The clan included such illustrious names as Frank Watt, Clint Ruin, Philip Toss and a seemingly infinite series of offshoot groups: Foetus Under Glass, Philip and his Foetus Vibrations, Foetus Over Frisco, Foetus Uber Alles, Foetus In Your Bed, Foetus Art Terrorism, Foetus On The Beach, You've Got Foetus On Your Breath and Scraping Foetus Off The Wheel. The fact that none of these groups were ever seen in public was not surprising, for the entire fleet consisted of one man alone — the mysterious J.G. Thirlwell.

By the end of 1981, Jim Foetus, as he is now commonly known, found himself at an unprecedented low ebb. He had invested almost all his income recording two albums, *Deaf* and *Ache*, and those long hours spent in the studio eventually cost him his day job. The albums were subsequently released under the group name You've Got Foetus On Your Breath, thereby ensuring that radio programmers and disc jockeys steered clear of Jim and his product. His reaction was to bury the name in favour of the equally offensive Scraping Foetus Off The Wheel. All this greatly appealed to the mischievous Stevo who perceived in Foetus an aggressive anarchic attitude that reminded him of his own earlier militancy. In particular, the 'positive negativism' expounded by Jim ('That which may initially seem purely negative often produces positive results by its very existence. If you're never miserable, you have nothing to compare happiness to') ably articulated Stevo's own feelings about the importance and purpose of Some Bizzare.

Stevo offered Jim Foetus the standard Some Bizzare management/recording contract, plus the dream of every struggling artiste: unlimited time in a 24-track recording studio and access to a mass audience on Foetus's own terms. When Jim finally delivered a completed tape, Stevo was ecstatic. Vistors to his Hammersmith house would be regaled with tales of the album's brilliance and Stevo even blew up his hi-fi speakers listening to a cassette copy at excruciatingly high volume. 'All this is by *one* guy' he would exclaim with wide-eyed astonishment. In private, he boasted of securing a big deal with any number of major record companies and accruing a sizeable advance into the bargain. For once, however, Stevo had overestimated his power in the industry and failed to convince A & R departments of Foetus's aesthetic or commercial viability.

Stevo was shocked and humbled by his failure to sell Foetus to the majors, though on one occasion he almost succeeded. One record company offered Jim a paltry advance which the by now desperate Stevo agreed to accept, but then came the bombshell. The corporate insisted that Jim drop the proposed group title, Scraping Foetus Off The Wheel, on the grounds that it was so tasteless and offensive that both the media and public would dismiss the record outright. In retrospect, the request was hardly onerous. Thirlwell had so many pseudonyms at his fingertips that a less repulsive Foetus-inspired name could easily have been substituted. Perversely, however, he refused even to consider such a *volte face* and coldly informed Stevo, 'No fear, no compromise'. The Some Bizzare supremo took great pleasure in rejecting the offer outright. It was as if Foetus had revived his evangelical zeal for absolute artistic control.

After some deliberation, Foetus's vinyl offering eventually appeared on Some Bizzare without the back up of corporate distribution. *Hole* documented several of Foetus's favourite themes: death, lust, sex, disease and spiritual decay. One critic called the album the product of a sick mind, a view with which Foetus wholeheartedly agrees. The follow up, *Nail*, offered much of the same, ensuring that Foetus was blacklisted by disc jockeys everywhere.

Foetus's chances of reaching a mass audience have been further hampered by an apparent aversion to live performances. As a one-man organization, he cannot produce his studio sound onstage without the use of extensive backing tapes. Nevertheless, the few Foetus performances witnessed over the years have been notable for their intensity and controversy. In November 1983, Foetus joined Marc Almond, Lydia Lunch and Nick Cave in a touring revue known as the Immaculate Consumptive. The concerts were memorable for their vitriolic abandon and Foetus (in his Clint Ruin persona) ended his performance surrounded by debris and broken glass.

The next recorded sighting of a live Foetus could not have been more contrasting. Early the following year, he was spotted playing saxophone with, of all people, Orange Juice. The urbane Edwyn Collins was even telling interviewers that Foetus was an important influence on the way he thought about music. It certainly seemed the oddest coupling of 1984. Here was Collins, the rather twee all-round pop sentimentalist, embracing the devilish positive negativism of a performer whose aural assaults and lyrical viciousness seemed diametrically opposed to the carefully structured work of Orange Juice. Sadly, the Foetus/Collins amalgam did not progress further, for it would surely have been a brilliant mixed marriage of pop and hard core capable of uniting both camps.

Foetus continues to record and appear with various offshoots. The affectionately named Stinkfist features soulmate Lydia Lunch, while Wiseblood combines the talents of Foetus and Rolli Mossiman of the Swans. Meanwhile, Foetus records continue to appear at odd moments. Prior to *Nail*, Some Bizzare released a boxed set, *The Foetus of Excellence* which soon scaled the independent album charts. Whether it qualified for such an honour is questionable, for the package consisted of only an empty box with a Foetus T-shirt inside. Hard Art indeed.

Foetus's favourite dictum, 'positive negativism', may well sum up the attitude of Stevo and virtually all the artistes on Some Bizzare, but it also leaves the label open to criticisms of self-indulgence and insularity. Former Human League manager Robert Last, whose career development has almost paralleled that of Stevo at times, puts forward the argument very lucidly:

> Stevo's got a set of ideas and he's playing the game of business for reasons other than business. And that's what I'm doing. But I don't agree with Stevo's vision of the world or his thoughts on matters. I think that he, and all his groups, imagine that by delving into the blacker aspects of life — this is somehow a healthy and cleansing activity. There's some truth in that view but I think all those groups are pissing around when it comes to delving into the darker aspects and deluding themselves. What they're actually doing is indulging their own problems.

Last has a point, for, in spite of embracing the darkness, it is difficult to accept that the artistes of Some Bizzare are ever endangering their own lives. The savage god of self-destruction that has transformed art into a loaded gun for many twentieth-century writers and performers will probably leave Some Bizzare unscathed. Their sleazy world of self-created darkness seems far removed from the real abyss of mental instability and mortification that can be found in a genuinely tragic sensibility.

Stevo has never welcomed criticism of his label or management style and arrogantly shrugs aside accusations of self-indulgence and elitism, preferring to place his faith in the unbridled egos of his more extreme artistes:

> Someone came up to me recently and said, 'Stevo, the trouble with you, your artistes and Some Bizzare is that you're too bigoted'. And I said, 'Yes, you're right, we are bigoted and we've got every right to be because we're superior'. The music of Some Bizzare is not a projection to the masses. It is something which is very self-indulgent. And, yes, it's a shame that you're 'élite' if you put over music that's intelligent, original, and projects attitudes. Some Bizzare has got its own variety in a very anti-structured framework. Maybe you can compare Neubauten to Cabaret Voltaire or PTV to Foetus; to me, there is no comparison. We widen variety, we support creativity, we discourage sycophantic adulation.

Stevo's faith in the integrity of Some Bizzare is mirrored by a powerful antipathy towards other independent labels and management set ups. Other managers are apparently only in it for the money while the indies are 'a giant arse with a balloon coming out saying, "HYPOCRISY"'. Ever since Stevo learned that some of his rivals diverted artiste royalties into interest-yielding international banks, his criticism of the independents has been caustic.

As for the majors and their ingratiating executive employees, Stevo cannot be disparaging enough:

> People who use false smiles are the enemy and the record business breeds stereotypes, which I don't like. I don't think they understand any integrity whatsoever other than selling records. The people inside those structures climb the bureaucratic ladder by false smiles and they end up with a permanent one. I have no time for these people. International companies are there to be used and that's all they are for. The people in these companies are sycophantic parasites.

In order to commemorate his legendary wrangling with the majors, Stevo had some brass ornaments made in the shape of a penis. Inscribed on the glans were the names of several prominent record companies. These weighty instruments were on display in the living room of Stevo's home as a provocative reminder of his political aversion to the corporates.

As a manager and label owner, Stevo has divorced himself from the orderliness of corporate mentality by establishing a company that frequently revels in 'complete chaos'. Although his artistes accept the politics of Some Bizzare, there is inevitably some disagreement over Stevo's methods. Matt Johnson explains his reservations:

> Stevo has got to learn to modify the way he deals with record companies; he needs to learn diplomacy. There are certain things at Some Bizzare that have to be changed. Stevo has efficiency confused with bureaucracy. At times, there's a lot of confusion and lack of communication. The idea is great, but the whole operation has to be improved.

It may prove difficult to reconcile Johnson's ordered vision with the playful self-destruction that Stevo apparently regards as an integral part of his organization:

> As soon as I feel Some Bizzare has made its point on a definitive level, it's then that Some Bizzare collapses. Major labels use Some Bizzare as the name to market something that's a little bit different, which is terrible for the state of art and the state of music. I hate commodities so I'd certainly like to change the name at some point, but at the moment it's too dangerous.

Stevo has since reconciled this dilemma by forming a subsidiary label, Kelvin 422. As well as featuring recordings by the Swans and Yello, the label intends to release soundtrack recordings by pseudonymous Some Bizzare groups.

Any hopes of expanding Some Bizzare are ultimately likely to be thwarted by budget control. Since the disbanding of Soft Cell, the purse strings have been tightened and Stevo has found himself subsidizing several acts in order to push projects through. The willingness to put his money where his mouth is separates him from his more rapacious contemporaries, for although such managerial altruism is not unique, it remains a rare quality:

> I've met millions of managers and I don't like them. 99.9 per cent of managers' aspirations are financial and I can't relate to that. I put my money into things that none of these people would. Everything I do everyone will say is insane. As soon as it's in a studio they get interested. Some Bizzare is not a financially successful label but it's artistically respected. Hopefully, we'll never have to sell our integrity to survive. Once, a major label tried to take us under with £18 000 unpaid bills. Eight times I've borrowed money from Matt, the Cabs and PTV to keep Some Bizzare going. We're always on the knife edge. It's ridiculous.

The relationship that has been forged between Stevo and his acts over the last few years is one of the strongest in the music business. Each party is acutely aware of the other's eccentricities and although there are often differences of opinion, the overall goals remain the same. Matt Johnson, along with the other Some Bizzare artistes, has learned to appreciate Stevo's strengths and weaknesses over a long period of time:

> Stevo's strength is his ear. He signs things other people wouldn't touch and nurtures artistes at their own pace. He can also be very heavy with the record companies and act as a buffer. His weakness is his paranoia; he's got so many things going on that it gets on top of him. Right now there aren't many big earners; most of the bands don't pay for themselves — he subsidizes them. Artistically, it's the right thing to do, business-wise it's tricky. He needs more staff and the money isn't there. It's Catch 22 — but it'll resolve itself. There was a lot of turbulence, but Some Bizzare seems a stronger unit now. I'm trying to push for it to clarify its aims and pursue them with vigour. It's got a lot to offer.

What the future holds for Stevo is anyone's guess. He may choose to follow in the steps of Chris Blackwell or Chris Wright and expand Some Bizzare, but his present ideals suggest otherwise. Yet the Mammon of the music industry has a fatal attraction, especially for budding entrepreneurs from underprivileged backgrounds.

The real personal test for Stevo is not whether he can keep Some Bizzare in operation, but whether he can sustain the almost puritanical zeal with which he dismisses capitalist record companies. Whatever else, he has chosen a rather odd industry in which to pursue the fulfilment of such radically artistic aspirations. He is not the first manager to confront the art versus money dichotomy and the paradox of his situation is that in order to keep his less commercial acts in operation he needs to shift vinyl. Without a money-earner in his stable, the corporates will hardly be tempted into signing Stevo's more esoteric acts and therein lies the rub. Stevo is adamant that he will overcome this dilemma, even if it means creating a subversive subsidiary, Strictly Financial Records, which would allow him to produce commercial material while retaining his playful sense of irony.

Stevo may see himself as an anti-manager in some respects, but in his role as middle man between the artiste and the corporation, he faces the same problems that have plagued his predecessors for the past thirty years.

In Search Of The Perfect Pop Manager

Any attempt to produce a definitive blueprint outlining the attributes of the 'perfect' pop manager demonstrates why such a creature cannot exist. Most of the desired qualities are mutually exclusive. The ideal candidate must be cautious yet innovative; intuitive yet empirical; forceful but sensitive to his artiste's feelings; aggressive in battle and reflective in victory; wise, but not intellectually intimidating; a rhetorician and a patient, sympathetic listener. The mythical 'perfect' pop manager lies somewhere between the hard businessman, the medical doctor and the dedicated schoolteacher — a powerful, worldly-wise entrepreneur who is professionally remote, yet acutely aware of the psychology of his artistes and how to get the best for and from them.

Presented with such a strange hybrid role model, most fledgling starmakers would no doubt throw up their hands in despair and scream, 'A good manager is born, not made.' In some respects, this objection is perfectly reasonable, for pop management strategies seem more a question of personality than policy. If you're naturally aggressive you'll become an autocrat, if altruistically diffident a sugar daddy, if ruthless a poacher, if lazy an inheritor, if flighty a dilettante, if resigned a fatalist, and so on. The preceding case studies and list of management types underline this argument most forcibly.

However, pop management and the problems it throws up cannot simply be referred to personality traits for a quick and easy answer. All pop managers, no matter how good or bad, are faced with a range of similar problems. Resolving those problems is a skilled process involving a finite number of considerations and requiring a methodology that is consistent and effective. Therefore, while it may not be possible to list the qualities of the 'perfect' pop svengali, there is enough data available to categorize the functions of pop management and pinpoint those characteristics which have proven most successful in establishing effective manager/artiste relations during the past thirty years.

The elements of successful pop management can be broken down into various sub-categories, and I have chosen nine that the reader may retrospectively apply to any figure in this study.

Defining Objectives

I was more interested in money than ego. I wasn't interested in self-aggrandizement or building up an empire like Shell oil.

Harvey Lisberg

With management you attach yourself to people who have incredibly powerful aims and need objects. Kids come to me and say, 'I want to go *there*'. And I say, 'Great, because I can tell you how to get there, so I'll be your manager and go with you'. Basically, that's what happens and it makes a perfect relationship because I never have any objectives pulling away from theirs. You never hear an artiste complain, 'The trouble with Simon Napier-Bell is that he's only managing me because he wants to do this'. That's because I have no objectives at all.

Simon Napier-Bell

Money wasn't my ambition. If I had an ambition, it was to try and reach as near the top of the ladder as I could . . . The ultimate was to reach the West End of London, then Broadway. I didn't want to stay a pop manager or a manager of artistes all my life.

Larry Parnes

I always looked for potential, not what an artiste is doing when I see them but what they might do next year or the year after, which I've always said is the essence of good management.

Ken Pitt

I see myself articulating things that are already there. Even without being aware of it, I'm encouraging certain things that are already there and discouraging things that aren't there.

Robert Last

Before ever making a managerial decision or signing a contract, a manager must be clear about his objectives and those of his artistes. If a manager and artiste are aware of, or in disagreement over, their respective aims (i.e. one party is interested *only* in profit; the other motivated *entirely* by artistic concerns) the relationship is unlikely to prosper. Obviously, the art/profit dichotomy can sometimes prove problematic, but it is seldom irreconcilable. Even extremely uncompromising artistes quickly realize that without adequate profits the confidence of record companies, booking agents, publishers, producers and impresarios cannot be retained. Similarly, the most hard-hearted financier cannot afford to ignore the artistic caprices of his charges without risking the loss of a substantial investment.

Planning Policies

> A manager's role is a creative one. He has to create a situation in which his artistes can happen.
>
> **Tony Stratton-Smith**

> The manager's job is putting the group into a framework where they can do what they themselves have the vision to see and do.
>
> **Simon Napier-Bell**

> My long-term strategy is to retain that element of things being close to the edge. There must always be the possibility of major change. Ironically, the effect of that, in the long term, is that you get a greater stability.
>
> **Robert Last**

After reconciling the aims of the artiste with his own general principles, the manager must formulate a policy. Without clear directives in respect to all his activities, the enterprise is likely to fail. Good planning ensures that there is a minimum of waste, thereby saving time, effort and money. A bad manager does not set aims or consider the results of his actions but is prone to spontaneous decisions which are frequently counter-productive. Abruptly firing a musician or singer, for example, may solve an immediate insubordination problem, but unless an effective plan has already been devised, the decision may cause unforeseen recruitment headaches, cancelled dates, a loss of morale and even the imminent dissolution of the group. A manager who has no plan is like a captain sailing through treacherous seas without a compass: when the storm breaks both parties will probably be driven towards perilous economic rocks and rapidly torn to pieces.

Communication

> I always used to sit down and talk for a long time with my artistes about their careers, their stage performances and what they were going to try and do.
>
> **Larry Parnes**

> If anyone conspires or speaks to you about the artiste, it must always be told. There must never be any secrets. The artiste must know everything . . .
>
> **Stevo**

In order to translate plans into actions, a manager must be capable of communicating his ideas cogently and precisely. Those managers who act on their own beliefs without consultation with their artistes are failing in a very important area. No matter how uninterested or stupid an artiste may seem, regular communication concerning changes in management strategy or career development are an absolute necessity. Good communication reinforces a sense of unity of purpose; unless the artiste is aware of what the manager is doing, an atmosphere of suspicion and mistrust will be the likely result. In such circumstances, the artiste becomes easy prey for a poacher.

Control

> If you can't control the destiny of your artistes how can you guarantee them anything?
>
> **Larry Page**

> When you get into the area of services for somebody the law is impossible to uphold. It can't hold contracts together on either side — management or artiste. It's got to be a relationship that works.
>
> **Simon Napier-Bell**

> The way you build power relationships into contracts is something that fascinates me, and a lot of people just have no idea the way subtle differences in your contract completely transform the power relationship.
>
> **Robert Last**

> You've got to be aware of the business to protect the artiste like a father.
>
> **Stevo**

Having budgeted a specific programme, a manager must ensure that his targets are met and, if they are not, locate the reasons before standards fall. It is the manager's job to evaluate the use of resources and the quality of the work in progress. This involves balancing the creative output of the artiste alongside the costs calculated to cover the enterprise, while also keeping abreast of changes in the economic climate and rock marketplace. All these considerations are likely to have profound effects upon morale, competence and career direction. Traditionally, the manager's most powerful weapon is his control, contractual or otherwise, over the distribution of income within his organization. The unscrupulous pop manager will abuse the control he has over income and contracts and exploit and damage his enterprise in order to line his pockets.

Coordination

There's a whole lot of different visions and, whether by design or default, I'm the person who ends up orchestrating which combination of visions is actually being operated on or ends up getting to the public.

Robert Last

You've got to have a partnership on the right terms. One theory I have is that just because the artiste doesn't happen you can't say, 'The artiste is no good'. You also can't say, 'The manager is no good'. It's a highly individual situation. I did well with Dusty but if I'd had Lulu it might not have happened for me'.

Vic Billings

What makes the business is the balance between the creative artiste and the record company. The manager is the balance in the middle who brings them together and sways both of them to see the other's point of view. And the manager never has that ability if he doesn't see the creative side as the dominant force. The managers who side with the record company aren't very good.

Simon Napier-Bell

One of the key factors in successful pop management is the ability to bring ideas and people together in order to accomplish an organizational goal. This requires some knowledge of how the music business functions as a whole and which people should be approached in order to enhance the artiste's chances of success. The choice of record company, road manager, producer, agent, solicitor and accountant should be carefully considered in the light of the group's aims and intentions. If the relationship between any of these parties becomes strained then the manager must eliminate such sources of disequilibrium quickly and effectively. Careful coordination is synonymous with efficiency.

Leadership

If you've got to rely purely on a piece of paper, you've got no management. You are bloody dead.

Larry Page

Larry Parnes was always considered to be right. Everything he said had to be right, which is what a good manager should feel. He has to have that kind of confidence.

Marty Wilde

If Tam Paton said 'jump' you jumped. He never threatened. It was absolutely voluntary . . . We were afraid of him. But don't ask me why. I haven't got a clue.

Ian Mitchell

Any authority I have is questioned or open to question at any single moment. But it's changing. I've noticed that with new groups we've taken on I have an aura and power, even if they're the same age as me. I now have a history and it does affect how you are received.

Robert Last

The rock manager is the President of the United States in terms of his acts. He should act as a chairman, analyse the information, and the group should make the decisions. Frequently, the manager offers his advice, the group refuse it, and the manager has to act on their behalf against his advice.

Simon Napier-Bell

Leadership requires confidence and the ability to win the interest and respect of other people — most crucially, the artiste. Some managers are too indulgent and spoil their groups while others have been known to intimidate them to such a degree that they scurry around like frightened schoolchildren. In both cases, the manager has failed in his role as leader. But poor supervision is not inevitably caused by personality. A manager may not bully or indulge his artistes, yet still prove fallible as a leader. This commonly occurs from failing to monitor the people with whom he works — their needs, interests, aims, intentions, abilities and problems. The ivory tower manager may successfully represent his artistes to the record business community, but his failure to involve himself in their lives can prove costly. For a time, he will be glamorized as a distant and omniscient presence, but once his artistes mature, the more prosaic image of the uncaring financier will be uppermost in their minds. Without the respect or admiration of his artistes, the manager cannot expect long-term involvements or complete success.

Delegation

I was apprehensive about delegation and watched it closely . . . I had a very good team. Everybody worked in the one room and could speak to each other. Everything we did was like a military campaign, a combined effort. I didn't do all this myself — no person could. It's a mistake a lot of people make. They think one person can do it.

Larry Parnes

One day Phil Solomon said to me, 'I'm getting out of this business'. And I said, 'But Philip, you've been involved in music all these years and have done so well out of it'. He said, 'Yes, but I can't have someone else running my business'. Typical attitude of an entrepreneur.

Dick Rowe

If anything was to happen to me, who would I hand my artistes over to?

Larry Page

I built the bands and backed off before the cream came . . . I didn't want to be traipsing around city to city, month after month, touring. If I had, the development of Charisma Records would have suffered. It was impossible to do both.

Tony Stratton-Smith

It's my intention to have, eventually, two or three managers in the company and a roster of six or seven acts and I won't be managing any of them myself.

Robert Last

The manager will only survive if he understands he has to get expert advice. All too often the manager emerges and doesn't appreciate to what degree it's an accident. You must get yourself surrounded by people who know what they're doing.

Simon Napier-Bell

Delegation was something I found very difficult to learn.

Stevo

'To delegate or not to delegate' is a question that has caused sleepless nights for even the most successful managers in pop history. Indeed, delegation could be described as the Achilles' heel of the great entrepreneur. By nature, the charismatic manager is a maverick whose philosophies are based on a rock-solid confidence in his own judgements. That confidence creates the drive that leads to entrepreneurial success, but herein lies a paradox. For success inevitably multiplies the work load to such a degree that the manager must go against his nature and seek help. If he tries to do everything, he will stretch himself to breaking point and the result will be a series of snap decisions leading to disastrous errors.

Even when a manager accepts that duties must be delegated, he can still make fundamental mistakes. The most common is inconsistency and lack of clarity in his instructions. He incorrectly perceives delegation as the surrendering of power and becomes obsessed with amounts and degrees. Is he giving too much power away or too little? Unless the manager understands the function of delegation he will forever be readjusting the power ratio, thereby causing confusion among his subordinates. For example, a road manager should not be placed in a position where he feels that his closeness to the group allows him to do anything he wants. Yet if he is powerless to make any important decision without consulting 'the boss', he may fail to take steps necessary to forestall a crisis. Successful delegation is not a matter of grudgingly surrendering chunks of power, but defining precisely the authority that is bestowed.

One reason why even the potentially great pop manager fails on the thorny question of delegation is his innate overconfidence. He struggles on defiantly and refuses to delegate until he is almost overwhelmed by chaos and inefficiency. The powerful manager whose confidence has festered into megalomania is ultimately a self-destructive creature. Usually, his reign ends with a bankruptcy or nervous breakdown.

Conflict and Ambiguity

> The groups that were put together in the sixties tended to come out with their manager's personality . . . The Yardbirds adopted Giorgio Gomelsky's personality. He believed in conflict. He believed that everything could be got from people by putting them in conflict with each other rather than putting them in harmony with each other. And he liked to stimulate disorder.
>
> **Simon Napier-Bell**

> If you do interviews, you're egotistical; if you don't, you're introverted. If you do nice artwork, you're pretentious; if you don't, you're a dickhead. I don't know . . .
>
> **Rob Gretton**

> I think the Jesus and Mary Chain thought I was going to be richer than they were, and they couldn't take that!
>
> **Alan McGee**

Any decision-making process inevitably involves a conflict of sorts and one of the biggest tests of a manager's skills is the ability to keep conflicting priorities in order. The manager who confidently claims that all priorities can be satisfied without prejudice to each other is either a fool or a liar. Some priorities must inevitably take precedence, but none can be ignored. This is a hard lesson for the inexperienced manager who often tends to ignore the priorities which he finds difficult or time-consuming. By contrast, the effective pop manager carefully orders his problems and acts upon them accordingly, frequently revising his decisions where necessary. In this respect, he is like a successful politician bombarded by conflicting demands, yet still capable of continuing with a consistent sense of purpose through all the chaos of adjustments and revisions until his final goal has been reached.

Innovation

> During the seventies, the business did regress absolutely . . . What we did in 1976-7 was an attempt to reverse that process.
>
> **Robert Last**

> The artiste must be unreasonable. Let's face it, any reasonable person *won't* be an artiste. A reasonable person is going to fit into his surroundings as they're presented and he's not going to cause a fuss. Any progress in an artiste's life has got to be made by being unreasonable. He's got to be asking for what *you* wouldn't ask for.
>
> **Simon Napier-Bell**

> Rock 'n' Roll . . . it's in people's adrenalin. It must be smashed out . . . You must stick by the one that inspires others and not the parasites that are inspired. Innovation — a lot of people dismiss it, but they're ignorant.
>
> **Stevo**

> The really great managers are the eccentrics who contributed hugely to what rock's become . . . Brian Epstein *has* to be there because the Beatles were the result of the tie-in with him. Oldham too. Anyone who created a group must be important.
>
> **Simon Napier-Bell**

A top group cannot be expected to remain static and artistic development is usually necessary for survival. Experimentation and innovation should not only be encouraged and rewarded but reflected by the manager. He must always be ready to discard old procedures that are no longer productive and seek new ways of improving the financial and artistic status of his charges. In the past, managers have demonstrated innovative qualities in a variety of ways. When Larry Parnes found that there were insufficient outlets to promote his artistes, he solved the problem by moving into impresario work. Other managers have ventured into music publishing, production, agency work and record label ownership in order to strengthen their standing in the business community. Such diversification often ensures that artistes are allowed to record and perform material which might otherwise have been dismissed as 'unsuitable' or 'uncommercial'. Unfortunately, it is also true that diversification can produce a conflict of interest, especially if a manager assumes too many roles. It is important, therefore, that any innovation on the part of the manager must be for the benefit of his artistes and not solely to promote his own interests.

Once there was a time when the managerial function was so simple that it was universally understood. The pop manager was the father figure, *in loco parentis*, sometimes benevolent, sometimes deleterious, but always the master of his realm. When Larry Parnes assumed the mantle of Britain's first great rock 'n' roll manager in the mid-fifties, he was still a young man, only several years older than his artistes, yet nobody dared question his authority. The music press called him the 'beat svengali' and it was assumed that his control over his artistes was absolute. By the end of the fifties, Parnes ruled an entire kingdom of pop stars and his apparently unlimited power ensured that there were seldom any problems involved in organizing their activities. The pop business was so neatly structured that Larry Parnes seemed omnipotent — the feudal lord of British rock 'n' roll.

When the Great Provider abdicated his managerial throne, the media found a new potentate in Brian Epstein. The Liverpudlian lacked Parnes's warm magisterial presence, but his remarkable coolness under pressure and aristocratic disdain for social inferiors were seen as the hallmarks of a great British leader. Like Parnes, Epstein was sometimes cast in the role of svengali, but the meaning of the word was changing. The original svengali, created by George Du Maurier in the novel *Trilby* and later immortalized in the 1931 movie *Svengali*, was a brilliant but ruthlessly maleficent hypnotist whose subjects obeyed his every command. Those critics who dubbed Parnes and Epstein svengalis, however, also saw them as devoted guardians whose concerns were not merely custodial, but philosophical and moral; they kept their boys in order and ensured that their public images were not tarnished by slovenly behaviour, bad language or confrontation with the law. Even John Lennon's characteristic rebelliousness was carefully held in check during the early days of Beatlemania. Paternal vigilance was always obligatory for a genuine British pop svengali.

'Power', 'authority', 'guidance' and 'instruction' had been the managerial watchwords of the late fifties, but the new decade brought some surprising changes. The post-war baby boom had created a surplus of teenagers and by 1963 ageism was rampant. The warrior cry 'Never trust anyone over 30' became a slogan that sent shivers down the spines of every would-be svengali. Most of the powerful managers of the day, including Don Arden, Phil Solomon and Peter Walsh, were already middle-aged, while the precocious Epstein was himself pushing 30. It was always assumed that some degree of senatorial maturity was obligatory for an effective pop entrepreneur, but the cult of youth challenged this viewpoint and, by 1964, that crucial age differential between manager and artiste had finally broken down. The man responsible was Andrew Oldham, whose outlandish self-promotion made him almost as notorious as the group he discovered in a Richmond club. If the Rolling Stones were the antithesis of the Beatles, then Oldham was their managerial equivalent. Unlike Parnes or Epstein, he did not suppress adolescent rebellion and bad behaviour, but actively encouraged yobbishness and transformed Michael Philip Jagger from a polite middle-class LSE student into the quintessence of sixties teenage moral degeneracy. Significantly, Oldham was never called a 'svengali' for he lacked the authoritarian image of the patrician pop manager. Rather, he was the 'brash young tycoon' or 'sixth Stone', epithets carefully chosen to reflect his close relationship with the group. Epstein could never have been a Beatle, but Oldham, a failed pop singer only two years before, would not have looked out of place in the Stones. In the wake of Oldham, other young managers such as Gordon Mills, Tony Secunda and Simon Napier-Bell jockeyed for power. They produced records, played instruments, wrote songs and became totally involved in the artistic process. They even looked like their own pop stars. When A&R representatives discovered new groups in the back rooms of pubs and clubs their first embarrassed words were usually: 'Now, which of you is the manager?' The old-style svengali had been superseded in the public imagination by the charismatic manager.

By the late sixties, the record business was such a powerful, money-spinning industry that more and more specialists entered the field. Pop managers had always employed accountants and solicitors but now these professional advisers were assuming positions of prominence. The notorious American business manager, Allen Klein, had already taken the Rolling Stones from Andrew Oldham and made no secret of the fact that he intended to wrest the Beatles from Brian Epstein. Other whizz-kid accountants and newly qualified solicitors also assumed managerial roles and their list of clients rapidly multiplied. The process was accelerated by changes in the economic climate which forced groups to think more and more about their financial future. Suddenly, good old-fashioned pop music was no longer fun and fewer untrained young kids were entering the management business. Meanwhile, Secunda, Oldham and Napier-Bell, the bright young men of mid-sixties British pop management, had either branched out into other areas of the music business or retired.

The general standard of British rock music during the first half of the seventies was quite dreadful. Pomp rock and heavy metal bloated the album charts while the singles market was glutted with the pubescent strains of David Cassidy and the Osmonds, occasionally relieved by the historically overrated glitter brigade. The distracting presence of Bowie and Roxy Music could not disguise the fact that something was very wrong. What's more, it progressively worsened. The most consistent chart artistes of 1974 and 1975 were the Wombles and Mud, respectively. But how did pop become so bad, so quickly? What we appeared to be witnessing was an unhealthy generation gap, with over-serious artistes and elitist record buyers concentrating almost entirely on the albums market, leaving the kids with undemanding factory fodder.

Interestingly, this creative nadir in British pop was reflected and arguably caused by the recent changes in management recruitment. Contrary to what Allen Klein and Tony DeFries may have thought, this was not the age of the charismatic accountant and lawyer. Most of the specialists in positions of power turned out to be boring and workmanlike, with no creative imagination whatsoever. The great visionaries, eccentrics, romantics and opportunists of the mid-sixties beat boom had been replaced by economic mechanics, anonymous agencies and management companies, which offered a professional service but little in the way of innovation. Suddenly, artistes were terribly alone. Many resigned themselves to life on the college circuit and supported sagging careers with the occasional mediocre album. The well-oiled agencies and management companies offered steady work for reasonable pay, without undue risk. There was little incentive for experimentation. The corporate mentality seemed all-pervasive.

Svengalis and charismatic managers may have seemed an anachronism by the mid-seventies, but they were still remembered with nostalgia, especially by those who craved something new or radical. 'Where are the next Beatles?' cried the media, instead of asking the far more pertinent question, 'Where is the next Larry Parnes or Brian Epstein?' As if to prove that every age must have its token svengali, the title was revived once more and applied to the Scottish patriarch Tam Paton. If only his creative energies and unquenchable passion had been put into something more worthwhile than the Bay City Rollers, how glorious those days might have been. Nevertheless, the hysteria produced by the Rollers and masterminded by their seemingly all-powerful mentor was to have an incalculable effect on Britain's next great manager.

Malcolm McLaren not only created a negative copy of the Rollers in the form of the controversial Sex Pistols, but ended up playing midwife at the birth of punk. As a manager, McLaren was extraordinary. His magpie mind seemed to assimilate and fuse a bizarre number of conflicting managerial styles, borrowed from figures as diverse as Larry Parnes, Andrew Oldham and Tam Paton. McLaren envied the power that the Great Provider wielded during the fifties, though he was uninterested in the strict codes of behaviour that both Parnes and Paton demanded of their artistes. McLaren enjoyed chaos and, like Oldham, provoked and revelled in his artistes' headline-grabbing outrages. Within a year, British pop music was back in the hands of youth and as hundreds of new groups stormed the capital, a fresh wave of entrepreneurs attempted to seize control from the corporate management companies. Even the once sprightly Simon Napier-Bell came out of retirement to join the fray.

The second half of the seventies promised the return of the charismatic manager of old, but most of the new wave entrepreneurs divided and diffused their interests. Figures such as Jake Riviera, Bill Drummond and Robert Last seemed more interested in founding independent record labels than following McLaren's managerial exploits. Much the same might be said of Rob Gretton and Stevo with their respective involvements in Factory and Some Bizzare. Recent trends suggest that the maverick manager may no longer be sufficient to take a group to the top. The Frankie phenomenon had less to do with management in its traditional sense than the efforts of a journalist turned record company executive and a hot-shot producer. In spite of McLaren's influence the old ego manager has not returned as the superstar svengali.

The svengali manager may presently be a dormant species but it would be a mistake to issue a death certificate. In spite of all the changes that have occurred in British popular music management over the past thirty years, the autocratic entrepreneur is still the image that the public most readily associates with the term 'pop manager'. The irresistible power and influence of the svengali, like that of the charismatic leader in politics, has a universal appeal that will ensure its cyclical revival at appropriate moments in future rock history.

While writing this book I researched the careers of several dozen British pop managers from the fifties to the present and was surprised to discover that a disproportionately high number of entrepreneurs from my sample groups fell into one of three categories: gay, Jewish and male. But what produced this unusual ethnic/sexual equation and why, in the case of homosexuals and Jews, was it valid predominantly from the early days of British pop until the late sixties? A broader observation of societal attitudes during those periods provided some important clues.

Few would disagree that there has always been a gay tradition in such 'artistic' occupations as dancing, painting and writing. Even in repressive periods, homosexuals were accepted by the artistic community, though the nature of their sexuality was often masked by euphemisms such as 'eccentric' or 'aesthete'. Historically, the gay movement has also been well represented in show business and other areas of entertainment. Since British pop music and traditional show business were inextricably linked, at least until the mid-sixties, the homosexual network during that period was particularly strong. Indeed, one sixties entrepreneur was confident enough to pontificate: 'The history of rock is based on homosexuality. That's how rock emerged in England. I don't think it would have started without it'.

Simon Napier-Bell, who ran with the gay set for most of the swinging sixties, maintains that the homosexual managers of his era were not only tolerated, but admired and respected by their impressionable charges:

> Any boy of 18-20 was brought up to feel the homosexual was something to be disliked, attacked and hated. But, everything about the 20-35-year-old man's gay lifestyle is what they aspire to. You don't have kids, you don't have a nice family, you live independently, you have a nice car and money to eat out every night. So suddenly there's this tremendous conflict in young kids ... They know they're never going to live like that but end up in this dreadful heterosexual rat race of kids and family ... Therefore, if they've any ability to *flex* their sexuality they do so. This is why sexually aggressive gays can always get exactly what they want because the boys are *desperate*. Many managers find it very easy to bring these people into their lives and keep them around. And if they're also offering potential stardom and all the things that go with the pop world, it's an absolute cinch.

This lurid picture of British pop as a cattle market in which capricious gay managers hired and fired aspiring artistes and brazenly indulged their homosexuality seems a slightly crude historical overview. However, when I accused Napier-Bell of sexual caricature, he drew upon his memories and experience of sixties pop management to ridicule my naïveté:

> I don't think you realize the degree to which sexuality can dominate someone's entire life. The only thing they care about when they wake up in the morning is who they're going to have sex with that day; everything else is peripheral. Of course, they want the income and the razzmatazz of show business, but that's all to give them the right panache to get sex. And that's the dominant factor. So when they are dismissive or curt with artistes they're not really being ruthless, but disinterested. Dilettante to the last degree. I could tell you half a dozen in the business that exist in that way today.

Indeed, Napier-Bell is remarkably frank about naming names and speculating, often in a gossipy way, about homosexual managers and their influence over young artistes. He even claims that the impressionable John Lennon went through a phase of sexual confusion, picking up boys at the Scotch of St James's and breaking into tears when his mentor snubbed him at a party in Liverpool. I remain sceptical. Even our ever-vigilant Sunday newspapers have yet to unearth a scandal in which a gay pop manager corrupted one of his own young artistes. The sexual promiscuity that Napier-Bell maintains was common in the sixties seems more likely to have been restricted to a small clique of his more excessive friends and associates. Generally, sexual relationships between managers and artistes have been taboo. Many gay managers have concealed their homosexuality from their charges and studiously avoided such liaisons as a matter of principle. Tam Paton, the most maligned gay entrepreneur of all, puts forward the argument against manager/artiste couplings most forcibly in his own chapter. In asking the question, 'What attracted gays towards pop management in the fifties and sixties?' we ultimately need a more convincing reply than Napier-Bell's flippant one word answer, 'boys'.

The psychology of the gay during this period is unquestionably the most crucial point of all. The life of a homosexual before the 1967 Sexual Offences Act was inevitably fraught with danger and emotional or physical pain. Denied sexual freedom by law, the homosexual was particularly prone to feelings of persecution and alienation. Loneliness, the need to feel wanted and the desire for power in personal politics were common. Clearly, the pop manager role provided an opportunity to yield a vicarious power — guiding and influencing the lives of adolescent artistes. The solidarity among gays in show business, and increasingly in the pop music sphere, allowed a manager of homosexual persuasion to feel, to belong, without the constant fear of peer group rejection.

Apart from homosexuals, the number of Jewish managers and impresarios in fifties and sixties pop is also remarkably high. Indeed, many of the figures included in this study, such as Parnes, Epstein, Arden, Solomon, Lisberg and McLaren, came from very solid Jewish backgrounds. Of course, the personalities and individual management strategies of these characters were frequently miles apart and there is common ground between only a few of them. Their achievements may well be connected to the traditional Jewish entrepreneurial role and it is interesting to note that the three most famous figures in British pop management history (Parnes, Epstein and McLaren) were former shopkeepers. It is also worth noting that, like gays, the Jewish community has always been well represented in show business and the record industry. This trend can no doubt be traced back further through Tin Pan Alley to the Hollywood movie barons such as Samuel Goldwyn and the Warner Brothers, with their related interests in the record business. But even accepting that a Jewish show business tradition exists does not explain fully why British pop management threw up so many Jewish managers during the fifties and sixties, or why there has been a noticeable decline in such trends during the seventies and eighties. The answer may well be linked to our discussion of homosexual prejudices during the same period.

In fifties Britain, post-war anti-semitism was still running high. Nowadays, people are apt to forget that blatantly racist epithets such as 'jew boy' and 'yid' were common expressions during that time, in the same way that 'paki shop' can today be heard in polite middle-class homes without causing comment. The insidious Nazi propaganda dealt a psychological blow which left the Jewish community almost as vulnerable to prejudice as their homosexual counterparts. That same need for solidarity, personal power, respect and a chance to influence and guide may well explain the sudden influx of young Jews into the pop management field. The phenomenon has never been discussed in the music press, but the Jewish writer Wolf Mankowitz was percipient enough to capture the flavour of the times in his neglected mini-masterpiece *Expresso Bongo*. In the film, Laurence Harvey plays Johnny Jackson, a young Jewish hustler, sharp as a razor and always on the look-out for a lucrative deal. When the film was shown in New York, it was warmly greeted by Jewish audiences who revelled in the East End Yiddish patter that Mankowitz had translated so accurately. It is interesting to note that the film inspired Andrew Oldham to become a pop manager and he later admitted to modelling himself on Harvey's role. No doubt, the real life exploits of the great Larry Parnes, and later Brian Epstein, inspired others along the same route. Of course, the liberalism of the sixties coupled with the youth explosion gradually broke down many of the old prejudices and stereotypes associated with Jewish managers. Thus there no longer appears to be a significantly high preponderance of Jews or gays entering British pop management.

While the previous two categories may be explained partly as a historical anomaly resulting from the social structure of Britain during the fifties and sixties, the third provokes more far-reaching questions. Even after 30 years of British pop history, male domination of the managerial role is almost absolute. Looking back over three decades, I search in vain for a female manager to rival the power and influence of Parnes, Epstein, McLaren, Oldham, Arden, Page or virtually any other person in this study. In the fifties and sixties there was the late Eve Taylor, the self-styled 'queen bee of show business', who managed Adam Faith, Sandie Shaw, Chris Andrews and Val Doonican. But Evie was generally regarded as a survivor from an earlier era who seldom felt at ease with pop, let alone the beat group scene, which she determinedly avoided. Looking back at the few women managers of the sixties and seventies, it is clear that the majority remained on the fringes of pop, veering close to MOR and Variety: Marion Massey (Lulu); Anne Calderwell (David and Jonathan; Genevieve); Jean Lincoln (Kenny Lynch; Elkie Brooks); Dorothy Solomon (The Bachelors; Lena Zavaroni); Linda Scharvona (Helen Shapiro); Freya Miller (post-rockabilly Shakin' Stevens; post-rock 'n' roll Joe Brown); Susan Johnson (Madelaine Bell; Karen Kay) and Nichola Martin (Buck's Fizz). Even in recent years the only notable female manager to achieve a standing in the industry is Stratton-Smith's former associate, Gail Colson, who handles Peter Gabriel.

Rock historians are apt to credit the explosion of punk as a form of emancipation for women in the pop world. Articles about 'New Wave Women' merrily pull together under one banner such diverse names as Joan Armatrading, Siouxsie, Chrissie Hynde, Debbie Harry, Kate Bush and Kim Wilde and rather feebly suggest that this demonstrates some major breakthrough. Since the worldwide success of Madonna several colour supplement commentators have decided that female liberation in rock has finally arrived. Scouring the charts for other girls, they have spotted such names as Alison

Moyet, Sade and Cyndi Lauper and so the case rests. What they fail to tell us is that there is nothing new about 'girls in pop' or indeed large numbers of them congregating in the charts at a particular time. In the period 1964-5, Cilla Black, Dusty Springfield, Sandie Shaw, Petula Clark and Lulu all figured prominently and there were many others too including Marianne Faithful, Twiggy, Jackie Trent and Françoise Hardy. The mid-sixties 'revolution' ultimately proved little more than a passing phase, not dissimilar to the brief proliferation of girl groups several years before. So 20 years on, what has really changed? Admittedly, the eighties girls generally seem more single-minded and independent, and the noticeable increase in female musicians since 1976 cannot be denied. Yet, neither punk nor feminist consciousness has done much to infiltrate the real positions of power. That familiar phrase A&R *man* accurately reflects the music business myth that the male is somehow a keener judge of artistic talent. During the fifties, Dick Rowe, Hugh Mendl, Jack Baverstock and their ilk dominated the talent-spotting role and, 30 years later, little has changed save the names. In other areas of the business, it is the same old story. How many major female record producers of the past three decades can the reader name? Frankly, I could not name even one minor female producer at present, let alone anyone to match the likes of Phil Spector, Leiber and Stoller, George Martin, Joe Meek, Brian Eno *et al.*[1] Of course, some will argue that such a trend is not unusual and drag in statistics confirming the lack of female technicians and engineers in many areas of business. But there is a big difference between those professions requiring specific skills and qualifications and the nebulously defined 'pop producer'. Several prominent sixties producers, including Andrew Oldham, Larry Page and Kit Lambert, were aspiring managers who walked in off the street, fiddled about with some knobs on a consul and 'created' their own sound. Technical brilliance was never requisite for a pop producer content to cut competent-sounding chart records. Similarly, general trends in management recruitment are a poor guide to understanding the lack of female representation in pop music. The lack of women

---

[1] Bert Muirhead's *The Record Producers' File* listed 1019 producers. Incredibly, the only female producers named were Emmylou Harris (a full-time performer who produced a one-off album for Delia Bell) and Suzi Jane Hokom (another American who produced the International Submarine Band's *Safe At Home*). Muirhead's list did not include Therese Bazar, Ann Dudley, Lotti Golden; the few female producers working on the periphery of the music industry; or the Jamaican-based Sonia Pottinger and Jahnet Enwright, but the figures are still harrowing reading — in fact, had he widened his study the 1019 to 2 ratio would have been increased substantially in favour of men.

in positions of power in commercial or industrial management is largely due to sexual stereotyping but the demands required of a high-powered executive are very different from those of a pop manager. The latter requires distinctive qualities, many of which might be termed 'maternal' — looking after sensitive artistes, ensuring that their needs are fulfilled and, more mundanely, making sure they dress correctly and appear on time. The average skilled housewife would regard many of these 'managerial' tasks as no more time-consuming than ensuring that a naughty child is well turned out and attends school punctually. Even a hardened chauvinist could not fail to observe that there are a whole range of managerial functions in pop that are perfectly suited to a 'feminine' sensibility. From a feminist viewpoint, it must be galling that such an unwarranted male preserve continues to exist. It is doubly ironic when you consider that successful female managers were actually far more common in the pre-rock 'n' roll days than in the emancipated eighties.

Although male domination of the record business is pervasive at present, it seems likely that feminist educators will eventually overcome and break down the old stereotyping. In all probability, the next managerial revolution in pop music will occur when women gradually reach the key positions of power. From there, we may actually see the first great female record producer and a record company board of directors that occasionally shows women in a majority. For the present, I can only conclude that the lack of female managers in British rock music over the past 30 years is a phenomenon that is not merely mysterious, but alarming.

INDEX

NB: The abbreviation *n*. refers to footnotes.